[ART OF THE 20TH CENTURY]

This book has been published
on occasion of the exhibition
German Expressionism: Art and Society
Palazzo Grassi, Venice
September 1997 -January 1998

First Published in Great Britain in 1997 by
Thames and Hudson Ltd, London

British Library Cataloguing-in-Publication Data

A catalogue record for this book is available from
the British Library

ISBN 0-500-23750-6

Printed and bound in Italy

© 1997 RCS Libri
1st edition Bompiani September 1997
via Mecenate 91, Milan

GERMAN EXPRESSIONISM: ART AND SOCIETY

by Stephanie Barron and Wolf-Dieter Dube

Thames and Hudson

Palazzo Grassi S.p.A.
San Samuele 3231, Venezia

This exhibition on German Expressionism, staged at Palazzo Grassi, Venice, offers an overview of a chapter in the history of European art that was not just important but fundamental to the development of the visual arts today.

The art of the previous century had explored forms of pictorial expression based on sensory impressions, seeking a *plein air* effect and deliberately straying from the established canons in search of nature, in which the person was laid bare and hence utterly essential. The Expressionists went far beyond this lingering romantic vision of things, their gaze penetrating to the core of contemporary society. The quintessence of man was no more to be found in his environment, but in his interior mechanisms, his inward gaze in search of the intimate liberty and freedom within his being.

The Expressionist aesthetic centered on a lively form of visual gesture that was echoed in the literature of the period.

This is the reason why Expressionism is also of such topical interest today – it was not just a chapter in the history of art, but, more importantly, it was a vital part of the society that produced it.

The Palazzo Grassi exhibition testifies to the extent to which the Expressionists were vitally in touch with their epoch, with the civilization around them – as much with art as with the breakthroughs in science and burgeoning new horizons, new worlds.

In this sense, this particular art form is in tune with Galileo's idea of our existence as an expression of striving for a new world.

Feliciano Benvenuti

Under the patronage of
the President of the Federal Republic of Germany Roman Herzog
the President of the Italian Republic Oscar Luigi Scalfaro

Tabula gratulatoria

Palazzo Grassi would like to thank
all those who have made
this exhibition possible

in particular
Costanza Caraffa
and also
Elfriede Kenitz and Ingrid Märtin
of the General Manager Secretariat
of the Staatliche Museen zu Berlin
Preußischen Kulturbesitz

Museums and institutions both public and private
that have generously contributed
by lending works of art
and all those who have wished
to remain anonymous

Lenders

Amsterdam, Stedelijk Museum
Berlin, Brücke-Museum
Berlin, Brücke-Museum, Karl und Emy Schmidt-Rottluff Stiftung
Berlin, Deutsches Historisches Museum
Berlin, Kunstbibliothek
Berlin, Kupferstichkabinett
Berlin, Nationalgalerie, Staatliche Museen zu Berlin
Berlin, Nationalgalerie, purchased with funds of the Vereins
    der Freunde der Nationalgalerie und des Bundes
Berlin, Nationalgalerie, Staatliche Museen zu Berlin
    purchased thanks to the Ernst von Siemens-Kunstfonds
Bern, Kunstmuseum Stiftung Othmar Huber
Bern-Davos, E.W. K. Collection
Beverly Hills, The Robert Gore Rifkind Foundation
Chicago, The Art Institute of Chicago, Arthur Jerome Eddy
    Memorial Collection
Cologne, Museum Ludwig, Stiftung Haubrich
Detroit, The Detroit Institute of Arts, Gift of Curt Valentin
Dortmund, Museum am Ostwall
Duisburg, Wilhelm Lehmbruck Museum
Düsseldorf, Kunstsammlung Nordrhein-Westfalen
Düsseldorf, Stadtmuseum
Emden, Kunsthalle, Stiftung Henri und Eske Nannen
Essen, Museum Folkwang
Frankfurt, Städelsches Kunstinstitut
    property of Städelschen Museums Verein e. V.
Frankfurt, Städtische Galerie im Städelsches Kunstinstitut
Frankfurt, Städelsches Kunstinstitut, Graphische Sammlung
Jerusalem, The Israel Museum, Sam Spiegel Collection
Halle, Staatliche Galerie Moritzburg
    Landeskunstumuseum Sachsen-Anhalt
Hannover, Sprengel Museum
Kassel, Staatliche Museen, Graphische Sammlung
Los Angeles, The Grunwald Center for the Graphic Arts
    UCLA, Gift of Mr. and Mrs. Stanley I. Talpis
Los Angeles, Los Angeles County Museum of Art
    The Robert Gore Rifkind Center for German Expressionist Studies
Ludwigshafen am Rhein, Wilhelm Hack Museum
Madrid, Foundation Collection Thyssen-Bornemisza
Milwaukee, The Marvin and Janet Fishman Collection
Munich, Bayerische Staatsgemäldesammlungen
    Staatsgalerie moderner Kunst
Munich, Städtische Galerie im Lenbachhaus
Münster, Westfälisches Landesmuseum
New York, The Museum of Modern Art
New York, The Solomon R. Guggenheim Museum
Nuremberg, Germanisches Nationalmuseum, on loan
    from a private collection
Portland, Portland Art Museum, Vivian and Gordon Gilkey
    Graphic Arts Collection
Schauffhausen, Museum zu Allerheiligen Sturzenegger-Stiftung
Sidney, The Art Gallery of New South Wales
Stuttgart, Galerie der Stadt
Stuttgart, Staatsgalerie Stuttgart
Toledo, The Toledo Museum of Art
    purchased with funds from the Libbey Endowment
Vienna, Museum moderner Kunst, Stiftung Ludwig
    loan of the Österreichische Galerie
Winterthur, Kunstmuseum
Wuppertal, Von der Heydt Museum
Zurich, Kunsthaus

Installations

Catalogue

Project
Gae Aulenti
with
Francesca Fenaroli

Graphic Design
Pierluigi Cerri
with
Dario Zannier

Lighting
Piero Castiglioni

Press Relations
Vladimiro Dan

Model of the Einstein Tower
Ercole Borsani
Giovanni Gianese

Multivision
Text and Direction
Andrea Frey
Janni Müller-Hauck

Multivision
Production
AV-OPTICS Berlin
Jurgen Krebs
Christoph Verbrüggen

Documents and Posters
Thomas Friedrich

Short Guide
Audio Guide
Chronology
Mural Texts
Andrea Frey
Janni Müller-Hauck

Musical Program
pieces by Alban Berg
Paul Hindemith
Arthur Honegger
Arnold Schönberg
Anton Webern
arranged by
Jurgen Liebing, Berlin

Editorial Director
Mario Andreose

Graphic Design
Pierluigi Cerri
with
Stefano Malobbia
Dario Zannier

Coordinating Editor
Simonetta Rasponi

Editorial Staff
Gianna Lonza
Maria Cristina Maiocchi
Valérie Viscardi

Translators
from German
Charles Axelrod
Jonathan Hunt
Michael Robinson
Stephen Wright
from Italian
Andrew Ellis
Jonathan Hunt
David Stanton

Iconographic Research
Carla Viazzoli

Coordination
Milena Bongi

Production Staff
Italo Cisilino
Sergio Daniotti
Carmen Garini
Daniele Marchesi
Rino Pasta
Stefano Premoli
Enrico Vida

Secretary
Luisa Gandolfi

Contents

previous pages
George Grosz, *Explosion*, 1917
oil on board, 47.8x68.2 cm
New York
The Museum of Modern Art
gift of Mr. and Mrs. Irving Moscovitz
cat. 93

Introduction

Wolf-Dieter Dube

When, in 1933, Alfred Barr organized the exhibition entitled "Deutsche Malerei und Bildhauerei" (German Painting and Sculpture) in the new Museum of Modern Art in New York, he wrote in the catalogue: "Much as it is admired or misunderstood abroad, German modern art is financed in Germany with extraordinary generosity at both a public and a private level. The directors of museums have the courage, the far-sightedness, and the competence to purchase works by avant-garde artists long before public opinion presses them to do so. As will be seen in the list, about fifty German museums support these artists, and in this way they educate the public to appreciate these works."

Alfred Barr was only thinking of the museums that were important at that time, but four years later raids that started with the campaign against "degenerate art" involved over a hundred state collections. This is a particularly significant fact. Only in Germany, in fact, was there such a range of innovative museums that the rulers of the Third Reich decided to intervene actively to put an end to this situation. Since it is certainly not correct, however, to begin with this event to explain the greater experience and receptivity of the Germans with regard to modern art in comparison with their neighbors, it is necessary to start to analyze the historical reasons for this.

Until 1871, the year the German Empire was founded, the political structure of Germany was characterized by single states and cities rather than a central power if, indeed, there was one. States and cities were the centers for cultural development, which was particularly variegated. The princes of the small German states soon realized that they counted for little among the Great Powers of Europe, and were not able to influence their policies in any way. Consequently many states, such as Saxony, abandoned any pretence of military power and concentrated all their efforts on art. The cultural independence of the cities – unless they were capitals or seats of the monarchy, such as Berlin and Munich – was impregnable, since it was assured by the financial support of the citizens. From the beginning of the twentieth century, in over thirty German cities, art societies devoted to contemporary art were founded; they financed themselves with exhibitions and the sale of works of art. Often these associations were the first step toward the setting up of municipal museums. For example, the Kunsthalle (Art Museum) in Bremen still belongs to the old Kunstverein (Art Society). Naturally, the establishment of a large number of museums, during and after the nineteenth century, led to the rapid growth of interest in art history and museology.

In 1871, with the foundation of the empire, it was not possible to absorb the regional museums, supported by enlightened and responsible citizens, into a national structure extending to the whole country. Thus, the individual states preserved their cultural independence, while the imperial government was only responsible for questions of cultural policy beyond the borders of the empire. The same criteria applied to the Weimar Republic and the Federal Republic of Germany: this is the basis of federalism. Meanwhile, this German peculiarity explains both the importance that Paris assumed for this multicentric nation and why any form of art that appeared in Paris – or was about to appear there – received so much attention in Germany. Since the country lacked a metropolis that could function as a cultural center, Paris took on this role. This situation only changed at the turn of the century, and we shall see how the coexistence of Paris and Berlin developed subsequently. Berlin was now able to become the political and cultural capital of Germany, and, supported by a liberal middle class free from prejudice – in Berlin this was largely Jewish – contemporary art began to appear in the museums. The works of a large number of leading French artists were present in the German museums long before they received any attention from the French museums. In 1914 it was estimated that there were about two hundred works by French artists, ranging from Ingres to the Cubists, in public collections in Germany, as against not more than a hundred in France. It is hardly surprising that sooner or later there was a reaction against this situation. In particular, Emperor William II, who considered his patronage to be a way of celebrating both his ancestors and himself, frequently condemned as degenerate the art that went beyond the limits he had imposed. From 1898 onward he insisted on personally approving every purchase by the Nationalgalerie, as well as its acceptance of any gifts. Thus the Nationalgalerie was effectively precluded from the possession of avant-garde works. In reality, however, the imperial prohibition only applied to the museums in Berlin, while the other Prussian cities took little notice of it. In 1903 the duke of Saxe-Weimar went so far as to comment: "It is just as well that the emperor is contrary to modern art, otherwise small states like ours would be left with nothing." And he was not only thinking of Weimar with its progressive Academy of Fine Arts, which, together with the School of Arts and Crafts, became the Bauhaus in 1919.

The rejection of Impressionism, Jugendstil, and the Secession – which were opposed by broad strata of society who felt they had the backing of the official cultural policy – was offset by the support that a large part of the affluent middle classes gave to the main currents of the most recent art. This situation was reversed by the arrival of Expressionism. The Expressionist utopia of the new man, informed by the principles of liberty, equality, and fraternity, and able to expedite the coming of a new era of the spirit, aimed to supersede a society based on materialism and selfishness. The alienation of man and his uprooting from his native soil was replaced by the concept of harmony between man and nature. Nonetheless, the naive hope of a better future cherished by the Expressionists soon came into conflict with the artificial reality of industry and urban life. The city became the metaphor for all the damage deriving from the transformation of the socioeconomic structure at the turn of the century, and was held to be the "worst evil for humanity" and "the grave of humankind." The serenity and *joie de vivre* of the Paris boulevards bathed in light that had been depicted by the Impressionists of the previous generation had disappeared. Impressionism was now identified with the ruling class, and it was time for a change in society. In 1916 Hermann Bahr wrote that "Impressionism represents the detachment of man from the spirit; the degeneration of man into the gramophone of the exterior world is Impressionist."

The suffering of man, his poverty, brutalization, and loneliness received increasing attention from the artist and, as a result, the atmosphere created by the Expressionists changed, as did their subjects. While, in the early years, there had been a preponderance of pleasant landscapes, often containing naked figures expressing a yearning for Arcadia, on the eve of the First World War there was a prevalence of images revealing the alienation of man, irresoluble human tensions, and a sense of gloom. These changes in theme need to be stressed because, in the case of German Expressionism, it was not a purely artistic question, but rather the result of a spiritual movement whose attitude toward society was extremely critical – in other words, it was a truly political aim. Painters and poets portrayed the apocalypse, destruction, and revolution, and hoped for violent subversion. In their eyes, war appeared to be the only way to create a new society for the new man and, when it finally broke out, they extolled it.

In 1914 Thomas Mann wrote: "Should not the artist – the soldier in the artist – have praised God for the collapse of a peaceful world that he now found terribly tedious? War! We perceived cleansing and liberation, and a great hope." At the same time Wassily Kandinsky asked: "What will happen afterward? I believe there will be a great unleashing of inner forces that will also generate fraternity." And Franc Marc declared: "There is no other path for the age of the spirit. Could the Augean stables – old Europe – only be cleansed, or is there a single person who does not want this war to take place?". Naivety once again! This is what Marc wrote to Kandinsky on the very day when August Macke fell at the front. He too fought in France, confident that Germany would win, but, if this nation had been victorious, would it have been transformed into the realm of the spirit? However, this attitude changed very rapidly: first-hand experience of the cruel reality led to the conviction that war was a crime, that revolution was inevitable, and every artist worthy of the name a precursor.

With the revolution of November 1918 in Germany it seemed that the aspirations of the Expressionists could become reality. The disappearance of the ruling dynasties from the political scene and the collapse of the whole apparatus of power did not only mean the end of an absurd war. The decline of the old order was compared to the death of the man of yesterday, and it was expected that the cataclysm would result in a new, improved world. The slaying of hundreds of thousands of human beings on the European fronts would thus have made sense. With almost divine afflatus, the artists greeted the resurrection of the new man who, freed from the chains of the past, aspired to be a social revolutionary and felt he was a part of an international society having a common spiritual destiny. This message was proclaimed in countless manifestoes, leaflets, and journals.

The painter Karl Jakob Hirsch described the prevailing atmosphere in Berlin thus: "This is the beginning! In our hearts we were ready to throw everything away – the old-fashioned ideas, the junk. Rubiner's plea for 'political art' had already stirred us. What did form matter to us? No, what counted were the contents. And these existed: liberty, equality, and fraternity. It was not necessary to paint a flagpole well, but rather to show the convictions represented by the flag fluttering in the wind. At a meeting in Berlin on the evening of 9 November 1918 a poet proclaimed: 'The revolution has won!' There was no room for sceptics."

The same applied to Dresden, where the poet Walter Rheiner wrote with regard to the new idealism: "This idealism is called 'Expressionism'. Thus Expressionism is not merely a question of technique or form, but, above all, a spiritual attitude (gnosiological, metaphysical, ethical) that has not appeared in human history overnight, but dates back thousands of years. In politics this idealism is called anti-nationalistic socialism; in any case, it requires radicality not only of the spirit, but also in action."

Nonetheless, the generation of 1880 that had founded Expressionism no longer felt involved. In particular, Ernst Ludwig Kirchner, Erich Heckel, and Karl Schmidt-Rottluff went back to the ideals of youth, no longer demanding or expecting, but harboring a faint hope. The artistic utopia and political ideology formed a symbiotic relationship that lasted until 1923. The autumn of that year proved to be a decisive turning point in German politics. The misery of the population was now even greater than it had been during the war years, and, in the country that had been worn out by the recent war and civil strife, the wave of strikes led to the Communist uprising in Hamburg, while in Thuringia and Saxony workers' governments were set up. The last revolutionary activities were suppressed with the aid of the army. The introduction of the Rentenmark in November 1923 determined the end of inflation and rapidly led to the stabilization of the economic situation and the consequent triumph of middle-class democracy. It was now quite clear that the Expressionist dream had failed, not only at a political level, but also at a spiritual and artistic one as well.

The anti-middle-class opposition, of which the artists felt they were an integral part, had already been obliged to abandon its hopes in 1919 when the armed clashes of the Spartacist revolt in Berlin concluded with the assassination of Karl Liebknecht and Rosa Luxemburg, and again, in May, when blood was shed as the experiment of the *Räterepublik* (Republic of the Counselors) in Munich, led by a group of writers, was crushed on the orders of the social democratic minister of defense, Noske. Revolutionary enthusiasm became resignation in some, while it drove others toward political radicalism. The painter Heinrich Vogeler wrote: "The resolute individual – the man of action – continued to be identified with the exponent of Expressionism, while the irresolute were branded as Impressionists." The same terminology was used to label political and philosophical beliefs: the social democrats were "socialist impressionists," while the communists were "socialist expressionists." Naturally, it was on this basis that the arguments for the campaign against contemporary art were prepared in the following years.

The symbiosis between Expressionism and politics caused the movement to be elevated to the status of the official artistic style of the state, as happened to Futurism in Fascist Italy; at any event, there was no longer antagonism between contemporary art and the cultural policy of the government. Certainly, before, and during, the First World War the museums had been able to purchase works by living artists, but now there were no longer any obstacles and it depended largely on the directors and their enthusiasm – which was not the same in all cases – how they built up their collections. Obviously, the depressing economic situation was a factor that had to be taken into account. Particularly significant was the case of Berlin: the imperial veto on purchases by the Nationalgalerie was now obsolete and the Prussian government – which was responsible for the museums in Berlin and, until 1932, was controlled by the social democrats – increased the size of its collection as far as was possible.

The fact that as early as 1919 the Kronprinzenpalais (the crown prince's palace) had been assigned to the Nationalgalerie so that it could have sufficient space to house its modern art collection certainly had political significance, as did the fact that majority of the works confiscated a few years later were among those that the Prussian minister of culture had purchased for the gallery. Since, with its own collections, the Nationalgalerie would not have been able to mount a sufficiently large display, Ludwig Justi, who directed it from 1909 to 1933, began, for the first time, to resort to borrowing works on a large scale; this procedure was later to have a serious effect on the German museums.

In only fourteen years, under the direction of Justi, a collection was built up that is still legendary today, and at the time had no equal in the rest of the world.

Following the political developments at the end of 1923, it was not only the middle-class forces that were strengthened, but also the reactionary ones. Immediately politically motivated attacks on modern art began, the effects of which varied considerably. The first victim was the director of the Städtische Kunstsammlungen in Dresden, Paul Ferdinand Schmidt, who was dismissed from his post after he had been accused of purchasing works by Expressionist artists. The war on modern art was fueled by the conflicts between left and right. The military defeat, the occupation of part of German territory, and the demands for war reparations that, according to the victorious powers, would not have been paid off until 1988, created an extremely favorable climate for nationalistic and reactionary forces. As an exercise in self-deception the legend of the fatherland stabbed in the back was concocted: according to this, the German army was not defeated on the battlefield, but was obliged to surrender by betrayal at home. Obviously those held responsible were the "expressionists" in politics and, together with them, the artists. A new Germany, founded on law and order must indeed have been welcome news at the end of the civil war. Friedrich von Schiller's maxim, "Power is only granted to the strong," was probably hammered into people's heads with great insistence. But power meant superiority, which had its roots in the privileged Nordic race.

Every time mention was made of the German people reference was only being made to a small part that only comprised the nationalists in the strict sense. In Germany these ideas had a long tradition, partly the result of the delay with which the country achieved national unity, but they were never seriously taken into consideration. From 1923 onward, on the other hand, a series of publications appeared that focussed on these concepts once again. These included *Rassenkunde des deutschen Volkes* (Ethnography of the German People) by Hans Günther, which by 1943 had reached its sixteenth edition. This book inspired the landscape architect Paul Schultze-Naumburg's *Rasse und Stil* (Race and Style, 1926) and *Ritter, Tod und Teufel, der heldische Gedanke* (The Knight, Death, and the Devil, the Heroic Thought, 1928). It is in these works that the origins of the artistic theory of National Socialism may be found, along with its demands that every artistic representation should respect the canon of the supremacy of the German race: the duty of art was to reproduce the model of Nordic man, the outcome of a long process of natural selection. Even the works of classical antiquity and the Middle Ages were re-examined from a clearly racist point of view.

The masterpieces of Greek art and the late Romanesque sculptures at Bamberg and Naumburg were considered to be exemplary in this sense, while Gothic was rejected *en bloc* because it was thought to be "influenced by the Orient." This tendency reached its apogee in the book by Alfred Rosenberg published in 1930, *Der Mythos des 20. Jahrhunderts* (The Myth of the Twentieth Century), in which one reads – just to quote one passage – that what Van Gogh, Gauguin, Picasso, and Signac had begun "emerged openly and uninhibitedly after the war: hybridism claimed the right to represent its bastard fetuses generated by spiritual syphilis and artistic infantilism, almost as if they were the expression of the soul." It goes without saying that such statements were not taken into consideration by the specialists, just as little importance was attached to Adolf Hitler's *Mein Kampf* at the time.

No one could have imagined the effect of these ideas on those lacking in culture; nor could they have foreseen that the destruction of art was at hand.

It was really believed that modern art caused the disintegration of the national identity and the culture of the people. Only Germany would be cleansed, so that the other peoples were welcome to degenerate art: it would be an effective means of self-destruction. This is why, during the occupation of Paris in the Second World War, the Germans did not interfere with exhibitions by French artists. Hitler merely remarked: "Is it in our interests that the French people is spiritually healthy? Let them degenerate by themselves. All the better for us!"

After 1930 the propaganda was progressively intensified. In the provinces, above all, every effort was made to ensure that any opposition would be crushed at once after the Nazis came to power in 1933. Artists and professors unpopular with the party were dismissed from their posts, as were directors and curators of museums. The first clearly discriminatory exhibition was held in Karlsruhe as early as April 1933.

Significantly, it was entitled "Regierungkunst 1918–1933" (Government Art 1918–1933). Hard on its heels came "Kulturbolschewistiche Bilder" (Paintings of the Bolshevik Culture) in Mannheim; "Schreckenskammer" (Chamber of Horrors) in Nuremburg, "Novembergeist: Kunst im Dienste der Zersetzung" (Spirit of November: Art in the Service of Demoralization) in Stuttgart; "Kunst, die nicht aus unserer Seele kom" (Art that Does Not Come from Our Soul) in Chemnitz; and "Entartete Kunst" (Degenerate Art) in Dresden. The latter exhibition toured to various cities in Germany up to 1936. In Berlin the resistance to the new course lasted longer, despite the fact that Hermann Göring was present in the capital as the Prussian prime minister. The various directors of the Nationalgalerie, none of whom lasted long in their posts, did their best to battle on, but in October 1936, shortly after the closure of the Olympic Games, the Kronprinzenpalais – which housed the modern art collection of the Nationalgalerie – was closed to the public.

"Give me four years" was Hitler's demand: and the fruit of the Nazi policy in the field of art were reaped at Munich in 1937 when the new Haus der Deutschen Kunst (House of German Art) was opened in the "Grossen Deutschen Kunstausstellung" (Great German Art Exhibition), while the recent past was pilloried in the "Entartete Kunst" exhibition mentioned above.

On 30 June 1937 the minister of propaganda, Joseph Goebbels, decided that the president of the Reichskunstkammer (German Art Association), the painter Ziegler, should be relieved of his post and that the works of the so-called degenerate German art dating from 1910 onward belonging to the central government, the *Länder* (federal states), and the municipalities should be selected for the exhibition and kept safely. In Goebbels's decree, "decadent" works were described as those that "offend the German national sentiment, destroy or distort the natural form, or are characterized by a lack of adequate manual or artistic skills." In just two weeks seven hundred works were sent from thirty-two museums to Munich, where the exhibition was officially opened on 19 July, the day after Hitler inaugurated the "Grossen Deutschen Kunstausstellung." The Führer had been present in person at the selection of the paintings.

Goebbels noted in his diary: "The sculpture is still acceptable, while the painting is a real catastrophe. Some of the works hanging on the walls are quite appalling. The Führer is trembling with rage." This attitude was also evident in the opening speech: "Among the paintings that have been sent here I have seen some works before which one can only suppose that the eyes of certain people see things differently from how they really are – in other words, there are men who depict our people as if they were depraved idiots. They paint – or experience as they would probably put it – blue meadows, green skies, sulphur-yellow clouds, and so on. I don't want to get involved in an argument as to whether they really see and feel things in this way, but in the name of the German people I would like to prevent these miserable wretches, who evidently have problems with their eyesight, from attempting to violently impose the products of their poor observation on their fellow men, or else try to pass it off as art.

No, there are two possibilities: either the so-called artists really see things in this way and believe in what they depict, and in this case we should find out whether their eyesight has been so reduced by disease or injury, or whether they have inherited this problem. In the first case, they are unfortunate people who are to be pitied, while, in the second case, the ministry of the interior of the Reich should step in to prevent further hereditary transmission of these repulsive visual defects. Or perhaps they themselves don't believe in the reality of such impressions, but, for other reasons, they do all they can to vex the nation with this humbug and, in this case, it is an offense that is within the competence of the criminal law."

Hitler threatened the artists in the same way that Stalin had been doing for some time; for decades in the Soviet Union this was the way socialist realism was imposed. The German artists and intellectuals suddenly realized that they were woefully mistaken in thinking that Hitler would be shown up for what he was – a caricature – and driven out by the people in a short space of time. Thus Max Beckmann, for instance, when he heard Hitler's speech on the radio, left for the Netherlands the following day.

The commission that selected the works for the "Entartete Kunst" exhibition later made a second appearance – in some museums a third – proposing to "cleanse" the existing collections once and for all. All attempts at opposition proved to be fruitless. Eberhard Hanfstaengl, the director of the Nationalgalerie, who had tried to resist, was immediately dismissed. Many curators attempted to hide the works, or, at night, replaced the paintings they had selected the day before with less valuable works because, in their haste, the commissioners had not drawn up a list, but had only noted the numbers of the works to be confiscated.

The commission went beyond its brief and also seized works executed before 1910 and ones by foreign artists. The pillage continued until 1938, and was legalized by the law on the expropriation of the products of degenerate art approved on 31 May of that year. All told, about 16,000 works – including paintings, sculptures, drawings, and prints by some 1,200 artists – were confiscated and sent to Berlin.

Very soon the Nazi authorities were faced with problem of what to do with this enormous quantity of artworks: the decision was reached to sell as many as possible abroad in exchange for hard currency, a practice that continued until 1941. It is now thought that approximately a third of the works were saved from destruction because they were sold abroad, another third, considered to be unusable, were burnt, while the fate of the last third is still unknown.

It was indeed a stroke of luck that the minister of propaganda entrusted Rolf Netsch with the registration and exploitation of these works. An art historian with publications on modern art to his name, Netsch took steps to return works that had been lent to museums to their rightful owners, the private collectors, and he did all that was in his power to save the most outstanding works by offering them for sale. And he always kept the prices low so that the art dealers, acting on behalf of potential purchasers, could successfully conclude the transaction.

The philosopher Ernst Bloch commented: "Please speak in a low voice. Someone is dying in the room: German culture is breathing its last. By order, in Germany not even the catacombs exist any longer, but only chambers of horrors where one is held up to the scorn of the rabble: a concentration camp open to the public. It's crazy, and it's getting worse."

Luckily, Bloch's prediction was not entirely fulfilled. There were still the private collectors' "catacombs," and there were the art dealers who covertly took the works threatened with destruction there, or even buried them. And I am not only referring to those who had been charged with the sale of the expropriated works, such as Hildebrand Gurlitt, who, as the result of his commitment to modern art, lost his job as director of the museum of Zwickau; these dealers were supported by a host of collectors.

It is important to remember that, with Expressionism, the character of the middle-class collector changed. The new generation of art lovers had a different sensibility and were emotionally involved. This is what Markus Kruss, an otherwise sober businessman, wrote to Emil Nolde: "Now inside me there is something that cries out as it seeks its flowers, the flowers of eternity, those dark blue, enigmatic flowers that draw the human soul into themselves and allow the hurly-burly of the world to be forgotten." Like many other collectors of Expressionist works, he had started in 1916–17. For this new generation of collectors it was no longer necessary to legitimize their affluence with art: in their eyes art had almost entirely lost its decorative character and had become an integral part of a particular world, the expression of an existential state. For them, Rainer Maria Rilke's plea "You must change your life" was valid. They were not willing to give in at that moment. On the contrary, they obtained foreign currency to allow the art dealers, who could only sell abroad, to camouflage their activities. In addition to them there were young people who, ironically enough, had been favorably impressed by the "Entartete Kunst" exhibition. Of these, it is sufficient to mention Bernhard Sprengel, who was later to found the Sprengel-Museum in Hannover.

Despite the surveillance, typical of dictatorships, many activities were still possible. It is well known, in fact, that in dictatorships, the left hand knows what the right hand is doing much less than in democracies. In this regard, one example will suffice: in a long letter of 1941, the notorious chief of the secret police, Reinhard Heydrich, informed the ministry of propaganda – especially the section of the SS responsible to it – that the Galerie Vömel in Düsseldorf exhibited and sold the controversial "degenerate art," thereby sabotaging the Führer's cultural policy. Heydrich also made it clear that he suspected that the trade in this forbidden art continued throughout Germany on a large scale.

"The odious Bolshevik and leader of the 'degenerate art,' Emil Nolde, in his tax return for 1940 has declared a sum of 80,000 marks," complained Heydrich in his report, which he concluded by asking for advice on how to put an end to this traffic. The ministry's reply was reassuring. While admitting that in Germany it was the so-called collectors' circles that were attempting sabotage, it observed that the term "degenerate art" should be applied to specific works of art rather than to the artists.

Although it is true that private collectors were not able to avert the destruction of the collections belonging to the German museums, it is also true that they did everything in their power to save some of these works, and they prevented the Nazi campaign against modern art from being a complete success. Using brutal methods, the Nazis managed to disperse the public collections of painting and sculpture, but they were not able to get the museums to accept works by the artists whom they approved and financed: the museums were simply not making any new purchases.

Although in some museums it is possible to find the occasional painting or sculpture in the official style of the regime, the provenances of these works are very varied, and they were acquired after the war. For the second time in a generation Germany had lost a world war. But, unlike 1918, in 1945 the traditions that should have carried on had been swept away; the country had been razed to the ground and occupied by foreign powers. About a third of the national territory had been lost, the rest was divided and about twenty-five percent of the population of West Germany consisted of refugees. The people – the word "society" is hardly applicable here – had to solve more pressing problems before they could think about art. It may well be true that we do not live on bread alone – but, without bread, we do not live at all.

The reconstruction, carried out rapidly thanks to both the renunciation of war reparations by the Allies and the Marshall Plan, went well beyond the mere elimination of the war damage: the country and the cities were rebuilt for a future in which there would be little room for the past. Many of the remains of the world of yesteryear that had survived the war, or could have been restored, were knocked down, and the obsession with demolition in the fifties and sixties, now greatly deplored, eliminated the rest of them for ever. Artists were no exception to this tendency. In reality, the older ones who were still alive were offered teaching posts in the art schools, but they carried little weight there. This was the same generation that, at the end of the First World War, realized that there were no artistic means for overcoming the horror they had seen on the battlefields, or that, at least, a long period was needed to find a style suitable for this purpose. In fact, the most outstanding antimilitarist novel – *All Quiet on the Western Front*, by Erich Maria Remarque – was only published in 1928, and Otto Dix painted his visions of the trenches in 1930. How was it possible, therefore, to represent in artistic form the horror, misery, and crimes now that they had increased out of all proportion? The focus of attention was no longer the recent past – it was only later that the nation came to terms with the past – but the bright future.

The majority of artists in West Germany – this officially became the Federal Republic of Germany in 1949 – were almost obliged to become abstractionists. Once again Paris became the model and the École de Paris tended to influence all the art forms. While Picasso was being reassessed in Paris, painters in the Federal Republic who had hitherto focused on the object, such as Karl Hofer, ceased to represent reality. The world that could not be dominated with artistic means was countered by the new abstract painting because it created an identity of the world and the spirit. In fact, abstraction juxtaposed an orderly artistic metaphor with the disparate visions of the world. For many critics this painting tended toward transcendence and numinosity.

This is where Wassily Kandinsky appeared on the scene and, at the same time, a tradition dating back to the Blaue Reiter was recognizable. Excessive importance should not be given to the great interest that Der Germans Hans Hartung and Wols aroused in Paris because both were heavily influenced by Paul Klee, Kandinsky, and Expressionism. In the mid-fifties it was generally believed that abstraction was the art form of the future.

The artists themselves were not interested in knowing what the attitude toward art of the new society might be. They were indifferent to this problem because, after the traumatic experience of the repression and destruction of art, the absolute freedom of the artist was postulated, a principle that was embodied in the constitution of the republic. Interference from, for instance, political organs was not tolerated because they would have been suspected of trying to condition art ideologically. The fame of the absolute independence of German art that also had official recognition spread beyond the country's borders and explains why the reconstruction of the "Entartete Kunst" exhibition in the United States in 1991 was so successful.

The consolidation of the Federal Republic soon highlighted the need for even a forward-looking society to have a positive spiritual tradition to which recourse could be made, and this appeared to be Expressionism. A concrete start was made with the Hochschule für Gestaltung in Ulm, founded in 1950 by the Swiss artist Max Bill, a former student of the Bauhaus who wanted to perpetuate its tradition. The same applied to the first Documenta in Kassel in 1955; the international exhibition kept this name even when the aims of its organizers changed. The choice of the provincial town of Kassel was further evidence of Germany's lack of a cultural center.

One of the reasons why Expressionism was favorably accepted everywhere was that all the regions of Germany had contributed to the movement. By contrast, the underlying reasons for its relevance became manifest when the so-called society of the economic miracle turned out to be very similar to the one that, from 1912 onward, the Expressionists had bitterly criticized because it was based on materialism and self-interest. On a political level, the revolt of youth at the time of the student protest had the same objective, while, on an artistic level, it was Joseph Beuys who personified this opposition.

Meanwhile the museums have been rebuilt and, in many cities, new ones have been constructed. They have all tended to favor contemporary art in the strict sense of the term, but, as a didactic basis, have chosen Expressionism, limiting themselves to the main exponents at a local or regional level. This, too, can be interpreted as a sign of the persistence of the romantic tradition in German art. However, a society without utopias, one that it is almost impossible to call liberal, was not – and is not – aware of critical positions. Rather, the profession of faith in Expressionism and the presumption of the freedom of contemporary artists have ensured social legitimation and, at the same time, have constituted an alibi.

The vast majority of private collectors who managed to save their works during the Third Reich subsequently donated their collections to the museums. These gifts formed a basis for the recreation of the public collections of Expressionist art, which they are still being completed with an active policy of purchases. The gaps left in the museums as a result of the Nazi campaign against "degenerate art" have now been filled, although many paintings are no longer displayed in the places where they were before 1937. Nonetheless, their presence is an essential part of the national conscience.

Stephanie Barron

Max Pechstein
Sommer in den Dünen 1911
Summer in the Dunes
oil on canvas
Berlin, Nationalgalerie

Ernst Ludwig Kirchner
Ins Meer Schreitende, 1912
Striding into the sea
oil on canvas
Stuttgart, Staatsgalerie

Karl Schmidt-Rottluff
Drei Akte, 1913
Three nudes
oil on canvas
Berlin, Nationalgalerie

Wassily Kandinsky, *Murnau mit Kirche I*
1910, *Murnau with Church I*
oil and watercolor on cardboard
Munich
Städtische Galerie im Lenbachhaus

From the beginning the German Expressionist artists were deeply involved with life beyond the studio. As they sought to break with pre-Wilhemenian society and conditions, they forswore the conventions of bourgeois life for the freedom (if only temporary) found in playing and posing in the countryside; their studios were filled with examples of art from exotic cultures; they were attracted to the vitality, with all its beauty and grittiness, of the growing metropolis. For some artists the city was filled with whores and drunks; for others it was the site of apocalyptic occurrences.

Traditional portraiture was incompatible with Expressionism; their portraits were a reflection of their new social world. They sought to expose the inner soul of the sitter, whether the subject was a friend or the artist himself.

These young idealistic artists embraced the impending Great War – it would, they thought, be the war to end all wars – and marched off to battle filled with the hopes and dreams that would very quickly be devastatingly altered at the front. Those who returned were quickly caught up in the fervor surrounding the 1918 revolution – a revolution in which they believed that they, as artists, were vitally important in order to carve out a new vision of mankind; a world in which they could make a difference.

Like its counterpart, the Russian avant-garde, German Expressionists encompassed all the arts; many were politically active, and both movements ended abruptly as totalitarian governments came to power. To explain German Expressionism one must look simultaneously at the artists, their art, and the society around them.

These artists not only worked in traditional media, but also wrote poetry and manifestoes; designed buildings; contributed to periodicals, and published portfolios for interested subscribers; organized exhibitions; designed for film and theater; and, for a brief time, even tried to assemble workers for political purposes.

For this reason this exhibition *German Expressionism: Art and Society* explores several different themes, and includes painting, sculpture, and works on paper, as well as posters, periodicals, manifestoes, exhibition catalogues, and examples of Expressionist film and music. The exhibition is divided into three large sections: the years before the war; the war experience itself; the November revolution and the years between 1918 and 1924. Within these three areas several specific themes related to the artists and society can be traced.

The Utopia of Nature – Naturutopien – "Wir lebten in absoluter Harmonie"
"We painter folk set out early every morning heavily laden with our gear, the models trailing behind with pockets full of eatables and drinkables. We lived in absolute harmony, working and bathing. If we found ourselves short of a male model, one of us stepped into the breach." (Max Pechstein)[1]

Around the turn of the century large sections of the German population, inspired by mystics and new cults, nudist societies, and outdoor movements, sought to celebrate the return to nature as a kind of religion. Nature and a belief in its healing powers took on a new significance. Nature was seen as the antidote to factory work and the frustrations of city life. For the Brücke artists, Kirchner, Heckel, Schmidt-Rottluff, Pechstein, and others, the landscape and the nude model in the out-of-doors epitomized this interest and celebration of nature. During summers they traveled throughout Germany, frequenting the stark beaches at the Baltic and North Seas, and the lush lakes of Moritzburg, near Dresden.

The artists sought to show human figures in natural surroundings, whether peaceful, domestic landscapes, Arcadian scenes inhabited by gypsies, or idyllic panoramas filled with naked men and women cavorting among trees, lakes, streams, and reeds. In contrast to academically posed compositions, these artists drew and painted spontaneously, capturing their nudes with intense colors, in compositions that overturned traditional ideas of morality and challenged social conventions.

These figures stride confidently into the sea; sunbathe proudly amidst dunes; and languorously observe one another swimming and playing outdoors. They seem at one with their natural environment, and reflect the harmony that the artists felt between life and art. Roads, houses, trees, and clouds seem to take on an expressive force against the background of unpopulated landscapes. Color and form are fused much in the same way that man seems to be an integral part of nature.

Franz Marc, *Die Hirten*, 1912
The Shepherds
oil on canvas
Munich
Bayerische Stadtsgemäldesammlungen

Berlin, Postdamer Platz, 1903

Ernst Ludwig Kirchner
Berliner Straßenszene, 1913–14
Berlin Street Scene
oil on canvas
Berlin, Brücke-Museum

Ernst Ludwig Kirchner
Rheinbrücke in Köln, 1914
Bridge on the Rhine in Cologne
oil on canvas
Berlin, Nationalgalerie

"We proceed from the belief that the artist, apart from the impressions he receives from the external world, Nature, continually collects experiences within an inner world. We search for artistic forms that reveal the penetration of these collected experiences, for forms that must be freed from all irrelevance, in order to forcefully express that which is essential, in short, for artistic synthesis." (Wassily Kandinsky)[2]

For Wassily Kandinsky, and the artists of the Blaue Reiter, evolving toward abstraction between 1909 and 1914, landscapes were not literal depictions of nature, rather they became cosmic landscapes, in which the scenes are filled with hints of familiar objects-mountains, towers, churches, horses and riders.

Retreating to the southern German town of Murnau in 1908, Kandinsky's style immediately began to change. From the Murnau landscape, Kandinsky derived the essential forms he used to construct dynamic impressions of nature, which came close to abstract painting. By flattening his compositions, exaggerating the rhythms that dance across the canvas, using powerful lines, and painting with bold colors, the artist made these works resonate with spiritual tension. Kandinsky's landscapes seem filled with a powerful force which frees the familiar from its recognizable context.

Franz Marc saw nature in a philosophical way; attempting to "intensify my feeling for the organic rhythm of all things; I seek pantheist sympathy with the vibration and flow of the blood of nature – in the trees, in the animals, in the air."[3] Marc tried to express this "inner truth" and felt that drawing directly from nature would not allow him to effect this. Rather he relied on his imagination and tried to construct animal forms that he felt paralleled nature. He simplified forms in an effort to convey the symbolism and mystery of nature. While his compositions were still based on recognizable natural forms, he subjected them to such rigorous formal conversion that they appear to function purely pictorially. Animals and nudes are no longer at home in nature, they are invented upon it.

The Big City

"The light of the modern city, together with the movement in the streets, continually gives me a fresh stimulus." (Ernst Ludwig Kirchner)[4]

For many of the German Expressionists, the modern city was a subject ripe with possibilities. Following the unification of Germany in 1871, Berlin had quickly emerged as its cultural and artistic capital. It experienced an unprecedented population explosion: in 1800 it had 170,000 inhabitants and by 1910 its population had skyrocketed to 1,4 million.

It was a city marked not by grand boulevards, expansive parks and public monuments, but rather by a density of modern buildings, a new underground railway, scandalous housing conditions for its expanding migrant population, and a city plan that grew out of a tangle of streets.

It was the antithesis to the idyllic natural setting celebrated just a few years earlier by artists in Dresden and Munich. Artists who were drawn to the city examined its character, its denizens, and were attracted to its diverse elements. Berlin street scenes present an alienating urban alternative to the liberated sexuality of the Baltic bather

As a newspaper article of 1917 described it: "What the artists of today seek in the city is not to obscure its ugliness with light and color; rather they have elevated precisely this ugliness to its characteristic feature."[5]

No artist more than Kirchner captured the essence of big city life in Berlin between 1911 and the outbreak of the war. He selected his subjects carefully. He avoided the extensive poverty and the desperate housing conditions; he ignored class tensions and the city at work. Rather he chose the cabaret and dance hall, the circuses, the cafes, and the prostitutes. The city at night is ripe for expressive interpretation.

Kirchner was attracted to urban alienation and the ambivalence he sensed and experienced in Berlin. His style would soon mirror the city's spirit; he seems to absorb the tempo and intensity of urban life with every fiber of his being. In his series *Straßenbilder* (Street Scenes) he celebrates the prostitute. She is the quintessential city inhabitant. She tries to seduce, but not too aggressively. She tries to attract the observer's attention. She is dressed in the latest fashions, replete with wildly plumed hats, brilliant shawls, gaudy necklaces, and elaborate furs.

Kirchner's city pictures introduce sharp angular lines, which split and fragment his subjects; every part of the picture is activated. The eye travels relentlessly across the picture's surface

Erich Heckel, *Müde* 1913, *Tired*
woodcut
Berlin, Kupferstichkabinett

Oskar Kokoschka, *Selbstbildnis* 1913
Self-Portrait
oil on canvas
New York, Museum of Modern Art

Ernst Ludwig Kirchner, *Selbstporträt
als Soldat*, 1915, *Self-portrait as Soldier*
oil on canvas
Oberlin, Allen Memorial Art Gallery

Ernst Barlach, *Der Rächer*, 1914
The Avenger, bronze
Ludwigshafen am Rhein
Wilhelm Hack Museum

searching in vain for balance. Kirchner establishes complex and jarring rhythms. Large groups of figures dominate the composition. These paintings seem to evoke an expression that perfectly captures the jostling, loud, chaotic atmosphere of the new metropolis. Yet the figures seem isolated and bound together only by their sameness of dress, movement, and attitude.

Portraits and Self-portraits

German Expressionist portraits, particularly in the years before the war, are frequently characterized by brooding, meditative, melancholic expressions. Sitters seem to reflect on deep issues or appear to be troubled by inner emotions.

Either individually or together, they are preoccupied, and rarely transmit the unbridled joy or free spirit that the early Die Brücke portraits conveyed. In graphics, many artists turned to woodcutting; the stark black and white carvings, such as those by Schmidt-Rottluff and Heckel, are powerful, solemn compositions.

Many artists were drawn to themes like "sick women", "tired women", "sad women"; which to presage the cataclysmic events that would unfold beginning in 1914. Jawlensky created a series of female figures, whose expressive faces and deeply rimmed, haunting eyes, seem isolated and meditative. With their oversize heads, and small hands, they convey unrelieved tension, distress, and isolation from the nature that surrounds them.

Landscapes, highly detailed, also convey unmitigated tension. Ochres, reds, browns, and dark greens all add to the melancholic feel of these pictures.

For the German Expressionists, the self-portrait held a special significance. Not only were they their own cheapest and readily available sitters, but through it they could understand more about their own personality and psyche – to discover more about themselves at a time when Freud was redefining human nature. For artists who were brought up in a society that was paternalistic and based on observance of authority, their portraits, which sought not to flatter but to expose the sitter, were a celebration of individualism.

With the outbreak of the war, many artists were drawn to reflect on their role as soldiers, medics, or victims. Otto Dix, who eagerly volunteered for war, served in heavy artillery in France, Flanders, and Russia, where he experienced desolation, and saw corpses, and bombardments. In 1914 he depicted himself before he experienced actual combat; he is seen expectant, defiant, powerful, and filled with energy.

For others the despondency that permeated Germany as the devastating effects of combat became known brought forth deeper psychological depictions of their inner souls. Kirchner, for example in *Selbs porträt als Soldat* (*Self-portrait as Soldier*), shows himself in full uniform, flanked by a nude model and a canvas, displaying a stump for a right hand; Kirchner projected himself as a casualty. In Der Trinker (*The Drinker*), painted shortly before his nervous breakdown, he reflects on his inner crisis, and hopelessness and despair suffuse the canvas.

Apocalypse and the War

Even before 1914, the apocalyptic spirit was brilliantly captured in a series of paintings by Ludwig Meidner. His exploding cataclysmic landscapes eerily foreshadowed the conflagrations that would, two years later, become all too commonplace. Most Germans approached the First World War, "the war to end all wars", with anticipation and elation. Artists, too, initially shared this enthusiasm.

Their changing attitude toward war can be seen in some of the periodicals of the time; *Kriegszeit, Der Bildermann*, and *Die Aktion*. Articles and illustrations show how their initial enthusiasm gave way to a growing pessimism. By 1916, Germany had sustained staggering casualties; the battle of Verdun alone resulted in hundreds of thousands of deaths. Trench warfare, poison gas, and tanks produced a war that was unimaginable in 1914. Quickly the initial fervor for the war turned to bitterness.

A number of artists volunteered for active duty: Macke, Marc, Kirchner, Dix, and Grosz all served in combat; Marc and Macke were both killed in the war. Others, such as Max Beckmann and Erich Heckel, were physically unsuited for the front, and volunteered instead for the medical corps. The idea of war captured the imagination of the artists: Barlach's *Der Rächer* (The Avenger, storms off to battle. Ludwig Meidner's city streets explode with bombs – both real and imaginary.

Ludwig Meidner
Apokalyiptische Vision, 1913
Apocalyptic Vision
indian ink and pencil on paper
Milwaukee
The Marvin and Janet Fishman
Collection

Wassily Kandinsky
Improvisation 30 (Kanonen), 1913
Improvisation 30 (Cannons)
oil on canvas
Chicago
The Art Institute of Chicago
Arthur Jermine Memorial Collection

Otto Dix, *Schädel*, 1924 *Skull*
etching with aquatint on copperplate
paper from the portfolio *Der Krieg*
Berlin, Kupferstichkabinett

Meidner's city is shaken to its foundation; house fronts contort and burst, buildings collapse; firestorms erupt. Human figures, dwarfed by the city, scurry in panic, seeking safety. The earth seems to burst forth, expel its underpinnings, rocks and convulse. These paintings feel like authentic witnesses to the end of the world.

Kandinsky had long held the opinion that a new world of the spirit could only come from a great judgment. A number of works in the years prior to 1914 have titles like *Deluge*, *Apocalyptic Rider*, and *Last Judgment*. Colors clash, forms seem to rock back and forth, the whole unstable landscape seems on the verge of collapse or explosion. Even before the outbreak of the war he painted *Improvisation 30*, in which a cannon unleashes its firepower across a colorful composition of hills, towers and other abstracted forms.

The German artists who survived service in the war were irrevocably scarred by it. Some of the most haunting scenes are those painted or drawn directly on the battlefield, such as Dix's shattering images of victims in trenches and on the battlefields. A few years later, Beckmann made horrifying prints and drawings from the operating room in Flanders and the morgue.

Dix produced one of the strongest graphic cycles condemning war – *Der Krieg* (War): fifty etchings documenting in great detail the victims, the mutilated and crippled, and the desolate, bombed landscape of war. For other victims, damage was perhaps not as immediately apparent – madness, and deep inner conflict and lack of confidence affected many.

In the graphic cycle, *Peter Schlemil*, Kirchner, who served for only six months before suffering a nervous collapse, transposed his horrifying experiences into figures illustrating *Peter Schlemil's Remarkable Story* by the Romantic writer, Adelbert von Chamisso. Von Chamisso's story of a man who sold his shadow and who tried in vain to get it back, became an allegory of Kirchner's own life.

If young German artists approached battle with the zeal and fervor of Barlach's *The Avenger* they returned, if at all, desolate, lonely, and defeated; while Barlach's figures signal the high point of early hope and nationalistic pride in the war, Lehmbruck's *Der Gestürzte* (The Fallen Man) represents the spiritual and moral collapse felt by the war's end.

Unlike traditional war memorials that usually celebrated victory, this elongated symbolic figure is nude; he stands for the war dead of Europe. Lehmbruck had served briefly as a medic, and after being deeply horrified at the slaughtering he witnessed to, he went to Zurich in 1916. Feeling greatly depressed, and that life had no more meaning, Lehmbruck committed suicide in 1919 at the age of thirty-eight.

Disillusionment and Revolution

"We stand on the fertile soil of the revolution. Our slogan is Liberty, Equality, and Fraternity!... We have come together because we share the same human and artistic beliefs. We regard it as our noblest duty to dedicate our efforts to the moral task of building Germany young and free." (*Manifesto der Novembristen*, 1918)[6]

Let painters and writers unite with the poor in sacred solidarity. (Ludwig Meidner)[7]

As German artists became increasingly aware of the imminent defeat, some sought to escape by turning inward and toward religious subject matter. Schmidt-Rottluff, Pechstein, Beckmann, Meidner and others painted or did graphic cycles of specifically religious subject matter – "Resurrection", "Deposition from the Cross", "The Lord's Prayer", "St. Sebastian", "The Mocking of Christ", "The Life of Christ", "The Last Judgment" all appear in Expressionist works after the war. In Beckmann's *Christus und die Ehebrecherin* (*Christ and the Women Taken in Adultery*) for example, the artist presents a secular interpretation of the Biblical theme, which now becomes a metaphor for the suffering of the German people and for men's shortcomings, complete with a Christ figure who bears a strong resemblance to the artist himself.

With the actual defeat, a period of uncontrollable economic chaos and widespread hunger ensued. Deserting soldiers roamed the streets, wounded war veterans and orphans were common sights. Kaiser Wilhelm II fled to Holland, and a few days later announced his abdication. The country was ripe for a change.

The November revolution of 1918 sought to replace the old regime with a system in which the leaders were responsible to the parliament. Between November of 1918 and the elections of January 1919, many artists became politically active.

Initially, artists sought direct involvement through revolutionary institutions and artist groups

Max Beckmann, *Christus und die Ehebrecherin*, 1917
Christ and the Adulteress
oil on canvas
St. Louis, Art Museum

Max Pechstein, *An alle Künstler!*, 1919
To All the Artists!
poster

Anonymous, *So führt Euch Spartakus!*
1919
How Spartakus leads you!
color lithograph, poster

Ernst Ludwig Kirchner
Wintermondnacht, 1919
Winter Landscape in Moonlight
oil on canvas
Detroit Institute of the Arts

that sprang up simultaneously in several German cities. Their goal was a close linkage between artists, government, and common people. Organizations such as the Novembergruppe and the Arbeitsrat für Kunst (Working Council for Art), the Dresdner Sezession 1919, and others were formed. In Bremen, Berlin, Bielefeld, Cologne, Darmstadt, Dresden, Düsseldorf, Halle, Hamburg, Hannover, Karlsruhe, Kiel, Magdeburg, and Munich short-lived politically engaged artists groups sought to create a "new man" in a new society that would replace the one with which they had become so disillusioned.

In Berlin, the Arbeitsrat für Kunst made several demands. They called for an influence and participation in all architectural and city planning projects; in the reformation of art schools; in the transformation of museum and state sponsored exhibitions, and in the awarding of exhibition spaces. They wanted to ensure that art would have a future in the new republic.

Through posters, manifestoes, broadsheets, questionnaires, newspapers, and periodicals they demanded a voice in the new Germany. In marked contrast to the censorship that had been so strictly enforced during the Kaiser's reign, German cities now became a riot of colors and slogans as strident messages covered kiosks and walls, and competing socialist parties – the Social Democrats, the Independent Social Democrats, and the Communists – sought control.

One of the most traumatic events occurred when Karl Liebknecht and Rosa Luxemburg, leaders of the Communist (Spartakus) party, were brutally murdered in Berlin. Several artists were moved to create memorials in their honor. Beckmann produced eleven lithographs as a portfolio, *Die Hölle (The Hell)*, in which several plates refer to the revolution and the bloody murders, and he depicts disabled veterans, beggars, prostitutes, and profiteers.

A number of artists were drawn to depicting workers and the proletariat. Conrad Felixmüller, a member of the Dresdner Sezession 1919 group, for example, when awarded the Rome Prize in 1920, went not to Italy, but to the Ruhr district of Germany to paint the coal workers. Felixmüller's political sympathies led him to join the Communist party and to engage in radical politics. This second generation or postwar expressionism is characterized by an emphasis on content and political and social issues.

Old Utopia – New Harmony

Many of the Brücke artists whose work characterized much of German Expressionism before 1914 initially joined in the revolutionary activity after the war. Yet soon many of them retreated to their studios, to the northern lakes, or to the mountains. Kirchner had moved to Davos in 1917 following his nervous collapse. There he painted landscapes, suffused with intense colors, which celebrate the heroic scale of the mountains and valleys that surrounded him. Traumatized by the war, then engaged briefly in revolutionary activity, Schmidt-Rottluff turned inward, seeking a harmony that he did not see around him.

He returned to landscapes with figures, but now calm and balance preside rather than tension. These artists continued to work in a similar style for many decades (Kirchner committed suicide in 1938). They were a generation profoundly affected by the events of the war and subsequent revolution; thereafter they sought to establish calm, order, and harmony in their work, perhaps as an antidote to the chaos they had witnessed.

Toward a New Order

Artists discovered in the early 1920s that the political revolution that intended to transform society was not compatible with an artistic revolution. A number of them, including Otto Dix and George Grosz were pioneers of a new style, a new objectivity, marked by diffidence and skepticism. They bore witness to contemporary events, often by indicting the participants. After the ecstasies of Expressionism, artists now reflected a more sober view of society, as the emotion of the previous decade gave way to unflinching reality.

Yet the fascination with the big city remained. They criticized the Weimar Republic in biting, satirical paintings and graphic cycles that attacked the "pillars of society" and those who ruthlessly exploited the working class; they thematized society's outcasts, racketeers, and sex murderers. The found their subjects not so much in nature as in the grittiness of the city, its factories, brothels, tenements.

Their work is characterized by an insistence on detail and overall clarity. The artists depict both victims and profiteers, whores and pimps, cripples and nouveau riche with merciless accuracy. In

George Grosz, *Stützen der Gesellschaft*
1926
The Pillars of society
Berlin, Nationalgalerie

Otto Dix, *Salon I*, 1921
oil on canvas
Stuttgart, Galerie der Stadt

Max Beckmann, *Tanz im Baden-Baden*
1923, *Dance in Baden-Baden*
Munich
Bayerische Staatsgemäldesammlungen
Stadtsgalerie moderner Kunst

Beckmann *Tanz im Baden-Baden* (*Dance in Baden-Baden*) of 1923, for example, a well-dressed crowd dance, but people do not look at one another; they are a group of marionette-like individuals engaged in various roles. Stiff and immobile, these men and women are crowded into a pictorial space, bound together by their greed.

In 1921 the Expressionist poet Ywan Goll, who in 1914 had described Expressionism as an art style less than a form of experience, wrote about the death of Expressionism. He emphasized the antimilitarist and Communist goals of the Expressionists and mourned the destruction of humanitarianism through the bitter political struggles of the various factions: "What has been whispered, smiled about, and suspected everywhere is now confirmed: once again an art is dying because of the times that betrayed it. Whether the art or times are at fault not important. Critically it could be proven, though, that Expressionism is choking on the carcass of the same revolution whose motherly Pythia it wanted to be."[8]

Ultimately Expressionism disappeared. Its practitioners did not suddenly abandon it. Certainly some of the founding artists such as Heckel, Schmidt-Rottluff and Kirchner continued to work in an Expressionist style, but it was no longer allied with the avant-garde. It had spent itself during the war and the subsequent revolution. The movements' ambitions and political engagement were passed over as ultimately ineffectual. A clear look at everyday life, an unsentimentality in detail, and the rise of an industrial society were all part of the new spirit. The slogan of the new generation would be new objectivity and new reality.

[1] George Biermann, "Max Pechstein", *Junge Kunst*, vol. 1, Leipzig, 1919.
[2] Wassily Kandinsky, "Vorwort", *Neue Künstler Vereinigung München*, exhibition catalogue. December 1-15, 1909, Moderne Galerie, second edition, München, 1909-10.
[3] Franz Marc, letter to Reinhard Piper, April 20, 1910; reprinted in Reinhard Piper, *Briefwechsel mit Autoren und Künstler 1903-1953*, München: R. Piper & Co. Verlag, 1979, p. 29-30.
[4] Ernst Ludwig Kirchner, "Über Leben und Arbeit", *Omnibus*, in Berlin 1931.
[5] E. Waldmann, "Die künstlerische Entdeckung der Grosstadt," *Vossische Zeitung*, 2 December 1917, Morgenblatt, Charles W. Haxthausen, "A New Beauty: Ernst Ludwig Kirchner's Images of Berlin", Charles W. Haxthausen and H. Suhr, eds., *Berlin: Culture and Metropolis*. Minneapolis: University of Minnesota Press, 1990, p. 60-61.
[6] Novembergruppe Manifesto, Helga Kleimann, *Die Novembergruppe*. Berlin: Gebr. Mann, 1969, p. 56.
[7] Ludwig Meidner, "An alle Künstler, Dichter, Maler", *Das Kunstblatt*, III, 1919, p. 29.
[8] Ywan Goll, "Der Expressionismus stirbt", *Zenit* (Zagreb), 1, no. 8, October 1921, p. 8-9; reprinted in Rose-Carol Washton Long, ed., *German Expressionism: documents from the End of the Wilhelmine Empire to the Rise of National Socialism*. New York: G.K. Hall, 1993, p. 288.

Expressionism in Imperial Germany

Peter Paret

At the beginning of the twentieth century, conditions in Germany inhibited but also favored the search for new forms of artistic expression. The country's political unification that had been completed with the victory over France in 1870 concentrated control of foreign and military affairs and of large areas of social and economic policy in the overlapping Prussian and imperial governments. But in cultural matters the twenty-five member states that made up the empire remained largely autonomous. Artists benefitted from the often competing cultural centers, each with its own social and political characteristics, a diversity that prevented any one set of opinions and rules from becoming dominant. The training and support of young artists, modes and extent of official patronage, censorship, and the administration and funding of museums varied from state to state, as did the attitudes toward the fine arts of the twenty-two reigning princes and of the senates of the city-republics of Hamburg, Bremen, and Lübeck. How significant these differences could be is exemplified by the two largest German states. In Bavaria, Prince-Regent Luitpold cared little for painting and sculpture, but his paternalistic sense of representing all Bavarians caused him to further even artists whose work he disliked or found puzzling. By contrast, William II, German emperor and king of Prussia, held strong personal convictions on art and its place in German life, opinions he rarely hesitated to express and often succeeded in imposing on the cultural bureaucracy and the general public. That his views tended to coincide with those of large segments of the upper and middle classes added force to his activist art policies.

Käthe Kollwitz
Storming the Gate, 1897
etching, plate 5
of *Weberaufstand Weavers' Uprising*
Washington, National Gallery of Art

An incident during the 1898 annual Berlin art exhibition, held under his patronage, indicates the attention William II paid to the arts, but also shows the limits that the federated structure of the empire placed on his authority. The jury voted to award a medal to Käthe Kollwitz for her cycle of lithographs and etchings, *Weberaufstand* (*Weavers' Uprising*). A memorandum to the emperor by the Prussian minister of culture suggested that "from a purely artistic point of view" an award might be justified, but that the subject matter and its uncompromising treatment made it inadvisable to single out the work for recognition.[1] The emperor agreed and took the unusual step of rejecting the jury's recommendation. In the following year the artist nevertheless won a medal in the annual Dresden art exhibition, the Saxon authorities feeling free to ignore the Prussian example.

Even within Prussia the emperor's cultural authority was far from absolute. Although the directors of the Prussian museums were state officials who could ill afford to antagonize him, they also possessed a measure of independence, which led to the acquisition by the Prussian state by gift or purchase of a significant number of Impressionist and post-Impressionist works in the decade-and-a-half before the First World War. William II's effort in 1908 to replace Hugo von Tschudi, the director of the Berlin Nationalgalerie and a determined proponent of modern art, caused such widespread resentment that the emperor was compelled to retain Tschudi. When Tschudi subsequently decided to leave Berlin after all, he was appointed director of the Bayerische Staatsgemäldesammlungen.[2]

Nor could the emperor prevent the growth of strong art organizations that were not subject to state control. Dissatisfaction with the annual contemporary art exhibitions sponsored by most German states, their halls crammed with hundreds of conventional works, led in the 1890s to secessionist movements throughout Germany. Most important were the Munich Secession (1892), the Vienna Secession (1897) with its many ties to German artists, and the Berlin Secession, founded in 1898, which in association with the art dealer and publisher Paul Cassirer became the principal institutional force of what has been called German Impressionism. The Secession and Cassirer in his private gallery exhibited recent foreign art as well, Cézanne and later Matisse being two examples. The 1901 spring exhibition of the Secession included five Van Goghs, the first time his work was shown in Germany; nineteen were again exhibited in the Cassirer gallery in December. The paintings were largely ignored, and only one was sold. After continuing to show Van Gogh's work in the following years, Cassirer assembled a major exhibition in 1905. This time ten paintings were sold, several to Tschudi, an indication that the new and unfamiliar was gradually gaining acceptance. The show also traveled to Dresden, where it had an overwhelming impact on three young artists – Kirchner, Pechstein, and Heckel – who a few months earlier had joined with a fourth – Schmidt-Rottluff – to form a working group of like-minded artists, the Brücke, a name possibly chosen to suggest that its members were building "a bridge" to the future.[3] It was the institutional beginning of Expressionism.

Vincent van Gogh
Plain near Auvers, 1890
oil on canvas
one of the paintings in the 1905
Dresden exhibition
bought by Hugo von Tschudi
Munich, Neue Pinakothek

Also in 1905 the dominance of the traditionalist national art association, the Allgemeine

Deutsche Kunstgenossenschaft, which over time had developed strong links to the cultural ministeries of the various states, was weakened by the founding of a rival association with modernist sympathies, the Deutsche Künstlerbund, under the chairmanship of Count Kessler. With their exhibitions and publications, their connections to modernist groups throughout Europe, and their influence on the art market, the new groups – the Deutsche Künstlerbund, the secessions, and the galleries representing recent and contemporary artists – coalesced into a powerful counterforce to state patronage and the official art establishment.

These developments were favored and in part made possible by the country's economic conditions. Between 1895 and 1913 the German economy experienced a boom, interrupted only by two sharp but brief declines. Most segments of the population shared in the economic expansion, but the greatest benefits accrued to the wealthiest five percent – the traditional elites, the new rich, and most of the still small propertied and educated middleclass. These were the same groups from which came the subscribers to art journals, the visitors to galleries, the buyers of art, and the officials who administered the cultural bureaucracy of the various states. They formed the essential core of the German art public, even if workers and the lower middleclass were part of the tens of thousands who enjoyed the historical scenes and the patriotic and sentimental images on view in the great state exhibitions. For economic as well as social reasons it is not surprising that when the Brücke artists added a category of "passive members" to their group, art lovers who for a fee received an annual report and a portfolio of graphics, they came without exception from the bourgeoisie.

The middleclass provided not only much of the art public but also most of the artists, whether traditional or avant-garde. Among the painters and sculptors who are commonly referred to as Expressionists even if they rejected the label, or whose work passed through an Expressionist phase, only a few came from poor or modest backgrounds – Lehmbruck, Nolde, and Pechstein are examples. Most were born into families of the traditional or new middleclass. Barlach's father was a physician; Beckmann's a flour merchant. Feininger was the son of a violinist and composer; Heckel, Kirchner, and Macke were the sons of engineers. After studying law and briefly serving in the Prussian bureaucracy, Käthe Kollwitz's father became a well-to-do building contractor. Marc was the son of a painter and grandson of a senior official who had received a patent of personal nobility. Müller's father was a Prussian officer, who after being severely wounded in the war of 1870 was employed in the tax administration. Schmidt-Rottluff's family had sufficient means for him to attend a gymnasium. Precariously hanging on at the lower edge of the middleclass were the fathers of Grosz, a restaurant manager, and Kokoschka, who writes that his father, a jeweler, goldsmith, and bookkeeper, was "the son of a patrician family in Prague."[4] Socially and culturally these artists were deeply influenced by German middleclass values of the end of the century and most retained throughout their lives the intellectual armature of a traditional secondary education with its emphasis on literature, history, and languages. German by adoption were Jawlensky and Kandinsky. Both came from the minor Russian nobility: Jawlensky's father was a colonel; Kandinsky's the director of a tea firm.

Angelo Jank, *The state-sponsored art exhibition as a phenomenon of mass culture*, drawing for *Jugend* 10 October 1896

Throughout the reign of William II the social groups from which most Expressionist artists came and which they addressed in their work continued to gain in size and significance. The traditional educated and propertied classes joined by the new technical specialists, administrators, and entrepreneurs powered the country's modernization. At the same time they experienced a crisis in function and values. On the national level the expanded middleclass was largely excluded from political power. Internally it was weakened by political divisions and the decline of liberalism. The growth of the Social Democrats, who gained nearly thirty-five percent of the votes in the Reichstag elections of 1912, seemed to squeeze the middleclass between uncompromising conservatives and the threat of proletarization and revolution.

The political dilemma was accompanied by a loss of confidence. How relevant were traditional ethics and the ideals of *Bildung* to the individual alienated in urban mass society or to the nation fighting the war of all against all in an international system in crisis? Religious faith weakened; its new substitutes – nationalism, materialism, and the belief in progress – raised as many problems as they solved. "The old truths are coming to an end," Nietzsche declared in his comments on *Twilight of the Idols* of 1888.[5] In his anger and despair at the decline of European moral and intellectual standards – especially the betrayal, in his eyes, of everything that was best in German culture – he proclaimed a reversal of all values. Morality was a lie, idealism a cowardly escape

Otto Dix
Büste Friedrich Nietzsche, 1912
Bust of Friedrich Nietzsche
plaster, now lost

from reality, the community a trap for the individual. With him and after him, a generation of critics identified bourgeois errors and hypocrisy, and ideologues ranging from anarchists and Marxists to ultra-nationalist saviors of German uniqueness and purity, did their best to politicize the cultural critique and the search for solutions to the ills of modern society.

The young Brücke artists responded to this crisis by depicting their world through prisms of conflict. They painted men and women at war with their surroundings and often with themselves. Even their nudes, playing and posing in the countryside, rarely lose the strained quality of people briefly released from the concrete cage of offices, factories and apartment houses. An assertive eroticism may help make life bearable for them, and its exploration gives the artist another tool for exposing the lies and decadence of society. Nor is sexuality always shown as a life-enhancing force: images of human degradation may destroy false ideals as effectively as do pastoral scenes.[6] Motifs borrowed from African and Oceanic tribal art and from Buddhist cave paintings further question the bourgeois world. But perhaps more important than the subjects of their work is the artist's revolutionary rejection of mimetic truth by means of distortion and of colors derived from the imagination rather than from the observed phenomenon.

This was an enormous achievement, at once destructive and liberating, and the searching, combative posture of the Brücke lends itself to romantic interpretations, which have not been lacking in the literature. Typical is the statement in a recent study of Heckel that "Expressionism was above all a protest: against the bourgeoisie, against aestheticizing, and against the dominant academic outlook."[7] But it is not clear what these words explain. By the time the Brücke was formed, the academic outlook no longer dominated German art but was a wounded force in retreat. Certainly, society in general either ignored or derided the contemporary avant-garde, and state art schools continued to follow conventional curricula; but those are constants of modern culture, and in 1900 mattered less than the slowly growing receptivity of the art public to varieties of modernism. Nor did the Brücke painters "protest" bourgeois values and the efforts of other artists to express one or the other concept of the beautiful. Whatever their feelings, in their work they necessarily had to go beyond the art that already existed, and their true enemy was not academic painting but the late followers of Impressionism, which only a few years earlier had been a liberating force but now could be experienced as oppressive in the broad acceptance it had won and in its domination of exhibitions and the art market. Even under different social conditions the Brücke painters would not have wanted to repeat what had already been done. It would be more accurate to say that the crisis of their society gave them some of the intellectual and emotional tools with which to clear a new path. That their work was almost wholly apolitical hardly needs adding. Although the Expressionism of the Brücke was among other things a revolt against aspects of bourgeois life, in the problems the young painters faced and in their ways of solving them they remained in the bourgeois world.

Above all, the Brücke cannot stand for Expressionism as such. Within a few years of the first the Brücke exhibition in 1905, Kokoschka showed his early paintings. Barlach – according to one scholar the greatest Expressionist "if the term *Expressionism* indicates an art which manifests in visible form the inner life of mankind" – produced his first wooden sculptures, most of which were calm, introspective figures in an ahistorical, classless world.[8] Beckmann's work was shown by the Berlin Secession and the Deutsche Künstlerbund. Kandinsky and Jawlensky exhibited with the New Artists Association, which in 1909 split off from the Munich Secession, and in 1911 Kandinsky with Marc assembled the first exhibition of the Blaue Reiter, the second great organized statement by Expressionist artists, which has often been called an antipode of the Brücke. With the possible exception of Kokoschka, none of these artists produced work that can be even remotely schematized as a protest against the bourgeoisie, unless creativity itself, whatever form it takes, is defined as protest. The enormous bursts of new concepts and images that swept across Central Europe in these years, from Kirchner's visions of the modern metropolis to Kandinsky's nonobjective compositions, possessed too much vitality to be subsumed under an ideological abstraction.

The further expansion of Expressionism was helped by the move of the Brücke artists to Berlin. Despite some relatively favorable reviews, Dresden had not proved receptive to their work. Pechstein's memoirs reveal the marginal existence to which lack of sales intermittently condemned the group. In 1908 he moved to Berlin, and was followed by Kirchner, Schmidt-Rottluff, and Heckel in 1911. The capital of Prussia and the empire was now also the center of the German art mar-

Ernst Barlach, *Die Verlassenen*, 1911
The Lonely Man
wood
Hamburg, Kunsthalle

Oskar Kokoschka, *Herwarth Walden*
pen-and-ink, in *Der Sturm*
19 May 1910

Max Liebermann
Badende Knaben, ca. 1910
Boys bathing
oil on canvas
Hannover, Niedersächsisches
Landesmuseum Landesgalerie

Lovis Corinth
Kain und Abel, 1919
Cain and Abel
woodcut
Washington, National Gallery of Art
Rosenwald Collection

ket, and with the Berlin Secession, the Cassirer gallery and publishing house, and Herwarth Walden's journal *Der Sturm* and the exhibitions connected to it, for a time the institutional center of modernism in Germany.

Some episodes in Berlin highlight the history of the Brücke in its last and most successful phase. Heckel, Kirchner, Schmidt-Rottluff, and Pechstein had exhibited with the Berlin Secession in 1908. Also represented was Nolde, who had joined the Brücke in 1906 but found the communal character of the group too enfolding and left again the following year. Soon he became a member of the Berlin Secession, which unlike the Brücke was not a small working group but a much larger association of artists formed for the exhibition and sale of the work of members and guests. In 1910 the jury for the summer exhibition of the Secession, which included Beckmann, accepted works of such modernists as Matisse, Van Dongen, and Barlach, but refused the entries of the Brücke painters. Pechstein and others reacted by organizing the New Secession, and showed the rejected works. It was in this exhibition that the Brücke artists became acquainted with the paintings of Otto Müller, whose sensuality if not the rather tame lyricism of his work struck a sympathetic chord, and invited him to join their group.

Although his entries to the summer exhibition had been turned down, Nolde remained a member of the Berlin Secession. It was not until the end of the year that he wrote a letter to the editor and critic Karl Scheffler that began as a complaint about Scheffler's comments on his work, but quickly turned into an attack on the character and ability of the president of the Berlin Secession, the German Impressionist painter Max Liebermann. Ignoring Liebermann's advice, the members of the Secession expelled Nolde by a vote of forty to two with three abstentions. Nolde sued the Secession, but lost the case and his appeal. The disproportionate violence of his accusations and their antisemitic overtones foretold Nolde's future course – his appraisal of aesthetic styles according to concepts of racial purity, his membership in the National Socialist party of Schleswig Holstein after the First World War, and his efforts after 1933 to win the approval and patronage of the Third Reich.[9]

The rejection by the Berlin Secession and the founding of the New Secession, which called attention to their work, helped rather than hindered the members of the Brücke. Sales and invitations to participate in other shows followed. Aside from smaller shows, they exhibited again with the New Secession in 1911 and with the International Sonderbund exhibition of 1912, the most important effort so far to present Expressionism in its historical and contemporary context. But that same year Pechstein again exhibited with the Berlin Secession. According to Kirchner, Pechstein's step was a "breach of trust," and Pechstein was expelled from the group.[10] Within a year the Brücke itself came to an end. The immediate cause may have been disagreements over Kirchner's brief history of the Brücke, which he wrote for friends and "passive members" of the group; but more decisive was the growing recognition each of the artists was gaining as his work developed in its own separate direction.

These incidents – the rejection of the Brücke painters by the Berlin Secession and the founding of the New Secession, Nolde's attack on Scheffler and Liebermann, and Pechstein's return to the Berlin Secession and his subsequent exclusion from the Brücke – point to general characteristics in the history of Expressionism in the years before 1914. Artists, art organizations, critics, and the art public were not grouped in two compact forces representing modernism on the one hand and the conventional on the other, but rather in many competing and coexisting factions. The war over modernism was not fought along a single front. Even modernist associations included different points of view and responded differently to new developments. The Berlin Secession rejected the Brücke, whose work it had shown earlier. Among its leading figures, Corinth displayed the greatest hostility to Expressionism, but in spirit and execution his own work was closer to Expressionism than that of any of his colleagues. Avant-garde artists could condemn each other's work with a vehemence that outdid the worst things William II said about modern art. After the first Matisse exhibition in Berlin, his paintings were dismissed by Beckmann as "one shameless piece of insolence after another," and Käthe Kollwitz consoled herself with the thought that his reputation would not last.[11] Nolde, according to Beckmann, "considers himself a genius, isn't one, but nevertheless wishes to be treated as one."[12] Beckmann and Marc derided each other's work in print, Kirchner rejected Futurism and Cubism, and Kandinsky thought that the work of the Brücke was of marginal significance.[13]

Such judgments are only to be expected from artists pursuing their own ideas. But they also af-

August Macke, *Promenade*, 1913
oil on canvas
Munich
Städtische Galerie im Lenbachhaus

Wassily Kandinsky
Kleine Freuden, 1913
Small Pleasures
oil on canvas
New York
Solomon R. Guggenheim Museum

Oskar Kokoschka, Poster for his play
Mörder - Hoffnung der Frauen, 1909
Murderer, Hope of Women
New York, Museum of Modern Art

fect the general situation. Art in Germany at the beginning of the twentieth century was often a battleground for modernism and its enemies, although not every innovative artist was at the center of the battle – Barlach in the years before the war is an example. But just as the country's political environment was not solidly hostile to innovation, so the conflict between different conceptions of art was not waged between two internally uniform forces in which the artist moved in lockstep with generally-held principles.

In 1912 Kandinsky and Marc published the *Blaue Reiter Almanac* – the "blue rider" on the cover of the volume signifying movement, exploration, and the slaying of the dragon Tradition. They articulated a vision of art centered on the "conception of compelling inner necessity ... independent of [either] abstraction or reality," and of an art that rejected the separation between images, sounds, and words.[14] The fifteen-hundred copies of the almanac were soon sold, an indication of the interest aroused by aesthetic experimentation.

While preparing the almanac, Kandinsky and Marc assembled the first Blaue Reiter exhibition, which opened in December 1911. The diversity of the works shown would, they hoped, demonstrate "how the artist's inner desire results in manifold forms."[15] "Inner desire" and "compelling inner necessity" are, of course, present whenever a work of art is created with a measure of originality; in Munich at the time these terms pointed to the artist's freedom, varying in kind and degree, from the representational. "A work of art," wrote Jawlensky, "is a world of its own, not an imitation of nature."[16] In the exhibition this freedom found a range of expressions, from Marc's increasingly abstract canvases and Macke's elegant urban scenes, their stylized forms painted in glowing colors, to Kandinsky's nonobjective compositions, with which the subjective distortions of the Brücke reached their logical conclusion. Making the inner world of the artist visible and giving it central significance not only shifted the task of the image but also affected the relationship between the artist and the public. That the unfolding of the artist's inner life, perhaps mediated by recognizable elements of the external world but never dependent on them, would lead to a dialogue between the artist and the newly intuitive viewer became one of the great hopes of Expressionism.

The founders of the Blaue Reiter, far more than the Brücke artists, occupied themselves with theory. New directions in aesthetics and art history explored by such scholars as Wilhelm Worringer helped clarify their ideas on the relationship of the artist to earlier art and to the present; for example, to recognize, in Marc's words, that "objects speak: objects possess will and form, why should we wish to interrupt them? We have nothing sensible to say to them. Haven't we learned in the last thousand years that the more we confront objects with the reflection of their appearance, the more silent they become?"[17] That Marc and Kandinsky were moving away from the objective reproduction of the visible world was clear enough. Less apparent was what they were moving toward, especially since their art as well as their argument continued to evolve. Still, particularly Kandinsky's writings had an impact on a generation of artists, who found support for their individual purposes in his interpretations of earlier art and in his faith in an intensely personal art of the future. In ways that could not yet be recognized this new art would set the artist free, and by eliminating the divisions between music, literature, and the fine arts at last achieve an integrated aesthetic experience.

It was not unusual for artists to convey their ideas in writing. Among German Impressionists, Liebermann was known for the brilliance of his essays. Corinth was the author of several books, among them a deeply-felt biography of his friend, the painter Walter Leistikow, one of the founders of the Berlin Secession. But for some permanent or temporary members of the Expressionist wave, literature became a medium of central importance. Lehmbruck wrote poetry, Kubin stories. Kokoschka's plays – the reduction and compression of their language creating violent effects that recall some of his paintings of the time – were soon staged and continue to be studied. In 1912 Barlach took a step toward Kandinsky's integrative ideal by publishing his first play illustrated with a series of his own lithographs. His subsequent dramas have made him a permanent presence in modern German literature. Nolde's four volumes of memoirs, written in a uniquely personal syntax, are an impressive monument to the man and his obsessions in a culturally and politically turbulent age.

But significant as these and other writings were, they characterized only one strand of the literature of the times. In painting and sculpture on the other hand, few modern works produced in Central Europe in the last years before the war remained untouched by Expressionist influences.

Ernst Barlach, *Stürzende Frau*
Falling Woman, lithograph for his play
Der tote Tag, 1912
Wedel, Ernst Barlach Museum

Max Beckmann, *Two Officers*, 1915
drypoint
The man on the right is Paul Cassirer

Franz Marc
Arsenal für eine Schöpfung, 1915
Arsenal for a Creation
pencil
Munich
Staatliche Graphische Sammlung

In the larger culture as well, Expressionism had arrived. Artists who a few years earlier had been ignored or derided were now seriously discussed, exhibited their work everywhere, and found a market for it.[18] When a second, slightly expanded edition of the *Blaue Reiter Almanac* was published in 1914, the number of copies printed was four times that of the first edition.

When war came the flaws and cruelty of modern society that had inspired some Expressionist art burst into the open with a violence that no one had foreseen. The cataclysm seemed all-encompassing, yet some artists avoided war as a subject. Others, like Beckmann, Kirchner, and the young Otto Dix, responded to the horror by raising their work to a new level. At the outbreak of the war Barlach sculpted *Der Rächer* (*The Avenger*), developing a subject that he had first addressed in 1910 with wooden and bronze versions of *Der Vertilger* (*The Berserk Man*). As many others, he responded to the enthusiasm and idealism that for the moment seemed to grip the entire country. But soon he followed *The Avenger* with lithographs and sculptures that expressed human suffering and helplessness before the inexplicable. He was called up as an over-age reservist, but saw no action. Others became psychic casualties, were wounded like Kokoschka, or were killed. Macke fell in the second month of the war; Marc a year-and-a-half later. In one of his last aphorisms Marc once more spoke as the explorer of the future: "Of the things that now lie behind us, what is still sacred to us today? From now on no one, no one can return across the sea of blood of this war to the past, and live from the past."[19]

Marc's hope that the war would be a new beginning points once more to the central energy of Expressionism. It was an achievement to destroy – or to continue the destruction – of a universally understood aesthetic in Western culture, and replace it with the liberated insights of the individual artist. The results of these insights varied in quality. Hundreds of painters, printmakers, and sculptors did little more than echo the innovators and expand Expressionism into a familiar cultural presence, as much at home in posters and store windows as in art exhibitions. But at its best, in the many different forms it assumed, the Expressionist vision enabled a few artists to reveal general truths about the world and humanity within the diseased and healthy context of European society and culture at the beginning of the century.

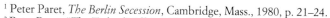

[1] Peter Paret, *The Berlin Secession*, Cambridge, Mass., 1980, p. 21–24.
[2] Peter Paret, "The Tschudi Affair," *The Journal of Modern History*, 53, 1981, 4. An expanded version "Die Tschudi-Affäre", appeared in *Manet bis van Gogh: Hugo von Tschudi und der Kampf um die Moderne*, Johann Georg Prince von Hohenzollern and Peter-Klaus Schuster, eds., München, 1996.
[3] On Paul Cassirer's Van Gogh exhibitions, see the detailed statistics in Walter Feilchenfeldt, *Vincent van Gogh & Paul Cassirer, Cahier Vincent* 2, Amsterdam, 1988. Fritz Schumacher mentions the reactions of the Brücke artists in his *Stufen des Lebens. Erinnerungen eines Baumeisters*, Stuttgart-Berlin, 1935, p. 283.
[4] Oskar Kokoschka, *Mein Leben*, München, 1971, p. 39.
[5] Friedrich Nietzsche, "Ecce homo," in *Nachgelassene Schriften*, vol. 6, of *Sämtliche Werke*, Giorgio Colli & Mazzino Montinari, eds., München, 1988, p. 354.
[6] Horst Jähner, *Künstlergruppe Brücke*, Berlin, 1986, p. 66.
[7] *Erich Heckel: Die frühen Jahre*, Serge Sabarsky, ed. Salzweg bei Passau, 1995, p. 9.
[8] Peter W. Guenther, "Barlach," in *German Expressionist Sculpture*, Stephanie Barron, ed., Los Angeles, 1983, p. 61.
[9] The episode is discussed in some detail in Paret, *The Berlin Secession*, p. 210–16.
[10] Ernst Ludwig Kirchner, *Chronik der Brücke*, printed in Jähner, *Künstlergruppe Brücke*, p. 246.
[11] Max Beckmann, Diary entry, 7 January 1909, printed in *Briefe*, vol. 1, Uwe M. Schneede, ed., Münich-Zürich, 1993, p. 419. Käthe Kollwitz, *Die Tagebücher*, Jutta Bohnke-Kollwitz, ed., Berlin, 1989, p. 779.
[12] Max Beckmann. Diary entry, 2 April 1909, *Briefe*, vol. 1, p. 413.
[13] Ernst Ludwig Kirchner, *Chronik der Brücke*, in Jähner, *Künstlergruppe Brücke*, p. 426.
[14] Paul Vogt, "Der Blaue Reiter," in *Expressionism: A German Intuition 1905–1920*, catalogue of the exhibition at the Solomon R. Guggenheim Museum, New York, and the San Francisco Museum of Modern Art, New York, 1980, p. 196.
[15] Catalogue of the first exhibition of the Blaue Reiter group, quoted in Peter Selz, *German Expressionist Painting*, Berkeley 1974, p. 206.
[16] Alexej von Jawlensky, quoted in Hans K. Roethel, *The Blue Rider*, New York, 1971, p. 50.
[17] Franz Marc, "Absolute Painting" (1911-12?), in *Briefe, Aufzeichnungen und Aphorismen*, Berlin, 1920, vol. 1, p. 124.
[18] Robin Lenman, *Die Kunst, die Macht und das Geld*, Frankfurt am Main, 1994, p. 97.
[19] Franz Marc, "Aphorism Nr. 85" (1915), in *Briefe, Aufzeichnungen und Aphorismen*, Berlin, 1920, vol. 1, p. 131.

Joan Weinstein

Introduction

In the name of the Expressionist artists exhibiting at the First German Autumn Salon in 1913, Herwarth Walden, founder of the Sturm Gallery, wrote in the exhibition catalogue: "Today we do not live in a time when art is a helpmate of life. What true art is created today ... is the equation drawn from life by abstractly oriented spirits, without desire, without purpose, and without restriction... That is the reason for our self-imposed seclusion from the demands the world makes on us. We do not wish to get mixed up with it".[1] Walden here summed up the radical construction of an exclusive marginality cultivated by the majority of the avant-garde in Germany in the years between 1905 and 1913. Whether it was Wassili Kandinsky's belief that an increasingly abstract art would play a leading role in the transformation from a decadent, materialist culture to an epoch of great spirituality, or the Brücke artists' eroticized subject matter and lifestyle as a repudiation of bourgeois morality, Expressionist artists positioned their art as a challenge to the repressive values and the naturalistic art of established Wilhelmine culture. The contrasting colors and dissonant chords of this art, the jagged brushstrokes and angular lines, probed "behind the veil of appearances" of Impressionist art for the "hidden aspects" and "inner, spiritual side" of nature, as Franz Marc put it in an essay on the new art in 1912.[2] Artists were not to be limited to depicting the visible forms of nature, but were to reflect a more profound, even cosmic inner form. The outbreak of the First World War forcefully challenged the bohemian marginality of the Expressionist artists. Their careers as artists interrupted by war service, their individuality threatened by conformity in the ranks of the military, Expressionist artists faced fundamental challenges to their art. All had to struggle with ways to reconcile the war and art. How would an art that claimed to be truly "modern" come to terms with the war, the most profound contemporary historical experience?

The essay that follows narrates the responses of a number of leading Expressionist artists to the First World War and its aftermath in Germany. It argues that the transformations introduced by the war completed an integration of Expressionist art into the mainstream of German culture, an integration that had begun already before the war. For the bloody events of the First World War and the brief, but violent, revolution that followed it in Germany, challenged the most fundamental notion of avant-garde art in the forefront of revolutionary change.

War Enthusiasm

When war was declared on August 1, 1914, Germans of all political persuasions joined in an outburst of patriotic fervor, filled with optimism and determination, confident of victory in a "defensive" war thrust upon them by "encircling" enemies. Kaiser Wilhelm II ratified the patriotic unanimity of the German people when he declared: "I know no parties any more, I know only Germans." In the first weeks of the war, the German army's lightning advance through Belgium and France, and the successful defense of a Russian invasion of East Prussia, confirmed the public's confidence. Even when the German advance was halted in September, even after the bloody battles of Ypres and Langemarck in late 1914 in which thousands of young German soldiers lost their lives, popular consensus in support of the war remained. They did not know that another three years of stalemate and a frightening technical war of attrition would follow.

The German art world, too, rallied to the cause. Rather typical was the patriotic fervor of Julius Meier-Graefe, a staunch supporter of Impressionism and Neo-Impressionism: "The war enriches us. We have changed since yesterday. The debate about words and programs is at an end ... We had theories. What we lacked was content, and that is being given to us, my brothers, by the times!... Unity has been granted us by the war. All parties have joined together to achieve the common goal. Art must follow!"[3] It was not just academic or Secession artists, however, who greeted the call to arms. Joining the fragile balance of forces supporting the war effort were Expressionist artists and their supporters as well. Many Expressionist artists volunteered for active duty, while still others volunteered for service as medics or with the Red Cross. Expressionist artists soon displayed their new work alongside academicians and Secessionists in privately sponsored exhibitions devoted to artists serving in the armed forces. In many ways, developments in the German art world had fostered this consensus already before 1914. In 1913 Secession artists were wooed by the government to participate in an exhibition to mark the twenty-fifth anniversary of the Kaiser's rule. Although in the end the Secession declined to participate, the government had recognized the artistic significance of their work.[4] Equally important, Expressionism had already begun to lose its marginal status in the German art world. By 1912 the Expressionists could count on a rapidly developing network of support. Their art was featured in a number of major exhibitions, including the 1912 Sonderbund exhibition and Walden's First German Autumn Salon the following year, and was promoted in journals such as Walden's *Der Sturm*. Berlin had also become one of the most internationally-minded art centers in Europe, regularly exhibiting modernist art from France, Russia, Italy, and Scandinavia.

Also fostering an integration of Expressionism into the wartime culture was the shift in the critical debate about Expressionism in the years immediately before the war. Before 1912 German artists, critics, and museum professionals had acknowledged the French role in the creation of modern art; indeed, they insisted on it, even while they sought to transform it into a more universal signpost of modern, urban, industrial culture. After 1912, however, the discussion about modernism began to take on more nationalist tones: modernity became a quintessential German experience.[5] As the influential critic Paul Fechter argued in his 1914 book *Der Expressionismus*, the first full-length defense of the movement, the "inner necessity" of Expressionism represented a fundamentally German spiritual disposition.[6] Similar arguments were now presented by other leading Expressionist critics. Adolf Behne wrote in winter 1915: "What is represented as seemingly oriented toward foreign countries under the confusing catchwords expressionism and cubism is German in its innermost essence, although the contrary is generally claimed. ... [E]xpressionism brings a strengthening of the national element in art, since it is built on will and on fantasy"...[7] Many cultural commentators believed that victory at the front would usher in a period of German economic and cultural preeminence, even if they did not agree what form that cultural preeminence might assume.

As Reinhold Heller has observed, during the first years of the war the subject matter of works shown in state-sponsored exhibitions by those who rejected traditional artistic vocabularies was similar to that of more traditional artists. Replacing the standard themes of nudes, landscapes, or still lifes were now scenes from occupied countries, soldiers in uniform, fighting, and the wounded, dying or dead.[8] Members of the former Berlin Secession were among the first to celebrate German victories and nationalist values (in 1913 the most prestigious members of the group had split over jury selections for their autumn exhibition and formed the Free Secession, headed by Max Liebermann). Max Liebermann, along with numerous others German academics and intellectuals, signed a declaration defending Germany's violation of Belgian neutrality. Lovis Corinth, head of the rump Berlin Secession, warned against the leveling effect of "Franco-Slavic internationalist art".[9] Both Liebermann and Corinth contributed to the periodical (*Kriegszeit*) and portfolio (*Krieg und Kunst*) published under the auspices of the Berlin Secession in support of the war. Corinth's 1915 lithograph for *Krieg und Kunst*, *'Barbaren': Immanuel Kant* (*'Barbarians': Immanuel Kant*), represented the quintessential "German" philosopher looking down at his native city of Königsberg, recently invaded by the Russians.[10] Corinth – or the editors' – inclusion of "barbarians" in the title reversed the epithet commonly hurled at the Germans for their destruction of cultural property and now directed it against their enemies. In the journal *Kriegszeit*, Ernst Barlach's *The heilige Krieg* (*The Holy War*) defended the notion that the war was a "defensive" one, thrust upon Germany. A giant figure wielding a sword attacks frontally toward the viewer, an expression of suffering on his face. The title, *Holy War*, suggested a war divinely ordained.

For many Expressionist artists, the war appeared as an unprecedented and enormous event pregnant with fate, one that would confirm rather than annihilate Expressionism. They shared with many other artists an intense aesthetic fascination with the war forged from front-line experience. Foremost among these artists were Franz Marc, one of the leading Expressionists of his generation Otto Dix, a young unknown artist from a working-class background, and Max Beckmann, an established figure in the German modern art world.

Max Beckmann had been elected to the governing body of the Berlin Secession in 1910 at the age of twenty-six (he left the Berlin Secession in 1913 to join the Free Secession). His large-scale figurative paintings, often of violent themes, gained him the attention–and admiration–of critics. Although he did not greet the war as enthusiastically as some of his colleagues, he traveled to the front in East Prussia in September 1914 as a civilian and volunteered as an orderly in a field hospital. In early 1915, he moved to Belgium where he volunteered for the medical corps. He was stationed first at a typhus hospital, then at an operating room at Courtrai. Beckmann recorded his experiences in letters to his wife, some of which were published in the

Ernst Barlach
Der heilige Krieg, 1914, *The Holy War*
litograph, *Kriegszeit*, no. 17
16 December 1914
Los Angeles County Museum of Art
Robert Gore Rifkind Center

journal *Kunst und Künstler* in December 1914 and July 1915, and later republished with thirty-five other letters under the title *Briefe im Kriege*. In these letters Beckmann mused on a seemingly mystical identification with death in war, and described the strangely illuminated, desolate landscape of the front as an apocalyptic spectacle: "... My will to live is presently stronger than ever, although I have already lived through terrible things and have already died several times with the dead. But the more often one dies, the more intensely one lives. I have drawn; that protects you against death and danger."[11] And: "After supper I again went up to my mountain fifteen minutes away from the hospital and saw the horizon constantly illuminated by the inverted pyramidal reflexes of the shrapnel and its somberly red, zigzaglike exploding flashes."[12] Beckmann seemed here to conform to the expectations of Karl Scheffler, editor of *Kunst und Künstler*. Scheffler claimed for Germany the future of Impressionism (linking it to German military and economic expansion),[13] and extolled the aesthetic appeal of battle, the intensification of artistic sensibilities promised by the war. The war promised, as Beckmann put it, "fodder for my art." During his time near the front Beckmann created more than a hundred and fifty sketches and drawings, mostly scenes of the field hospital. These drawings were largely reminiscent of his pre-war imagery of strained bodies in poses of suffering and struggle. In *Soldatenbad* (*Soldier's Bath*), the artist joined his keen observation of life at the front with his pre-war interest in bodies in forceful movement. Beckmann's last letter from the front was dated June 12, 1915. By late 1915, the artist had suffered a nervous breakdown; he returned to Frankfurt to undergo psychiatric treatment and remained there for the duration of the war.

Max Beckmann, *Soldatenbad*, 1915
Soldier's Bath, pen and ink wash
Sammlung Garve

Beckmann came before the public again one year later in the summer of 1916 with a series of etchings, quite different from his confident posture at the beginning of the war. They were marked by Expressionist distortions (probably influenced by the work of Ludwig Meidner) and caricatural elements. By the time they were exhibited, they corresponded to a new, more critical mood that had entered the modern art world.

Franz Marc, a member of the Neue Künstlervereinigung and the Blaue Reiter, also saw the war as a positive experience for his own development as an artist, one that offered a state of hypersensitivity and intensified vision. Marc volunteered for active service on August 6, 1914 and by September was at the Alsatian front. He was quickly promoted through the ranks, to sergeant, platoon leader, master sergeant, and finally lieutenant. In an endless stream of letters to friends and family, he wrote his thoughts on the war: "The war is nothing different from the evil times before the war; what one previously committed in one's mind is now committed in deeds; but why? Because the sham of European propriety is no longer tolerable. Better blood than eternal deception; the war is just as much atonement as voluntary sacrifice to which Europe subjected itself in order to 'come clean' with itself."[14] Marc experienced the war in mythic terms as a medium of cultural renewal, an apocalyptic cataclysm predicted by his own art – paintings such as the 1913 *Tierschicksale* (*Fates of Animals*), which retrospectively conveyed a sense of the mounting political tensions in Europe.

Marc's letters reveal a thoroughgoing aesthetic fascination with his military experience. "These artillery combats have something unspeakably impressive and mystical about them," he wrote. "Battles, wounds, movements have such a mystical, unreal effect, as though they meant something quite different from what their names signify."[15] Marc, though, made little art at the front, aside from sketchbook drawings in pencil that were ideas for large-scale compositions he planned to paint after his return from the war. One of these, *Streit* (*Struggle*), was reminiscent of *Fates of Animals* with its interpenetrating diagonals. Other drawings depicted idyllic scenes in nature, with horses in mountain landscapes. Marc fell back on his prewar abstract art, rather than invent any new forms to capture his experience of the war, consistent with the belief that the new art would be confirmed by the war. On March 4, 1916, Marc was killed in action near Verdun. He was immediately celebrated in the press as the leading Expressionist artist in Germany, his art tied to his identity as a soldier.

Max Beckmann, *Gesellschaft*, 1915
Society, etching

Although Otto Dix later became known as the foremost anti-war artist in Weimar Germany, particularly though his 1924 portfolio *Der Krieg* (*War*), he, too, believed in the war experience as a profound life experience. Almost fifty years after the war, he still asserted: "The war was a horrible thing, but there was something tremendous about it, too. I didn't want to miss it at any price."[16] His most famous diary entry, "In the final analysis, all wars are waged over and because of the vulva,"[17] asserted the erotic energy of combat and war as a test of manliness.

The twenty-three-year-old Dix volunteered for military service in the fall of 1914. He underwent training as an artilleryman and machine gunner, seeing action on both the eastern and western fronts. As late as 1918 he volunteered as a candidate aerial observer to see the war from a new perspective. Promoted to the rank of master sergeant, he received both the Iron Cross for valor and the Friedrich-August medal after being wounded by grenade fragments.

While still training as a machine gunner, Dix painted himself as the god of war, *Selbstbildnis als Mars* (*Self-Portrait as Mars*). In this composition of abstracted force lines, the artist combined an artillery helmet with the helmet of Greek mythology, its spikes transformed into stars around his head, an allusion to Nietzsche's *Zarathustra*: "You must still have chaos within you in order to be able to give birth to a dancing star." A tumultuous landscape of bleeding faces, collapsing buildings, and the crosses of a cemetery surround the artist's head. Dix's choice of a Futurist style for the self-portrait was inherently linked to the war enthusiasm of the Italian Futurists who had first developed it.

Franz Marc, *Tierschicksal*, 1913
Fates of Animals, oil on canvas
Basel, Kunstmuseum

Not all artists, of course, succumbed to the war enthusiasm. Among the exceptions was Ernst Ludwig Kirchner, the leading member of the Brücke group who, perhaps more than other artists, embodied the extreme bohemian marginality of the avant-garde before the war. Kirchner had developed an intense phobia of the military ever since he was detained briefly on the island of Fehmarn in 1914 by military authorities who mistook him for a spy. In spring 1915 Kirchner volunteered for the artillery as a driver in order to avoid being drafted into the infantry. In July he was called up into a replacement artillery unit; his mental state, however, became so precarious that he was released on the condition that he seek psychiatric treatment. At the end of 1915 Kirchner traveled to Königstein im Taunus, where he checked into a sanitarium. He remained in Switzerland until his suicide in 1938.

Franz Marc, *Streit*, 1915
Struggle
from the war sketchbook

In 1915 Kirchner painted *Selbstbildnis als Soldat* (*Self-Portrait as Soldier*) a work that captured the acute anxiety he experienced that year. Dressed in a military uniform, flanked on either side by a nude model and a painted canvas, his right arm amputated, Kirchner depicted himself as a wartime casualty, with military service threatening his individuality, his sexuality, and his ability to make art.[18] Similarly, his painting *Soldier's Bath* showed an anguished experience of military service. Compared with Beckmann's drawing of the same subject, Kirchner's is a painful image of awkward bodies, unwanted physical contact, and loss of privacy and individuality.

Franz Marc, untitled, 1915
from the war sketchbook

War Disillusionment

By the middle of 1916 Germany had suffered staggering reversals on the battlefield; the siege at Verdun alone resulted in hundreds of thousands of casualties. It was a kind of mechanized warfare that no one had imagined, marked by poison gas attacks and agonizingly protracted trench warfare. German losses mounted, while civil unrest hit Berlin in 1917 as a result of food shortages. When the spring 1918 offensive on the western front did not succeed, the precarious military situation forced the German command to face defeat.

When the German offensive collapsed after 1916, the chauvinistic fervor of the war's initial years waned. Artists increasingly agonized over their inability to reconcile the war and their art. The Expressionist artist Karl Schmidt-Rottluff wrote despairingly in early 1917: "Either you are a painter and you shit on the whole caboodle or you join in and kiss painting good-bye."[19] Patriotic commitment gave way to detachment, disillusionment, defeatist cynicism, and in a few cases outright political opposition.

What generally prevailed in the German art world was a new promotion of art as a spiritual compensation for the misery of war. Paul Cassirer ceased publication of *Kriegszeit* and published in its place the pacifist *Der Bildermann*. The introduction to the first issue declared: "Despite the horror of the times, our spirit has remained faithful to the old gods; in the midst of war we want to use our eyes as we used them before the war, even take pleasure as we once did. The strain of war has taught us to look horror calmly in the face, but it has also reawakened our longing for higher and purer things."[20]

With the awareness of possible defeat, art was increasingly projected as an alternative to the war, as a spiritual escape from its horrors. Expressionism, too, participated in this general trend.[21] Its promoters could point to interpretations from before the war that had conspicuously advertised it as a turning inward from historical reality and as a regeneration in the midst of catastrophe.[22] The spiritual element in Expressionism, its speculative nature, had been there

Otto Gulbransson
"Bei den Futuristen" (At the futurists)
Simplicissimus 21, no. 4
16 Mai 1916

from the start, but now a broader public dissatisfied with the war seemed to discover it. Under these circumstances, Expressionism began to achieve new success with a buying public. The founding of the journal *Das Kunstblatt*, oriented toward Expressionist art, and its almost immediate success, point to the burgeoning new public for modern art. So did the inclusion of Expressionist art in exhibitions at the Cassirer and Gurlitt galleries. This success was the result not only of an ideological convergence between Expressionist art and a war-weary public, but also its conjuncture with economic conditions. High profits in the armaments industry and few available consumer goods led to a boom in the art market. Many of the Expressionists' patrons now came from the newer industrial and financial sectors.

The satirical journals of the period testify to the growing acceptance of Expressionist art, and to its very centrality to debates about art. Typical is a 1916 cartoon by Olaf Gulbransson for the Munich journal *Simplicissimus*, one of many cartoons designed to inspire laughter over the absurdities of a distorted and fragmented art. Gulbransson showed a wounded soldier visiting an exhibition of "Futurist" art; the soldier concludes that the war was nowhere as bad as it is portrayed in the explosive, inhuman world of modernist art. As Beth Lewis has argued, the process of parodying avant-garde art served to establish it as a norm that one might reject or vilify, but whose dominance could not be denied.[23]

As part of a turn to "spiritual" values, an increasing number of modernist artists after 1916 turned toward religious subject matter, including Ludwig Meidner. When war was declared, Meidner had not enlisted. After his closest friend and collaborator died in battle in the first month of the war, Meidner, who had seen no actual fighting, embarked on a series of battle scenes featuring French soldiers. Several, including *Französiche Soldaten (French Soldiers)*, which showed the retreat of frightened French soldiers who leave behind an injured comrade, corresponded to the prevailing war propaganda despite their gruesomeness. By September, though, Meidner had apparently turned against the war. A planned cycle of drawings entitled "Europe 1914–15", which was never published, included the bitter titles "Dedicated to the Peace Kaiser" and "The German Socialists Tear Up the Banner of Humanity". In the summer of 1916 Meidner was drafted, posted to Sedan, but soon transferred to Kottbus, where he served as a French translator in a prisoner-of-war camp. There he wrote pacifist texts and turned to first Catholic, then Jewish religious subjects that emphasized admonishment.

In June 1917, the Mannheim curator Gustav Hartlaub published a long article in *Das Kunstblatt* titled "Art and the New Gnosticism", in which he predicted that Expressionism might serve as a prelude to a religious monumental art.[24] Hartlaub soon began preparations for a large exhibition, New Religious Art, that would address the stress and pain of war from the standpoint of modern art. The exhibition, which consisted primarily of Expressionist works, opened in Mannheim in January 1918.

Ludwig Meidner, *Prophet*, 1916
The Prophet, drawing for *Im Nacken das Sternemeer*
On the head a sea of stars

Also among the artists whose work turned to religious subjects emphasizing apocalypse, resurrection, and redemption was Max Beckmann. Finally discharged from the military and living in Frankfurt, Beckmann took up oil painting again in 1917 and produced several large-scale works with religious themes, including *Kreuzabnahme (Deposition from the Cross)*. The turn to religious imagery in his work had begun the year before with *Resurrection*, a work never completed that combined recollections of the war with depictions of Beckmann, his friends, and family on the homefront. The solid composition of *Deposition from the Cross*, despite its unnatural perspective, is reminiscent of Beckmann's prewar paintings. The angular body of Christ, however, derived from his wartime drawings of figures in the field hospital. Beckmann took as his model medieval passion pictures; his emaciated Christ, with blank expression, left little room for comfort or consolation.

During his brief home leaves Dix also must have observed the new attitude of the war-weary public. His war images, too, now took on vaguely apocalyptic and religious overtones. Although gouache works such as *Schützengraben (Trenches)*, with their struggling bodies, bleeding faces, skeletal remains, grasping hands, and explosions, suggest the horrors of war, others, such as *Awakening*, suggest a religious hope for redemption from its disasters.

Ludwig Meidner
Französische Soldaten, 1914
French Soldiers
pen and ink wash
Recklinghausen, Städtische Kunsthalle

Few artists in these years exhibited outright political opposition in their art, although a few expressionist journals turned increasingly toward radical politics. Franz Pfemfert's journal *Die Aktion* now devoted whole issues to Karl Marx. (Because of strict censorship, his opposition to the war had previously been expressed primarily by reproducing works of modern art from enemy countries.) In Dresden, the painters Conrad Felixmüller and Raoul Hausmann, along with the writers Walter Rheiner and Felix Stiemer, formed the Expressionist Working Group (Expressionistische Arbeitsgemeinschaft Dresden), simultaneously promoting Expressionism and radical politics. The Dresden Expressionist journal *Menschen* repudiated any spiritual comfort for the miseries of the war, distancing itself from the "spiritualization" of Expressionism.

The most radical provocation, however, emerged from the Berlin Dada movement. Dada first came to Berlin from Zurich in 1917 in the person of the poet/physician Richard Huelsenbeck, whose antiwar stance was quickly taken up by a number of artists and writers who became known as the Berlin Dada group. The core group consisted of George Grosz, a bohemian artist of working-class origins; the brothers Wieland Herzfelde and John Heartfield, sons of the socialist poet Franz Held and the working-class activist Alice Stolzenberg; and Raoul Hausmann, co-editor of the anarchist journal *Die freie Straße*. Their scorn for the war and for German society soon manifested itself in a series of outrageous performances modeled on the programs of the Cabaret Voltaire. In one of the most famous, Grosz performed an obscene tap dance in which he relieved himself in pantomime before a Lovis Corinth painting with the words "Art is shit."[25] Grosz and Heartfield even anglicized their names to protest anti-British propaganda.

This combination of insult and humor was directed at the hypocrisy of German society: its reverence for culture – and its penchant for brutality. The mocking skepticism with which they confronted the world around them soon found an outlet in the Malik Verlag, a clandestine publishing house they founded and which was always one step ahead of the censors. The first George Grosz portfolio, published by the Malik Verlag in 1917, included a number of hard-edged drawings of rape, murder, assault, and insanity in the big city–symbols of a society gone absolutely mad. One of the Dadaists' prime targets soon became the Expressionists, whose growing success – and "spiritualization" – they saw as part of an escapist bourgeois culture responsible for the war and its carnage. The attack on Expressionism went public when Huelsenbeck read the First German Dada Manifesto at an April 1918 Dada evening in Berlin. Here Huelsenbeck challenged the widening appeal of Expressionist art as symptomatic of a withdrawal from the brutal realities of war: "The highest art will be that which ... has been visibly shattered by the explosion of the last week, which is forever trying to collect its limbs after yesterday's crash ... Has expressionism fulfilled our expectations for such an art?

No! No! No!

Under the pretense of internalization, the Expressionists in literature and in painting have joined together to form a generation which already today longingly awaits its literary and art historical appreciation and is a candidate for honorable recognition by the bourgeoisie. Under the pretense of propagating the soul, they have ... found their way back to those abstract-pathetic gestures which presuppose an empty, comfortable, and inflexible life."[26] By 1918, Grosz's work took a turn toward radical politics, first with the large-scale painting *Leikenbegängnis – Widmung an Oscar Panizza* (*Dedicated to Oskar Panizza*) and then with caustic drawings such as *Die Gesundbeter* (*The Faithhealers*). Oskar Panizza was the author of a virulently anticlerical play *The Council of Love*, published in 1894.

The play purported to document the first outbreak of syphilis in Europe in 1445, tracing it to the moral degeneracy of the papal court. In his play, Panizza mocked, among others, Christ, Mary, and God. Panizza was brought to trial on charges of "crimes against religion" and was imprisoned in 1895. Grosz's painting showed what he later described as a "hellish" funeral procession of dehumanized figures representing alcohol, syphilis, and pestilence. In *Faithhealers* an army doctor examines the decomposed skeleton of a dead soldier, proclaiming him "fit for active service." The background setting, with its blocks of workers' tenement housing, suggests the unfair toll of the draft on the working class.

Revolution

In late 1918 Germany experienced military defeat, economic collapse, and revolution, all within the space of a few months. In its earliest phase, this "people's revolution" was marked by optimistic proclamations of socialist equality and the brotherhood of mankind. On the morning of November 9, enthusiastic processions of factory workers and soldiers streamed into the city of Berlin. Meeting no resistance, they quickly took possession of public buildings, planting the red flag of the revolution on the rooftops and in the doorways. The capital fell into the hands of the

Otto Dix, *Schützengraben*, ca. 1918
Trench, gouache
Private collection

George Grosz
Pandämonium, August 1914
Pandemonium, August 1914
drawing

workers and soldiers, who spontaneously set up councils modeled after Russian soviets. Ignited by the events around them, many Expressionist artists, including Karl Schmidt-Rottluff, Max Pechstein, Paul Klee, and Otto Dix, formed their own artists' "councils."[27] The names they gave these organizations were meant to proclaim their revolutionary aspirations: the Working Council for Art, the November Group, the Action Committee of Revolutionary Artists. Once more artists were confronted with the uncertainty of their dependence on an art market catering to the wealthy – a market that had suffered a serious setback in mid-1918. As Ludwig Meidner melodramatically lamented: "Is our position in society much better and safer than the proletarian's? Aren't we, like beggars, dependent on the whims of the art-collecting bourgeoisie?"[28] With confidence in their mission, these artists issued excited manifestoes that called for complete artistic freedom, an end to the capitalist art market, the dismantling of the old imperial arts institutions, and the creation of a new proletarian audience for their art. They assumed that the triumph of the revolution would mean the triumph of Expressionism, particularly since their art had been labeled with the epithets "radical" and "revolutionary" before the war. What they disregarded for the moment was the complicated history of Expressionism during the war, as well as the dilemma of how an art supposedly predicated on opposition to society could now be reclaimed as a catalyst to social integration.

George Grosz
Leichenbegängnis-Widmung an Oscar Panizza, 1917–18
Dedicated to Oskar Panizza
oil on canvas
Stuttgart, Staatsgalerie

The optimistic events of November 1918 soon gave way to a political struggle for control of the revolution. At issue was the choice between proletarian revolution and parliamentary democracy. The competing socialist parties – the Social Democrats, Independent Social Democrats, and the Communists – fought each other at every turn. By January, the revolution was in trouble: the tenuous socialist government had collapsed, the councils were largely neutralized, and elections to a National Constituent Assembly were imminent, which the newly-formed Communist Party promised to boycott.

In an atmosphere of approaching civil war, armed communists in January occupied a number of buildings in Berlin, declaring the government deposed. The Social Democrats, in response, called out the Freikorps, a temporary armed force composed mainly of anti-republican adventurers. The Communist Party leaders Karl Liebknecht and Rosa Luxemburg were captured and summarily murdered.

The bloody street fighting forced Expressionist artists to examine their vague confidence in the revolution to transform the art world. The political struggle for control and containment of the revolution put into doubt the indiscriminate use of a term such as "revolutionary." Accrued power was often defended through revolutionary rhetoric, and retained by counter-revolutionary action. What could it mean, then, to call Expressionism revolutionary?

At least one Berlin artists' group, the Working Council for Art (Arbeitsrat für Kunst), now turned its opposition to imperial art policies into opposition to the Social Democratric government. Convinced that little support could be expected from the government, they attempted to reach a proletarian audience in a series of unusual exhibitions. At the Exhibition for Unknown Architects, the group showed utopian architectural drawings by predominantly unknown artists. Many of the "buildings" were clearly fanciful, Cubist-inspired towers or anthropomorphic shapes that seemed to grow organically from the earth. The exhibition questioned prevailing conceptions of what counted as architecture, who was an architect, how an exhibition was to be organized, and how it was to be advertised. Their open attack on architectural standards and institutions struck a raw nerve with critics, who for the most part were hostile to the works on show.

George Grosz, *Die Gesundbeter,* 1917
The Faithhealers, in *Die Pleite*

A number of artists took a different political course and initially supported the social democratic government. One of these artists was Max Pechstein, a leading member of the November Group. The son of a textile worker, Pechstein had studied at the Dresden School of Applied Arts. He first gained a reputation as a member of the Brücke and as a cofounder of the New Secession. By 1912, though, he had returned to exhibiting with the Berlin Secession, and had a degree of success with this more mainstream profile.

Between January and March 1917 Max Pechstein contributed work to a short-lived journal *An die Laterne. An die Laterne* generally warned against anarchy and terrorism by the extreme left while promoting the social democrats as the protectors of socialism. Pechstein also created an advertising poster for the journal that showed a dead body hanging from a lamp-post as an angry, threatening procession of clench-fisted figures carrying red flags marches past, and small figures flee in terror. Closest to the viewer, the face of the figure at the rear of the procession

Johannes Molzahn
Architekturidee, 1919
Architectural Idea
pencil on trasparency

Max Pechstein, advertising poster
for *An die Laterne,* 1919
color lithograph
Los Angeles County Museum of Art
Robert Gore Rifkind Center

displays a prominent "Jewish nose," reinforcing anti-Semitic charges that bolshevism was an alien import to Germany, the result of a Jewish conspiracy. Only a few artists took as their subject matter the events of the November Revolution. Käthe Kollwitz created the work that came to be most closely associated with its events. By 1919 the 52-year-old Kollwitz was one of the best-known artists in Germany. She was the granddaughter of an 1848 revolutionary, sister of an editor of the social democratic newspaper, wife of a physician who worked for a trade union insurance fund, resident of a working-class suburb in northern Berlin. Her first public success had come in 1898 with etchings of the 1880's weavers' uprising in Silesia, inspired by a play by Gerhard Hauptmann.

As with so many other German artists, the war proved a critical test for Kollwitz's art. Her diaries reveal a woman resigned to the necessity of war, even admiring of the willingness of German youth to sacrifice themselves for the cause. Much of her art during the war reflected this resolve, even after the death of her second son Peter in action. It was only in the very last stages of the war that Kollwitz publicly assumed an antiwar stance.

With the revolution, Kollwitz joined a short-lived artists' group known as the Cooperative Society of Socialist Artists. Membership in a socialist party was a prerequisite for joining the group, which was organized on a cooperative basis. The group staged exhibitions in factories and union halls, making inexpensive graphics available to a working-class audience. Kollwitz left the Cooperative Society when it became too closely aligned with the Communist Party.

After the murder of Karl Liebknecht, Kollwitz considered creating a memorial to the slain communist leader, even though she was not a follower and had voted social democratic in the elections. Kollwitz, her husband, and her son gained access to the morgue where Liebknecht's body awaited burial. There she completed several sketches of the body. Over the next two years, Kollwitz tried to find an appropriate form for her work, successively abandoning etching and lithography. She finally experimented with woodcut, inspired by her friend Ernst Barlach. The simplified, even crude technique heightened the stylization of the figures, and helped achieve a greater compactness.

The final form embodied an uneasy political balance: on the one hand, the resolute faces of the workers created a heroic depiction of the working class; on the other hand, she attempted no politically charged image of Liebknecht's murder. The title inscribed on the work reflected this ambivalence. It read: *Die Lebenden dem Toten. Erinnerung an den 15. Januar 1919* (The Living to the Dead. Remembrance of January 15, 1919). The first part was a transposition of Friedrich Freiligrath's poem of the 1848 revolution, *The Dead to the Living.* The reversal of the title altered the political meaning; the living were no longer called upon to carry on the struggle, but only to mourn the dead.

Max Beckmann also responded to the double murders of Liebknecht and Luxemburg as part of his 1919 lithographic portfolio *Die Hölle* (*The Hell*). *Das Martyrium* (*Martyrdom*) was published along with ten other lithographs, several of which made reference to the events of the revolution. The large-format lithograph showed several soldiers dragging the body of Luxemburg from an illuminated entranceway toward a waiting automobile. Many of the details corresponded with press accounts of the murder. Beckmann's lithograph was no simple act of reportage, however; these were not portraits, and the narrowness of the space and lack of unified viewpoint confused rather than clarified the scene. Rather, *The Hell* seemed an extension of Beckmann's critical production of graphics in 1916. In the series, he criticized both left and right, with the artist himself as the only seeing witness to the revolutionary "hell" of the title where killers and victims were equally blind.

By June 1919 a degree of political and economic stabilization had returned to Germany. The government elected in Weimar had a familiar look; it was basically a reconstructed coalition of the parties that had been in power in October 1918. Approval by the National Assembly of a new constitution, and the signing of the Versailles Treaty, were the signposts of this new order. Of importance to the artists' councils, a new government policy toward the arts emerged, one that increasingly sought to include Expressionism as part of a broad-based democratic program including all directions in the arts.

One of the first signs of this new policy was the promotion of a new gallery for contemporary art as part of the National Gallery. Before 1918 Expressionist art was barely represented in public museums throughout Germany; the National Gallery did not own a single Expressionist

Käthe Kollwitz, *Die Lebenden
dem Toten. Erinnerung
an den 15. Januar 1919*, 1919–20
The Living to the Dead. Remembrance
of January 15, 1919
woodcut
Berlin, Kupferstichkabinett

Max Beckmann
cover with self-portrait
for the portfolio *Die Hölle*, 1918–19
The Hell, lithograph
Berlin, Kupferstichkabinett

George Grosz, *Prost Noske!
das Proletariat ist entwaffnet!
Prost Noske!
The Proletariat is Disarmed*
cover for *Die Pleite*, no. 3, 1919

painting. Redress of this exclusion had been among the high priorities of the artists' councils. When the new contemporary wing of the National Gallery opened in August 1919, it included works by almost every major German Expressionist artist, acquired either through new purchases or (for the most part) lent by collectors. With the museum as the apex of the commercial system, Expressionism had achieved a final act of validation. The accommodation of Expressionism was also fostered by a resurgent art market, which assured Expressionist artists economic opportunity in the new republic. The coalition government had already signaled its commitment to a capitalist economy, and industrialists soon used inflation to rebuild – which had as one result a thriving art market.

Most Expressionist artists soon adapted themselves to the new culture of the parliamentary democracy, their artistic freedom of expression and financial opportunities assured. Expressionism seemed perfectly suited to represent the greatest cultural achievement of the new government policy, the illusion of successful revolution.

Toward a "New Objectivity"

By early 1920 the choice for artists became one between artistic accommodation and outright political opposition to the new republic. But even for those who chose the latter, the form that opposition would take was still open to debate. Was the only consciously revolutionary art anti-art, either collections of the mundane refuse of contemporary life or satirical cartoons attacking the ruling class? Or was a more positive, even heroic, art of the working class possible?

Among those who now sought to discredit the new republic in their art were George Grosz, Otto Dix, and Conrad Felixmüller. Grosz had joined the German Communist Party at its founding, receiving his membership card from Rosa Luxemburg herself.[29] With the murders of Liebknecht and Luxemburg, Grosz devoted himself to fighting the "traitors" of the revolution. He contributed satirical drawings such as *Prost Noske! – das Proletariat ist ertwaffnet! (Prost Noske!–The Proletariat is Disarmed)* to the journal *Die Pleite. Prost Noske!* depicted the prototype of a Prussian officer (it was Gustav Noske who called in the Freikorps for the social democratic government) with a wine glass and bloody saber, celebrating his victory over the bodies and barbed wire below him.

An alternative oppositional art was offered by the Dresden artist Conrad Felixmüller. The son of a factory blacksmith, Felixmüller had achieved considerable success as an artist after leaving the Dresden Academy in 1915. Sometime in 1917 Felixmüller was drafted. His wartime experience as a military hospital orderly intensified his opposition to the war; he now began contributing graphics to *Die Aktion*, and participated in the Dresden Expressionist Working Group. Only twenty-two years old in 1919, he was a cofounder of the Dresden Secession Group. By late 1919 Felixmüller had become an adherent of Otto Rühle, a renegade Dresden communist who founded the syndicalist Communist Workers Party of Germany. With Felixmüller's intensified political commitment came a change in his art. When in 1920 he won the Rome prize he traveled not to Italy but to the Ruhr.

He painted a number of pictures inspired by workers' militancy in the region, including the events of the Kapp Putsch, a right-wing attempt to oust the government which failed when workers went out on strike and an army of more than fifty thousand formed in the Ruhr. Felixmüller's *Ruhrrevier II (Ruhr District II)* depicts members of this red army. He retained the expressive color and even the exaggerated features of his earlier art, but now tied them to a politically conscious subject matter. Felixmüller explained his new position in a letter to one of his patrons: "There [the Ruhr] I felt again Schiller's words: All men become (are!) brothers–and understood still more strongly that work is holy ... I am still more convinced after this trip... that it is bad and repugnant to be a "dadaist;" that is, to make fun of everything, to cause an upheaval. For man certainly becomes noble through serious work."[30]

Felixmüller's belief in a positive, expressive partisan art, and his rejection of Dada, brought him into conflict with his protégé Otto Dix. The two had met after Felixmüller saw Dix's work at an exhibition and invited him to join the Dresden Secession Group. Dix, too, soon developed a politically committed art, but one quite different from Felixmüller's. Dix's new socially conscious paintings and collages of 1920, works such as *Die Skatspieler (The Skat Players)* and *Prager Straße* used caricature to attack the persistence of militarism in the Weimar Republic. Their incorporation of collage elements contributed to their anti-art aura. Felixmüller, Dix, and Grosz, though,

Conrad Felixmüller
Sezession Gruppe 1919, poster
for the Exhibition
of the Dresden Secession Group, 1919

posed another unresolved dilemma of the revolution. Their work found its way into the private collections of wealthy, though politically enlightened, patrons. While distancing themselves from Expressionism, they continued to exhibit in Expressionist shows. Subversion of the establishment could be tolerated, it seems, as long as it was accompanied by a simultaneous compromise with it. The acceptance of Expressionism as an official style had about it a somewhat funereal aspect. The affirmative thrust of an art supported by and supporting the Weimar state became alarming to those who saw it in conjunction with the many signs of the republic's political regression. By 1920, many critics proclaimed the "death" of Expressionism. Wilhelm Hausenstein, an early supporter of Expressionism, wrote the movement's epitaph: "Expressionism today has its Glass Palace [official exhibition space]. It has its salon. No cigarette poster, no nightclub manages without Expressionism. It is loathsome."[31]

What critics such as Hausenstein meant was not that Expressionism had disappeared, not that its practitioners suddenly abandoned it or its patrons deserted it, but that its fateful history during the war and the revolution, its institutionalization, had destroyed confidence in its ability to serve the avant-garde notion of art in the forefront of revolutionary politics.

Otto Dix, *Die Skatspieler*, 1920
The Skat Players
oil and collage on canvas
Berlin, Kupferstichkabinett

[1] Die Aussteller, "Vorwort," *Erster Deutscher Herbstsalon: Berlin 1913* (Berlin 1913), 9; quoted in Reinhold Heller, ed. *Art in Germany 1909–1936. From Expressionism to Resistance*, Munich, 1990, p. 19.

[2] Franz Marc, "Die neue Malerei," *Pan* 2, no. 16 (7 March 1912), p. 469.

[3] Julius Meier-Graefe, "Der Krieg beschert uns," *Kriegszeit: Künstlerflugblätter* 1, no.1 (31 August 1914), 4; quoted in Heller, *Art in Germany 1909–1936*. p. 19.

[4] O.K. Werckmeister, *German Art in the First World War*. Unpublished manuscript, 1984.

[5] See Robert Jensen, *Marketing Modernism in Fin-de-Siècle Europe*. Princeton, 1994, especially chapter 8.

[6] Paul Fechter, *Der Expressionismus*. Munich, 1914.

[7] Adolf Behne, "Organisation, Deutschtum und Kunst," *Zeit-Echo* 1, nos. 23-24 (1915–16), p. 364.

[8] Heller, *Art in Germany 1909-1936*. p. 20.

[9] Reprinted in Lovis Corinth, *Selbstbiographie*. Leipzig, 1926, p. 129.

[10] Horst Uhr, *Lovis Corinth*, Berkeley 1990, 234.

[11] Max Beckmann, *Briefe im Kriege*. Berlin, 1916, p. 13.

[12] Letter Max Beckmann to Minna Beckmann-Tube (18 April 1915), reprinted in Barbara Copeland Buenger, ed. *Max Beckmann. Self-Portrait in Words*. Chicago, 1997, p. 159.

[13] Karl Scheffler, "Der Deutsche," *Kunst und Künstler* 13, no. 2 (1 November 1914), p. 49-51.

[14] Letter Franz Marc to Maria Marc, 6 April 1915, reprinted in Rose Carol Washton-Long, ed. *German Expressionism. Documents from the End of the Wilhelmine Empire to the Rise of National Socialism*. Berkeley, 1993, p. 164.

[15] Letter Franz Marc to Maria Marc, 12 September 1914, reprinted in Washton-Long, ed., *German Expressionism*. p. 162.

[16] *Stuttgarter Zeitung* (30 November 1961), quoted in Dietrich Schubert. *Otto Dix in Selbstzeugnissen und Bilddokumenten*. Reinbek, 1980, p. 24.

[17] Quoted in Otto Conzelmann, *Der andere Dix. Sein Bild vom Menschen und vom Krieg*. Stuttgart, 1983, p. 133.

[18] Irit Rogoff, "The Anxious Art–Ideological Mobilisations of the Self in German Modernism," in Irit Rogoff, ed. *The Divided Heritage*. Lindon, 1991, p. 116-47.

[19] Quoted in Theda Shapiro, *Painters and Politics: The European Avant-Garde and Society 1900–1925*. New York, 1976, p. 154.

[20] Paul Cassirer and Leo Kestenberg, "Zur Einführung," *Der Bildermann* 1, no. 1 (5 April 1916); quoted in Peter Paret, *The Berlin Secession*. Cambridge, 1980, p. 240.

[21] See O.K. Werckmeister, "Klee im Ersten Weltkrieg," in *Versuche über Paul Klee*. Frankfurt am Main, 1981, p. 86-87.

[22] See, for instance, Wilhelm Worringer, *Abstraktion und Einfühlung*, München. 1908.

[23] This point was made by Beth Irwin Lewis in an unpublished talk, "War and Contemporary Art: Perceptions and Promotion in Wartime Journals," presented at the symposium "Revolution, Republic, Repression: Art and Politics in Weimar Germany" at the Block Gallery, Northwestern University, January 1994.

[24] Gustav Hartlaub, "Die Kunst und die neue Gnosis," *Das Kunstblatt* 6 (June 1917), p. 166-69.

[25] Beth Irwin Lewis, *George Grosz: Art and Politics in the Weimar Republic*. Madison, 1971, p. 57.

[26] Richard Huelsenbeck, "First German Dada Manifesto," quoted in Raoul Hausmann, *Am Anfang war Dada*. First edition, Steinbach/Giessen, 1972, p. 23-24.

[27] For a more complete history of artists involvement in the November Revolution see Joan Weinstein, *The End of Expressionism. Art and the November Revolution in Germany*. Chicago, 1990.

[28] Ludwig Meidner, "An alle Künstler, Dichter, Musiker," *An alle Künstler!* (Berlin, 1919), p. 8.

[29] Lewis, *George Grosz*, p. 59.

[30] Letter from Conrad Felixmüller to Heinrich Kirchhoff, 27 July 1920, reprinted in *1920–1980: Sechzig Jahre Galerie Nierendorf*. Berlin, 1980, p. 18.

[31] Wilhelm Hausenstein, *Die Kunst in diesem Augenblick*. München, 1920, p. 17.

Otto Dix, *Prager Straße*, 1920
oil on canvas
Stuttgart, Galerie der Stadt

Supporters and Collectors of Expressionism[1]

Shulamith Behr

"The picture [*The Tempest*] will cause a stir when it is made public, my greatest and most powerful work, the masterpiece of all Expressionist strivings. Are you coming to Vienna before New Year? Buy it for yourself, and, with your ability to make the most of modern painting, you could have an international success... The picture ought to go to America where my name is slowly filtering through".[2] Kokoschka's letter to the Berlin-based dealer and publicist Herwarth Walden (1878-1942) testifies to the complex structures of avant-garde activity in the early twentieth century. During the 1890s, the founding of urban-based secessions, which veered away from academic and related professional associations, was symptomatic of the changing cultural, social and economic status of the artist.[3] One of the cornerstones of avant-gardism, which is the alienation of the artist from the training and supportive mechanisms of the state, necessitated the construction of alternative networks for reaching a public.[4] Artistic survival depended on establishing viable commercial or professional outlets, on seeking sponsorship and media promotion in order to secure a niche in the competitive market economy of late Imperial Germany.[5] Herwarth Walden (a *nom-de-plume* for George Lewin), initially trained as a concert pianist and composer, provided such opportunities through his Sturm Gallery (Storm), established in Berlin in 1912, and his publishing of the periodical *Der Sturm* (1910-1932), featuring art criticism and theory, poetry, literature and, as it developed, the reproduction of contemporary graphics and drawings. Hence, prior to his participation in the opening group exhibition of the Sturm Gallery in March 1912, Kokoschka functioned as editor responsible for the publication of *Der Sturm* in Austria from October 1910 until October 1911.[6] At this time, the journal served as the outlet for his series of title-page portraits, *Menschenköpfe* (Heads)[7] and for the text and illustrations of his Expressionist drama *Mörder - Hoffnung der Frauen* (*Murderer, Hope of Women*).[8] Kokoschka's poster for *Der Sturm* in 1910, in portraying his self-portrait in the guise of an ascetic martyr, demonstrates that, however fictional, Expressionists created images of "alienation" in forefronting their unique and distorting style in the face of increasing commercialization.[9] By 1912, the object of this promotional exercise was realized when Paul Cassirer, largely known for his dealership in modern French and secessionist art, brought Kokoschka his first real income in the form of a contract.[10] Moreover, the photograph of Kokoschka in the print-room of Walden's private residence in 1916, posed against a background of the artist's graphics, shows the dealer's continuing status as both collector and patron.

Oskar Kokoschka, *"Der Sturm" with Self-portrait*, 1910, poster from Hans Peter Thurn *Der Kunsthändler: Wandlungen eines Berufes*. Munich: Hirmer, 1994

Whereas Kokoschka was one of the first artists to benefit from the Sturm enterprise, during the prewar period the gallery also displayed the works of other artists deemed to be Expressionist – the members of the Blaue Reiter and Ludwig Meidner from the group known as the Pathetiker.[11] In particular, through Walden's propaganda in *Der Sturm*, the artist Wassily Kandinsky came to be regarded as one of the movement's chief exponents in Germany.[12] His publications in 1912 were pivotal to Walden's mystical definition of the Expressionist process: "The painter paints whatever he sees with his innermost senses, the expression of his being ... his inner apparitions".[13] Yet Walden equally championed European avant-garde art – Futurism, Cubism, Orphism – and his Erster Deutscher Herbstsalon (First German Autumn Salon), held in Berlin in 1913, was a significant international event, involving the display of works from fourteen countries.[14] As the quotation from Kokoschka's letter confirms, in expressing a desire to reach an American public, it is evident that Walden's promotional skills were not limited to marketing Expressionism in Germany. In order to ensure a wider audience, travelling exhibitions were sent to Scandinavia, Finland and Tokyo before the outbreak of the First World War.[15]

Walden's particular style of dealership that exploited the concept of a burgeoning publishing industry, improved communications and the growth of an international art market was not wholly unprecedented in the Berlin context. He benefited from over a decade of rapid development of this city, with its political and mercantile concentration, as a major art capital.[16] By comparison, the commercial climate for contemporary art in Munich improved only marginally in 1908 when Heinrich Thannhauser became more active in his partner's, Hans Josef Brakl's, Moderne Kunsthandlung. Thannhauser established his own Moderne Galerie in Autumn 1909 which proved both beneficial and attractive to the annual group exhibitions of the Neue Künstlervereinigung München (NVKM) between 1909 and 1912[17] and the first exhibition of the editors of the Blaue Reiter at the year end of 1911.[18] After the second exhibition of the Blaue Reiter, consisting exclusively of original graphics, was held at the bookstore of Hans Goltz in 1912, the dealer opened his gallery Neue Kunst – Hans Goltz which became an important outlet for many Expressionists, in particular the artist Paul Klee.[19]

Oskar Kokoschka in conversation with Herwarth Walden, Berlin, 1916 Pöchlarm, Kokoschka Archive

August Macke
Bildnis Bernhard Koehler, 1910
(Portrait of Bernhard Koehler)
oil on canvas
Munich, Städtische Galerie
im Lenbachhaus

Yet the expansion of dealership in the marketing of Expressionism, while being a significant factor in informing a range of supporters, was only one of several conditions that led to an upsurge in the collecting of contemporary art. A new art-buying public, drawn from the ranks of the educated and the affluent middle class, constituted a strong social entity in developing a direct relationship with artists.[20] The wealthy Berlin manufacturer Bernard Koehler (1849–1927) is a case in point. He already owned a substantial collection, ranging from El Greco to Cézanne, but turned to patronizing the works of the Blaue Reiter group based in Munich. He was an uncle of August Macke's wife Elizabeth and, through their introduction, sponsored Franz Marc for 200 Marks per month from mid-1910 onward, providing, as well, a guarantee of 3000 Marks to the publisher Reinhard Piper for the publication of *Der Blaue Reiter Almanac*.[21] Hence, active in public and private life, the supporters of Expressionism ranged from influential museum directors, professional people, publishers, art historians and critics to bankers, industrial *entrepreneurs* and businessmen. Indeed it remains largely unacknowledged that the phenomenon of women's increasing emergence into modern public life and their role as consumers was crucial to the positive reception and championing of male avant-gardism.

Significantly, this was accompanied by the construction of the modern patron, informed by the expanding function of the public museum and its societies, by women's cultural groups, in addition to the role played by "print-capitalism" in the age of modernity. As Benedict Anderson has observed, the latter factor "made it possible for rapidly growing numbers of people to think about themselves, and to relate to others, in profoundly new ways" and was critical to the search "for a new way of linking fraternity, power and time meaningfully together".[22] For, in its alignment with the anti-naturalistic tendencies of "foreign" modern art, Expressionism was firmly entrenched in the cultural politics of the Wilhelmine period.

In 1911 xenophobic outbursts against the collecting and importation of foreign works reached a climax in the publication of Carl Vinnen's *Ein Protest Deutscher Künstler* (A Protest of German Artists).[23] This forced the supporters of early modernism in their reply, *Im Kampf um die Kunst – Die Antwort auf den "Protest Deutscher Künstler"* (The Struggle for Art: The Answer to the "Protest of German Artists"), to close ranks in defining the benefits of cosmopolitanism to German culture.[24] However, as has been argued, there is much evidence to show that Expressionism was deemed a distinctly German rather than an imported phenomenon and the political inflections of the First World War consolidated on this viewpoint.[25] As discussed below, before 1914, the role of the museum director and patron Karl Ernst Osthaus, in sponsoring Expressionism in the public domain, was redolent with ideas of reforming German national culture in accordance with a vitalist, modernising aesthetic. In that a resurgence of Wagnerian ideas led many Expressionists to explore the interrelationships between the visual arts, music and literature and to experiment in different media, be it graphics, sculpture, painting or the applied arts, Expressionism permeated German culture at various levels.[26] This involved a self-conscious definition, on the part of practitioner and patron alike, as to what constituted modern art theory and practice. Defined in opposition to both official taste and the Impressionist *sensation* of external appearances, Expressionism was aligned with what was considered to be the most authentic and progressive in contemporary art. The perceived threat of its "foreignness" was no doubt partially due to economic considerations and the growth of an international art market, aspects of which formulated the acquisition and didactic policies of enlightened museum directors.

A new type of gallery director[27]
By the turn of the century, it was clear from the rapid expansion of public museums in Germany that various tensions would arise between insular state bureaucracies and the outward-looking aspirations of a new generation of directors. Concordant with the rise of the bourgeoisie in German society, these establishments were founded around the collections of private bequests or propagated by voluntary associations, such as the Kunstvereine.[28] As this phenomenon was fairly widespread in the major as well as regional centers of Germany, consideration of the directors of three differently formed institutions in Hagen, Berlin, and Hamburg illuminates how their activities and publications impinged on the promotion and collection of Expressionism.[29]

Of all three discussed, the case of Karl Ernst Osthaus (1874–1921) is rather unique since, as founder, owner and director of the Museum Folkwang in Hagen, he was reponsible for an unusual degree of public patronage with private funds. Osthaus came from a wealthy background; his fa-

Karl Ernst Osthaus photograph
Berlin, Nationalgalerie

Interior of Museum Folkwang, Essen
with paintings by Emil Nolde
tribal masks and non-Western
sculptural objects (before 1933–34)

ther owned a bank in Hagen and the family was well connected with industrialists and business-men. After inheriting 65 million Marks from his maternal grandparents, he was able to fulfill his ambition of bringing modern visual culture to the Ruhr.[30] Completed in 1902, the interior of the museum itself was crafted around Osthaus's collection of modern European and non-Western art, the design being effected by Henry van de Velde (1863–1957), the Belgian architect and designer. A notable supporter of the Applied Arts movement, Van de Velde played a crucial role in dissem-inating the style known as Jugendstil in Germany. He was a committed internationalist and it has been suggested that he tempered the less salubrious features of Osthaus's affiliation with right-wing, anti-semitic groups during his student career.[31] Hence, the principle of *Lebensreform*, of re-uniting art and craft in improving the environment of a modern, industrial society was of enduring significance to Osthaus's dedication to the display of the decorative arts and to his on-going in-volvement in the Deutsche Werkbund (Works Union). Furthermore, he played a decisive role in making the Museum Folkwang the initiating venue for the traveling exhibitions of the Deutsches Museum für Kunst in Handel und Gewerbe (German Museum for Art in Commerce and Trade).[32] Through his capacity as a patron and collector, Osthaus was of notable importance to the promo-tion of Expressionism.[33] While his collection of modern French works was purchased through art dealers such as Paul Cassirer, Osthaus soon became directly involved in patronizing contemporary German art.[34] He first bought a painting from Emil Nolde in 1906 and was a source of continuous encouragement to the artist during times of extreme difficulty. As a consequence of Nolde's inter-action with the Brücke artists in Dresden, the group held major exhibitions in the Museum Folk-wang in late 1907 and 1910. Importantly, it has been suggested that one of the unique features of Osthaus's museology, his installation of modern art juxtaposed with the tribal art of Africa and oth-er non-Western cultures, was of seminal significance to the "primitivist" reorientation of the group.[35] An installation photograph of three of Nolde's paintings (fig. 5), interspersed with tribal masks and abutted by three dimensional sculpture, demonstrates that this principle was continued after the collection was moved to the Museum Folkwang in Essen.[36]

Osthaus appeared unperturbed by the stylistic pluralism of early Expressionism and invited the NKVM and the Blaue Reiter to exhibit, acquiring works of Kandinsky and Alexej Jawlensky for his permanent collection by 1912. Evident, as well, is the extent to which Osthaus offered women prac-titioners opportunities. Between 1910 and 1918, the Expressionist sculptor Milly Steger (1880-1941) was associated with the Museum Folkwang, executing commissions in Hagen and working in the artists' colony at Hohenhof, the director's mansion.[37] Moreover, through his interest in hand-made craft, he promoted the finely woven rugs and pillows made by Ada Nolde (1877–1945), wife of Emil.[38] The director also forged links in Rhenish Westphalia by joining Der Sonderbund West-deutscher Kunstfreunde und Künstler (The Association of West German Artists and Friends of Artists) in 1910, whose members were dedicated to promoting local artists.[39] Under Osthaus's di-rection, however, the annual Sonderbund (Special Exhibition) assumed an international character, the most famous being that held at the Cologne Kunsthalle in 1912. Undaunted by the chauvinist accusations of Vinnen's *Ein Protest Deutscher Künstler*, the jury selected works by artists from France, Germany, Russia, Austro-Hungary, Switzerland, Holland and Norway.

The sponsorship of international modernism sits uneasily with Osthaus's efforts to locate the Mu-seum Folkwang and its program at the heart of national regeneration. His pronouncements res-onate with *völkisch* sentiments: "Culture is today not a question of class, it is a question of a peo-ple [*Volksfrage*]".[40] However, in attempting to foster and develop the civic virtues of regional and industrial communities, he was pivotal to the decentralization of Prussian dominance in cultural matters. Being privately financed, the Museum Folkwang could well ignore the ramifications of the so-called "Tschudi-affair" currently being waged in Berlin.

There, the founding of a national museum of modern art was spurred by the donation of a private collection by the banker Consul Wagener to the Prussian state. Completed in 1876, the National-galerie was imbued with the significance of the recent unification of Germany and dedicated to the display of German art.[41] In consultation with the gallery dealer Paul Cassirer, Hugo von Tschudi (1851–1911), director of the Berlin Nationalgalerie between 1896 and 1908, systematically enriched the collection with the works of nineteenth-century French Realists and Impressionists.[42] Although these were largely acquired through bequests and donations, such actions led to open confrontation with the emperor, Wilhelm II, who cherished notions of an idealized national culture. Tschudi's po-sition in Berlin was made untenable and he subsequently accepted an offer to head the Bavarian

Photograph by Bruckmann
of *Hugo von Tschudi*
Berlin, Nationalgalerie, 1996

state museums in Munich, from 1909 until his untimely death in 1911. The publicity surrounding Tschudi's championing of both foreign and modern art was welcomed by contemporary artists. In Munich, Kandinsky elicited the director's support in informing him of the theoretical preoccupations of the recently formed NKVM: "Our still small community thinks that art is not merely the embodiment of 'beauty'... but the work of art has an *inner* subjective life, an inner, subjective *essence*... the atmosphere, that takes in the bud of the future and causes it to flourish". In responding to this letter, Tschudi invited Kandinsky to meet him at the Pinakothek.[44] Evidently, it was also through the auspices of the director that the NKVM held their first exhibition in the Modernen Galerie of Heinrich Thannhauser in December 1909. This venue, with its compelling installations apparently inspired by Tschudi's example, was crucial to the public display of the works of the NKVM and the Blaue Reiter group.[45] Significantly, *Der Blaue Reiter Almanac*, edited by Kandinsky and Franz Marc and published in early 1912, was dedicated to the memory of Hugo von Tschudi.[46]

This chain of events underscores the dynamism of the museum director in interacting with dealers and artists. Moreover, in communicating his ideas on the function of the modern director as collector, Tschudi's writings resonate with features of early modernist theory: "This new gallery director of the twentieth century now also steps side by side with a new type of collector. As the one supervises and restores, so the other builds up. Not according to art historical points of view, and also not with those specific collector's passions ... but with the excited abandon of the spirited art lover, who ... seizes quickly there, where his artistic feelings become transposed into strong vibrations".[47] This extract, a form of aesthetic testament, highlights the importance of the experiential process in selecting works of art, irrespective of their national or chronological boundaries. However, it would be a misrepresentation to label this approach as purely "formalist." While he was not alone in entertaining such criteria, Tschudi's efforts testify to his attempt to define national heritage in accordance with an unparochial, contemporary living tradition. As is made clear in his lecture "Kunst und Publikum" of 1899, the context for Tschudi's theoretical departure was based on a rejection of official history painting in favor of the immediacy of Impressionist subject matter.[48] However, in contrast to his mentor and colleague Alfred Lichtwark, director of the Hamburg Kunsthalle between 1886 and 1914, Tschudi maintained an elitist viewpoint in asserting that modern art was beyond the sensibility of the masses.[49]

Like Osthaus and Tschudi, Lichtwark (1852–1914) was profoundly dissatisfied with the cultural development of Germany since 1871, claiming that there was a lack of cultivation, of an informed taste for (as distinct from knowledge of) the arts. The relative political and economic autonomy of Hamburg, induced by liberal doctrines of free enterprise and *laissez faire*, resulted in the forceful presence of a wealthy business community.[50] The Kunsthalle itself was founded in the mid-nineteenth century on the initiative of the local Kunstverein and subsequently donated as a gift to the state.[51] Lichtwark wanted to instill civic pride and to harness the energies of the affluent middle class. Thereby he dedicated himself to the task of reforming and educating a literate bourgeois audience in the value of the visual arts for everyday life. At the core of this project was the Enlightenment concept of *Bildung* which Lichtwark developed in the article "Selbsterziehung" (Self-education) of 1896. Here he zealously advised adults to take art into their own home and to respond to it with the senses: "Treat it as a friend at your hearth and in constant communion with it expand your own sensitivity, increase and strengthen your ability to recognize and appreciate art."[52]

To this effect he revived the term and concept "dilettante," purging it of its pejorative connotations, a re-evaluation that was argued in his essay "Wege und Ziele des Dilettantismus" (Paths and Goals of Dilettantism).[53] In 1893 he founded the Gesellschaft Hamburgischer Kunstfreunde (Society of Hamburg Art-lovers), a group of charitable and influential citizens, whose tasks included the curating of exhibitions, the commissioning and fostering of the local arts. In that original graphics were financially accessible for middle-class consumption, Lichtwark recommended these would serve as an important means to self-improvement, a process that would spiritually benefit the broader community and ultimately the nation.[54] By 1911 Lichtwark's agenda was summarised in the discourse "Der Sammler" (The Collector) in which he stated that the bourgeoisie should model themselves on the nobility of the eighteenth century. Collecting should involve the elements of patronage and aesthetic self-education through the "Gymnastik der Sammeltätigkeit" (the gymnastics of collecting activity).[55]

While Lichtwark was not a staunch supporter of Expressionism, his contribution toward establishing the discursive framework of the modern patron was of paramount importance within his

Photograph by Rudolf Dührkoop
of Alfred Lichtwark, 1890
Berlin, Nationalgalerie

lifetime. Like Tschudi, he stressed the values of empirical response to the work of art but firmly believed that "aesthetic sensitivity" was a matter of education and not class. Accordingly, while cultivating an informed "taste" among adults, he also laid the foundation for the reform of school education.[56] Members of his Gesellschaft Hamburgischer Kunstfreunde participated in the public life of the Kunsthalle while concurrently purchasing contemporary German art for their private collections. Emil Waldmann, who from 1914 was director of the Bremen Kunsthalle, recognized this interaction between the public and private spheres, commenting as follows: "In general, the fostering of private art collecting in German cities goes in hand in hand with the activities of museums, particularly when these occupy a leading position in German artistic life. When in Hamburg the greatest German art campaigner [*Kunstpolitiker*] of recent time, Alfred Lichtwark, began his work of reorganization, exciting times also arose for the Hamburg art lovers and collectors of paintings".[57] This observation, introducing an article on "Die Sammlung Rauerts in Hamburg," focused on the impact of Lichtwark's legacy on the well-known lawyer, active *Kunstfreund* and collector of Expressionist works Dr Paul Rauert (1863–1938). Not surprisingly, Waldmann confidently concluded in his book *Sammler und Ihresgleichen* (The Collector and His Kind) that the "true promoter" of modern art was "the collector and buyer".[58]

The development of the modern patron: the Hamburg case

In the absence of arrangements with commercial galleries, the formation of communal artists groups dedicated toward self-sponsorship and the securing of alternative exhibiting venues is best exemplified by the group known as Die Brücke. As architectural students in Dresden, Ernst Ludwig Kirchner, Erich Heckel, Karl Schmidt-Rottluff, and Fritz Bleyl banded together in 1905 both in order to promote shared aesthetic ideals and to create a viable studio existence. While their manifesto declared their commitment to the new epoch, to authenticity of approach in rejecting academic practice, they nonetheless recognized the need for reaching like-minded spectators. As their words proclaimed: "With faith in progress and in a new generation of creators and *spectators*, we call together all youth."[59] With such aims in mind they recruited so-called "passive Mitglieder" (passive members) who, in return for a subscription (which started at 12 Marks and later increased to 25 Marks), received a membership card, an annual portfolio of prints and an annual report. Invariably these members remained long standing patrons of the individual artists well after the Brücke disbanded in Berlin during 1913.

Instructively, the majority of the passive members of the Brücke community recorded by 1910 were based in Hamburg, where networking among supporters was well entrenched. Of these, Gustav Schiefler (1857–1935) was one of the earliest to be listed. Soon after his arrival in Hamburg in 1888 to take up his position as a district judge, Schiefler was drawn into Lichtwark's inner circle.[60] In 1893 he became secretary of the Gesellschaft Hamburgischer Kunstfreunde and his dedication served to set Lichtwark's ideas in motion. As the director advised, Schiefler channeled his interests into collecting contemporary original graphics, his first major discovery being the prints of Edvard Munch. He met the artist in 1902 and remained a constant friend and patron, publishing the catalogue raisonné of Munch's graphics in two volumes in 1907 and 1927.[61] His home became a venue for cultural evenings, the so-called "Schiefler-Abende," establishing a forum in which patrons, artists, writers and performers could mingle. In a similar manner, he first met Emil Nolde in 1906 and was enlisted by Karl Schmidt-Rottluff to promote the Brücke in the same year. Far from being a "passive" member, Schiefler's friendly interest extended to visiting their studio in Dresden in 1910, as evidenced in the postcard sketched by Kirchner, and his enduring legacy as a patron resides in his preparation of catalogues of the graphics of both Nolde and Kirchner.[62]

Whether or not Kirchner and his fellow-associates intended spectatorship to bridge the gender divide is debatable. Yet closer scrutiny of the membership lists reveals that eleven of the passive members based in Hamburg were women.[63] Not all the individuals fulfilled the "call to all youth," however, and ranged from the wives of the professional upper middle class (Martha Rauert, wife of Paul Rauert), to practitioners (Minya Diez-Dührkoop, the photographer)[64] and single, professional women (Dr Rosa Schapire, the art historian). These observations point to the residue of an older tradition of salon-derived patronage within the significant discourses of the demand for political equality and the role of the female consumer.[65] Importantly, the late Wilhelmine period corresponded to the height of the German women's movement, when feminist-inspired activities had been at an intense pitch for roughly a quarter of a century, achieving political emancipation in 1919.

Karl Schmidt-Rottluff
Brücke passives Mitglied 1911
(Passive Members Card 1911)
woodcut
Berlin, Brücke-Museum

Ernst Ludwig Kirchner, *Lists of Passive Members*, 1906–10, woodcut from the catalogue of the Dresden Brücke exhibition Galerie Arnold, 1910

Generally, those women involved in circles of patronage were active in groups raising awareness about feminist issues. Hence, in addition to the societies established by public museums, the founding of women's clubs in regional centers under the inspiration of the Allgemeiner Deutscher Frauenverein (German Women's General Association) contributed to the development of the modern woman patron. In Hamburg, one of the future passive members of the Brücke, the notable art collector Bertha Rohlsen established and became chair of the Frauenklub (Women's Club) at the Antoine-Feillschehaus in 1906.[66] In this she was assisted by Ida Dehmel who became a well-known supporter of the vote for women.[67] The club was dedicated to the organization of cultural activities for its members and was the venue for literary events, recitals, exhibitions and lectures – in that winter one by Elizabeth Förster-Nietzsche. The formation of a sub-committee called the Frauen-Künstlerhilfe (Women's Aid for Artists), moreover, established a pattern of charging an entrance fee so that the proceeds could be used toward the support of artists, the purchase of works, providing, as well, the opportunity for women in the crafts to sell their ware.[68] Indeed, the Frauen-Künstlerhilfe was responsible for sponsoring a major exhibition of contemporary works by Hamburg artists at a commercial gallery, the Commeter, in 1915.[69]

It was in such an ambience that Rosa Schapire, during a short sojourn in Hamburg in 1906, was first introduced to the work of the Brücke artists when she attended an evening gathering at the Women's Club. Luise Schiefler (1865–1967), wife of the patron Gustav, delivered an informal lecture based on two of Emil Nolde's graphics drawn from their collection which were circulated among the attendants for their perusal.[70] During 1907 Schapire met Nolde who, at that time, was an active member of the Brücke group in Dresden and she was recruited as a passive member. From 1910 onward, however, she devoted herself more fully to developing the career of Karl Schmidt-Rottluff. That Schapire was not alone in this task is illuminated in Gerhard Wietek's publication on *Schmidt-Rottluff: Oldenburger Jahre 1907–1912*, the most intensive and fascinating account of the artist's interaction with his circle of patrons.[71]

The success of the Women's Club in cultivating the patronage of contemporary art and its nexus with the rise of female consumerism can be gauged from the promotion of the *Kunstgewerbe* or applied arts. Irene Eucken was an astute business woman who had her own *Stickstube* (embroidery studio) and who, in 1916, sponsored a fashion show of her designs for the Bremen Women's Club which was established in 1908. She was better known as the wife of Rudolf Eucken, the famous Nobel Prize winner and Professor of Philosophy at Jena University. Her introduction to the catalogue of fashionware has the impact of a manifesto in stating the following: "We aspire in Germany, for some time, to an independent existence of fashion ... However, to convert the aspiration into deed, we now need urgently to strengthen cooperation of creative artists. They must give us new forms and colors. They must teach us the application of our highly developed arts and crafts, therewith really wearable, new designer clothes [*Kleidermodelle*] originate ... In my embroidery room some skillful artists will now have opportunity to bring their ideas to completion."[72] Importantly, the "skilful" artist to whom she referred and who was commissioned to produce the woodcut prints for her catalogue was Ernst Ludwig Kirchner. Indeed, at a time of intense psychological suffering after his military service in 1916, Kirchner wrote about this commission in letters to Gustav Schiefler.[73]

Eucken's sentiments demonstrate that awareness and sponsorship of modernist manifestations in Germany extended beyond the realms of fine art production to embrace the commercial.[74] This, in itself, was not uncommon in view of the aspirations of Jugendstil at the turn of the century and Osthaus's efforts to inspire contemporary artists to engage in the applied arts. Interestingly, in Berlin, Kirchner and Pechstein had attempted to extend their involvement in tutoring the decorative arts by opening the MUIM – Institut (Moderner Unterricht in Malerei; Course in Modern Painting) in November 1911.[75] But Eucken's words resonate with a Nietzschean-derived emphasis on the importance of eternal striving for personal expression and of her centrality to the enterprise: her attempt to promote originality and authenticity in modern German fashion through the reference to a contemporary and vital artistic practice. Rosa Schapire's activities as an art historian, critic, patron and collector similarly reveal a self-conscious resoluteness about her role in modern life.[76] Not unlike her male colleagues, her professional status and upper middle-class cosmopolitanism served to anchor her interaction with the public as part of the individual's commitment to civic responsibility, an evocation of progressive modernity espoused since the Enlightenment. Schapire (1874–1954) was born in Brody, Galicia, in Poland, the second youngest of five daughters in a Jewish family. She was no mere "dilettante" and her foray into the male-dominated profession of art history at the turn of the

Ernst Ludwig Kirchner
Gustav Schiefler in Dresden, 1910
pen and ink and wax crayon
Private Collection

Ernst Ludwig Kirchner
*Ausstellung von Kleidern
aus der Stickstube von Frau Eucken*
1916, (Exhibition of clothing designs
from the atelier of Frau Eucken)
woodcut, frontispiece of the catalogue
Los Angeles, County Museum of Art,
Robert Gore Rifkind Center

Karl Schmidt-Rottluff
Bildnis Rosa Schapire, 1919
Portrait of Rosa Schapire
oil on canvas
London, Tate Gallery

century was most unusual, indicative of her allegiance to feminist aspirations for equal opportunity and political emancipation.[77] Having gained a doctoral degree from Heidelberg in 1904 and having spent a semester studying under Heinrich Wölfflin at Berlin University, she settled in Hamburg from 1908 onward. There, she played an active role in the art scene as a lecturer, reviewer, critic, editor and translator. Though her doctoral work was devoted to the eighteenth-century Frankfurt landscapist, Johann Morgenstern,[78] she turned her attention to promoting Expressionist art, the climax of which was her publication of a catalogue raisonné of Schmidt-Rottluff's graphic works in 1924.[79]

Schapire's patterns of collecting and commissioning led to the adornment of the private sphere as a total entity. Views of the living-room interior of her apartment in Osterbekstraße in 1921 testify to the integration of art and life and to the aesthetic unity of applied and fine art, whether sculpture, relief, or easel art. One of the six oil paintings by Schmidt-Rottluff from her collection, *Woman with a Bag*, was displayed prominently. In a letter to the Tate Gallery she stated that it came straight from his studio in Berlin and was painted in autumn 1915, "a few weeks before he had to do his military duty and go to the Front in Russia."[80] The furniture was designed by Schmidt-Rottluff and executed in the workshops of the manufacturer Jack Goldschmidt in Hamburg. Their shapes are simple and geometric, controlling the organic configuration appropriated from various primitive sources and the strident coloration of yellows, browns and ultramarine blues. It is not difficult to see that the classical context of *Bildung*, which involved the pursuit of an inward culture, was at the core of both Schapire's feminism and patronage. Yet she was not immune to having photographs of the interior made up as postcards to circulate to friends and acquaintances.[81]

Her public activities assumed national dimensions during the First World War. In the regional centers of Germany, there was a general recognition that lack of local support for young artists was seen as a reason for their departure to larger cities, particularly Munich and Berlin. While working largely within the framework of patriarchal institutions, Schapire spearheaded in 1916 the formation of the Frauenbund zur Förderung Deutscher bildenden Kunst (Women's Society for the Advancement of German Art) for the sponsorship of contemporary art in Hamburg, a precedent which assumed national dimensions by 1919, once branches had been founded in Berlin, Bremen, Elberfeld, Dresden, Essen, Hagen, Heidelberg, Kiel, Lübeck, and Mannheim.[82] Due to the privations of war and a reduction in purchasing budgets of official galleries and museums, Schapire considered it necessary for the Frauenbund to donate works as gifts to the state. Thereby, the Nietzschean ideal of cultural renewal could be achieved through constant reference to a living, creative tradition.[83] Evoking the period before the war when she had been recruited for ambassadorial work by the Brücke as a passive member, Schapire instituted an annual fee of 20 Marks for membership of the society, 300 Marks for life-membership, for which, in return, subscribers received an annual portfolio of graphics. As a consequence of these strategies, a *Still-Life with Dahlias* (1912) by Schmidt-Rottluff was donated to the Hamburg Kunsthalle in 1917, a Kirchner *Landscape at Fehmarn* and a Rohlfs *City-Scene at Soest* to the Kunsthallen in Bremen and Mannheim respectively in 1918, and a *Portrait of a Woman* by a certain Fräulein Friedrichs to the Kaiser-Friedrich-Museum in Elberfeld in 1919. No less important was the Frauenbund's sponsorship of exhibitions, the most ambitious being that of November 1917 at the Kunsthalle of new German art selected from private collections in Hamburg. This display contained one hundred and thirty-four works, including those from Schapire's collection, eight Nolde works from Martha and Paul Rauert, seven Pechstein from Minya Diez-Dührkoop, two Hofer works from the Dehmels and works by Van Gogh and Munch from Gustav Schiefler.[84]

As was observed of this occasion: "That in Hamburg, in the last decade of Expressionism, from Munch and Van Gogh until Heckel, Nolde and Kokoschka, a place of loving care found scarcely in another German city, one saw with full surprise the organized loan exhibition in Winter 1917 of the Women's Society for the Advancement of German Art."[85] In many ways the relationship between public and private had become inverted and it was the "taste" of the private patrons for contemporary art that generated and spurred this public event. During the war years, through the bequests of the Frauenbund and other notable patrons, the works of major Expressionists secured their place in public collections. While the Hamburg Kunsthalle cautiously pursued new purchases, such as the acquisition of Franz Marc's *Der Mandrill* (*Mandrill*) (1913) in 1918 which generated intense public controversy, these were nonetheless given prominent installation in a hall of Expressionist works.[86] The completion of the new section of the Kunsthalle, started in 1911 under Lichtwark, was opened to the public in 1919. Gustav Pauli, the director since 1914, commissioned

Photograph of Dr Rosa Schapire's living room, Hamburg, Osterbekstraße 1921, interior and furniture designed by Karl Schmidt-Rottluff

second generation Expressionists – members of the Hamburg Secession[87] – to decorate the interior.[88] Assisted by the media explosion of the early Weimar period, Rosa Schapire dedicated herself to cultivating the "newest Expressionist art". She acted as co-editor of and contributor to two Expressionist broadsheets featuring original prints, literature and reviews – *Die rote Erde* (The Red Earth) and *Kündung* (Herald).[89] Understandably then, by 1923, she was acclaimed by Hans Fischer as "an untiring propagandist for young art."[90]

Second generation Expressionists, dealers and collectors

It seems uncanny that dealership and the expansion of private collections continued unabated during the First World War. Herwarth Walden, for instance, while ceasing his interaction with the French and Italian avant-garde, made strenuous efforts to export Expressionist exhibitions, primarily the works of the Blaue Reiter, to the neutral countries of Holland, Denmark, Norway and Sweden. Indeed recently published evidence confirms that Walden's activities were endorsed and sponsored by the Zentralstelle für Auslandsdienst (Central Office of the Foreign Service) in Berlin.[91] This brings into question the political neutrality and ascribed internationalism of the Sturm enterprise during this period. Whatever officialdom thought of Expressionism in private was concealed in favor of recognizing its function as propaganda. In the face of an increasingly hostile international press, with the assistance of Walden, the Foreign Office sought to promote a view of German culture that was tolerant of artistic radicalism and expressive freedom.

The ascendance of Expressionism coincided with a recovery of the art market. The growth of the war industry during 1915 had steadily boosted the money supply and one of the consequences of this increased purchasing power was an investment in art works, a situation that reached boom proportions by 1917.[92] Tax exemptions on the work of living artists also benefited the Expressionists who drew advantage from a war-weary bourgeois public.[93] Though second generation Expressionists were widespread in regional centers throughout Germany, they were more cohesively defined by their anti-war sentiments and political engagement in the revolutionary fervor of the early Weimar Republic. At the heart of Expressionist theory lay the paradox that the personal "strivings" and subjective expression of the artist could nonetheless rekindle utopian notions of spiritual community and identity.[94]

Conrad Felixmüller
Bildnis Heinrich Kirchhoff, 1918
Portrait of Heinrich Kirchhoff
lithograph
Hamburg
Titus Felixmüller Collection

In negotiating these complex economic and ideological conditions, the early career of the Dresden-based artist Conrad Felixmüller is fascinating from the viewpoint of his interaction with diverse private collectors, commercial and media outlets. In 1917, at the age of twenty, he participated in a group exhibition at the Galerie Arnold called New Art in Saxony which, in its display, deliberately linked the works of second generation Expressionists with those of the Brücke. The well known collector and patron, the banker August von der Heydt (1851–1929) of Elberfeld, viewed this exhibition and became one of the artist's earliest collectors.[95] However, Felixmüller's career established a firmer base when the building developer, Heinrich Kirchhoff (1874–1934) of Wiesbaden, drew up a contract for two years guaranteeing the artist a monthly allowance between 1918 and 1920. As a consequence, Kirchhoff had first option on his paintings and assembled a collection of twenty-two oil paintings and a sizable graphic *oeuvre*. Felixmüller, who was self-trained as a graphic artist, gained early public recognition beyond Dresden through the exhibition of his prints in the graphic gallery of Israel Ber Neumann in Berlin in 1914.[96] Established in 1910 as a specialist bookshop, art dealer, and publisher of modern graphics, the monthly, temporary exhibitions held at this venue provide some measure of the growth in demand for graphic production.[97]

Yet Felixmüller also found commissions for his provocative political statements in the numerous Expressionist journals that were circulated during the war. The anti-war periodical *Die Aktion* was one of the foremost vehicles for left-wing radicalism and after his introduction to the editor, Franz Pfemfert, Felixmüller contributed over fifty woodcuts to the journal between 1917 and 1924.[98] Notwithstanding their incendiary statement, Felixmüller's prints held joint appeal for upper-middle-class businessmen and anti-bourgeois circles alike. But the upsurge in the demand for print culture and works on paper was due, as well, to a *Luxussteuer*, or luxury tax, instituted on 24 December 1919 by the financially beleaguered postwar German government which levied charges on items such as paintings. The burden of the tax of ten percent, rising soon after to fifteen percent, fell on art dealers who had to pay the government while not being able to pass on the additional cost to their customers for fear of losing them.[99] Nonetheless, Expressionists benefited from retroactive repeal of the tax program for the work of living artists in early 1920.[100]

Photograph of the exterior of the Neue Kunst Frau Ey, 1919, Düsseldorf Hindenburgwall 11

Photograph of *Barricadenkampf auf dem Düsseldorf Ey-Wall* *Barricade-Battle at the Ey-Wall* Düsseldorf, 24 December 1919

Photograph of the interior of the Neue Kunst Frau Ey: Johanna Ey Karl Schwesig and Maria Ey with Gert Wollheim's painting *Self-portrait in a Garret*, 1924

Werner Gothein *Porträt Rosy Fischer*, 1918 *Portrait of Rosy Fischer* woodcut USA, Nachlass Ludwig und Rosy Fischer Collection

Felixmüller subtly negotiated the nuances of the art market, diversifying his practice and audience. As such, in 1920, he advised the artist Otto Dix, who had recently returned to Dresden after his military service, to "make graphics; they are easily sold, one arrives immediately at the intended expression of ideas, and working expenses and the cost of materials are considerably less than painting."[101] Just as artists needed to engage with the implications of modernity – an urban-based, commodified existence – so dealers too faced urgent commercial considerations.[102] In Düsseldorf, Johanna Ey (1864-1947), in her search for appropriate gallery premises, eventually found a shop in the Hindenburgwall with two display windows which she named Neue Kunst Frau Ey in 1919.[103] Ey's adoption of confrontational tactics to attract a clientele is one of the most intriguing aspects of her dealership.[104] Seizing on the modernity implicit in glass-fronted shops, she seduced the public gaze by displaying controversial works in the windows of her gallery. Furthermore, while the dealer's gallery was a focus of the more conservative members of Das Junge Rheinland, formed in 1919, she encouraged the notion of spectacality by sponsoring artists who attracted official scandal. Otto Pankok (1893–1966) and Gert Wollheim (1894–1974) were lured to Düsseldorf to join a group of left-wing dissident war veterans known as the Aktivistenbund 1919 (Activist League 1919).[105] Both artists had been severely wounded on the front and their anti-war statement precipitated their move. When Wollheim's triptych *The Wounded One* (1919), of which only the central panel with its tormented, lacerated figure remains, was included in an exhibition of new purchases at the Düsseldorf Kunsthalle in February 1920, public protest forced its removal.[106] Whatever events transpired, the triptych found its way into one of the most intimate spaces of Ey's private realm, above the bed in her bedroom.[107] Indeed, it would appear that the dealer favored a more *sachlich* interpretation of war imagery and encouraged Wollheim to generate further paintings with pacifist sentiments, such as *The Condemned Man* of 1921.[108] Otto Dix was also prompted to complete his unfinished painting *Schützengraben* (*The Trench*) once he joined Johanna Ey's circle in 1923. The work itself attracted notoriety, endorsing the observation that in the highly competitive art market during the great inflation of the early twenties, public or professional scandal could secure artist's careers.[109] The politicized nature of war themes admirably leant itself to this procedure and, significantly, Dix's Berlin dealer and publisher at this time, Karl Nierendorf, commissioned the artist to produce the print portfolio *Der Krieg* (*War*).[110]

A photograph of 24 December 1919 *Barrikadenkampf auf dem Düsseldorfer Ey-Wall* (Barricade-Battle at the Ey-Wall in Düsseldorf), functions as a display of avant-garde transgressive behavior, a painting by Max Ernst (*Lime-preparation from Bones*) performing a protective barrier.[111] It is appropriate, therefore, that Ey's reminiscences, published in 1930, were entitled *Das rote Malkästle* (The Red Fortress). The inferences of rebellion and deviancy are more self-evident when the inner sanctum of Ey's gallery is compared to that of Alfred Flechtheim's (1878–1937), another notable dealer in the fashionable district of Düsseldorf. Behind the group of Ey, her daughter and the artist Karl Schwesig, is Wollheim's sober *Self-portrait in a Garret* (1924), unframed sketches to the left and right and informally hung paintings that contrast with Flechtheim's more elitist aspirations and sponsorship of international modernism.[112]

Johanna Ey's role has not escaped the realms of mythical categorization but the attribution of the name "Mutter Ey" belies the subversiveness of her tactics. Her forging of a space in a public arena differs greatly from that of Rosy Fischer (1869–1926) who, after her husband's death in 1922, decided to become a dealer and promoter of "Neuzeitliche Kunst" (Modern Art) from the privacy of her residence in Mendelsohnstraße, Frankfurt am Main.[113] Set against a background of the spiraling inflation at the time, this was as much a feature of economic necessity as a desire to explore a modern self-determined identity. Between 1916 and 1922, the Fischers assembled an incomparable collection of over five hundred Expressionist works, including major paintings, sculpture, works on paper and graphics. As a businessman, Ludwig Fischer (1860–1922) would have been aware of the benefit of investing in contemporary art in the economic boom during the war, however, their interest was generated, as well, by a legacy of enlightened Jewish patronage in the city. They were also introduced to contemporary art by the dealer Ludwig Schames (1852–1922) whose new Kunstsalon, founded in August 1913, became central to the promotion of Expressionism in Frankfurt. The Fischers' particular fascination for the works of Kirchner can be evinced from photographs of the dining-room taken in 1923. His paintings dominate the interior, their modernity being made all the more explicit by their contrast with the domestic setting. Among others, their collection included paintings by Nolde, Heckel, Schmidt-Rottluff, Kokosch-

Conrad Felixmüller
Bildnis des Kunstsammlers
Ludwig Fischer, 1922
Portrait of the Art Collector
Ludwig Fischer
etching and drypoint
Düsseldorf im Ehrenhof Kunstmuseum

Photograph by Paul Wolf
of the dining-room of Ludwig
and Rosy Fischer, Frankfurt am Main
with paintings by Kirchner, 1923

ka, Jakob Steinhardt and Otto Müller; sculpture by Kirchner, Lehmbruck, Gerhard Marcks, Milly Steger, and Gustav Wolff. From 1921 they also started collecting works of second generation Expressionists – the Dresden artists Felixmüller, Dix, and Lasar Segall – who were promoted by Rosy Fischer in her temporary exhibitions. Due to the hyperinflation of 1923 and the subsequent revaluation of the Mark, trade in the Galerie Fischer dwindled. On behalf of the Städtische Museum für Kunst und Gewerbe in Halle, Max Sauerlandt negotiated for the purchase of twenty-four works in exchange for a life annuity for Rosy Fischer.[114] The Halle acquisition was greeted with immense public approval, an indication of the degree to which Expressionism had made inroads into state collections since its inception.[115] As Vernon Lidtke has commented, this convergence led to an alliance of cultural modernism with more traditional notions of German patriotism.[116] Whereas the movement started out as a marginalized experience of semi-private viewing among select patrons, it was now recognized as a mainstream and organic development of modernism. Unlike the fate of most private and public collections of Expressionism during the Third Reich, at least half of the Fischer collection was salvaged and kept intact by their son Ernst Fischer, who immigrated to the United States in 1934.[117] The Fischers' activities, as representative of the climax of Jewish participation in the project of modernity, serve to highlight the extremely fragile and short-lived path of this so-called renaissance.[118]

[1] The research for this essay was partially undertaken while a Scholar-in-Residence at the Robert Gore Rifkind Center for German Expressionist Studies at the Los Angeles County Museum of Art. I am grateful to Robert Gore Rifkind and Stephanie Barron for their kind interest, to the Associate Curator Timothy O. Benson, the Librarian Susan Trauger and her Assistant Registrar Christine Vigiletti for their expert assistance. The architect Titus Felixmüller in Hamburg has consistently availed me of his time. I would also like to thank Ines Schlenker for the assistance and the Tate Gallery Archive for allowing me access to their correspondence with Dr Rosa Schapire.
[2] Oskar Kokoschka, *Letters 1905–1976*. London: Thames and Hudson, 1992, p. 48–49, 267 n. The painting *The Tempest* (oil on canvas, 181 x 220 cms) was referred to as *Tristan and Isolde* by Kokoschka, receiving its title *Die Windsbraut* after Georg Trakl's visit to the artist's studio.
[3] The secessions were formed in Munich in 1892, in Vienna in 1897 and in Berlin in 1898. See Maria Makela, *The Munich Secession: Art and Artists in Turn-of-the-Century Munich*. Princeton, New Jersey: Princeton University Press, 1990, and Peter Paret, *The Berlin Secession. Modernism and its Enemies in Imperial Germany*, Cambridge Mass., Belknap Press, 1980. For an incisive account of the spread of the secessionist idea see Robert Jensen's chapter on "Secessionism" in *Marketing Modernism in Fin-de-Siècle Europe*, Princeton, New Jersey, Princeton University Press, 1994, pp. 167–200.
[4] Reinhold Heller outlines the conditions for identifying an artistic avant-garde as involving: the rejection of established aesthetic values, the formulation of shared innovative ones based on a 'yearning for the future', the foundation of alternative exhibitions and other propagating collective groupings and the search for new circles of patronage. See his "'Das Schwarze Ferkel' and the Institution of an Avant-Garde in Berlin 1892–1895" in Thomas W. Gaehtgens, ed., *Künstlerischer Austausch. Artistic Exchange. Akten des XXVIII Internationalen Kongresses für Kunstgeschichte*, Berlin, 15–20 Juli 1992, vol. III, Berlin 1993, p. 509.
[5] Volker R. Berghahn, *Economy, Society and Culture of Imperial Germany 1870-1914*. Providence and Oxford: Berghahn, 1994, p. 15–17, pinpoints the intense period of economic expansion to the years ca. 1893–1913.
[6] Maurice Godé, *"Der Sturm" de Herwarth Walden ou l'utopie d'un art autonome*. Nancy: University of Nancy Press, 1990, p. 26.
[7] The series comprised the pen and ink drawings of K. Kraus, A. Loos, H. Walden, P. Scheerbart, A. Kerr, R. Dehmel, K. Michaelis.
[8] Beatrix Nobis, "'Expressionismus ist ein Kampfwort...'. Ein idealistcher Revolutionär. Herwarth Walden und der Sturm'", in Henrike Junge ed., *Avantgarde und Publikum: Zur Rezeption avant-gardistischer Kunst in Deutschland 1905–1933*, Cologne: Böhlau, 1992, p. 323.
[9] Robert Jensen explores this feature in greater detail in his article, "Selling Martyrdom", *Art and America*, vol. 80, April 1992, p. 138–145.
[10] Godé, *"Der Sturm"*, p. 29. Cassirer (1871–1926) had already featured an exhibition of Kokoschka's portraits in July 1910. About the dealer's background and gallery, established in 1898, see Paret, *The Berlin Secession*, p. 70-79. His publishing business is dealt by Eva Casper, *Paul Cassirer und die Pan-Presse: Ein Beitrag zur deutschen Buchillustration und Graphik im 20. Jahrhunder.* Frankfurt am Main: Buchhändler-Vereinigung, 1986.
[11] The Blaue Reiter was included in the launching exhibition of the Sturm Gallery in Tiergartenstraße 34a in March 1912 and the Pathetiker in König-Augustastraße in November 1912.
[12] See Marit Werenskiold, *The Concept of Expressionism: Origin and Metamorphoses.* Oslo: Universitetsforlaget, 1984, p. 47 and n. 45, p. 176. In 1913, *Der Sturm* published a Kandinsky Album, *Wassily Kandinsky: Rückblicke 1901–1913*.
[13] Herwarth Walden, "Vorrede", *Erster Deutscher Herbstsalon*, Der Sturm, Berlin, p. 5–8, as cited in Rose-Carol Washton Long ed., *German Expressionism: Documents from the End of the Wilhelmine Empire to the Rise of National Socialism.* New York, G.K. Hall, p. 57–58. Kandinsky's *Über das Geistige in der Kunst* was published by Piper, Munich, 1912.

[14] See Magdalena M. Moeller, "Erster Deutscher Herbstsalon", Eberhard Roters *Stationen der Moderne: Die bedeutenden Kunstausstellungen des 20. Jahrhunderts in Deutschland*, ed., Berlinische Galerie, 1988, p. 130–153.

[15] Nell Walden, *Herwarth Walden: Ein Lebensbild*. Berlin: Florian Kupferberg, 1963, p. 71.

[16] See Jensen, *Marketing Modernism*, p. 70–1, for the *fin-de-siècle* context of dealership.

[17] For an outline of the NKVM see Shulamith Behr, "Neue Künstlerveinigung München", in *The Dictionary of Art*, vol. 22, Grove, London, 1996, p. 921.

[18] Heinrich Thannhauser (1859–1934) was a sleeping partner in the gallery of Franz Josef Brakl, Goethestraße 64, from 1904 onwards. His private gallery was established in the former Arco-Palais (Theatinerstraße 7) in Autumn 1909. For a detailed account of his dealership see Mario-Andreas von Lüttichau, "Die Moderne Galerie Heinrich Thannhauser in München", in *Avantgarde und Publikum*, p. 299–306.

[19] Kathrin Lochmaier, "Die Galerie 'Neue Kunst Hans Goltz' in München", in *Avantgarde und Publikum*, p. 103–110.

[20] Robin Reisenfeld, *The German Print Portfolio 1890–1930: Serials for the Private Sphere*. London: Philip Wilson, 1992, p. 28–29. The *Bildungsbürgertum* or educated middle class refers to civil servants and university-trained professionals. As industrialization took hold in the later nineteenth century, the number of businessmen obviously underwent a rapid increase. For an analysis of the *Besitz- und Bildungsbürgertum* shared interests in the realm of cultural and social identity "in the broadest sense", see David Blackbourn's introduction to the anthology, *The German Bourgeoisie: Essays on the social history of the German middle class from the late eighteenth century to the early twentieth century*, David Blackbourn and Richard J. Evans, eds. London and New York: Routledge, 1991, p. 9.

[21] Klaus Lankheit (ed.), commentary to documentary edition of Franz Marc and Wassily Kandinsky eds., *Der Blaue Reiter* (1912), Munich, Piper, 1984, pp. 274-277.

[22] Benedict Anderson, *Imagined Communities: Reflections on the Origin and Spread of Nationalism* (1983). New York: Verso, revised edition 1991, p. 36. In investigating circles of patronage, I have adopted the framework from Anderson's compelling reminder that "nations" are "imagined political communities", which can be explored through the specific nexus connecting intellectuals to the printing industries and which loses its monolithic character when considering the multiplicity of print communities.

[23] Carl Vinnen, *Ein Protest Deutscher Künstler*. Jena, Eugen Diederichs, 1911. The catalyst for Vinnen's essay "Quousque Tandem", was the purchase of Van Gogh *Poppy Field* 1889-90 by the director of the Bremen Kunsthalle, Gustav Pauli (1868–1938). Vinnen (1863–1922), a former landscapist of the Worpswede school, railed against the acquisition of inferior French works, the inflation of the art market and their corruptive influence on German culture. See Wulf Herzogenrath, "'Ein Schaukelpferd von einem Berserker geritten'; Gustav Pauli, Carl Vinnen und der 'Protest Deutscher Künstler'", in *Manet bis van Gogh: Hugo von Tschudi und der Kampf um die Moderne*, Johann Georg, Prinz von Hohenzollern, and Peter-Klaus Schuster eds, Nationalgalerie, Berlin, 1996, p. 264–273.

[24] *Im Kampf um die Kunst–Die Antwort auf den "Protest Deutscher Künstle"*, *Galerieleiter, Sammler und Schriftsteller*, was organized by Gustav Pauli through his Munich-based friend Alfred Walter Heymel and the artist Franz Marc. It was published by Piper, Munich, 1911.

[25] The literature on the derivations and meanings of Expressionism is extensive. Recent contributions to the field argue with the findings of Donald E. Gordon, as expressed in his pivotal article, "On the Origin of the Word 'Expressionism'", *Journal of the Warburg and Courtauld Institute*, vol. XXIX, 1966, pp. 368–385. See Marit Werenskiold, *The Concept of Expressionism: Origin and Metamorphoses*, 1984, and Ron Manheim, "Expressionismus – Zur Enstehung eines Kunsthistorischen Stil- und Periodenbegriffes", in *Zeitschrift für Kunstgeschichte I*, vol. 49, Heft I, 1986, p. 73–91.

[26] For an outline of the multi-disciplinary features of the movement see Shulamith Behr and David Fanning eds., *Expressionism Reassessed*. Manchester: Manchester University Press, 1993.

[27] Quoted from Hugo von Tschudi, Introduction to the catalogue *Der Sammlung des Kgl. Rates Marczell von Nemes, Budapest*, Alte Pinakothek, Munich, 1911, in *Gesammelte Schriften zur neueren Kunst von Hugo von Tschudi*, Dr. E. Schwedeler-Meyer, ed. Munich 1912, p. 228 ff: "ein neuer Typ des Galeriedirektors".

[28] Walter Grasskamp outlines this phenomenon in his essay, "Die Einbürgerung der Kunst: Korporative Kunstförderung in 19. Jahrhundert", in *Sammler, Stifter und Museen: Kunstförderung in Deutschland im 19. und 20. Jahrhundert*, Ekkehard Mai and Peter Paret, eds. Cologne: Böhlau, 1993, p. 104–113.

[29] The restriction to these examples is due to limitations of space. Clearly, the role of Harry Graf Kessler, director of Weimar's museums between 1902 and 1906, was of equal significance to promoting Weimar as a major centre of modernism during the empire. See Thomas Föhl, "Ein Museum der Moderne: Harry Graf Kessler und das Neue Weimar", in *Manet bis van Gogh*, p. 288–301.

[30] See Carmen Luise Stonge, *Karl Ernst Osthaus: The Folkwang Museum and the dissemination of international modernism*, Ph. D., City University of New York, 1993.

[31] *Ibid.*, p. 58–69, for Osthaus's early art historical training; p. 78-100 for the role of Van de Velde.

[32] For an exploration of Osthaus in relation to the Deutsche Werkbund (founded in 1907) and the Deutsches Museum für Kunst in Handel und Gewerbe (co-founded by Osthaus and the Werkbund in 1909), see the exhibition catalogue, *Der Westdeutsche Impuls 1900-1914. Kunst und Umweltgestaltung im Industriegebiet. Die Deutsche Werkbund-Ausstellung Cöln 1914*, Kölnischer Kunstverein, 1984, pp. 80-92; Sebastian Müller, "Das Deutsche Museum für Kunst in Handel und Gewerbe", in *Karl Ernst Osthaus: Leben und Werk*, Herta Hesse-Frielinghaus, ed. Recklinghausen, 1971, p. 259–342.

[33] Herta Hesse-Frielinghaus, ed., documents the acquisitions and provenance of the collection in the essay "Folkwang 1. Teil", in *Karl Ernst Osthaus. Leben und Werk*, Recklinghausen: Aurel Bongers, 1971, p. 192 ff.

[34] Andres Lepik discusses the purchase of modern French paintings in "Die Zurückführung der Kunst ins Leben. Karl Ernst Osthaus und das Museum Folkwang", in *Manet bis van Gogh*, p. 302–7.

[35] Stonge, p. 114, 146; Jill Lloyd, *German Expressionism: Primitivism and Modernity*. Yale: Yale University Press, 1991, p. 8–12.

[36] Martin Urban, *Emil Nolde. Catalogue Raisonné of the Oil Paintings 1895-1914*, London: vol. I, 1987, Sotheby's, p. 27. After Osthaus's death in 1921, the city of Hagen was unwilling to keep the collection intact, as stipulated in his will. As a consequence, the city of Essen raised the fifteen million marks required and the new Folkwang Museum opened on 29 October 1922. The collection was dismantled after 1933, however.

[37] See Magdalena Bushart, "Der Formsinn des Weibes: Bildhauerinnen in den zwanziger und dreißiger Jahren", in *Profession ohne Tradition. 125 Jahre Verein der Berliner Künstlerinnen*, Berlinischen Galerie, 1992, p. 135–150; Birgit Schulte, "Milly Steger. Stadtbihauerin von Hagen", in *Hagener Impuls*, Heft 9, September 1994, p. 27–36. Birgit Schulte also documents Osthaus's exhibiting of eighty works by Elsa Lasker Schüler (1869–1945), the Expressionist poet, in 1916, in "Zwischen Theben und Hagen. Else Lasker Schülers Begegnung mit Karl Ernst Osthaus, Milly Steger und Christian Rohlfs", in *Hagener Impuls*, Heft 11, June 1995, p. 7–15.

[38] Stonge, *Karl Ernst Osthaus* p. 204–5.

[39] For an outline of this association see Magdalena M. Moeller, *Der Sonderbund: Seine Voraussetzungen und Anfänge*. Cologne: Rheinland, 1984.

[40] Karl Ernst Osthaus, "Die Museen als Volksbildungsstätten", 1904, quoted in Monika Lahme-Schlenger, "Karl Ernst Osthaus", *Avantgarde und Publikum*, p. 228: "Die Kultur ist heute keine Klassenfrage, sie ist eine Volksfrage, ist die große Frage unserer Zeit".

[41] Peter-Klaus Schuster, "Hugo von Tschudi und der Kampf die Moderne", in *Manet bis van Gogh*, p. 25 ff.

[42] For a definitive account, see Paret, "The Tschudi Affair", *The Journal of Modern History*, vol. 53, no. 4, December 1981, p. 589–618. This article has been updated in his "Die Tschudi-Affäre", in *Manet bis van Gogh*, p. 396–401.

[43] See Carla Schulz-Hoffmann, "Hugo von Tschudi - Avantgardist mit Augenmaß", in *Manet bis van Gogh*, p. 441, quoting Kandinsky's letter to Tschudi, 4.7.1909, in the Gabriele Münter- und Johannes Eichner-Stiftung, Munich: "Unsere noch kleine Gemeinde denkt, daß die Kunst nicht nur eine Verkörperung des >Schönen< ist... sondern daß ein Kunstwerk ein *inneres* subjektives Leben hat, ein inneres subjektives *Wesen* ist... der Atmosphäre, die die Keime der Zukunft aufnimmt u. zum Gedeihen bringt".

[44] *Ibid.*, Letter from Tschudi to Kandinsky, 8.7.1909, Gabriel Münter- und Johannes Eichner-Stiftung, Munich.

[45] See Mario-Andreas von Lüttichau, "Der Blaue Reiter", in *Stationen der Moderne*. Berlinische Galerie, 1988, p. 108–129.

[46] Wassily Kandinsky and Franz Marc, eds., *Der Blaue Reiter*. München: Piper, 1912.

[47] Hugo von Tschudi, Introduction to the catalogue *Der Sammlung des Kgl. Marczell von Nemes Collection*, 1911, München, 1912, p. 228: "Diesem neuen Galeriedirektor des 20. Jahrhunderts tritt nun auch ein neuer Sammlertyp an die Seite. Wie jener verwaltet und ergänzt, so baut dieser auf. Nicht auf kunsthistorischen Gesichtspunkten, auch nicht mit jener spezifischen Sammlerleidenschaft, der es um Vollständigkeit zu tun ist, sondern mit der erregten Hingabe des temperament vollen Kunstfreundes, der nur da, aber da rasch zugreift, wo sein künstlerisches Empfinden in starken Schwingungen versetz wurde".

[48] See Thomas W. Gaehtgens, "Tschudis Impressionismusverständnis: Historienmalerei als Darstellung erlebten Lebens", in *Manet bis van Gogh*, p. 360–363.

[49] *Ibid.*, p. 362, quoting Hugo von Tschudi, "Kunst und Publikum", 1899, from *Gesammelte Schriften*, p. 75.

[50] See Richard J. Evans, "Family and Class in the Hamburg grand bourgeoisie 1815–1914", in *The German Bourgeoisie*, p. 117–119.

[51] See introduction in Eva Maria Krafft and Carl-Wolfgang Schumann, *Katalog der Meister des 19. Jahrhunderts in der Hamburger Kunsthalle*, vol. II, Hamburg, 1969. The Kunsthalle was founded in 1846 around the bequest of P. Delaroche and was initially called the Öffentliche Städtische Gemäldegalerie.

[52] Alfred Lichtwark, "Selbsterziehung", *Pan*, vol. 2, Heft 4, 1968–87, p. 302, as cited in Reinhold Heller, *Stark Impressions: Graphic Production in Germany 1918–1933*. Mary and Leigh Block Gallery, Northwestern University, 1993, p. 10.

[53] Alfred Lichtwark, "Wege und Ziele des Diletantismus" (1894), in *Die Grundlagen der Künstlerischen Bildung: Studien aus den Vörtragen an der Kunsthalle*. Berlin: Bruno Cassirer Verlag, 1918. See Clive Ashwin, *Drawing and Education in German-speaking Europe 1800-1900*. Ann Arbor: UMI Research Press, 1981, p. 148–149.

[54] Alfred Lichtwark, "Glitza-Blätter", in exhibition catalogue of the fourth annual exhibition of the Gesellschaft Hamburgischer Kunstfreunde, Hamburg, 1898, p. 17 ff., as cited in Henrike Junge, "Alfred Lichtwark und die 'Gymnastik der Sammeltätigkeit'", in *Sammler, Stifter und Museen*, p. 205.

[55] Alfred Lichtwark, "Der Sammler", *Kunst und Künstler*, vol. X, 1911–12, p. 288, as cited in Junge, *ibid*, p. 204.

[56] Clive Ashwin, *Drawing*, p. 146 ff.

[57] Emil Waldmann, "Die Sammlung Rauerts in Hamburg" *Kunst und Künstler*, vol. 17, 1919, p. 427: "Im allgemeinen pflegt das private Kunstsammeln in deutschen Städten Hand in Hand zu gehen mit der Tätigkeit der Museen, besonders wenn diese im deutschen Kunstleben eine führende Stellung einnehmen. Als in Hamburg der grösste deutsche Kunstpolitiker der Neuzeit, Alfred Lichtwark, sein Reorganisationswerk begann, stiegen auch für die Hamburger Kunstfreunde und Bildersammler anregende Zeiten herauf".

[58] Emil Waldmann, *Sammler und ihresgleichen*. Berlin: Bruno Cassirer Verlag, 1920, p. 70: "der wahre Förderer... der Sammler und der Käufer".

[59] See Magdalena M. Moeller, "Die Jahresmappen der Brücke 1906–1912," in *Brücke-Archiv*, Heft 17, 1989, p. 17, Ernst Ludwig Kirchner, *Programm der Brücke* 1906–1912," in *Brücke*, Text, 1906, woodcut: "Mit dem Glauben an Entwicklung, an eine neue Generation der Schaffenden wie der Genießenden, rufen wir alle Jugend zusammen...".

[60] See Indina Kampf, "Gustav Schiefler (1857-1935) Der programmatische Dilettant", in *Avantgarde und Publikum*, p. 291–97.

[61] "Gustav Schiefler, *Verzeichnis des graphischen Werks Edvard Munchs bis 1906*, Berlin, 1907; *Edvard Munch. Das Graphische Werk, 1906–1926*, Berlin, 1927.

[62] Gustav Schiefler, *Das graphische Werk Emil Noldes bis 1910*, Berlin, 1911; *Das graphische Werk von Emil Nolde 1910-1925*, Berlin, 1927; *Die Graphik Ernst Ludwig Kirchners*, Berlin, 1924 and 1931.

[63] The members Rosa Schapire and Martha Rauert were listed in 1907. All names were included in the catalogue of the Brücke exhibition held in September 1910 at the Galerie Arnold, Dresden: Bertha Rohlsen, Henny Droste, H. Schroeter and A. Philippi, I. Deutschmann, Diez-Dührkoop, Frl. Cl. Goldschmidt, E. Hopf, Helene Simon.

[64] Minya Diez-Dührkoop (1873–1929) was the daughter of the photographer Rudolf Dührkoop (1848-1918) and was trained in his studio.

[65] See Ute Frevert, *Women in German History: From Bourgeois Emancipation to Sexual Liberation*, Oxford 58, Berg, 1989, p. 54–58. The salon of the late eighteenth century was a typically middle class institution that bridged the schism between the private and the public, the bourgeoisie and the aristocracy.

[66] Gustav Schiefler, *Eine Hamburgische Kulturgeschichte 1890–1920*. Hamburg: Verein für Hamburgische Geschichte, 1985, p. 300-301. Bertha Rohlsen (1852– 1928, *née* Rauert) was the older sister of the collector Paul Rauert and widow of the businessman Consul Gustav Rohlsen.

[67] Ida Dehmel (1870–1942, *née* Coblenzer), the second wife of the poet Richard Dehmel (1863–1920) founded the group GEDOK (Gemeinschaft Deutscher und Österreichischer Künstlerinnen und Kunstfreunde) in 1926.

[68] Schiefler, *Eine Hamburgische Kulturgeschichte*, p. 526–527.

[69] See Gerhard Wietek, "Dr phil. Rosa Schapire", in *Jahrbuch der Hamburger Kunstsammlungen*, vol. 9, 1964, p. 120, note 1. Apparently, this was achieved through Schapire's initiative.

[70] Hans Platte and Luise Schiefler, *Gustav Schiefler: aus der Erinnerungen von Luise Schiefler*. Hamburg: Hans Christians, 1965, pp. 28-29.

[71] Gerhard Wietek, *Schmidt Rottluff: Oldenburger Jahre 1907–1912*. Mainz: Zabern, 1995.

[72] Irene Eucken, "Zur Einführung", in *Ausstellung von Kleidern aus der Stickstube von Frau Eucken*, Bremer Frauenklub von 1908, Bremen, 1916: "Seit einem Jahre erstreben wir in Deutschland ein Selbständigwerden der Mode... Um aber das Streben in Tat umzusetzen, bedürfen wir jetzt dringend der kräftigen Mitarbeit schaffender Künstler. Sie müssen uns neue Formen und Farben geben. Sie müssen uns neue Formen und Farben geben. Sie müssen uns die Anwendung unseres hochentwickelten Kunstgewerbes lehren, damit wirklich tragbare, neue Kleidermodelle entstehen. In meiner Stickstube werden nun einige tüchtige Künstler Gelegenheit haben, ihre Ideen zur Ausführung zu bringen...".

[73] Ernst Ludwig Kirchner and Gustav Schiefler, *Briefwechsel 1910–1935–1938*. Stuttgart: Belser, 1990, p. 80–83, letters dated 22 September and 19 October 1916.

[74] Sherwin Simmons (University of Oregon, Eugen) discusses this context in a paper "Expressionism in the Discourse of Fashion", delivered in a session devoted to Art and Patronage in Germany 1870–1945, Association of Art Historians Conference, Courtauld Institute of Art, London, 4-6 April 1997.

[75] See Lloyd, *German Expressionism*, p. 9.

[76] For a definitive account of her contribution and publications see Wietek 1964, Schmidt-Rottluff ..., p. 115–160. Regarding her role as patron and collector, see Shulamith Behr, "Anatomy of the woman as collector and dealer in the Weimar period: Rosa Schapire and Johanna Ey," in *Visions of the "neue Frau": Women and the Visual Arts in Weimar Germany*, Shearer West and Marsha Meskimmon, eds. London: Scolar, 1995, p. 96–107.

[77] See Rosa Schapire, "Ein Wort zur Frauenemanzipation", in *Sozialistische Monatshefte*, vol. 1, 1897, p. 510–517.

[78] Rosa Schapire, "Der Frankfurter Maler Johann Ludwig Ernst Morgenstern 1738–1819", Ruprecht-Karls-Universität zu Heidelberg, 1904.

[79] Rosa Schapire, *Karl Schmidt-Rottluffs Graphisches Werk bis 1923*, Berlin, 1924.

[80] Tate Gallery Archive: Rosa Schapire letter to Mr. Hollon, 6 January 1951. Another letter to Mr Reid 27 July 1950 records that the Tate had accepted the gift of the painting *Woman with a Bag* 1915 (oil on canvas, 95.2 x 87.3 cms). Schapire arrived in London on 18 August 1939 on a transit visa. For her period in exile see Shulamith Behr, "Dr Rosa Schapire - Art Historian and Critic in Exile", in *Hitler's Gift to Britain*, Proceedings of the Second International Symposium on German and Austrian Exiles in Great Britain, Institute for Germanic Studies, London, forthcoming.

[81] Wietek, "Dr phil. Rosa Schapire," 1964, p. 132.

[82] Rosa Schapire, "Der Frauenbund zur Förderung deutscher bildenden Kunst", *Neue Blätter für Kunst und Dichtung*, November 1919, no. 2, p. 166–167.

[83] *Ibid.*, p. 167: "Er will sein Teil dazu beitragen, daß den Kunstwerken der Gegenwart ihr Platz rechtzeitig in jenen Stätten angewiesen werde... Er möchte jene Atmosphäre mitschaffen, die, nach ein schönen Wort Nietzsches, alles Lebendige zu seiner Entwicklung bedarf".

[84] See Maike Bruhns, "Rosa Schapire und der Frauenbund zur Förderung Deutscher Bildenden Kunst", in *Avantgarde und Publikum*, p. 274, 280 note 28.

[85] Emil Waldmann, "Die Sammlung Rauerts in Hamburg", *Kunst und Künstler*, vol. 17, 1919, p. 427– 428: "Dass in Hamburg im vergangenen Jahrzent der Expressionismus, von Munch und van Gogh bis Heckel und Nolde und Kokoschka eine Stätte so liebevoller Pflege fand wie kaum in einer andren deutschen Stadt, sah man voll Überraschung und der vom 'Frauenbund zur Förderung bildender Kunst' im Winter 1917 organisierten Leih-Ausstellung..."

[86] See *Zinnober: Kunstszene Hamburg 1919–1933*, Roland Jaeger and Cornelius Steckner eds, Szene, Hamburg, 1983, p. 32–33.

[87] In Hamburg, in the wake of the November Revolution, a purely advisory body, the Künstlerrat, was formed to provide the city council with suggestions for assisting artists. The largely conservative Kunstverein was challenged

by the formation of Kräfte (Forces) in 1919, a branch of the Berlin Novembergruppe, and by the group known as the Hamburgische Secession. See Peter W. Guenther, "A Survey of Artists' Groups: Their Rise, Rhetoric and Demise", in *German Expressionism 1915-1925: The Second Generation*, Stephanie Barron, ed. München: Prestel, 1988, p. 108–110.

[88] See Jaeger and Cornelius Steckner eds., *Zinnober*, p. 32–33.

[89] *Die Rote Erde* was co-edited with Karl Lorenz between 1919 and 1920, *Kündung* with Wilhelm Niemeyer between 1920 and 1921.

[90] Hans W. Fischer, *Hamburger Kulturbilderbogen*, Hamburg, 1923, p. 225, as cited in Jaeger and Steckner, *Zinnober*, p. 21: "eine unermüdliche Werberin für junge Kunst".

[91] See Kate Winskell, "The Art of Propaganda: Herwarth Walden and 'Der Sturm', 1914–1919", in *Art History*, vol. 18, no. 3, September 1995, p. 315–344.

[92] See Otto Karl Werckmeister, *The Making of Paul Klee's Career 1914– 1920*. Chicago: University of Chicago Press, 1984, p. 35–36, 86–88.

[93] Joan Weinstein, *The End of Expressionism*. Chicago: University of Chicago Press, 1990, p. 20, observes that "this was the result not only of an ideological convergence between Expressionist art and a war-weary bourgeois public, but also its conjuncture with economic conditions". See also in this catalogue, Joan Weinstein, "Expressionism in War and Revolution".

[94] It is evident that such aesthetic criteria, dependent on a complex of Nietzschean and Wagnerian ideas, could be appropriate to a range of ideologies, whether left- or right- wing. See Rhys Williams, "Culture and Anarchy in Expressionist Drama", in *Expressionism Reassessed*, p. 201–211, and the writings of the Expressionist poet Gottfried Benn, who turned to Nazism during the early 1930s, "Expressionismus" 1934 (The Conversion of an Expressionist) in *Voices of German Expressionism*, Victor Miesel, ed. New Jersey, 1970, p. 192–203.

[95] Jutta Penndorf, "Conrad Felixmüller und seine Sammler in den Dresdner Jahre (1917–1934)", in *Conrad Felixmüller: Monographie und Werkverzeichnis der Gemälde*, Heinz Spielmann, ed. Cologne: Wienand, 1996, p. 32–45.

[96] See Shulamith Behr, *Conrad Felixmüller 1897-1977: Works on Paper*. London: Courtauld Institute Galleries, 1994, p. 15 ff.

[97] For details of I.B. Neumann (1880–1958), see Karl-Heinz Meißner, "Israel Ber Neumann– Kunsthandler–Verleger", in *Avantgarde und Publikum*, p. 215–224.

[98] Behr, *Conrad Felixmüller*, p. 16–23.

[99] For the protest of German art dealers against the tax measures see Felix Szkolny, "Die Besteuerung der Kunst", *Kunst und Künstler*, vol. 17, Heft 3, 1919, p. 116–117.

[100] See Felix Szkolny, "Die neue Unsatz- und Luxussteuer", *Kunst und Künstler*, vol. 18, Heft 9/10, 1920, p. 337–338, and *Memorandum on German Taxes*. London: Price Waterhouse, August 1927, p. 14–16.

[101] Conrad Felixmüller, *Legenden 1912–1976*, G.H. Herzog, ed. Tübingen: Wasmuth, 1977, p. 54.

[102] For the context of dealership in this period see Hans Peter Thurn, *Der Kunsthändler: Wandlungen eines Berufes*. München: Hirmer, 1994, p. 115–138.

[103] See Anna Klapheck, *Mutter Ey: Eine Düsseldorfer Künstlerlegende* (1958), fourth edition Düsseldorf: Droste, 1984, p. 9–19, and Beata Ermacora, "Neue Kunst, Frau Ey", in *Avantgarde und Publikum*, p. 59–67.

[104] Behr, "Anatomy of the woman", p. 102–103.

[105] Johanna Ey, "Das rote Malkästle", *Das Kunstblatt*, vol. 14, 1930, p. 80.

[106] See Barron, *German Expressionism 1915–1925*, fig. 1, p. 80 (oil on wood, 156 x 178 cms, private collection), produced in Remels, East Friesland (April 1919), where Wollheim and Pankok were hoping to establish an artists' colony.

[107] Ey, "Das rote Malkästle," p. 80.

[108] Stephanie Barron, *German Expressionism 1915–1925*, fig. 9, p. 87 (oil on canvas, 123 x 99 cms, private collection).

[109] See Wolfgang Schröck-Schmidt, "Der Schicksalweg des Schützengraben", in *Otto Dix zum 100. Geburtstag 1891–1900*, Wulf Herzogenrath and Johann-Karl Schmidt (eds.), Städtische Galerie Albstadt, 1991, p. 159–164 (oil on canvas, lost or destroyed).

[110] Wulf Herzogenrath, "Die Mappe *Der Krieg* 1923–24", in *ibid.*, p. 167–175.

[111] The photograph, while taken on Christmas Eve 1919, was published in the magazine *Das Stachelschwein*, 1925, p. 31.

[112] See *Alfred Flechtheim: Sammler, Kunsthändler, Verleger*, Hans Albert Peters and Stephan von Wiese, eds. Düsseldorf: Kunstmuseum, 1987, p. 163.

[113] For a detailed discussion see *Expressionismus und Exil: Die Sammlung Ludwig und Rosy Fischer, Frankfurt am Main*. Georg Heuberger, ed. München: Prestel, 1990.

[114] Max Sauerlandt (1880–1934), as director of the Hamburg Museum für Kunst und Gewerbe between 1919 and 1933, had broken with tradition in initiating the acquisition of over 300 works drawn from contemporary arts and craft. For an account of his support of Expressionism and museology, see Andreas Hüneke, "Von der Verantwortung des Museumdirektors-Max Sauerlandt", in *Avantgarde und Publikum*, p. 261–268.

[115] For an account of the reception see Cordula Frowein, "Die Sammlung Rosy und Ludwig Fischer in Frankfurt am Main", in *Avantgarde und Publikum*, p. 75.

[116] Vernon L. Lidtke, "Museen und die Zeitgenössische Kunst in der Weimarer Republik", in *Sammler, Stifter und Museen*, p. 233–24.

[117] Cordula Frowein, "Schicksal der Sammlung Fischer", in *Expressionismus und Exil*, p. 116–119.

[118] Peter Paret elaborates on this context in his essay, "Bemerkungen zu dem Thema: Jüdische Kunstsammler, Stifer und Kunsthändler", in *Sammler, Stifter und Museen*, p. 171–185.

German Expressionism and Italian Art

Maurizio Calvesi

Our overall perspective on the development of the avant-garde movements that started the new century, including German Expressionism, has become a question of hindsight, and so is the unbiased assessment which I propose in this essay. What still need to be investigated, perhaps, are the ideological and cultural aspects of Expressionism – a task this exhibition aims to fulfill by means of its broad spectrum of historical documentation – and also in relation to the frequently underplayed "ethnic" question. Before the Third Reich's sinister philosophy of race took hold, the Expressionists had candidly touted a racial idea of German art, believing it could be sourced back to some legendary cultural roots.

The cultural influences that determined the figurative content of Expressionist art are easy to trace: Edvard Munch, Vincent van Gogh, and James Ensor; the Fauves in France; the return to "primitive" art forms; imported art works from Oceania and Africa; the revival of archaisms and of the woodcut, an important part of German tradition. From the literally standpoint, the Expressionists read their Nietzsche, but also Ibsen, Strindberg, Wedekind, and Whitman.

The new art form was characterized by heavy, harsh lines and clashing colors. The Fauves also used pure colors, though with a more radiant and gratifying result epitomized by Matisse's unbridled *joie de vivre*, in which the limpid application of color and the lack of shadows was the utter antithesis of the sense of tragedy conveyed by the Expressionists, with their crude reds and yellows clashing with blacks, deep blues, and nocturnal violets; with their jagged geometry that was neither geometrical nor the fruit of rational analysis like that of the Cubists, but rather a materialization of their cry of dismay, a macabre sword dance or masquerade.

The bitterness that informed Expressionist painting was not so much innate as provoked. It was an outspoken reaction to an existential condition and acute state of awareness; it was motivated by the urge to rebel against the suffocating mediocrity of urban middle-class society, against an academic and authoritarian vision of culture; against the brutality of the military ethos, which imposed its rules and behavior; against the ongoing "Prussianization" of the country. Theirs was indeed the first form of rebel art.

However, the Expressionists did not have a political outlook as such, though they aspired to various vaguely anarchical and communitarian ideals, and felt that modern man, prey and victim of an existential angst, had to break free and draw on his uninhibited, innermost spirit and on the popular ethos, or, as Nolde thought, on the "obscure magmatic energies of Mother Earth."

It is hard to define exactly what void is actually straddled by the bridge implied by the group's name, Die Brücke. It was, certainly, an appeal to "bridge the communication gap," to communicate with others and group together (some members of the Brücke were "inactive," and made an annual contribution for membership, receiving a portfolio of works and an almanac). The Brücke also symbolized a bridge toward the inner self, leading to the painful and discordant interior world of the member artists, testifying to their spiritual crisis and attempts to override the euphemistic framework of classicism.

When he and his associates were dubbed Fauves by a critic at the Salon d'Automne of 1905, Matisse was already thirty-six years old, and had therefore reached artistic maturity. The Brücke movement formed in Dresden that same year, and its members were all very young: the group's theoretician Kirchner was only twenty-five, Heckel twenty-two, Schmidt-Rottluff twenty-one. The oldest was Nolde, who joined in 1906, only to leave the following year. Another figure who joined in 1906 was Max Pechstein, then twenty-five; while Otto Müller joined in 1910. By 1913, however, the group had all but disbanded. Forerunners of the rebel spirit of later generations, the Expressionists wore their youth like a medal. Kirchner's woodcut manifesto of 1906 was unequivocal in its appeal to young artists – and to the public – to endorse their claim for freedom of expression and to shake off the trammels of the entrenched status quo.

This ebullience – and the combative harshness that accompanied it – was the artists' response to the authoritarianism and intransigence of the oppressive society around them.

The ethnic question is more important than it seems at first sight, and is one of the issues that attracts scholars to German Expressionism. The ethnic component in art is somewhat taboo, and has been declared "politically incorrect," particularly in Italy, where anyone who attempts to pin down the specifically national characteristics of Italian painting is quickly dismissed, when in fact the "ethnic" and "cultural" by no means exclude each other. There is no question that the Expressionists' choice of early Germanic models, for instance, was prompted by a deeply rooted national identity, combined with precise cultural factors of the moment.

Umberto Boccioni
Stati d'animo. Gli addii, 1911
States of Mind: The Farewells
oil on canvas
New York, The Museum of Modern Art
gift of Nelson A. Rockefeller, 1979

Umberto Boccioni
Stati d'animo. Quelli che vanno, 1911
States of Mind: Those who go
oil on canvas
New York, The Museum of Modern Art
gift of Nelson A. Rockefeller, 1979

Umberto Boccioni
Stati d'animo. Quelli che restano, 1911
States of Mind: Those who stay
oil on canvas
New York, The Museum of Modern Art
gift of Nelson A. Rockefeller, 1979

Arturo Martini
Fanciulla verso sera, 1919
Twilight girl
plaster
Venice, Galleria Internazionale
d'Arte Moderna - Ca' Pesaro

Umberto Boccioni, *Il lutto*, 1910
Mourning, oil on canvas
Private Collection

We might make similar considerations regarding the comeback in the last few decades of New Expressionism in Germany, whose spokesman Anselm Kiefer made such an impression at the last Venice Biennale.

Albeit with different results, the same applies to Italian art: if we strip off the layers of classicism and Renaissance we find the supposed ethnic factor, that is, the inherent Mediterranean ingredient that underlies the national sense of equilibrium, or where this is lacking (as in Futurism), we find the characteristic openness and innate radiance. This quite opposite ethnic spirit explains the reluctance of Italian artists to embrace the Expressionist aesthetic, except when events here in Italy took a more dramatic turn, and artists turned to social protest.

In 1917 Herwarth Walden published his critique of what he considered the three major spearheads of the international avant-garde (*Einblick in Kunst. Expressionismus, Futurismus, Kubismus*, Berlin, 1917). Walden's first encounter with Futurism dates back to 1912, when the painters in Marinetti's group took their exhibition to Berlin; that same year Boccioni made three pen drawings entitled *Stati d'animo* (*States of Mind*), which were transferred to woodcut for the magazine *Der Sturm*.[1] The following year the Futurists took part in the September Sturm exhibition in Berlin.

The Futurists' exchange with their German colleagues ended here. There was effectively little for them to communicate over, given that in some respects the two outlooks were antithetical.

There were certain points, however, where they overlapped. For both movements, art was not merely a question of aesthetics, but a means for changing society; both were youth cults and loathed the staid academic outlook. They were also drawn to the colorful repertory of everyday social matters, to "modern life," and the theme of the metropolis. But whereas while the Futurists saw the city as the crucible of progress and sang the triumphs of industry and of the victory of "artificiality" over nature (the refuge of the backward-looking), their Expressionist counterparts condemned the frustrations of modern city life, hard work, and the alienation of the metropolis, peopling their works with drunkards and prostitutes (whom the Futurists, incidentally, saw as an example of the thrills of city night life), symbolizing an urban malaise for which their suggested remedy was to return to nature.

Given this marked divergence of outlook it is hardly surprising that Futurism was largely impermeable to the Expressionist ethos and its fruits, though the latter movement was more receptive to developments taking place in Italy. Indeed, Kandinsky (whose expressionism was *sui generis*) read the Futurist manifestoes out loud to his students at the Bauhaus; and Marc and Grosz may have drawn inspiration from the Futurist idea of *linee di forza*, or lines of force. More generally speaking, however, the Expressionist imprint is altogether absent from Italian art over the same period, save for certain stylistic reflections from Barlach in the early works of Arturo Martini, who may have become acquainted with the graphic works of the Brücke group during his stay in Munich in 1909.[2] The work of anarchist painter and writer Lorenzo Viani evinces traits of Expressionism, but this stems from Munch and French sources, such as Daumier, Van Dongen, and Toulouse-Lautrec.

Leaving aside his militant pro-Futurist stance, the artist closest to the restive spirit of Expressionism is Umberto Boccioni, although his influences are evidently not from the Brücke as such, but stem from Van Gogh and Ensor, certainly the graphic works of Munch, most likely of the engravings of Otto Greiner, and the paintings of Franz von Stuck (whose works were displayed at Munich and at the Venice Biennale of 1907), and not least Corinth, Slevogt (or perhaps Liebermann?). He was evidently attracted by their "spurious impressionism informed with plastic energy and prone to expressionist slants."[3] It also looks as if sometime between 1908 and 1910 Boccioni came across the graphic works of Käthe Kollwitz[4] who had exhibited at the 1909 and 1910 Biennales with thirteen and three engravings respectively; her work was also shown at the Rome Secession exhibition in 1915, together with Munch, Pechstein, and Kirchner. Like her compatriots Max Beckmann and Barlach, Kollwitz also received the coveted Florentine Villa Romana award, though no traces of the period show through in her work.

One isolated case remains, however, and that is Boccioni's cousin Adriana Bisi Fabbri, who was enthralled by the heady Futurist palette and migrated from caricatural studies in 1917–18 toward the spirit of Otto Dix,[5] as did Dudreville shortly afterward.[6]

The Brücke artists and their followers were actually unknown in Italy, except for Nolde and Pechstein, and even they had only been represented by a single engraving each in the 1910 Bien-

Mario Sironi, *Paesaggio urbano*, 1922
Urban landscape
oil on canvas
Private Collection

Scipione
Gli uomini che si voltano, 1930
Men tourning round
oil on canvas
Rome
Galleria Nazionale d'Arte Moderna

Mario Mafai, *Fantasie*, 1939-43
Fantasies
oil on canvas
Rome, Città del Vaticano

Renato Guttuso, *Crocifissione*, 1941
Crucifixion
oil on canvas
Rome
Galleria Nazionale d'Arte Moderna

nale. Pechstein was later to resurface, together with Kirchner, at the aforementioned Secession exhibition staged in Rome in 1915. It was not until the 1922 Biennale that German Expressionism breached the Italian scene in any force: Ernst Barlach with three sculptures and eleven engravings; Max Beckmann with six engravings; Erich Heckel with five paintings and five engravings; Kirchner with three paintings and six engravings; Kollwitz with three engravings; Wilhelm Lehmbruck with three sculptures and two engravings; Franz Marc with three engravings; Otto Müller with two engravings; Max Pechstein with two paintings and three engravings; Karl Schmidt-Rottluff with three paintings; and not least Oskar Kokoschka with fifteen paintings and three engravings.

In 1926 Otto Dix exhibited at Venice with one painting; alongside him were Barlach, Beckmann, Heckel, and Kokoschka. The 1928 Biennale saw the return of Nolde, Kirchner, Lehmbruck, Marc, Beckmann, Dix, Heckel, Müller, Pechstein, Schmidt-Rottluff, and August Macke. Marc and Pechstein took part in the second Biennale in Rome, held in 1924. Grosz did not appear until the 1930 Venice Biennale, with five paintings.

It is legitimate, therefore, to say that German Expression did not really receive any exposure in Italy until the 1920s, during the acme of the Valori Plastici movement, in whose journal, *Valori Plastici*, the group's exponents voiced their interest in those aspects of Neue Sachlichkeit that indicated a return to more traditional figurative values. A symptom of this affinity is the group's monograph on George Grosz, which followed those on Picasso, the Austrian painter Georg Schrimpf, and André Derain. Much to Beckmann's annoyance,[7] the reigning critics of the German scene at the time (e.g., Franz Roh, and G. F. Hartlaub) had even credited the Valori Plastici artists with having steered the Germans toward their present exploration of Neue Sachlichkeit. The expressive medium of the Novecento movement was diametrically opposite to the Expressionist spirit; an exception may be made of the pessimistic vision of Mario Sironi, however, whose desolate urban settings were likened to those of Kirchner's Berlin in the early 1910s.[8] Sironi's penchant for Nordic settings was largely drawn from the work of the Belgian painter Constant Permeke, from whose commanding but expended human figures Sironi distilled a fateful gloom of his own.

In 1927 a dealer by the name of Mino Maccari opened a new gallery, the Galleria del Selvaggio. The gallery and its journal began to follow the works of Expressionist artists, from Ensor and Grosz to Kubin and Kokoschka. Given the growing if ambivalent mood of anti-Fascism in Italy, what particularly appealed to Maccari and his company was the vein of heavy satire and caricature running through the German artists' work, together with the mordant graphics and ever-present hint of the grotesque.

The murmurs of anti-Fascism grew increasingly explicit, bringing with it a greater receptiveness to the Expressionist canon, whose implications of social criticism and political critique had previously had no voice in the otherwise peaceable Italian artistic scene.

The change of political mood took substance in the offshoot of Expressionist art that sprouted in Rome with Scipione (Gino Bonichi) – a great admirer of Grosz, Soutine, Ensor, and Pascin – together with the couple Mario Mafai and his lifelong companion Antonietta Raphael Mafai. In these artist the dissatisfaction with the Novecento movement was secretly fueled (particularly in Mafai's case) by a political dissatisfaction that manifested itself in pathos. Scipione, who died shortly after in 1933, expressed it through his portrayal of a dissolute and crumbling Catholic capital; his *Uomini che si voltano* (Men turning round), bears traces of Nolde's stamp. Then there was the Rome of Mafai's "demolitions," cryptically at odds with the jingoistic imperialism that prevailed in Fascist Rome; these were followed in 1939–43 by the *Fantasie* (Fantasies), inspired by the horrific events of war, with manifest overtones of Goya and northern Expressionism. A combination of naiveté and expressionist bent is present in the works of Antonietta Raphael Mafai, who had studied under Epstein in London, and had mixed with Rouault, Soutine in Paris, and had witnessed the visionary poetics of Chagall.

This climate was the starting point for the work of Renato Guttuso, an artist who had always kept himself regularly informed of developments outside the country in reaction to the autarchy and isolation imposed by Fascism. His solid, highly plastic imprint began to take on its characteristically restless torsions at the start of the 1930s; during this decade and the one that followed his work was shot through with a vigorous expressionist slant which, alongside the influence of the Roman artists (and Antonietta Raphael Mafai in particular), reveals an

Emilio Vedova
Assalto alle prigioni, 1945
Assault in the prisons
oil and mixed technique on paper
transferred on canvas
Venice, collection of the Artist

inequivocable awareness of the work of Emil Nolde (at the 1932 Venice Biennale Nolde was represented by fourteen paintings) and also of Max Beckmann.[9]

The Novecento movement spreads from Rome to Milan, home of the so-called Corrente group, founded in 1938 to foster openness to European culture, an endeavor that also expressed a political commitment that became so evident in 1940 that its magazine was suppressed by the Fascist government. Alongside Guttuso in the Corrente group were Birolli, Badodi, Broggini, Cassinari, Migneco, Sassu, Vedova, each in his own way affected by an expressionism of German and French provenance.

In the aftermath of war and the inevitable cessation of political agitation new models first from France and later from the United States seized the attention of the Italian artists. Those who retained their allegiance to expressionist poetics were Guttuso, who transferred his commitment to the Communist Party, allaying the former tensions with a more inert brand of realism; and Emilio Vedova, who, more than his American counterparts of action painting, deserves to be branded as an abstract expressionist.

[1] Until recently these drawings were considered merely preparatory to the painting *Stati d'animo*; but see Maurizio Calvesi, *Umberto Boccioni. Incisioni e disegni*. Firenze: La Nuova Italia, 1973, no. 36.

[2] See Carlo Pirovano, *Scultura italiana del Novecento*. Milan: Electa, 1991, p. 115.

[3] Maurizio Calvesi, "Boccioni prefuturista," in *Boccioni. L'opera completa*, Maurizio Calvesi and Est Coen, eds., Milano: Electa, 1983, p. 35. See pages 35-41 for an outline of Boccioni's figurative background during the years that presaged the emergence of Futurism.

[4] Ibid., pp. 37-38.

[5] Giovanni Anzani, Carlo Pirovano, "La pittura in Lombardia nel primo Novecento (1900–1945)," in *La pittura in Italia. Il Novecento. 1900-1945*, vol. I, Carlo Pirovano, ed. Milano: Electa, 1992, p. 133.

[6] Ibid., p. 170.

[7] See Augusta Monferini, "Un diverso rapporto con la tradizione," in *Max Beckmann* (exhibition catalogue, Rome 1996), Torino, 1996, pp. 17-20.

[8] Enrico Crispolti, "Per un'introduzione a Sironi," in *Mario Sironi* (exhibition catalogue, Rome, Galleria "Il Collezionista"), Roma, 1970, p. 16.

[9] See Stephan von Wiese, "Guttuso und Beckmann," in *Renato Guttuso* (exhibition catalogue, Tübingen 1991). Stuttgart: Hatje, 1991, pp. 31-37.

Roland März

Ferdinand Dorsch
Die Schumannsche Träumerei, 1904
The Schumannesque Reverie
detail
Dresden, Great Art Exhibition

Ernst Ludwig Kirchner
Paar im Zimmer, 1912
A Couple in a Bedroom
oil on canvas
Private Collection

"The yearning for the indivisible Being is the fundamental tendency of all art" (Franz Marc).
As early as August 1808, in a letter to Friedrich Wilhelm Riemer, Goethe observed: "Far from being natural or authentic, what is described as Romantic is false, studied, exaggerated, excessive and bizarre to the point of distortion and caricature." The decidedly negative judgement of the "healthy" classicist Goethe on "sick" Romanticism of his day now appears to be fairly similar to the severe criticism of the "primitives" who, a century later, not only shocked the fossilized society of the Wilhelmine period with their brightly colored caricatures, but also sought a new form of life. At the beginning of the twentieth century, early German Romanticism – characterized by a fondness for fragility, the ironic perception of distance, and black humor in a society that was felt to be increasingly alien – had been completely forgotten by the general public. In a period of deceptive cemeterial silence nothing survived of the early nineteenth-century Romanticism except the kitsch choreographies of the intimist idylls "in the bower" and the "Schumannesque reveries" of artists such as Ferdinand Dorsch in his nostalgia for the reassuring civic character of the citizens of yore. The great artistic exhibitions in Berlin, Dresden, and Munich were packed with these slipshod works overflowing with the sentimentalism of an "inner life protected by the powers-that-be," as Thomas Mann put it. Nonetheless, "being German" in the Kaiser's day called for the chauvinistic cultivation of an intimate spiritual sentiment: a flicker in the mist of the German soul and simulation of depth where there was nothing but a void.
The first to refer to the forgotten ideals of Romanticism was Ricarda Huch in 1899 in her book *Blütezeit der Romantik* (The Flowering of Romanticism). It was only in 1906, however, that Hugo von Tschudi, director of the Nationalgalerie in Berlin, albeit from an "Impressionist" point of view, rediscovered as "true art" the legacy of the great German painters – Caspar David Friedrich, first and foremost – in the legendary Exhibition of a Hundred Years of German Art 1775–1875 for which he was responsible. Hard on the heels of this exhibition came the publication of the writings of the authors, poets and philosophers of early Romanticism: Clemens M. Brentano, Adalbert von Chamisso, Ernst Theodor Amadeus Hoffmann, Novalis, Friedrich Wilhelm Josef von Schelling, and the brothers August Wilhelm and Friedrich von Schlegel. It was not von Tschudi's fault if William II's cultural ideologists immediately led the revolutionary impetus of Romanticism back onto the highway of the harmonization of the emerging social contradictions. Only the artistic avant-garde, after the initial hesitation, put their visual powers to the test by probing the dual aspect of Romanticism – which looked back to the past and heralded the future – because, as the critic Carl Einstein put it, "Romantic millenarism is concealed in modern art." From the outset, Expressionist art shared with early Romanticism the eschatological expectation of "an authentic art" and a new reformable society and, together with this, the dualism of endings and new beginnings, and decline and hope.
But initially, in 1905, Expressionism burst out in Germany without any reference to Romanticism. Rather than with *Zwei Männer in Betrachtung des Mondes* (*Two Men Contemplating the Moon*) by Caspar David Friedrich at the Gemäldegalerie in Dresden, the Brücke artists had affinities with what the critic Werner Hofmann described as "the flight of Gauguin from the ghetto of civilization, a romantic gesture." With Jean Jacques Rousseau's "return to nature," it was clear that the source of Expressionism was not introspection or meditation, but rather the vitalistic call of the primigenial world at the origin of life; this call was followed by the abandoning of the impressionistic descriptiveness of nature. Initially the monastic isolation of Friedrich's studio was alien to the Brücke artists; rather they replaced the introvert ego with the collective id in the Freudian sense. In contrast with the Lukasbund, or Guild of St. Luke, of the Nazarenes Franz Pforr and Friedrich Overbeck, founded in Vienna in 1809, the Romantic idea of the community was excluded from the consciences of the Brücke painters; in their scanty writings there is no reference at all to the Romantics of any kind. Their starting-point was absolutely non-Romantic, since they wanted "to achieve freedom of life and action against the long-established older forces." They were, in fact, convinced that strength lay in unity. The young artists who joined the Brücke did not take the oath of allegiance of the Romantics or share their concept of the hubris of the spirit; rather they looked to the *élan vital* of Henri Bergson and the revolutionary Dionysian vitalism of Friedrich Nietzsche.
Already at the beginning of the nineteenth century the Romantics were aware of the gulf that

Wilhelm von Schadow
*Selbstbildnis mit seinem Bruder Ridolfo
und Thorvaldsen*, 1815–16
*Self-portrait with his Brother Ridolfo
and Thorvaldsen*
oil on canvas
Berlin, Nationalgalerie

had widened between town and countryside, while, as soon as the process of industrialization was underway, the painters belonging to the Brücke and the Neue Künstlervereinigung-München (New Artist's Association of Munich, or NKV) did all they could to revitalize the rural idyll so that their Arcadian paradises could contrast sharply with the city of Moloch. On the shores of the small lakes near Dresden and the Baltic Sea, and at Murnau in Upper Bavaria, near Munich, an attempt was made to return to the harmony of man and nature, a state of innocence that was still considered to be possible. Thus they painted naked men and women bathing together and in amorous poses in the natural environment; these were visions of the innocence of humanity before the Fall of Man. And once again Pantheism made an appearance; while it rejected the classicizing mythology of the neo-Romantic Symbolist Arnold Böcklin, at the same time it carried on along this path.

The academic style of the early Romantics continued to be distant from the Expressionists whose irrepressible desire to be "expressive" in their use of color and form derived from French modern art. In the maelstrom charged with energy of pure, bright colors, Ernst Ludwig Kirchner proclaimed the "ecstasy of seeing things for the first time," Emil Nolde "organic growth identical to that of nature," and Karl Schmidt-Rottluff "the experience of the transcendental nature of the earthly sphere." The earthly paradises of the artists of Dresden and Munich overflowed with sounds and rhythms of the present that had been directly experienced. In Carl Einstein's words, "the paintings of the early Expressionists depicted a poeticized natural world; they were conceived as an emotional idyll in contrast with the city. One could speak of urban Romanticism, the protest of a primitivism that was almost moralizing." Following Gauguin in his search for paradise, in 1914, before the outbreak of war – again according to Einstein – Nolde and Max Pechstein, "the geographical romantics, went to the South Seas, convinced that Rome could wait until they had seen the Marquesas Islands." Confronted by a "primitive" culture that had already been half-destroyed by the colonialists, these artists adhered to ethnological exoticism at the same time as the artistic failure of Expressionism. The dream of the archetypal beginning in far-off countries was over.

At first the Brücke was still *Sturm und Drang*: the spontaneous desire for expression prevailed over the intellect and philosophical reflection. The situation changed radically in 1911, with the foundation of the Blaue Reiter in Munich. The first spokesman for the reawakening of Romanticism in the artistic circle of "spirituality in art" was Franz Marc, who described himself as "coming from the land of German dreamers, poets, and thinkers." Instead of the "neo-decadent Parisians and the nature-men" of the Brücke (in 1926 Kirchner dedicated a monument to it, thus continuing the tradition of the romantic "friendship" paintings of Wilhelm von Schadow), a group of individuals with a tendency to reflect was formed in association with the *Blaue Reiter Almanac*; with missionary zeal they upheld "spiritualism" against the ignoble materialism and rationalism of their day. Their motto was "Speak of secrets using mystery." As Marc put it, art, by forming "a bridge with the realm of the spirits, should have brought necromancy to humanity." In the program of this spiritual elite there was room for the blue flower of Romanticism in Novalis's unfinished novel *Heinrich von Ofterdingen*. The circular letter founding the NKV in Munich in 1910 alludes to the "inner world" of the artist and his "aspiration to artistic 'synthesis';" both of these already formed the basis of Romanticism. In the *Blaue Reiter Almanac*, Marc thought that the "primitives," like bifront Janus, faced two ways and observed: "Mysticism has reawakened in the souls and, together with this, primordial elements ... Their thought has a different objective: that of creating the symbols of their time that are to be placed on the altars of the future spiritual religions behind which the demiurge of technology disappears." In the almanac, next to the illustration of a Romantic text, Kandinsky's *Lyrisches* (*Lyrics*) was reproduced; Marc declared himself to be a follower of Caspar David Friedrich, Philipp Otto Runge, Moritz von Schwind, and Alfred Rethel. The aim of every representation was believed to be the spiritualization of art and life, as well as the elevation of imperfect reality thanks to a mystic idea and the visualization of the invisible in art. With this profession of faith, Marc felt he was himself part of the Romantic tradition. The new and modern elements in our lives were only the obligation – after Nietzsche's proclamation that "God is dead" and the rejection of metaphysics – to accept the "spirituality in art" as a substitute for religion. Carl Einstein later observed that "probably every kind of aesthetic admiration is nothing

Ernst Ludwig Kirchner
*Eine Künstlergruppe (Otto Müller
Ernst Ludwig Kirchner, Erich Heckel
Karl Schmidt-Rottluff)*, 1926–27
*A Group of Artists (Otto Müller
Ernst Ludwig Kirchner, Erich Heckel
Karl Schmidt-Rottluff)*
oil on canvas
Cologne, Museum Ludwig

Caspar David Friedrich
Frau in der Morgensonne, ca. 1820
Woman in the Morning Sun
oil on canvas
Essen, Museum Folkwang

Franz Marc
Pferd in der Landschaft, 1910
Horse in a Landscape
oil on canvas
Essen, Museum Folkwang

more than degenerate devotion, a substitute." The return to the old Romanticism had reawakened the unsatisfied yearning for what August Macke described as a lost "invisible god" and Marc's concept of the "indivisibility of the being" in the link between man, nature, and cosmos. The dream and the unconscious were one of the themes of Romanticism, which was brought up-to-date in Sigmund Freud's *Interpretation of Dreams*, but was, however, only fully accomplished by the Surrealists, who Carl Einstein described as "the true Romantic generation." The debate on early Romanticism and the Romanticized "Roman-Germans" associated with Arnold Böcklin, Anselm Feuerbach, and Hans von Marées at the end of the century was replaced by the new metaphysics of the lost paradises produced by modern means. The demonization of the image assumed greater importance thanks to magic, mystery, and astonishment, so that the image became symbolic and then archetypal. Finally, Marc clearly saw spirituality in art being transformed into a golden altarpiece in the predicted aesthetic churches of the future. Around 1800, early Romanticism was still specifically German and patriotic; the Blaue Reiter, on the other hand, had a cosmopolitan program, in particular because it comprised artists from other countries.

While, for the Brücke artists, the god Pan was still present in this world, in the pantheism of the Blaue Reiter a transcendent, "German" dimension developed that was inspired by Wilhelm Worringer's essay *Abstraktion und Einfühlung* (Abstraction and Empathy). Marc, however, wanted to become part of "the organic rhythm of everything," following the maxims of Novalis, "everything in life is rhythm," and that of Philipp Otto Runge, "the symbols of the eternal rhythm of the universe." Novalis's writings, including *Fragmenten* (Fragments), were Marc's favorite reading; the influence of this poet and philosopher is evident in the style of the artist's *100 Aphorismen* (100 Aphorisms). Already in Ludwig Tieck's novel *Franz Sternbalds Wanderungen* (Franz Sternbald's Wanderings), the animal had begun to replace man in the natural world. His conviction that man was mean and impure led Marc along the path of the "animalization of art" to the symbolic image of the animal: "Not man but the deer has feelings." The painter loved his blue horses; his precept on the theory of color, "Blue is the male principle, severe and spiritual," was derived from Runge. With regard to the topos of the figure seen from behind, his *Pferd in der Landschaft* (*Horse in a Landscape*) – depicting a red horse "meditating" – is reminiscent of the absorbed silhouettes of Caspar David Friedrich mediated by Edvard Munch, whose fellow-countryman Johan Christian Clausen Dahl associated with Friedrich in Dresden. Moreover, the art historian Andreas Aubert, a friend of Munch, had published his studies on Friedrich and Runge in Germany. Similarly, the Blaue Reiter sought to provide interior images of the soul "vibrating with the contrasting tension and reflecting the continuous mutability of the world." With his *Scream* and the melancholy girls seen from behind on the beach at Aasgaard, Munch had a decisive influence that was not limited to the Brücke group. In Friedrich's paintings the figures portrayed from behind seem at times to be frozen in the tragic gesture of separation, while in Marc's work they symbolize hope for the total harmony of man, nature, and transcendence.

For Marc, the animal – the symbol and embodiment of the "pure ideas forming the basis of the construction of the world" – represented only an intermediate stage before reaching the dematerialized and abstract representation where there are echoes of Albert Einstein's theory of relativity, Max Planck's quantum theory, Wilhelm Ostwald's theories on energy, and Niels Bohr's model of the atom. Marc wanted to capture "the passage through things" and found the spiritual character of the world in abstraction, which brought him close to Kandinsky. On the eve of the world war he attempted to link catharsis, redemption, and Messianism in the mistaken belief that "a new religion had spread through the country." But the war shattered the dream of a private mythology, and, once again, utopia failed in its confrontation with reality; what Friedrich von Schlegel described as the "unavoidable conflict" and the "unattainable coincidence" turned out to be the Romantic fate of the Expressionists too. Thus, as modern art came into being, illusion and reality diverged; but something of this innocent faith remained, as may be seen in Novalis's aphorism "Zukunftslehre des Lebens" (Future Doctrine of Mankind): "The world is not a dream, but it ought to become one, and perhaps it will."

Marc's spiritual identity with German Romanticism was only shared to a limited extent by his comrade-in-arms, Kandinsky. Kandinsky's Romanticism was, in fact, also rooted in Russian mysticism and in the anthroposophy and theosophy of Helena Blavatsky and Rudolf Steiner.

Caspar David Friedrich
Schweizer Landschaft, 1823–24
Swiss Landscape
oil on canvas, destroyed in 1945

Erich Heckel, *Gläserner Tag*, 1913
Crystalline Day
oil on canvas
Munich, Staatsgalerie moderner Kunst

Kandinsky had provided his friends with the programatic axiom relating to the "inner necessity" that cannot be renounced in life, thought, and nature. His cosmic improvisations are full of "inner sound": "The world resounds. It is a cosmos of beings that act on a spiritual level. Even dead matter is living spirit." Thus, while in Marc there is spiritual ascesis and pictorial intensity, in Kandinsky, on the contrary, there is total fluency and freedom in his cosmic expressive formulations.

The two modes could not have been more different. Already the Romantics found the model for their painting in music, which E. T. A. Hoffmann described as "the most romantic of all the arts." Spurred by Runge's idea of the *Gesamtkunstwerk* (total work of art), in *Tageszeiten* (*Moments of the Day*) Kandinsky created the synesthesia of painting, music, and theatre. He worked with all modern artistic media on his project to integrate the art forms that, in the twenties, became reality – albeit in a fragmentary form – in the Bauhaus at Weimar and Dessau. Romantic thought, with its ambivalence of cosmic sublimity and boundless demonism, has found expression in every period. The artist who brought the dark side of Romanticism into the Blaue Reiter group was Alfred Kubin; the obsessive draftsman of *Dämonen und Nachtgesichte* (*Demons and Nocturnal Visions*), he was clearly inspired by Hoffmann's *Die Elixiere des Teufels* (The Devil's Elixir). Lyonel Feininger also gazed at the fantastic pages of the nocturnal side of existence with a mixture of admiration and terror. And so did Paul Klee, who noted in his diary: "He [Kandinsky] fled this world because he was physically unable to bear it any longer. Halfway he stopped, yearning for crystallinity: but he was not able to free himself from the mud of the phenomenal world. His art conceives the world as poison, as decay." Traces of this gallows humor, with its apocalyptic tones, are to be found in the early graphic work by Feininger, Grosz, and Klee. Here, in the typically German phenomenon of the grotesque, with the dualism of ideality and trivial reality – both of these seen in a fantastic dimension – a large part of what links modern art to this aspect of Romanticism is concentrated: chaos and fragment, the roots of the principle of the collage and the structure of the open artwork of the twentieth century.

The Romanticizing grotesque reflects the absurdity of a world in decline, while, in Franz Marc's vitreous constructions of the spirit, the portents of the impending tragedy of war are evident. In Marc's paintings the animal is a metaphor for the human being, and catastrophe irrupts with a cathartic function, driving away his horses until the *Turm der blauen Pferde* (*Tower of the Blue Horse*) and the vitreous *Skizzen aus dem Felde* (*Sketches from the Front*) – what remains of the unpainted pictures – disintegrate amidst the drumfire. With the death of Lieutenant Franz Marc at Verdun in 1916, the painter's Romantic vocation found its final, premature fulfillment — in his own words, "death marks the beginning of real existence around which us living beings flutter like moths around the light." The pictorial crystal of Marc and Erich Heckel was destroyed; in 1913, Heckel, in the tradition of the icy mountain peaks of Joseph Anton Koch and Caspar David Friedrich, celebrated the unity of man, nature, and the cosmos in *Gläserner Tag* (*Crystalline Day*). Despite this, for a certain period, the pacifist Paul Klee continued to cling to the artistic symbol of the crystal, transformed by Cubism into a different inner life that was no longer Romantic: "This earthly sphere is abandoned and, instead, one goes beyond to build, in an ultramundane region: abstraction. The cold Romanticism of this style without pathos is incredible ... A landslide of artificial elements for the formation of impure crystals. Today it's like this ... I thought I'd die, war and death. But can I die, I who am a crystal?" With his forms imitated by the structure of crystals, the pacifist Klee distanced himself from the patriotic euphoria and the voracious monster that was war: he planned his *Gärten der Mysterien* (*Gardens of Mystery*), which were inspired by the Runge's *Tageszeiten* (Moments of the Day) as far as their attention to the vegetable element and the enigma of light was concerned. Also the Romantic flight from the "storms of steel" of the times to the moon and the stars was a gesture of survival.

When faced with the threat of annihilation posed by military service and the war, Kirchner's attitude was different from that of Marc and Klee. His colored woodcuts for *Peter Schlemihls wundersame Geschichte* (The Marvelous Tale of Peter Schlemihl) by Adalbert von Chamisso are not illustrations for Romantic poetry, but existential metaphors of Kirchner's personal situation on the verge of madness and death. It is the story of a man without a shadow who, forever in flight, is threatened by the extinction of his artistic ego and the loss of his remaining

Philipp Otto Runge, *Der Morgen (Gesamtkomposition)*, 1808
Morning (Composition)
pen and ink
Berlin, Kupferstichkabinett

identity. In the series of woodcuts by Kirchner – one of the most outstanding examples of Expressionist graphic art – every trace of optimistic Romantic utopia has disappeared. During the war, in Zürich, the Dadaists scornfully opposed Expressionism and the "metaphysical beefsteak." In this regard, in his diary entitled *Die Flucht aus der Zeit* (The Flight from Time), Hugo Ball asserted: "Arp is opposed to the arrogance of the painters who think they are God Almighty (the Expressionists). Marc's bulls are too fat for him; the cosmogonies and crazy stars of Baumann and Meidner remind him of Bölsche and Carus Sterne ... He feels the planimetry in contrast with the painted rise and fall of the world." The Romantic visions of the rising and setting of the moon and the Expressionists' apocalyptic "rise and fall of the world" were the first to come to an end: the horrendous battles fought at the front swept away the eccentricity of the Expressionist utopia and the vision of the new man. The artists of the Blaue Reiter, who had emerged from what W. Haftmann described as "the romantic heart of central Europe," had mostly "fallen fighting for the fatherland" – August Macke and Franz Marc, for instance. But, in 1919, the year the Weimar Republic was founded, the few survivors, worn-out by the experience of war, met with renewed optimism at the Bauhaus.

Nineteen nineteen was, therefore, a year for new departures. The veteran Erich Heckel portrayed himself with the facial features of Christ on the walls of his studio at Osterholz, which were entirely covered with Arcadian scenes. Thus there was the return of the blue flower of the Romantics – a memento of his friend Franz Marc who had fallen at Verdun, but also a sign of hope. Heckel wrote to Lyonel Feininger: "It is just as well we both live in the peace and quiet of the countryside. Certainly, all the memories of the war years re-emerge more powerfully in me, but perhaps they are losing their oppressive character." The artists tended to focus once again on their inner lives, but subject to the constraints of Neoclassicism. The Dadaists staged a brief trial of art and its metaphysical extraneity to life; in 1919, with his *Mondweib* (*Lunar Woman*), Otto Dix dared to poke fun at the Romantic myth of the moon in the manner of Caspar David Friedrich, while in Hanover the artist who invented "Merz," Kurt Schwitters, began to work on his *Kathedrale des erotischen Elends* (*Cathedral of Erotic Misery*).

It is significant that the visions of the Gothic cathedrals of the Romantics euphorically introduced "Neo-Romanticism" in 1919 after the disaster of the First World War. Nobody was more suitable – or he may even have been predestined – for this operation than the German-American Lyonel Feininger with his *Element of Longing*, which was influenced by the Blaue Reiter. The views of Gothic cathedrals of the Romantics Friedrich and Karl Friedrich Schinkel, described by Adolf Knoblauch as "solitary guardians of the submerged cities," inspired Feininger's prismatic cathedrals flooded with light. In Romanticism, architecture was, as Schinkel put it, a form of "crystallized nature." Feininger, too, adhered to this tradition when, at the beginning of his artistic career in 1907, he wrote: "What one sees must be inwardly remolded and crystallized." The next step was Schinkel's cathedral of freedom, "faithful to the national tradition of the medieval wooden hut," proceeding to Bruno Taut's Glasarchitektur (glass architecture), the projects of the group of architects known as "Die gläserne Kette" (Glass Chain), and finally the woodcut with Feininger's cathedral for the cover of the four-page manifesto of Walter Gropius's Bauhaus: "Together let us desire, conceive, and create the new building of the future that, in a single form, will include everything – architecture, sculpture, and painting – and that one day will rise toward heaven from the hands of millions of craftspeople as the crystal symbol of a new faith." The legacy of the Blaue Reiter is clearly perceptible in this rhetorical proclamation: the idea of community, the *Gesamtkunstwerk* (total work of art), purism, and the future. To a large degree, Lyonel Feininger, Wassily Kandinsky, Paul Klee, Johannes Itten, and Georg Muche – the "Romantic" Expressionists – were the protagonists of the Romantic period of the Bauhaus in Weimar, which lasted until 1923. At that time the architect Mies van der Rohe firmly opposed these attempts to revitalize the metaphysical dimension: "The efforts of the mystics will remain as mere episodes. Despite the deepening of our concepts of life, we shall not build any cathedrals ... Even the great gesture of the Romantics means nothing to us because we perceive the form as emptiness. Our times do not have pathos; it is not the great impetus that we hold in esteem, but rather reason and reality."

In 1924 Kandinsky, Feininger, Klee, and Alexei von Jawlensky, supported by Galka Scheyer, founded Die Blauen Vier (The Blue Four) and attempted to recreate and spread the ideas of

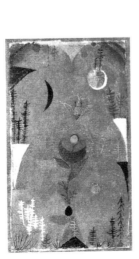

Paul Klee, *Blumenmythos*, 1918
Flower Myth, watercolor
Hannover, Sprengel Museum

Karl Friedrich Schinkel
Gotischer Dom am Wasser, 1813–14
Gothic Cathedral by the Water
copy by F. Ahlborn
detail, oil on canvas
Berlin, Nationalgalerie

Lyonel Feininger, *Kathedrale*, 1919
Cathedral
woodcut for the Bauhaus manifesto

the Blaue Reiter – above all, in the United States. The sigh with which Paul Klee renounced ("The people aren't supporting us," he lamented) became particularly poignant when they turned to the public and social spheres, especially in view of the fact that these *retardataire* – or penultimate – Romantics wanted to be something more than mere "masters of the Bauhaus." But it was not so much the group as the single artists who were involved in the transformation of Expressionism, which, by distancing itself from the stereotyped spirituality of László Moholy-Nagy, had used certain aspects of the artistic tenets of the pre-war Expressionist movement to produce very original works of art in the nineteen twenties and thirties too. The Late-Expressionist Romanticism of the painters working at the Bauhaus was in marked contrast to the interpretation of Romanticism in the twenties in works by the exponents of Magic Realism (Franz Radziwill), Neue Sachlichkeit (Alexander Kanoldt, Franz Lenk, Georg Schrimpf), and Surrealism (Max Ernst), where the painting of Caspar David Friedrich – with his myth of nature – played a major role. Only very few attained the profundity of this tragically solitary figure; of his successors, only Paul Klee, described by Emil Nolde as his "cousin in profundity," has allowed the essential legacy of Romanticism to survive until today in a broader, all-embracing relationship with existence: "Art behaves allegorically with creation." Novalis's aphorism "Becoming a man is an art" immediately brings to mind Joseph Beuys.

The nostalgic visits to the lost paradises of Friedrich and Runge, and then those of Marc, Feininger, Klee, and Beuys, will continue to the end of this century and beyond. In every period of German art, the Romantics have been linked by their common sense with regard to life and an escape from time through high flights of spirituality, and they have failed in their encounter with the destructive events in life. Although this is the "German destiny," one fact must be taken into consideration: in the modern era Romanticism, as Peter-Klaus Schuster put it, "is not at all a mere retreat into an inner life, but, on the contrary, the great step forward taken to represent ... the entirety of modern life." Despite all the current prognostications of the "final cessation" of metaphysics at the end of this century, it is certain that the ideals and utopias of Romanticism will not be honored. We continue to feel a yearning for gratification, and the magic circle has not been closed for some time now. In fact, on 28 November 1925 Wassily Kandinsky wrote to Will Grohmann: "At times the circle that I use so often cannot but be described as a romantic circle. And the Romanticism of the future is truly profound, beautiful (one must use the outmoded word 'beautiful'), fraught with contents, and a bearer of joy – it is a piece of ice in which a flame burns. If men only manage to see the ice and not the flame, that's their bad luck. But many will notice it soon..."

Riccardo Dottori

Friedrich Wilhelm Nietzsche
(1884-1900)

The influence of Nietzsche

Expressionism flourished in Germany during a period when the thought of Friedrich Nietzsche enjoyed a wide diffusion. Not a professional philosopher, for his training was in classical studies, Nietzsche was an apostate from his Christian faith, on which he had been nurtured until early manhood, when he had studied theology and cherished the dream of becoming a pastor. He was an apostate from the university: after ten years of extremely conscientious teaching he left the University of Basel, where he had been appointed to a lectureship at a very early age. He was an apostate from his own country, because he did not return there after leaving University, coming instead to Italy, where he wrote his major works, and stayed until the time of his mental collapse, with the exception of a few visits to Engadina and Nice. Finally, he was an apostate, not so much from his teacher in classical philology, but from the only philosopher whom he read avidly and who had an influence on him, Arthur Schopenhauer, and from the man who represented his true ideal of the artist and who was his real spiritual master, Richard Wagner. His temperament, then, was rebellious, but it was a rebellion that did not burn itself out in mere revolt but marked an opening-out of genuinely new paths, the diagnosis of a spiritual situation which was rapidly changing and in which his exceptionally lively intelligence perceived the crisis of stale traditional values. In reality no one understood Wagner better than Nietzsche, and no one remained more loyal to him – despite the recriminations – because no one understood and appreciated better than he did the new spirit of music, which he called Dionysiac: Nietzsche understood art not as mere skill and pleasure, but as the *justification of existence*, perhaps the only authentic legitimation of existence, that legitimation otherwise always sought in metaphysics, ethics and religion. The Dionysiac was what was still left – and embodied in the music of Wagner – of ancient tragedy, that is, of classical Greek religious sensibility; only the Dionysiac could the justification of existence and the victory over nihilism be entrusted. Where does it come from, what is it, Nietzsche asked himself, this guest that stands before our door, this most perturbing of all guests, nihilism? Nihilism arises when the greatest values are devalued: "The purpose is lacking, the reply to the question why is lacking." But what is hidden in this devaluation of the greatest values? Is it only "a state of social necessity," or a physiological degeneration, that *décadence* which finds a body and a voice in *fin de siècle* culture? For Nietzsche, and this demonstrates his acute sense of cultural and social analysis, it is neither one nor the other: it is rather the consequence of the "death of God," which casts its shadows over us. And with the death of the Christian God, the world of truth, the Platonic world of Ideas, has also become a fable: no truth is possible any longer, and nothing is left of the truth.

But there are nihilisms and nihilisms. Nietzsche, who claims to be the first, the most complete and authentic nihilist in the entire history of philosophy, distinguishes the simply passive nihilism of those who are in nihilism, are not aware of it and do not react (that is, naturalists and decadentists), from the active and realized nihilism of those who are conscious of the sense of history, and therefore are able, in the twilight of all values, to arrive at the complete negation of the existent, with the purpose of creating and affirming new values. This is the role that Nietzsche again assigns to culture, and in particular to art. The creation of new values makes possible that self-surpassing of life, which cannot be understood in purely vitalistic or Darwinian terms. When Zarathustra leaves the mountains and goes to the town, he apostrophizes the men gathered in the market with these words: "All beings have created something above themselves, and do you wish to be only the ebb in this great tide, and recede to the beasts rather than surpass man?" In order to create, however, it is necessary to know how to command and to know how to obey; only he who has learned to command and serve himself will not have to obey another: this is Nietzsche's aristocratism, which concerns both life in itself and art. "Thus life spoke to me", says Zarathustra again, "behold, I am she who must continually surpass herself." This self-surpassing is the increase of power, the growth of energy in new and higher forms of life, which are most clearly and fully realized in art; only in art is an authentic surpassing of nihilism achieved, so that from the destruction and the rejection of the old values, of the faded and decadent forms of life, new forms and new values may arise.

This concept of artistic creation as a reinvigoration of life, a growth of strength and a surpassing of nihilism, is expounded in the aphorisms collected and published by his sister and his most loyal pupil and friend – Elisabeth Förster Nietzsche and Peter Gast – under the title *Der Wille zur Macht*[1] (*The Will to Power*). In particular, the fourth chapter of Book III, which was given the title "Der Wille zur Macht als Kunst" (The Will to Power as Art), brings together the notes from the late 1880s concerning this theme. Anticipating Freud, in these aphorisms Nietzsche traces the artist's creativity, and all vital creativity in general, to the sexual impulse (cf. Aph. 804, 805, 806, 808, 815); but it is also true that while this may

Friedrich Wilhelm Nietzsche
Thus Spoke Zarathustra
Biblioteca di Scienze Moderne, no 7
frontispiece

Edvard Munch
Portrait of Friedrich Nietzsche
Stockholm, Thielska Galleriet

be the cause, in the result of the artistic transfiguration there is something more, namely the perfection that flows from this transfiguration. Nietzsche even goes so far as to speak of beauty and ugliness as judgements related to our "preservation values" (Aph. 804), but it would be wrong to take this affirmation in a purely biologistic sense, accepting the interpretation of Nietzschean thought later adopted by National Socialism. For in the same aphorism the philosopher also states that, in addition to the aesthetic instinct, other perfections of the most diverse origins come into play, acting and crystallizing around the particular beauty. Therefore, in this state of affairs there can be no *objectivity*; whatever this energy may be which is the basis of the aesthetic instinct, it still is an energy which *interprets*. Certainly the interpretation may contain a considerable amount of untruth; but untruth is necessary to existence: "The truth is ugly. We have art so as not to perish because of the truth" (Aph. 822). Drawing on his primal distinction between Apollinean and Dionysiac – the two stages, or rather the two constitutive forces of classical tragedy, deriving from the two fundamental states of the human mind, dream and inebriation – Nietzsche now inclines in particular to the Dionysiac and to inebriation, in which he sees the ultimate root of artistic creation, including that of antiquity, including that ideal and harmonious beauty which fed on the dream vision, the sculptoreal beauty of ideal forms, of those who "philosophized with the hammer." Classical beauty itself is now seen as an increase in strength, in power, inasmuch as a vital instinct succeeds in dominating and balancing everything. It is extraordinary that Nietzsche goes on to add an observation in which one can sense the indication of a parallel path, the path taken by Paul Klee: "Logical and geometrical simplification is a consequence of the increase in strength; and the *perception* of this simplification in its turn increases the feeling of strength... The grand style is the peak of evolution."

All this leads to the concept of the *grand style*, which is a new point of dispute with Wagner, Late Romanticism and Decadentism, but also a lesson – or perhaps again a prophecy – for what is to become the new art of the twentieth century: "This style has in common with grand passion its refusal to please; its forgetting to persuade; its commanding, its *willing*... To become master of that chaos which one is; to force one's chaos to become form; to become logical, simple, univocal, mathematical, to become *law* – that is the grand ambition" (Aph. 842). In comparison with all this the dualism between classical and romantic becomes insignificant; both, when they are authentic manifestations of art as "organic function," are not simply an expression of dissatisfaction with existence, nor gratitude for a happiness enjoyed; the very will to eternize can be both the dithyrambic expression of apotheosis and romantic pessimism, which wishes to imprint on everything the image of its own torture, like Schopenhauer's philosophy of the will, or non–will, and Wagner's music. True Romanticism, not decadent Romanticism, should be capable of appreciating and of matching true tragic art, in that superabundance of force and energy which makes it possible to express the judgement of "beautiful" even in conditions which impotence may judge to be odious and ugly. In this sense, there is for Nietzsche a consonance between pessimism, that basking in selfhood of the inferior romantic spirit, which is incapable of rising to the strength of tragic art, and the nihilism of the artists of the *décadence*, who "take refuge in the *beauty of form* – in *noble* things, in which nature has become perfect and is *grand and beautiful* with indifference ... The 'love of the beautiful' may therefore be different from the *faculty* of *seeing* something beautiful, of *creating* the beautiful: it may be indeed the expression of the *inability* to do it" (Aph. 852). We know how powerful a hatred for ornament there was to be in Expressionist art, and we feel once again how prophetic all this sounds. Even more significant are the last aphorisms in the same section which refer explicitly to *The Birth of Tragedy*. They read almost like a catalogue of the principles of Expressionist art, especially the art of those Expressionists who were active around the time of the First World War: "Art is nothing else but art! It is what makes life possible, the great seductress of life, the great stimulant of life ... Art is like the *redemption of him who knows* – of him who sees the terrible and enigmatic nature of existence, who wants to see it, who knows tragically. Art as the *redemption of the man of action* – of him who not only sees the terrible and enigmatic nature of existence, but who lives it and wants to live it, of the tragic and warlike man, of the hero. Art as the *redemption of the sufferer* – the way toward conditions in which suffering becomes willed, transfigured, divinized, in which suffering is a form of great rapture." (Aph. 853)[2]

Thus, for Nietzsche, who had been brought up with a deep faith in Christianity and had abandoned it, art becomes the final refuge which still enables him to accept existence; "metaphysics, ethics, religion, and science" meet in it, like so many stages in the flight from the truth, or in the will to untruth. In this way, however, the artist according to Nietzsche – and the same will be true of Kafka – feels like a "fragment of reality, of truth, of nature," which in order to accept life and existence must also become "a fragment of the genius of untruth." For if truth, as Aphorism 493 of the same collection states, is nothing but "that *kind of error* without which a certain kind of living being could not live," so that "ultimately it decides the value for life;" or if, as Aphorism 534 states, "the criterion of truth is found in the increase of the feeling of power," the conclusion can only be that "art does not have more value than the truth," a precise allusion to the words of the Preface to *The Birth of Tragedy*, where Wagner was mentioned explicitly: "Art is the true task of life, art is its *metaphysical* activity..." But this also means that in this rapture of art which equals religious enthusiasm, in this supreme affirmation of existence which is the tragico-Dionysiac condition, "man has become the master of 'matter'! Master of the truth!...," so much so as to be able to enjoy untruth as his own power. And this implies a clear rejection of naturalism, both in art and in philosophy, as well as of the materialism and positivism implicit in it; this, and nothing but this, is the way to Expressionism. We may truly affirm that Nietzsche gave Expressionism its "artist's gospel." This gospel, or prophecy of the new art, we find expressed in another famous aphorism of *Beyond Good and Evil*. Profoundly attentive to all that was going on around him with regard to politics, society and costume, culture and above all art, Nietzsche had become aware that the resonance of every artistic phenomenon was now European (even for Wagner Paris had been indispensable), and that consequently the formation of the new artistic currents, too, crossed the borders between the national cultures beloved of Romanticism. Moreover, he had grown aware of how the various arts were intimately linked to each other; of what would be the natural outcome of the new art that evolved on the basis of a resumption of the researches of Late Romanticism, and on the rejection of Impressionism and Naturalism. It is worth reading this passage, because in this mature consciousness of the artistic problems of Late Romanticism we find a true anticipation of the Expressionistic canons, and of the very concept of Expressionism: "But who could express exactly what all these masters of new linguistic means were not able to express clearly? It is certain that they were tormented by the same tempest and the same impulse, and that they *sought* in the same way, these last great searchers! Dominated, all of them, even in their sight and hearing, by literature – these first artists with a worldwide literary training – for the most part even writers, poets, mediators and amalgamators themselves of the arts and the senses (as a musician Wagner counts among the painters, as a poet among the musicians, as an artist in general among the comedians); all fanatics of *expression* 'at all costs' – I emphasize the strong affinity between Delacroix and Wagner – all great discoverers in the realm of the sublime, and also of the ugly and the horrible, and even greater discoverers in the effect, in the show, in the art of the shopwindow, all talents beyond their genius ... in short a rashly bold, splendidly violent, upward-flying and upward-pulling species of superior men, who must, above all, teach their century – which is the century of *multitude* – the idea of the "superior man ..." (ß 256).

Debates and polemics
That Nietzsche's philosophy was widespread throughout German artistic circles is now an established fact. This resonance, deriving in particular from his critique of Decadentism, from his vitalism, from his reawakening of sensibility and liberation of its energy, has made it possible to speak of a group of "Left-wing Nietzscheans." [3] The two main leaders were Kurt Hiller and Erwin Lewenson, who in March 1909 founded in Berlin the literary circle *Der neue Club*. Subsequently, Hiller founded the *Neopathetisches Kabarett*, where there were discussions of the new "pathos," an idea of Stefan Zweig's, and readings of extracts from Nietzsche, chiefly taken from the *The Gay Science*, *The Twilight of the Gods*, and *The Will to Power*. The new pathos of which Lewenson and Zweig talked was Nietzschean pathos, the pathos of the tragic "saying yes" to life. By now the cult of Nietzsche was spreading widely among artists and generating a Nietzschean fashion, which was not right-wing (though on the right, too, there was considerable support for Nietzsche), but above all an Expressionist fashion. The Nietzschean revolt against Bismarck's Prussia had become the Expressionist revolt against Wilhelmine Germany, in the name of the Nietzschean revaluation of sensibility, sensuality and creative force, the three elements seen as the basis of artistic creation, of its legitimation of existence and of the cultural and social function of art. These ideas patently coincided with those of the post-Impressionist artists, notably Gauguin, Van Gogh, and Cézanne, to whom all the Expressionist painters looked for inspiration. But it was above all Herwart Walden and Franz Pfemfert, the founders and editors of *Der Sturm* and *Die Aktion*, the two most committed journals, who spread Expressionist ideas. The principles propounded by Walden in his journal were Nietzschean principles, especially in the aim of changing society through culture and art, an aim which was maintained until the postwar period, when Walden opted for political action, and became a communist. The contributors to the journal were intellectuals and artists of the first rank, such as Else

Stefan Zweig (1881–1942)
Vienna
Österreichische Nationalbibliothek

Lasker–Schüler, Salomon Friedländer, Alfred Döblin, Paul Scheebart, Gottfried Benn, and many others. Their impact on the cultural life of Berlin, thanks to the numerous debates, soirées, and exhibitions organized by this journal, was particularly intense: blending Nietzsche and Expressionism meant advocating a change in society through art and culture, which it was hoped would lead to the creation of the new man. The journal *Die Aktion*, founded in 1911, also in Berlin, by Franz Pfemfert, was born, by contrast, with explicit political intentions, and called itself a "weekly journal of politics, literature and the arts." Pfemfert cannot be described as a Nietzschean, since he had frequented anarchist and radical circles; at all events, the first issue of *Die Aktion* revived the old, originally politico-clerical concept of *Kulturkampf* (cultural conflict), in support of a great German left, and therefore at the service of a new political party, to be formed outside the Social Democratic party. Naturally, both Pfemfert and his contributors were convinced that Nietzsche was useful for this purpose, indeed one issue of the journal was dedicated to an anthology of the philosopher's writings, drawn chiefly from *Thus Spoke Zarathustra* (the section *Of Ancient Tables and New*). Furthermore, the anti-bourgeois polemic centred on the concept of the "philistine of culture," philistinism being a concept previously used by Nietzsche in the first of his *Untimely Considerations on History*, consisting of a critique of David Strauss; the philistine of culture was seen as the bourgeois, the polemical target of the Expressionists. Despite the avowedly political objective of the journal, a certain elitist spirit eventually prevailed among its authors, that elitist spirit which was generated in every bohemia by the revolt against bourgeois society, and which remained fundamental throughout Expressionism: an indelible sign of Nietzschean aristocratism, that orientation which gained Nietzsche the sympathies of the right and of the so-called conservative revolution. Even Thomas Mann, in his *Reflections of an Unpolitical Man*, criticized Nietzsche for staying out of politics, locked up in a sort of ivory tower of culture, thus abandoning politics to the conservative conformism of the bourgeois class and to the reactionary orientation of the nobility and the warmongering military. Nevertheless, not everyone on the left agreed with this appraisal and this use of Nietzschean ideas. György Lukacs, in particular, attacked both Nietzsche and Expressionism and directed his ideological struggle against the alleged "irrationalism" of Nietzsche and against Expressionist "vitalism," on the grounds that it was susceptible of a National Socialist interpretation.[4] And what of "official philosophy"? The cult of Nietzsche had spread among the artists, but not in the universities, partly because he had never aimed at the academic audience. The poet Stefan George's circle in Heidelberg was certainly closer to Nietzsche but, despite its influence on the history of literature and science, it remained outside the academic world in the true sense of the term, and outside academic philosophy. This circle, whose importance in German cultural life is gaining increasingly wide recognition, was an extraordinary one, considering that it included among its members both the architect Albert Speer, the future minister under Hitler, and Hitler's attempted assassin, Stauffenberg.

The aesthetic debate
From the acute observations formulated by Wilhelm Worringer, the critic and theorist of Expressionist painting, in his fundamental book *Abstraction and Empathy* (originally his doctoral dissertation, 1908), the philosophical and theoretical background to this artistic movement emerges. The fundamental theses concern the metaphysical basis of the new painting, namely the necessity of recurring to the Platonic Ideas in order to overcome the simple *impressions* filtered through light and registered as if the subject remained merely passive before them. Moreover, the author calls for a return to the primitives, to medieval and Gothic art, even to the Egyptian, and for a revaluation of popular and folk art. Liberation from the rules, liberation of the force of color, as well as the liberation of line, the distortion and exaggeration of figurative features, the allocation of an increasing amount of space to plane surfaces, avoiding the perspective illusion, are all means of acquiring greater freedom and greater expressive force. However, these are synthetist ideas, and Expressionism took them entirely from Gaugin. Together with the artists of the so-called Pont–Aven School, Gaugin had developed them as part of a theory influenced in turn by Baudelaire and his reflections on the work of Delacroix (here, too, Nietzsche had shown remarkable perception in stressing the importance of Delacroix and his affinity with Wagner).[5]
If Van Gogh was the artist most congenial to the Expressionist painters, because in him the subjectivity of the artist and the expressive force of color and line are predominant, the great master of the return to the primitive was Gauguin, both because of the subjects of his pictures and because of his flight from Paris to Tahiti. Nor should we forget Cézanne, who fully developed the ideas that Gauguin had intuitively perceived and expounded in theory, thus bringing the work of art to a true perfection of construction, through colors, lines and planes, so that he may justly be regarded as the precursor of all twen-

tieth-century art. Strangely enough, Cézanne, who came to the very threshold of abstraction, was less aware than Gauguin of the theoretical implications of his practice. Writing to his friend Schuffenecker, Gauguin urged: "Never paint by copying nature; the work of art is an abstraction;" whereas Gauguin expressed dissatisfaction with his own results, declaring: "I tried to copy nature; I didn't succeed:" he never saw that the secret of the nature which he wanted to grasp was already inside him, in his work.[6] But all this is extremely significant, because it raises once again the romantic (in fact, idealistic) problem of the correspondence between inside and outside, between idea and nature, or rather between the idea that is in the subject and the idea in nature. Were the Expressionists aware of this problem? The painters of the Brücke may have felt it, in their desire to return to nature, to an original state and a purity of nature in which they could express their sensibility freely and achieve through art a harmony between external nature and their own feelings.

For the Blaue Reiter – that is, for Marc and Kandinsky – the situation is identical but opposite. While they are very close to Nietzsche in their belief in the potential of art – the Introduction to the *Blaue Reiter's Almanac* talked of a new epoch in art, a new era in human affairs, a world that is changing and needs a new art – they have a different concept of sensibility, which for them is totally absorbed into spirituality and the idea of "inner need." This is an even stronger Romanticism, because it is the task of the spirit, not of the sensibility, to achieve through art that correspondence between inside and outside, content and form, which is the goal of artistic activity. Therefore, abandoning Nietzsche, Marc and Kandinsky move towards Novalis and Rudolf Steiner, that is, toward anthroposophy.

A further link between Expressionism and philosophy, in addition to that centring on Nietzsche, has recently been suggested in the influence of Edmund Husserl's phenomenology on the work of Paul Klee: Husserl's theory of *Abschattungen*, shadings, has been seen as lying behind Klee's concern with catching the various shades and passages of color which approach the object and at the same time prevent any unitary perception of it, any ultimate point of view free of perceptive variability. However, these observations on Klee could be applied with even more justification to Cézanne, although Cézanne did not know Husserl, nor Husserl Cézanne. In the absence of any objective evidence – that objective evidence which abounds in the case of the relationship between Nietzsche and the Expressionists – such considerations are nothing more than interpretative conjectures. Similarly, with respect to Ernst Mach and his empirio-criticism, some scholars claim that through his psychologism Mach had an influence on Viennese Expressionism as a whole and not just on Musil, who studied for a doctorate under him at the University of Vienna. The further question which I would raise at this point is whether the Expressionist movement was only a carrier of Nietzsche's influence, or whether it elaborated an autonomous philosophy of its own. That is to say, whether it is possible to speak of an Expressionist philosophy and point to any philosopher who lived in the Expressionist period and dedicated himself to an Expressionist philosophy which was not simply a rehash of Nietzsche's ideas. I think it is possible to answer this question in the affirmative, citing the name of Ernst Bloch, whose first work, *The Spirit of Utopia*, was conceived in an Expressionist environment and in the midst of the themes of Expressionist culture.

The spirit of utopia

The war shook the whole Expressionist movement to the core. It has been rightly said that the end of the war was a time not just for counting the dead but also for taking stock of fallen causes and ideologies. One attempt at doing this was made by Ernst Bloch, who, in 1918, after the end of hostilities, tried to draw up an assessment of what, in addition to human lives, had been lost, and therefore also of Expressionism. This assessment is set out in his first book, *The Spirit of Utopia*, first published in 1918, a work which develops within Expressionist thought, and is a product of its problems and its historical evolution. The themes dealt with are those of Expressionism, the style is Expressionist, the language is Expressionist. One might say that the Expressionist ideal of life relives in it, in its positive appraisal of the experiences of the past, and in its attempt to avoid a surrender, despite the war. Bloch's attitude is not one of resignation; on the contrary, his first concern is a polemic against what he considers to be still a romantic heritage, but one which has now grown pessimistic after the recent experiences, so that it preserves nothing of Romanticism but a hopeless suffering, an inner torment, and despairs of rebuilding the unity of idea and nature in the Ego, in the spirit and through the spirit. But how is one to go beyond Romanticism without falling either into dangerous illusions on the one hand or despair on the other? The long discussion of music which forms the central part of Bloch's book seems to revive, without naming it, the Nietzschean aim of a legitimation of existence through art, and in particular through music, that is to say, through the Dionysiac which it expresses. While Bloch has no qualms about dusting

Paul Gauguin
The Yellow Christ, 1889
oil on canvas
Buffalo, New York Albright-Knox
Art Gallery

off the old terms "thing in itself" and "metaphysics" with respect to music, they are, however, a new metaphysics and a new thing in itself. The thing in itself is that of self-perceiving, or self-encountering; the metaphysics that is built on its foundation, on the extension of the principle to all reality, is that of utopia. Not only can one enjoy self-perception, in music; this encounter with the self contains an inevitable otherness which must be reassembled, a gap which must be filled, a beginning which we do not know and which we will only be able to know when we have reached our goal. We know nothing of our being, of the thing in itself that is most crystalline to us, but this tension which is called utopia; we are obscure to ourselves even in this crystallinity which is our ethical moment, that ethical commitment which saves us from the pointlessness of life, from nothingness, from senselessness. Therefore utopia finds a reality of its own, which is firstly ethical reality, and secondly historical reality, that historical reality which is implicit in the manifold forms of art, and which gives them meaning. Thus the desire to be reunited with the Goths, the Egyptians, the Jews, the Papuans, is a form of utopia; what utopia could be greater than that of Gauguin, who wishes to paint new altars and new temples, and who mingles Paris and Tahiti? But this utopia is present and real above all in our will to be reunited with the Christ, as it is in his will to identify himself with us, to call us to him as he dies on the Cross; an identification which is that of the community, of the Church, to which Christ calls us in a sort of "downward transcendence," since the Church is his bride, whom he has sought and called. The utopia of Expressionistic art coincides, therefore, with the "reverse transcendence" of the Christian faith, and in this coincidence both acquire their sense, the sense of utopia, which is at once aesthetic, ethical, and historical.

The crystalline transparency of the encounter with the self which is achieved in music and in the other arts implies the crystalline transparency of the ethical relationship, and eventually the historical transparency of the moment of the achievement of utopia, which as such links the beginning with the end. Utopian tension constitutes the secret of the world and of history; and only the loss of this secret – that is, of this non-true world – makes it possible to enter the other world. The only surpassing of romanticism is the utopia which resolves it in itself, without false illusions and without despair. The saying yes to suffering and to the obscurity of existence, which for Nietzsche is achieved in art, the justifier of existence, is not kept exclusively to the aesthetic and existential level by Bloch, but is transferred to the historical – that is, the political – level. This political result of Expressionism at the end of the war, as Bloch understands it (although through Marx he too eventually falls into the illusion of a perfect match between inside and outside), should not make us forget that any surpassing of Romanticism is in danger of remaining romantic if one does not appreciate that the justification for existence through art has its own place and its own laws in the economy of being in the world, that of the *spiritual in art*. He who "philosophizes with the hammer" may indeed construct an image of man which satisfies the spirit, or the "sensibility", the conscience, etc.; but the philosopher who reflects still has the task of separating this legitimation of existence through art from that legitimation which awaits us when the model itself has to be brought on to the field of the law and the struggle for "the right" or for "rights"; in order to defend this model, and prevent it from being distorted or misrepresented.

Wassily Kandinsky, woodcut for *Über das Geistige in der Kunst* (*The Spiritual in Art*), 1912

[1] First in the pocket edition of Naumann (vols IX and X), then again in 1911 in an edition revised by Otto Weiss in Kroener's *Gross–Oktav Ausgabe*.
[2] See Seth Taylor, *Left–wing Nietzscheans: the politics of German Expressionism, 1910–1920*. Berlin–New York: De Gruyter, 1990, a volume which is extremely rich in documentation and references; see, for example: Eva Kolinsky, *Engagierter Expressionismus*, Stuttgart, 1970; Gunter Martens, *Vitalismus und Expressionismus: Ein Beitrag zur Genese und Deutung expressionistiischer Strukturen und Motiven*, Stuttgart, 1971; *Karl Marx und Friedrich Nietzsche*, Reinhold Grimm and Joseph Hermann eds., Frankfurt am Main, 1978; on p. 6 of his Introduction Taylor states programmatically: "Expressionism was a revolt, based largely on Nietzsche's philosophy, against an authoritarian regime for the sake of individual autonomy."
[3] See Stephan Zweig, "Der neue Pathos," *Das literarische Echo*, II, 1909, 24; reprinted in *Expressionismus: Der Kampf um eine literarische Bewegung*, München, 1965.
[4] His systematic criticism of Nietzsche's ideas was set out at length in the well-known volume *Die Zerstörung der Vernunft* of 1952; but the first attack was made in 1934, see G. Lukacs, "Expressionismus: seine Bedeutung und Verfall", in *Internationale Literatur*, I, (1934), pp.153–73; reprinted in *Die Expressionismus–Debattte: Materialien zu einer marxistischen Realismuskonzeption*, Hans–Jürgen Schmitt, ed., Frankfurt am Main, 1973; for a discussion of the contributions see Eugene Lunn, *Marxism and Modernism*, Berkeley, 1982.
[5] See my essay *Paul Gauguin. Il contemporaneo ed il primitivo*. Palermo: Aesthetica–Preprint, 1989.
[6] Here too I must refer to an essay of mine, *Paul Cèzanne. L'opera d'arte come assoluto*. Palermo: Aesthetica Preprint, 1994, in which I cite the source of Cezanne's statement; for Gauguin's letter see my study quoted earlier.

Friedrich Rothe

Fritz Kortner in *Die Wandlung*
(*The metamorphosis*) by Ernst Toller
Berlin, Tribüne, 1919

Leopold Jeßner, scenography
for *Wilhelm Tell*

Walter Hasenclever, ca. 1917

Scene of *Die Entscheidung*
(*The vertict*) by Walter Hasenclever
Berlin, Tribüne, 1919

It is difficult to be impartial or unbiased about expressionist drama. For their contemporaries the performances of expressionist dramas were spectacular events. Such dramas as *Der Sohn* by Walter Hasencleaver as performed at the Court and National Theater in Mannheim in January of 1918 (directed by Richard Weichert) and Ernst Toller's *Die Wandlung* at the end of September 1919 in The Tribune (Berlin), with Fritz Kortner in the leading role left enduring impressions. These productions would have been unthinkable without the excited and exacerbated atmosphere of the endphase of World War I and the beginning of the November Revolution in Germany. Both of these occurences helped the expressionist dramatists to fulfill their wishes for attention beyond a limited circle of admirers and defined the picture of the expressionist movement for the broader public. The conventional box and peep-hole stage was transformed through a variety of innovations. These included innovations in the areas of lighting, theater of movement, and stylistics, many of which young directors even today claim to be their own discoveries, although their origins date back to the brief period of expressionist development between 1918–25. Nor did the performance of the classics remain un-influenced by the innovativeness of the expressionist dramatists of the period. Leopold Jessner's productions as director of the state theater (Berlin) for instance sent a clear signal in this respect. The so-called "Jessner-Stairway" upon which Kortner played Richard III was widely discussed. A particular source or irritation for conservatives was his production of *Wilhelm Tell* which also used the same stairway as well as the fact that in this production all references to Switzerland were eliminated and the difference between the good and the bad characters is underscored by the wearing of black or white costumes.

Despite their significance for the breakthrough of The Modern, these dramatic works neither belong to the repertoires of established theaters, nor do they enjoy anywhere near the same degree of attention or stature as expressionist poetry or prose by a reading or viewing public today. Walter Hasenclever's tragedy is no exception in this respect: the son, having failed his Abitur, wishes to commit suicide, but manages to strengthen himself by joining the club Zur Erhaltung der Freude modeled on Schiller's *Die Räuber* and which has as its objective the resolution of conflicts in dealing with tyrannical fathers. The son in Hasenclever's drama has reached the point of wanting to shoot down his father in order to save humanity. Just as their confrontation reaches a peak and the father wants to call the police, he dies of a heart attack under the threat of the son waving a pistol at him.

External actions and fantasy of the protagonists in these dramas are nearly inseparable. Much the same as in a dream, thought and perception become visible reality. Similarly, the author changes from prose to poetry – rhymed iambic pentameters – suddenly and without warning. Common to both forms however is the use of an ecstatic and elevated tone which uniquely combines Schillerian pathos with the melancholic tempo of speech of Büchner. Hasenclever's intention here and the reason for his achieving such an enormous impact upon his public was that he attempts to deal with the inavoidable and universal problem of the rebellion of sons against their fathers, who are seen to be inadequately suited to deal with this situation. The piece by Hasenclever functions almost as a dramatized commentary to Freud's work, *Totem und Tabu* (1914) which appeared in the same year as Hasenclever's drama. For Hasenclever, much the same as for Freud, the evolution of civilization derives from the act of killing the father (patricide). The mythical guilt of the self-tormented and rebellious son represents for both, in other words, the animus of culture. The convergence of ideas between Freud and Hasenclever directs our attention to the centrifical intensity of the epoch, and consciously or unknowingly also directs our attention to and anticipates the emergence of Fascism, or at least some of its features. In contrast to Freud for whom the above-defined schemata of patricide is problematical, Hasencleaver is more at ease with this problem and to some extent even identifies himself with these motives and intentions of the epoch.

The search of the "Neuen Menschen" goes together with or is joined up with the theme of the celebration of the sacrificial death. Self-sacrifice in the form of suicide or self-redemption through patricide or parental murder also belong to the basic themes of such authors as Arnolt Bronnen (*Vatermord*, written 1914–20), Reinhard Johannes Sorge (*Der Bettler*, 1912), Georg Kaiser (*Die Bürger von Calais*, 1914), Hanns Johst (*Der junge Mensch*, 1916) and Fritz von Unruh (*Ein Genschlecht*, 1917). Characters reduced to their stereotypical essence (Father-Son, Man-Woman, General-Soldier etc.) are sharply drawn in black-and-white contrast then step onto the stage and speak ecstatically. Monologues and appeals are dominant. In the protagonists of these dramas there is an astounding renaissance of heroic and mythological elements. It is

Ernst Toller at Niederschönfeld
fortress-gaol, 1919–24

almost as if the development toward an episodical theater, as exemplified by Ibsen, Maeterlinck and Chekov had never taken place. The characters act as models of awakening and uprising as well as inner emancipation. In their personae the birth of the new and transformed individual is supposed to be experienced. The theatrical production creates a sense of communality. Choruses or the simultaneous speaking of several characters accentuate the anti-individualist and archaic qualities of the expressionist drama and transform the experience of the theater into a form of cult experience.

Ernst Toller's *Die Wandlung* (written in 1917/1918) marks a high point in connection with the above-mentioned features and additionally reflects a combination between Messianism and the union or meeting of souls. His drama portrays the fate of a Jewish sculptor who voluntarily registers for the military, and thereafter becomes an opponent of war and eventually a revolutionary leader. Toller himself is clearly identified with the level of pathos suggested here. He had himself registered voluntarily to do military service at the front in order to extinguish or compensate for the feeling of being a "Jewish outsider." Toller had also been a revolutionary leader and political agitator for the USDP, as a result of which he clearly understood how to address and mobilize the masses. During the January strikes of the munition workers (1918) he had taken up a leading role and had served as the head-of-state in the revolutionary Münchner Räter-Republik in April of 1919. At the end of his drama *Die Wandlung* the masses arrive at an "ever-strengthening movement, some of them kneeling and others crying and burying their faces in their hands." The piece thus culminates in a gripping communal experience and in a tone reminiscent of *Zarathustra*.

Oskar Kokoschka's dark drama *Mörder, Hoffnung der Frauen*, which exists in an astounding variety of different versions (1907–17) is typical of the expressionist's attitude toward women and the question of sexuality. Kokoschka sets his drama in Greek antiquity and portrays a sexual struggle in which man and woman are torn between self-defense and desire and self-destructively battling for redemption. As suggested by the title the only hope for the woman is to be murdered. As a result of the mere touch of the *geistige* hand of the male, the woman sinks dead to the earth at the end of the play. The sexual fantasies of the expressionists are combined with feelings of loathing and in general everything associated with the body reflects anxiety and discomfort. Body, earth and death come into close association with one another which has its dramatic appeal on the one hand, but is also equally frightening on the other. In Arnolt Bronnen's *Vatermord*, is a family tragedy in which the mother is to be seen on stage with hear breasts exposed and prodding her son into murdering his father. Expressionist drama here reaches one of its most drastic high points in which the author unrelentingly and mercilessly exposes the fundamental dynamics of the oedipal triangle.

Expressionist drama does not remain limited to any specifically self-defined criteria. On the contrary, in the decade between 1909–19, pieces are written and performed in which the stylized pathos is not quite as extreme but which nevertheless possess a radicalness, the provocative power of which is undeniable even today. To these works belong *Der Wupper* by Else Lasker-Schüler which the authoress herself reads at the "Neopathetischen Cabaret" in Berlin. In this work, the author-ess/lyricist tightly connects the factory-owner's villa with a working-class milieu and in so doing turns all of the traditional notions about socially engaged drama upside down. Behind the facade of a realistically portrayed social reality, there is a dimension of inwardly surrealistically structured movement, a method which reveals her ties to Strindberg. The inclusion of surrealist elements, however, at no point obscures the borders between bourgeoisie and workers. The tragic constellation consists of the interplay of the pipe dreams and wishful thinking by the workers which is directed at a better life as represented by the factory-owner's villa. The villa with it's blossoming garden, fountain, and pavilion succeed in arousing the envy of some of the workers while in others the wish and hope of upward mobility is awakened. The life of the factory-owner and his family is played out directly before the eyes of the workers. They subordinate themselves, but while so doing, they observe each and every step of their social superiors. The climax of the drama comes in the Third Act in which a grotesque carnival atmosphere is unfolded. Rapturous sentiments of love and social tension collide with one another, ectasy and bitter poverty are the basis of a quick and sudden transition which leaves the impression of inconsolable and abysmal emptiness behind.

Carl Sternheim employs the traditionally enlightenment oriented form of the comedy in order

Oskar Kokoschka, poster
for his drama
Mörder - Hoffnung der Frauen
(*Murderer, Hope of Women*)
on show at Hamburg
Hamburger Museum für Kunst
und Gewerbe, 1965

Alexander Granach as a cashier
in *Von morgens bis mitternachts*
(*From morning to midnight*)
by Georg Kaiser, Berlin, 1926

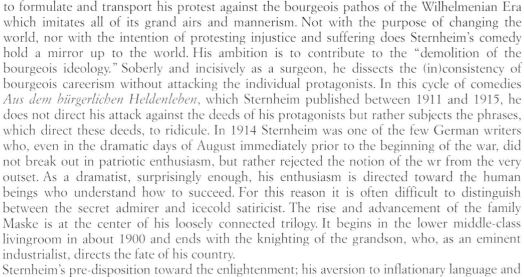

to formulate and transport his protest against the bourgeois pathos of the Wilhelmenian Era which imitates all of its grand airs and mannerism. Not with the purpose of changing the world, nor with the intention of protesting injustice and suffering does Sternheim's comedy hold a mirror up to the world. His ambition is to contribute to the "demolition of the bourgeois ideology." Soberly and incisively as a surgeon, he dissects the (in)consistency of bourgeois careerism without attacking the individual protagonists. In this cycle of comedies *Aus dem bürgerlichen Heldenleben*, which Sternheim published between 1911 and 1915, he does not direct his attack against the deeds of his protagonists but rather subjects the phrases, which direct these deeds, to ridicule. In 1914 Sternheim was one of the few German writers who, even in the dramatic days of August immediately prior to the beginning of the war, did not break out in patriotic enthusiasm, but rather rejected the notion of the wr from the very outset. As a dramatist, surprisingly enough, his enthusiasm is directed toward the human beings who understand how to succeed. For this reason it is often difficult to distinguish between the secret admirer and icecold satiricist. The rise and advancement of the family Maske is at the center of his loosely connected trilogy. It begins in the lower middle-class livingroom in about 1900 and ends with the knighting of the grandson, who, as an eminent industrialist, directs the fate of his country.

Sternheim's pre-disposition toward the enlightenment; his aversion to inflationary language and his ambivalent relationship to his protagonists leads to a language, which compared to the meagreness of the story lines of his dramatic works, by and large attains a life of its own. The language nearly fully constructs the characters of his dramatic figures. He employs a coldly manneristic diction which exposes excessive pathos. Hardly to be differentiated from this are the terse abridgements of language which enable the speaker to establish himself as master of his situation and lay bare his "own nuance" as an individual. One Sternheimer hero, the verbally radical Wilhelm Ständer, concludes one of Sternheim's dramas *Tabula rasa* (1916) by stepping into a free space and uttering the following: "Für mich Ständer," stehe ich. Welch Glück, dass man keine Kinder hat!" Similar to the distinctiveness of the language is also the syntax, which twisted nearly to the point of being grotesque, additionally distorts the speakers of his satire to the point of (un)recognizability. Sternheim's highest priority on the stage is to exhibit and generate a sense of the disintegration of values which in turn is supposed to encourage his viewers to find their "eigene Nuance."

Georg Kaiser did not only write drama *Die Bürger von Calais* which overflows with self-sacraficial pathos and for which he was best known, but he was also responsible for the stormiest drama to have appeared during this period: *Von morgens bis mitternachts* (1916). Urban scenes of the Megapolis Berlin: – settings in the sport palace, in the chambre séparée of a dancehall and a meeting place of the Salvation Army dominate the happenings in this drama. The play is comprised of the passage through one day in the life of a bank clerk and his despairing attempts at escape into ectasy. Kaiser leads his drama away from declamatory stylization into a seething metropolitan inferno which belongs to the same thematic repertoire as the pictures of Kirchner, Beckmann, and Grosz. Although *Von morgens bis mitternachts* mercilessly demonstrates the hopelessness of earthly existence and thus belongs to the category of the expressionist drama of redemption, it is the tempo of the dialogue and the story, the utilization of music and the use of lighting and sound effects which constitute the essentially distinctive features of this drama by Kaiser and which also directs our attention to the dramatic revues of the 1920s as well as the increasing significance of the film for literature.

Die letzten Tage der Menschheit a tragedy in five acts by Karl Kraus is a piece of expressionist anti-war literature which has by no means lost its punch, even for the contemporary reader or viewer. Karl Kraust who persisted in the publication of his magazine under the particulary difficult conditions of censorship during World War I completed this work in three summer visits to Switzerland between 1915–17. He published scenes from it in *Die Fackel* and by means of public readings achieved a considerable impact upon his audiences and no less so upon the censorship authorities. Counting both prologue and epilogue in *Die Fackel* edition of the work (1919) it is nearly 700 pages in length and is intended by the author to be performed in a gigantic arena ("Marstheater"), the huge dimensions of which are thought by him to be appropriate to the immensity of the proceedings represented in the piece itself. For this literary achievement the author demands no particular recognition. On the contrary, he perceives

Paul Edwin Roth
in *Draußen vor der Tür*
(*Outside, in front of the door*)
by Wolfgang Borchert, Berlin
Hebbel Theater, 1948
directed by Rudolf Noelte

himself merely as a chronicler of everyday events; his sole and inexhaustible source for this work being the daily press which is available to anyone.

The story or course of action of Kraus's piece concentrates upon the life in Vienna and not on the various battlefronts of the war. Kraus sees the war as a heightened continuation of the mundane everyday world. The war itself is pre-ordained in Kraus's view, by the inability of humans to think and their inadequate capacity for perception. In more than an hundred scenes *Die letzten Tagen der Menschheit* Kraus tries to track down a mentality which clings to certain phrases in order to assure itself of the normality of its actions in the midst of the crisis situation of the war. On the way into the catastrophe a highly peculiar form of motionlessness exists which is expressed in the repetition of highly verbalized, not to say hysterically verbalized, sequences. The cast is constantly increased to the point where the register of speakers or performers takes up three narrowly printed pages. Finally, in the epilogue the voice of God is to be heard quoting Emperor Wilhelm II and concluding the drama as cosmic catastrophe in outer space: "Ich habe es nicht gewollt." From the hope of the "Neuen Menschen," which had been nourished and sustained by the pathos of the expressionist drama, there is nothing left in the view of Kraus except for the catastrophe. It was the catastrophe which, in the view of the expressionists, was supposed to give birth to the new era.

Not only Karl Kraus but also Hasenclever, Toller and Kaiser belong to the rows of the distraught and disillusioned. This however did not prevent the coming of a blossoming of the expressionist drama at the beginning of the 1920s. The censorship had been lifted and the theaters competed with one another for the pieces by the new and as yet unknown dramatists. Such authors as Arnolt Bronnen, Ernst Barlach, and Hans Henny Jahn, among others, now received the opportunity to be performed. Despite the attention which these new pieces aroused, owing frequently to their being loaded with sensation and scandal, they could not conceal their debt of origin to the expressionist drama which had preceded them. By comparison to the new trends and tendencies such as Functionalism (Sachlichkeit), cabaret-type of entertainment, and the increasing political orientation, the expressionist dramas were hopelessly ineffective and even clumsy. With the appearance of Wolfgang Borchert's drama *Draussen vor der Tür*, there was a short-lived and heart-wrenching revival of the expressionist drama after 1945. Borchert's drama became one of the most frequently staged plays in postwar Germany.

Quirino Principe

The stylistic seal of Expressionism appears very early in European music, in years contemporaneous with the birth and development of Expressionistic poetics in other artistic languages such as the visual arts, poetry and the theatre, which were their true "seed-beds" and incubators. One circumstance is particularly significant: the avant-garde musicians who at the beginning of the twentieth century adopted features of style and expression convergent with those which the leading exponents of Expressionism in painting and literature were beginning to produce, were fully conscious of this convergence. Just as Oskar Kokoschka, from the beginnings of his creative work as painter and writer, showed the efficacy of his aggressive language in paintings and drawings, but also in his provocative and scandalous plays, so Arnold Schönberg implicitly proclaimed the consanguineity of the new method of composing music by means of sequences of twelve notes with the disturbing stylemes of Kokoschka himself, Emil Nolde, Egon Schiele, or Paul Klee. Besides, Schönberg was a painter in his own right, and a painter of great originality, though still belonging to the stylistic sphere typical of those artists.

Despite these strong affinities, and despite the awareness which the avant-garde composers – especially those of the Vienna School – had of them, it was only at a later stage that talk of "musical Expressionism" began in the field of art history and criticism. It is a singular fact that the first discussions were conducted not dispassionately and in a spirit of serious, objective historical assessment (this happened only later, in the years immediately following the Second World War), but in an accusatory spirit and in a venemously polemical, indeed intolerant atmosphere. In the thirties, the Austro-German area was pervaded by a fierce censorship, promoted by the National Socialist guardians of the Beautiful, of "degenerate art" (*entartete Kunst*); and the painting of Klee, Kokoschka, Schiele, Franz Marc, the whole group which formed under the banner Der Blaue Reiter, and countless other artists, was banned. But an analogous censorship, a logical consequence of the former, also targeted the "degenerate music" (*entartete Musik*) of Schönberg, Berg, Webern, Hindemith, Křenek, Korngold, and Zemlinsky, not to mention Mahler. The programmes of the concert seasons were sanitized and purified of the plague of degeneration. Many titles were conspicuously excluded from the opera seasons. Berg's *Wozzeck* (which was, besides, a defeatist and antimilitaristic work), Hindemith's *Cardillac*, Křenek's *Jonny spielt auf* (Jonny plays music), Berthold Goldschmidt's *Der gewaltige Hahnrei* (The wonderful cuckold), even Korngold's *Das Wunder der Heliane* (The wonder of Heliane), were banned from the theaters, as of course was all the music, whether theatrical or not, of Kurt Weill, doubly censurable in view of his artistic partnership with Bertolt Brecht. These are only the more celebrated examples; the excluded were legion. In strictly musical terms, bearing in mind the aesthetic predilections of National Socialism, the hostility unleashed on Hindemith, Berg, Schönberg, Křenek and Weill is understandable; but the "stylistic" reason for the censorship of Korngold is a mystery. His theatrical works, from *Der Ring des Polykrates* (The ring of Polykrates), *Violanta*, and *Die tote Stadt* (The dead city), to the incriminated *Das Wunder der Heliane*, are works of a late-romantic nature which emanate an atmosphere very similar to that which one finds, for example, in the *Mona Lisa* of Max von Schilling, an author of firm National Socialist convictions and therefore celebrated, even after his death in the fatal year of 1933, by Hitler's regime. In fact what was decisive in Korngold's case was not so much a judgement on his musical language as the underlying anti-Jewish factor, which linked the composer of *Das Wunder der Heliane* with Schönberg, Goldschmidt, and, of course, retrospectively with Mahler, and before him Mendelssohn. This lengthy but necessary preamble brings into focus a curious fact. While it is true that we should always beware of transposing the features of a movement like Expressionism to fields collateral to the ones in which the movement originated (in this case, from the visual arts to music), and while it is true that as far as Expressionism is concerned a large dose of critical caution is necessary in assimilating poetic stylemes and aims, it is also true that, before the mature critical reflection which has evolved since the fifties, that very adjective, *entartet* (degenerate) – the very concept of degeneration – was paradoxically the first critical tool which was to clarify the stylistic affinities between Kokoschka and Schönberg, or between Schiele and Berg.

This is equally true of Italian musical culture, into which a knowledge of the Austro-German musical avant-gardes filtered rather earlier than has often been claimed, since Giannotto Bastianelli had already performed the function of a pioneer and herald in the years immediately preceding the First World War. Certainly, in Italy, as elsewhere, it was not until fairly late – after the Second World War – that an organic and well-informed body of critical opinion began to formulate a definition of musical Expressionism. The first result was the volume published by the Italian

Arnold Schönberg
Der rote Blick, May 1910
The red glance, oil on canvas
Munich, Städtische Galerie

Zum Wozzeckskandal am Prager tschechischen Nationaltheater
16 November 1926
Of the scandal raised by Wozzeck at the Tschechischen Nationaltheater Prague, a report

Entartete Musik
Eine Abrechnung von Staatsrat
Dr. H. S. Ziegler
Degenerate music by regulation
of the Council of State
Dr. H. S. Ziegler, booklet

Books burning in Opernplatz
Germany, May 1933

B.F. Dolbin, *Arnold Schönberg*
und Alban Berg bei einer Probe
des Kolisch-Quartetts, 1923
Arnold Schönberg and Alban Berg
at a rehearsal of the Kolisch Quartet
drawing

state broadcasting company, ERI, in 1953 for the series "Etichette del nostro tempo" (Labels of Our Time), and edited by Luigi Rognoni and Enzo Paci, in which the former, a distinguished musicologist, sketched a first fascinating panorama of Expressionism embracing poets like August Stramm and Georg Kaiser, painters like Franz Marc and Oskar Kokoschka, composers like Schönberg, Berg, Webern, Hindemith and Weill; this was followed by Rognoni's distinguished long essay *Espressionismo e dodecafonia* (Expressionism and the Twelve-Note System, 1954), which provided two or three generations of scholars with food for meditation; later, dedicating less space to music, came an elegant volume by Ladislao Mittner published in 1965.[1] But in singular parallel with the aforementioned critical prejudices of National Socialism during the thirties, in Italy, too, something similar to the censorial critical tool of "unification" or "pooling" adopted in the Austro-German area had appeared during the same decade, and that something was, significantly, a linguistic signal. In a book published in 1932 (and therefore before Nazism had seized power in Germany), Guido Pannain talked of "degeneration" in music, and, commenting on Schönberg's chamber music, wrote: "In *Quartet* op. 10 there is already that imperfection of the spirit which is the prelude to Expressionism"[2] where "Expressionism," in Pannain's intentions, meant Evil. Rather than simply dismissing the concepts of "degeneration" and "imperfection of the spirit" as expressions of an attitude that we hope has been irrevocably defeated, I would suggest that, whatever their intentions, they bore within them a sort of mirror-image of the truth: a fragment of truth whose algebraic sign needs to be changed. If we really try to get to the primary roots common to the various Expressionist poetics and to the various artistic languages, I believe it is correct to indicate three situations of the spirit which have an archetypal presence in the visual arts as in literature, in drama as in music: a) *trauma*, which greets with a cry of anguish (like Munch's "shriek") a horrifying revelation or a tragedy of unprecedented dimensions; b) *destabilization*, which shakes the ground on which the certainties rested and which prefigures the catastrophe; c) *solitude*, which creates a void around the individual and places him in an inorganic, artificial, dehumanized world. These three archetypes of the Expressionistic psyche have one common outcome: *fear* which is clothed in darkness. The Expressionists' universe is nocturnal, sick, enigmatic and malign. Its revealed truth is the deformation of the appearances previously regarded as "natural": the real world is the deformed, menacing one in which the subject feels persecuted and condemned *ab initio*, and music, with the linguistic tools peculiar to it, is perhaps the art which best manifests the terror and despair of those who expose themselves to this sinister discovery. Therefore in Expressionist poetics there really is a degeneration, but it is the world that has degenerated from its origins, not art; it is the world that bears within it the signs of imperfection and sickness, not the spirit that denounces them with despairing boldness. As Edgar Wind wrote in *Art and Anarchy* (1963), those who persecute art as something dangerous to order and society (as did National Socialism, or Stalinism, or Catholic censorship in its grimmest phases) honour art more than those who tolerate artists as harmless, decorative and ultimately unimportant figures, even protecting them, out of concern for any "relapse" of their own image. "Art is – let us face up to it – an uncomfortable business, and particularly uncomfortable for the artist himself. The forces of the imagination, from which he draws his strength, have a disruptive and capricious power which he must manage with economy. If he indulges his imagination too freely, it may run wild and destroy him and his work by excess."[3]

In any discussion of musical Expressionism, the greatest difficulty arises from the fact that no composer can be described as an "Expressionist" except temporarily, with reference to a particular period of his creative output and a restricted number of compositions. In view of his often very close relations with painters and writers representative of expressionistic poetics, Arnold Schönberg (Vienna, 13 September 1874 – Los Angeles, 13 July 1951) is the composer whom it is most appropriate to identify with Expressionism in music in the pre-1914 period. Those of his compositions which may be described in these terms, starting with the traumatic *Erwartung* (Wait) of 1909, are the result of a slow psychological, poetic, and theoretical evolution, and the story of their origins is different from what happens in the itinerary of the Expressionists born after 1890, for whom the decisive stylistic choice was inseparable from the trauma of the First World War and a consequent changed awareness in the face of the spectral revelation of what the world "is." Besides, the themes of trauma, the intimation of menacing cataclysms in civilization, and solitude, were familiar ingredients of the Viennese cultural environment during Schönberg's youth. The horrors of war, that horrific mutilator of bodies and souls, were less important in the

Arnold Schönberg
Herzgewächse op. 20, 1911
front page, autographic manuscript
facsimile
Munich, Archiv Piper Verlag

Richard Gerstl
Arnold Schönberg
oil on canvas
Vienna

Alban Berg (1885–1935)
with Arnold Schönberg (1874–1951)

history of Expressionism than the dream-visions which the Viennese scientific milieu delighted in analyzing and which soon pervaded the imagination of artists. In 1899 Sigmund Freud's *Die Traumdeutung* (The Interpretation of Dreams) was published; in the same year Schönberg completed *Verklärte Nacht*, the composition for string sextet whose poetic "programme" was a poem by Richard Dehmel permeated by dreams and by ambiguous relationships between sleep and wakefulness. Schönberg absorbed the Expressionistic moods of Viennese poetry: he associated with Peter Altenberg, Else Lasker-Schüler, and Georg Trakl. But in his vocal compositions he preferred different poets, drawing rather on the realm of Symbolism: Stefan George for the *Lieder* op. 15 (1909), Rainer Maria Rilke for the last three of the *Vier Lieder* op. 22 (1913–15), and Maurice Maeterlinck for *Herzgewächse* op. 20 (1911). He chose minor or downright mediocre poets like Marie Pappenheim for *Erwartung* op. 17 (1909), Albert Giraud translated by Otto Erich Hartleben for *Pierrot lunaire* op. 21 (1912), a composition in which the typically Expressionistic themes of the grotesque deformation and the disturbing dream are emphasized by the vocal style of *Sprechgesang*, long-drawn-out or shouted words which tend toward song without ever identifying with it. He himself wrote the text for *Die glückliche Hand* op. 18 (1908–13).

The importance of *Erwartung* and *Die glückliche Hand* (The glad hand), authentic examples of musical Expressionism in Schönberg's *œuvre*, is accentuated by the fact that these are two compositions for the theatre. For the musical theatre is the point of convergence of the Expressionistic stylemes in music, the context in which the unmasking of reality and the revelation of its spectral, nocturnal horrors is rendered more eloquent through sounds. *Erwartung* is a *Monodram*, a drama with a single character. In a forest, by night, under a pale, bloodless but blood-presaging moon, a woman searches for the corpse of her lover. The music passes from one melodic and harmonic cell to another, cancelling every syntactic connection at the very moment when the listener expects it. The only element of formal connection is perhaps the general pause in bar 158, when the horrified woman discovers the corpse. Schönberg exploits to the full the technique, already present in Mahler, of the *Klangfarbenmelodie* ("Melody of timbres"): in each melodic fragment, each ones of the notes is given to a completely different instrument, creating the sense of a world that is disintegrating and fragmenting. *Die glückliche Hand*, a *Drama mit Musik*, has a subject which may have been suggested to Schönberg by the suicide, two years earlier, of the painter Richard Gerstl. The Man and the Woman love one another, but on the appearance of the Lord the Woman leaves the Man and throws herself into the arms of the other. In vain the Man tries to win the Woman back by passing difficult tests and forging a splendid golden jewel: a mass of stone detaches itself from the fortress which is the Lord's dominion and buries the Man. The Woman and the Lord are silent characters who only mime their actions; the entire text is given to the Man. At the beginning and the end of the action, a monster, a nightmare image, is seen with its teeth planted in the back of the Man's neck; it disappears in all the other scenes of the drama. This monster is a symbol of the anguish which oppresses human life from birth to death. Fragments of music of the past, tonal and dancelike, pervade the score like ghosts, and are immediately deformed and demolished. A large, variegated orchestra, of Mahlerian or Straussian complexity, acts on three levels of sonority: a *continuum* consisting of a tremolo of violas, violins, harp and kettledrum; a texture of orchestra and song, continually deconstructed and transformed into *Sprechgesang*; and the irruption of flashes of melody in which the use of *Klangfarbenmelodie* is taken to an extreme. In *Die glückliche Hand* the characters only have symbolic names, in accordance with the idea of anonymous universality dear to the purest type of Expressionistic theatre. But Schönberg had no links with the leading playwrights of the mature phase of Expressionism, Walter Hasenclever (1890–1940), Reinhard Sorge (1892-1916), and Georg Kaiser (1878–1945). However, one model that was very familiar to him was what Ladislao Mittner has called the first "truly" Expressionistic play, Oskar Kokoschka's *Mörder, Hoffnung der Frauen* (*Murderer, Hope of Women*, 1907). However, he opted for a different tone, replacing Kokoschka's bloodthirsty cruelty (the murderer's knife, the disembowelled woman) with anguish and terror. The more sanguinary elements of Kokoschka's play are rather to be seen in Berg's *Lulu*, whose ending is an extension *ad infinitum* of the Expressionistic "shriek". In short, the Expressionistic characteristics of Schönberg's musical theater lie more in the music than in the subjects and texts. Similarly, Schönberg's two greatest pupils, Anton Webern (Vienna, 3 December 1883 – Mittersill near Salzburg, 15 September 1945) and Alban Berg (Vienna, 9 February 1885 – Vienna, in the night between 23 and 24 December 1935), both of whom went through an Expressionistic phase (which in Berg's case

Alban Berg (1885–1935)
with Anton von Webern
(1883–1945), on the right

Alban Berg
*Vier Lieder für eine Singstimme
mit Klavier Opus 2 nach Gedichten
von Hebbel und Mombert*
4 Lieders for a singing voice
and piano op. 2
on poems by Hebbel and Mombert
frontispiece

Remusat, *Paul Hindemith*, drawing
Paris, A. Meyer Collection

continued, in his musical dramas, to the very end), rarely turned to poets who were truly representative of that stylistic and poetic movement. In Webern's vocal music, the only truly Expressionist poet who appears as an author of texts is Georg Trakl (*Sechs Lieder* op. 14, 1917–21). Peter Altenberg, an Expressionist only in some respects, is present in Berg's *Lieder* op. 4 (1912). For the rest, Berg chose poets whom we may consider precursors of Expressionism, such as Alfred Mombert (*Vier Lieder* op. 2, 1908–09), or Romantics (Nicolaus Lenau), Late Romantics (Theodor Storm), or Symbolists (Rainer Maria Rilke, Otto Erich Hartleben) in the beautiful *Sieben frühe Lieder* (1905–08). For *Lulu*, composed to his own libretto, he drew on a playwright, Frank Wedekind, in whose poetics perhaps only one (albeit very accentuated) element, the spirit of revolt, may be considered consanguineous with Expressionism. For the earlier opera *Wozzeck*, also composed to his own libretto, he drew the subject and the dramatization from an early-nineteenth-century author, Georg Büchner, whose links with Expressionism are purely analogical; though admittedly the analogy is an irresistibly attractive one.

The nature of the relations and affinities changes profoundly with the emergence of a new generation of musicians, the generation which produced its first works after 1918. Essentially this means the four composers born around the turn of the century who, together with Schönberg, Berg and Webern, and with the Vienna School whose greatest exponents these three were, constitute the main group of composers involved, to varying extents, in the poetics of Expressionism. Of these four musicians, two, Weill and especially Hindemith, moved away from the Expressionistic style in the later period of their lives; the other two, Křenek and especially Eisler, remained close to Expressionism almost to the very end.

These four composers, unlike the masters of the Vienna School, drew abundant inspiration from Expressionistic texts. Paul Hindemith (Hanau, 16 November 1895 – Frankfurt am Main, 28 December 1963), used Kokoschka's play *Mörder, Hoffnung der Frauen* for his first theatrical work of the same name (1919), and set to music texts by Lasker-Schüler in *Lieder* op. 9 (1917) and poems by Trakl, and again Lasker-Schüler, in *Acht Lieder* op. 18 (1920). Later, in the oratorio *Das Unaufhörliche* (1931), he turned to Gottfried Benn, the poet who represented German literary Expressionism with originality and continuity in its concluding (one might say "posthumous") phase. Ernst Křenek (Vienna, 28 August 1900 - Palm Springs, California, 24 December 1991) set to music texts by Franz Werfel in his stage cantata *Zwingburg* (Stronghold) op. 14 (1922) and by Oskar Kokoschka in the opera *Orpheus und Eurydike* (1923); later he was to use poems by Karl Kraus in the Lieder cycle *Durch die Nacht* (During the night) op. 67 and in the concert aria *Die Nachtigall* (The nightingale) op. 68, both written in 1931. Kurt Weill (Dessau, 2 March 1900 - New York, 3 April 1950) composed two operas on subjects from Georg Kaiser, *Der Protagonist* (The protagonist) op. 14 (1925–26) and *Der Zar läßt sich photographieren* (The Czar lets himself to be photographed) op. 21 (1927–28), and took from Ywan Goll the idea for the "Ballet-Opera" *Royal Palace* op. 17 (1927), before beginning his celebrated collaboration with Brecht. Hanns Eisler (Leipzig, 6 July 1898 - Berlin, 6 September 1962), one of Schönberg's Berlin pupils, on three occasions used poetic texts by Trakl in the Lieder written before 1923.

As far as conscious participation in the poetics and central ideas of the Expressionistic movement is concerned, Hindemith, Křenek, Weill and Eisler had a common attitude: all four of them, in different situations, without themselves abusing the term "Expressionism," tacitly agreed to be placed, by the use of this term on the part of critics and essayists, within a definite category of style and culture. Very different – reluctant and even irritable – was the attitude of the Vienna School, whose exponents belonged to the two preceding generations. In 1922, Schönberg wrote some extremely harsh words on the subject to Wassily Kandinsky, rejecting the cavalier attachment of labels: "I have no great liking for all these movements ... Nothing more quickly comes to a standstill than these movements that everyone is always calling into being. And it's our skin – yours and mine – that all these people are peddling."[4] Distancing himself from the proliferation of 'isms', he wrote to Berg that Expressionism had become the "trade-mark of a manufactured product."[5] In more serious vein, he expounded his ideas in a 1932 lecture on his *Vier Lieder* op. 22.[6] "In the first place, I was forced to renounce the construction of great forms, and at the same time I was obliged to avoid the use of great melodies and all those formal elements of music which depend on the frequent repetition of motifs. In the circumstances, it seemed impossible to find, among the means at a musician's disposal, anything equivalent to the great forms and great melodies. Involuntarily, and therefore rightly, I found an aid where music always finds it when it reaches a crucial point in its development. *This, and this alone*, is the origin of what is called Expressionism. A musical work does not create its formal shape starting from the logic of its *own* material, rather, guided by a sense of the internal and external procedures, and bringing these *to expression*, it bases itself on their logic and builds itself on the foundations of this logic."

Only one composer, the naturalized Swiss of Russo-German origin, Wladimir Vogel (Moscow, 29 February 1896 – Zurich, 19 June 1984), who, though never really Schönberg's pupil, was strongly influenced by him, used the term Expressionism, in its adjectival form, in the title of one of his piano compositions, *Nature vivante, six pièces expressionnistes* (1917–21). The Expressionistic aura, which in western music surrounded many great composers of the early twentieth century, flowed for decades into collateral phenomena on the borders of popular music: and these, in turn, inspired the militant masters in the sphere of art music. Pre-eminent among these phenomena was the cabaret tradition, especially that of Vienna, Munich and Berlin: what in the Austro-German area was called *Tingeltangel*, a word of uncertain etymology which may derive from a corruption of the French *café chantant* or from an onomatopoeic sequence imitating the sound of two idiophonic percussion instruments, the so-called "Chinese hat," a hollow metal cone with a very open point, also used in jazz ensembles ("ting"), and the cymbals ("tang"). The first literary cabaret in Germany was the celebrated Buntes Theater in Berlin, also known as Überbrettl, in which Schönberg participated during his time in the German capital. It was inaugurated on 17 January 1901 with a midnight show in a hall of the Berlin Philharmonie. Irony, grotesque deformation, desecration, the corrosive critique of the certainties of the bourgeoisie and the social order, and the revelation of spectral aspects of reality, were typical themes of the Überbrettl, which was frequented by "rebellious" writers, artists and musicians (foremost among them Ernst von Wolzogen) who had blood ties with the poetics of Expressionism. Prominent writers of songs for the Austro-German cabaret were the Prague-born Kurt Robitschek (1890–1950), the Hungaro-Slav Alexander Rosenfeld, alias Roda-Roda (1872–1945), and the Berliner Kurt Tucholsky (1890–1935). The historical experience of the cabaret and its atmosphere was a decisive influence on the poetico-musical development of Kurt Weill, and nurtured within itself, through a process of transfiguration on the one hand and radicalization on the other, the well-known theatrical works in para-expressionistic style written by Weill in collaboration with Brecht: *Mahagonny* (1927), *Die Dreigroschenoper* (The three-pence opera, 1928), *Aufstieg und Fall der Stadt Mahagonny* (The rise and fall of Mahagonny, 1930), *Happy End* (1929), and *Der Jasager* (The yes-man, 1930).

If the link between musical Expressionism and cabaret music, with its grotesque, corrosive deformation, is something perceptible even at a first hearing, far more problematic is the relationship between Expressionism and the twelve-note system, which is one of the major inventions of twentieth-century music, and indeed of all modern music. Certainly, in its beginnings the twelve-note system may have seemed, to the ear traditionally attuned to the *temperamentum aequabile* and the system based on the tonalities, something "deforming," dreamlike and spectral: in short, it may have seemed like a "poetics" typical of the Expressionistic climate. But in fact, as it developed and evolved, the technique of composition with twelve notes (the twelve semitones into which the "natural" octave is subdivided), and with sequences of notes rigorously chosen from the twelve and stably fixed, so as to constitute an "order" taking the place of the old tonality, it contained within itself the potential for repudiating the Expressionistic tendency, which was by definition anarchic and destabilizing. This happened especially in Schönberg, who was the great inventor and theorist of the twelve-note system, though his claim to chronological precedence in the invention was bitterly contested by Joseph Mathias Hauer (Wiener Neustadt, 19 March 1883 – Vienna, 22 September 1959). It happened to a lesser degree in those other composers, mentioned above, who accepted Expressionism as part of their creative physiognomy; it did not happen, least of all in their theatrical works, in Schönberg's two greatest heirs, Berg and Webern. Schönberg was an Expressionist in the period during which, moving away from the youthful works which show a strong influence from Wagner, Brahms and Mahler (*Verklärte Nacht, Pelleas und Mélisande, Gurrelieder*), he created magisterial, experimental, visionary works written within the ambit of suspended or indefinite tonality and of atonality (or properly speaking, as Schönberg himself pointed out, "polytonality," since there is not a single bar of music before the twelve-tone system that "does not have" a tonality). He was an Expressionist, as we have seen, in works such as *Pierrot lunaire, Erwartung*, and *Die glückliche Hand*. Certainly, in that period there were premonitions of twelve-tone and serial music: a sequence of six ascending notes, all at intervals of a fourth

Die Theoretiker der Atonalität!
The theorists of atonality!
Nazi document
against modern music

(D, G, C, F, B flat, E flat) opens the *Kammersymphonie* op. 9 (1906); a complete series of twelve notes is an apparition, for the first time in Schönberg,[7] in the Scherzo of a symphonic sketch of 1914–15. But they were just that, apparitions, which have the effect of a ghost suddenly looming toward us. The Expressionistic climate is thereby accentuated. But from 1923, with the rigorous application of the twelve-note series in *Fünf Klavierstücke* op. 23, Schönberg's musical language tends to build itself up as a rational, mathematical and perfectly stable system, leaving the expressionistic experience behind it. Toward the end of the twenties, in Austria and Germany, another stylistic tendency supplanted Expressionism, though inheriting its anti-rhetoricity and its anti-bourgeois spirit: this was the *Neue Sachlichkeit* (New Objectivity), the inspiration for an art that was "useful," beneficial to society, didactic and pedagogic. Hindemith was its greatest representative in music between the late twenties and the early forties, but Schönberg, too, adhered to the new poetics in some of his compositions, such as the choral pieces of op. 35 and 44, and the vocal and instrumental *Canons* of the thirties. In the case of Berg and Webern, however, the adoption of the twelve-note language did not take the composers away from the poetics of Expressionism. On the contrary, trauma, anguish and solitude quiver with immense energy in *Wozzeck* and *Lulu*, and pervade Webern's *Drei Gesänge* op. 23 and *Drei Lieder* op. 25. Here we are in the presence of Expressionistic masterpieces "outside their time," especially by virtue of a vocality which in Berg and Webern reaches its expressive peak in underpinning, through the emotions, the negativity of the world. And yet a very strong Expressionistic echo still rings on, "outside its time," until the beginning of the thirties, in a composition of Schönberg's, the *Begleitmusik für eine Lichtspielszene* ("Music to Accompany a Scene from a Film"), of 1929–30, divided into three parts with unequivocal titles: "Danger Threatening," "Fear," "Catastrophe." The film, which was never completed, or even planned, has been imagined in more recent years by the film director Jean-Marie Straub, who "modelled" it on Schönberg's music which in 1930 had been left a spirit without a body. The score was in fact commissioned from Schönberg by a German musical publishing house which had suggested to various composers that they write a piece for a hypothetical film. This was all part, in the days of the silent film (already under threat from the talkie in 1929), of a practice widespread in the film industry: that of keeping in reserve "cue sheets," ready-made music of a particular type, to be used as an interchangeable repertoire for a wide variety of films. This might lead us on to another theme, that of the relationship between music and the cinema. But the alluring topic of expressionistic cinema would require a specific discussion of its own.[8]

Alban Berg, "Interludium"
Lulù, unfinished
page 58, autographic manuscript
facsimile
Vienna
Archiv der Universal Edition

[1] *L'espressionismo*, edited by Luigi Rognoni, *L'esistenzialismo*, edited by Enzo Paci Torino: Edizioni Radio Italiana (E.R.I.),1953; Luigi Rognoni, *Espressionismo e dodecafonia*. Torino: Einaudi, 1954, revised under the title *La scuola musicale di Vienna*. Torino: Einaudi, 1966; Ladislao Mittner, *L'espressionismo*. Bari: Laterza, 1965.

[2] Guido Pannain, *Musicisti dei tempi nuovi*. Torino: Paravia, 1932, p. 59.

[3] Edgar Wind, *Art and Anarchy. The Rieth Lectures 1960 Revised and Enlarged*. London: Faber and Faber, 1963, p. 2.

[4] Letter from Traunkirchen, 20 July 1922: "Ich stehe allen diesen Bewegungen mit nicht viel Sympathie gegenüber [...] Nicht kommt rascher zum Stillstand, als diese Bewegungen, die von so vielen hervorgerufen werden. Übrigens tragen ja alle diese Leute bloß unsere Haut - Ihre und meine - zu Markte" (Arnold Schönberg, *Briefe*, ausgewählt und herausgegeben von Erwin Stein. Mainz: Schott, 1958, p. 70).

[5] This letter, too, is dated Traunkirchen, 20 July 1922 (Schönberg, *Briefe*, prints only part of it, not including the brief passage referred to here).

[6] The lecture was published in a booklet that accompanied the recorder version of op. 22 directed by Robert Craft.

[7] For the first time in Schönberg, but not for the first time ever. As is well known, Luigi Dallapiccola pointed out that there is an unmistakable, perfect series of twelve notes in Mozart's *Don Giovanni*, in the final statue scene, to the words "Non si pasce di cibo mortale chi si pasce di cibo celeste."

[8] For those who wish to go further into the themes touched on here, the following are recommended as essential introductory reading: Luigi Rognoni, *La scuola musicale di Vienna*. Torino: Einaudi, 1966; Alain Poirier, *L'expressionisme et la musique*. Paris: Fayard, 1996; *Théorie des Expressionismus*. Stuttgart: Reclam, 1976 (with texts by Benn, Däubler, Döblin, Goll, Hasenclever, Kaiser, Kandinsky, Kokoschka, and others); Klaus Budzinski, *Das Kabarett*. Düsseldorf: Econ Taschenbuch, 1985; Mario Bortolotto, s.v. *Espressionismo*, in *Dizionario enciclopedico universale della musica e dei musicisti*: Lessico, vol. II. Torino: Utet, 1983, p. 145-52.

Thomas Friedrich

"What did the Patheticists want? They wanted to give content to the pictures. They wanted great stirring content. They wanted to once again create art that would seize hold of the people and of humanity, not just satisfy the aesthetic fancies of a small faction."[1] It was in these terms that Jakob Steinhardt, a member of the Patheticist art group, who penned these lines, expressed one of the most widely held sentiments among the artists and poets of Expressionism. The style of these Expressionist activists degenerated inevitably into sermonizing, exhortation or rebellion, according to one account[2] which claims the movement made a principled "turn toward the public", fundamentally distancing itself from art and poetry toward the beginning of this century. In its original form, the radical Expressionist message was noisily and publicly proclaimed, often through the use of posters. The Expressionists are praised for their commitment to making their message public, both in poetry and in the visual arts.

"Instead of breaking off into ever smaller factions as they did around 1900 and painstakingly isolating themselves from the majority of the population, by venerating a style of aristocratic reserve that had an elitist ring to it, movements of artists like Die Brücke (The Bridge) or Der Blaue Reiter (The Blue Rider) were established. This opened their work up to a broader audience which they set about to influence in their own way. In the course of this public turn the Expressionist painters were only too willing to set themselves up as activists, devoting themselves to woodcuts, newspaper and magazine illustrations… intending to reach the greatest possible number of people with their work."[3]

This argument sounds convincing, particularly in light of the vociferously proclaimed declarations of many Expressionists. Less persuasive is the argument that the secessionists were adverse to opening up to the public.[4] In this context it should however be questioned to what extent the Expressionists didn't just pay lip service to the "Publicity Principle" but actually practised it.

In 1905 – the year the art group the Brücke was founded in Dresden – the art critic Max Osborn, in his work on the history of woodcuts, argued that over the course of the nineteenth century the woodcut progressively shifted from being an artistic to being a booksellers' concern. "We scarcely come across any famous names anymore, and the few we do encounter did not earn their reputation in this domain."[5]

Observing the most immediate past however, Osborn came to the opposite conclusion: that thanks to the reception of Japanese woodcut art, a new era had begun for European woodcuts. As European pioneers of a new woodcut art, he cites notably William Morris, Felix Vallotton and, in the realm of German culture, Otto Eckmann, Peter Behrens and Emil Orlik. And considering the works of Viennese artists affiliated with the review *Ver Sacrum* and similar tendencies in Germany, it would appear, Osborn claims, that throngs of talent in all art centers were pressing to "delve into this forgotten area of art." He even chanced the prediction that "the next few years will witness an even more significant and lively interest in this area." Obviously the old folk's art aspect of woodcuts was long gone. Lithography and photomechanical techniques had relegated woodcuts to a very minor role as far as mass reproduction procedures were concerned, making them an object of ever more graphical refinement. In essence, the democrat who fitted in everywhere with the people had become a sensitive, highly refined aristocrat, addressing only a small circle and satisfied when he met with their approval.[6]

Max Osborn thus inadvertently described the dilemma that was shortly to confront Expressionist groups as they turned away from the conventional art world – which in their eyes also included the secessionist modern movements – in their quest for a new unity between artists and the people, between art and life. They were not long in electing the woodcut initially as their exclusive, and later as their preferred graphic medium, consequently relying on the work of those artists mentioned by Osborn, such as Emil Orlik (others, particularly Edvard Munch, should also be noted in this context)[7],. And yet the Expressionists systematically appealed to the techniques of old German woodcutting and its (real or supposed) proximity to the everyday reality of the people, all the more so as the robust hand-craftsmanship of the woodcutters was in contradiction to their self-perception as artists. Ernst Ludwig Kirchner for instance never tired of holding up Albrecht Dürer as an example for the work of the Brücke artists.[8]

In the context of such justifications – by no means rare in Kirchner's case – the influence of contemporary artists is all the more valuable. The Brücke artists in fact were familiar with periodicals like *Pan*, *Die Insel* and *Kunst und Künstler* which kept Germany up to date on modern European art and featured the work of illustrators like Bruno Paul whose "sweeping curved Art

Max Pechstein, poster for *An die Laterne*, 1919, color lithography

Nouveau style lines appeared to exert a lingering influence on more than a few woodcuts by the Brücke artists."[9] These artists also had to escape the all powerful effect of Art Nouveau in publishing and illustrating, which had "on the whole paved the way for Expressionism".[10]

Above and beyond such considerations, the turn toward woodcuts had another perfectly trivial reason: it was lack of money pure and simple that led the not so very well off artists to pick up gouges and chisels. There were also financial reasons which pushed the Brücke artists to cut various commercial artworks in wood, including printing membership and invitation cards, lists of their "passive members" (friends and patrons of the artists), progress reports, and posters. Even their early exhibition catalogues contained original woodcuts based on works being shown, that the artists "reproduced in woodcut for purely financial reasons."[11] This "however" touches upon the dilemma of the Expressionist woodcutter, that Max Osborn had pointed to in his "democratic–aristocratic" opposition.

If graphic artists were to reach the public with their works, chiefly woodcuts, they not only had to present their exhibitions, they had to take steps to ensure the reproduction of their work. Photographs were expensive, and if the artists didn't have the financial means to reproduce the works – for instance in a large circulation magazine – they were obliged to disseminate them as original graphics, in other words print woodcuts from their stocks, which only allowed for a limited number of copies.

This predicament led the artists – at any rate in the early and flourishing years of Expressionist book illustrating – to turn toward an elite circle of bibliophiles and book collectors. In the worst cases, their works remained unprinted for decades or even for their whole lives: Erich Heckel's woodcut for Oscar Wilde's *Ballad of Reading Gaol*, was done in 1907 and only came out in book form in 1963, seven years before Heckels' death; or Ernst Ludwig Kirchner's seven woodcuts in color done in 1915–16 for Adelbert von Charnisso's "Peter Schlemihl", which in fact only came out in 1974, decades after the artist's death (1938). The first series of publications to open their pages to Expressionist illustrators were the *Lyrischen Flugblätter* (*Lyrical Leaflets*) founded in 1907 by the small Berlin publisher A. R. Meyer. In 1913, Ludwig Meidner and Else Lasker-Schuler contributed front-page drawings to various issues. One of the series' highpoints came in 1913 with the publication of Alfred Döblin's short novel *Das Stifsfräulein und der Tod* (The Canoness and Death) with woodcuts by Ernst Ludwig Kirchner. Exceptions aside, it is true that up until 1914 only some 500 copies of he *Lyrischen Flugblätter* were printed:[12] it reached only a tiny, connoisseur public.

This situation only changed profoundly after the 1918 November revolution when Expressionist artists sought to reach not only the lovers of avant-garde literature with their book-jacket drawings and illustrations, but also a politically agitated mass public. Wouldn't what has just been said about the situation of book illustrating not also hold for the equally limited editions of posters done by Expressionist artists? While the extremely limited collectors' editions were destined for an elect public, posters, even if printed in small quantities, are by definition publicly oriented. For the time being, the new start, and in particular the posters of artists like Oskar Kokoschka, Wassily Kandinsky and members of the Brücke artists with their innovative pictorial language and formal composition, was "not yet prevalent on the poster wall.

The development into modernity, the clear-sighted break with the inherited ideal of beauty was brought about in painters' studios instead. The place where these revolutionary events showed up in posters was consequently not on the poster wall, but was in the art dealer's show window and in collectors' files."[13] Accordingly the Expressionists' posters were a unique species: "Original Artists' Posters."[14]

For all of that, the "original artist's poster" was not entirely unprecedented. Artistically designed posters for art exhibitions date back to the beginning of the history of modern posters,[15] and among the designers one finds many such illustrious names as Ludwig von Hoffmann and Franz von Stuck. It seemed perfectly natural for instance for the newly founded Berlin secession to challenge the "Great Berlin Art Exhibition's" poster with their own.[16] As shown in a shot of the Spittelmarkt, a lively square in Berlin's business district, by the Berlin photographer W. Titzenthaler, posters advertising the exhibition of the Berlin secession were put up even in the city center: Thomas Theodor Heine's poster for the 1901 secession exhibition can be spotted on an advertising kiosk in the middle of the square. The poster caused quite a stir among onlookers: "It was lauded and it was decried, but everybody remembered it", observed one contemporary.[17] On

Ernst Ludwig Kirchner, frontispiece for *Das Stiftsfräulein und der Tod* (The Canoness and Death) by A. Döblin woodcut

Oskar Kokoschka drawing for the cover of *Der Sturm* no. 20, 14 July 1910

Conrad Felixmüller
cover for *Die Aktion*, February 1921
woodcut

Richard Seewald, cover for *Revolution*
no. 1, 15 October 1913

César Klein, *Arbeiter Bürger
Bauern Soldaten*, poster for the elections
of the representatives
to the National Assembly, 1919
color lithography

some occasions, art exhibition posters also featured statements on current issues: a poster also designed by Thomas Theodor Heine in 1905 made ironic reference to Kaiser Wilhelm II's notorious remark about "gutter art."[18]

In this context, the Brücke artists made themselves known through the posters they had been making since 1906 to publicize their own exhibitions. It is very probable they were aware of how frequently in previous years posters had led to sensation and even scandal. Nothing is known of the public reception the Brücke's exhibition posters met with during the Dresden years; what has however been established is the outraged reaction of certain art critics toward Max Pechstein's poster for the first exhibition of the "New Secession" (in partnership with the other Brücke artists) in Berlin in 1910. "The exhibition catalogue shows a plump, naked Indian woman, her bow in firing position. Here is the message: the revolt of a raw, primitive art instinct against civilization, culture and taste in art", was the judgment passed by the Munich magazine *Der Kunstwart*.[19] While the Expressionists failed to gain access to a wider public in book illustrating and only seldom managed to do so in poster art, their ultimate success in building up a journalistic network of periodicals and collections was all the more remarkable.

It was indeed a journalistic constellation at the beginning of the century which forced them outright to turn toward the public in their own reviews. While periodicals created at the turn of the century (*Kunst und Künstler* for instance) came to be a forum for artists of the modern secession movements, in which thorough and generally favorable accounts were given of their activities and especially their exhibitions, just the opposite held true for the Expressionists: "Right from the beginning the Expressionists had their troubles with the critical clique. The press played on every register, from head-shaking incomprehension to furious attacks."[20]

It was two Berlin editors who ventured the first step to autonomy by creating periodicals independent of one another, which in terms both of content and form were to play an exemplary role for Expressionist publications on the whole. The tone was set in March 1910 by Herwarth Walden with the founding of the periodical *Der Sturm*. In the first issue he stated: "We have resolved to be our own publisher. We have done so because we believe that culture and the arts can still be dealt with in the domain of journalism and feuilletonism."[21] For three years *Der Sturm* came out as a weekly, later as a bimonthly, then from 1918 on as a monthly, and for its first nine years in a format which was unusually large for a periodical. From the eighth number on, *Der Sturm* printed drawings, linocuts and woodcuts on the cover page, thus acquiring its distinctive look, a poster-like blend of title headings, script and pictures. The effect of the twentieth issue, which came out on 14 July 1910, was epoch-making, featuring a play by Oskar Kokoschka and one of his drawings on the title page. Before long, Walden had transformed the periodical, which he quickly affiliated with a publishing house and a gallery (where evening readings were organized and, from 1918 on, plays were staged), from being a vehicle of the artists of the Brücke and the Blaue Reiter, into a forum for the European cultural avant-garde, whose graphics (often original woodcuts) were at the heart of the *Sturm* circle right up until the time of the First World War. On 20 February 1911, the first issue of the review *Die Aktion*, edited by Franz Pfemfert, came out; for almost a decade, from 1913 on, it was to create its own unmistakable look, its front cover featuring illustrations, and especially woodcuts or drawings, by Ludwig Meidner, Max Oppenheimer, and Conrad Felixmüller amongst others. Its example would occasionally be imitated by others, as by *Revolution* which came out in Munich in 1913.

Aside from the personal rivalry and different focuses of the editors of *Der Sturm* and *Die Aktion* (Walden tended to favor the artistic, and Pfemfert the literary avant-garde), the two periodicals complemented each other, even if the contributors' circles were partially overlapping. Following the Berlin example, other, often very short-lived operations started up: in May 1914, there were at least fifteen Expressionist-leaning reviews, six others had already folded. The world war in no way curtailed the setting-up of still further reviews, and after the 1918–19 revolution there was a positive flurry of review creation.

One bibliographical index enumerates 100 periodicals, 52 yearbooks, collective editions and almanacs as well as 30 book series,[22] an output creating a communications network all the more unparalleled as it was wholly brought about by the personal initiative of Expressionist journalists, poets and artists, outside the sphere of established publishing.

With the November 1918 revolution and the abolition of censorship, the political freedom of the periodicals increased, bringing about more dramatic changes in the public impact of poster art

Erich Ludwig Stahl, Otto Arpke
poster for *Das Cabinet des Dr. Caligari*
(*The Cabinet of Dr. Caligari*)
by Robert Wiene, 1920
color lithography

Josef Fenneker, *Luna-park
Berlin-Halensee*
poster for Berlin-Halensee funfair, 1921
color lithography

than of book illustrating. Previously, Expressionists' posters were only seldom able to attract attention; after the collapse of the empire however the situation turned completely around. It was artists like Max Pechstein and Cesar Klein, from the so-called November groups controlled by the Expressionists, who between 1918–19 picked up government contracts to design posters calling for public participation in the rebuilding of the republic, and above all encouraging people to get out and vote in the February 1919 national elections.[23] "A new chapter in the history of the poster" was how the arts journalist Adolf Behne saw the posters' design and emotive form: "A reaching beyond the habitual… the most essential part of which was the urgency with which they broke with convention."[24]

It was the first time that Expressionist artists were given a commission, in this case by the social-democratic government, to produce posters and to bring them out in massive editions. Their impact was controversial and there were no further contracts. For the next one or two years, the Expressionist poster was used primarily for advertising Expressionist films, petering out with the latter. The same went for book cover illustrations and similar work done by Expressionist artists: after a "boom" in 1919–20, the Expressionist wave soon ebbed away.

The ending of inflation in November 1923, and the mental and socio-economic changes it brought with it, is often put forth as the first important break in German history after the First World War and at the same time the cause of the "death of Expressionism". While naturally linked to this, the collapse of Expressionist publicity had still other causes. In the Weimar Republic, *Der Sturm* turned into an art review like the rest, only more poorly printed, while people who had supported the avant-garde since 1917 were behind Paul Westheim's *Kunstblatt*, far more professional in terms of its print quality. *Die Aktion* became more and more a sectarian paper with a radical left agenda, in which art came to be used only as a weapon. Generally speaking, under the new circumstances, the Expressionist papers, conceived as organs of struggle against an ubiquitous philistinism, ceased to be relevant. And if after 1918, Expressionism, in degenerate form, became fashionable for a short while, the fate of Expressionist commercial art was that of every fashion – it was superseded by the next one. Thus for the Expressionists, the (unrestrained) turn toward the public proved to be not an elixir for life, but rather the beginning of the end.

[1] In his posthumous "Kurzen Lebenslauf". Quoted in Gerda Breuer and Ines Wagemann, *Ludwig Meidner, Zeichner, Maler, Literat 1884–1966*, vol. II, Stuttgart, 1991, p. 18.

[2] Richard Hamann and Jost Hermand, "Expressionismus" (*Deutsche Kunst und Kultur von der Gründerzeit bis zum Expressionismus*, vol. IV), Berlin, 1975, p. 41.

[3] R. Hamann and J. Hermand, "Expressionismus", p. 55.

[4] On the contrary, nothing is more characteristic for the Berlin secession around Max Liebermann as its great public resonance which secessionist members actively worked at bringing about through exhibitions along with posters and catalogues.

[5] Max Osborn, *Der Holzschnitt* (Collection of Illustrated Monographs, 16), Bielefeld and Leipzig, 1905, p.106.

[6] Ibid., pp. 13, 146, 150.

[7] Concerning the influences on the early pictorial language of the Brücke artists, see Alexander Drückers, *Graphik der "Brücke" im Berliner Kupferstichkabinett*, Berlin, 1984, p. 10.

[8] Horst Jähner, *Künstlergruppe Brücke. Geschichte einer Gemeinschaft und das Lebenswerk ihrer Repräsentanten*, Berlin, 1984, p. 26. Ernst Ludwig Kirchner, *Chronik KG Brücke*, 1913, quoted from the reprint in Heinz Spielmann, Christian Rathke and Hermann Gerlinger, eds., *Die Maler der "Brücke"*, Hermann Gerlinger Collection, Stuttgart, 1995, p. 124.

[9] Hans Bolliger, *Die Publikationen und Dokumente der Künstlergruppe "Brücke"* [1959]. Quoted from the reprint in Magdalena M. Moeller, ed., *Die Jahresmappen der "Brücke" 1906–1912*, Berlin, Brücke-Archiv 17/1989, p. 14.

[10] Lothar Lang, *Expressionistische Buchillustrationen in Deutschland 1907-1927*, Leipzig, 1975, p. 14.

[11] H. Bolliger, *Die Pubblicationen…*, (fn. 9), p. 23.

[12] Paul Raabe, *Die Zeitschriften und Sammlungen des literarischen Expressionismus. Repertorium der Zeitschriften, Jahrbücher, Anthologien, Sammelwerke, Schriftenreihen und Almanache 1910-1921*, Stuttgart, 1964, p. 168.

[13] Herbert Schindler, *Monografie des Plakats. Entwicklung Stil Design*, München, 1972, p. 149.

[14] Schindler, *Monografie…*

[15] See the illustrations in *Kunst! Kommerz! Visionen! Deutsche Plakate 1888-1933*, exhibition catalogue, Berlin, German Historical Museum, 1992, p. 39 ff.

[16] See the illustrations of the poster designed by Wilhelm Schulz for the second exhibition of the Berlin Secession in 1900, in *Kunst! Kommerz! Visionen!*, p. 63.

[17] Klaus von Rheden, "Plakate und Plakatstil," in *Velhagen & Klasings Monatshefte*, Jg. 18 (1903–04), H. 3. p. 310.

[18] An illustration of the poster may be found in *Kunst! Kommerz! Visionen!*, (fn. 15), p. 67.

[19] Quoted *in Expressionisten. Die Avantgarde in Deutschland 1905–1920*, exhibition catalogue, Staatliche Museen zu Berlin, Nationalgalerie und Kupferstichkabinett, Berlin, 1986, p. 90.

[20] Corona Hepp, *Avantgarde, Moderne Kunst, Kulturkritik und Reformbewegungen nach der Jahrhundertswende*, Munich, 1987, p. 109.

[21] Quoted in Paul Raabe, loc. cit. (fn.12), p. 25.

[22] Paul Raabe, loc. cit. (fn. 12), p. V-VIII.

[23] See Klaus Popitz, *Plakate der Zwanziger Jahre aus der Kunstbibliothek Berlin*, Berlin, 1977, p. 12.

[24] Adolf Behne, "Alte und neue Plakate", in *Das politische Plakat*, official edition, Berlin, 1919, p. 11.

Das Cabinet des Dr. Caligari
(Decla, 1920), by Robert Wiene
sets by Hermann Warm
Walter Reimann, Walter Röhrig
Bologna, Cineteca Comunale

Expressionist Film as an "Angewandte Kunst"*

Leonardo Quaresima

The term "Expressionist film" enjoys wide currency and notoriety, and yet as a definition its edges have been regarded with reservation as being too blurry and extensive. The uncertainty does not only concern the appropriateness of the term itself, however; the real issue at stake is the very field the definition is supposed to designate. Furthermore, the borders of the area of discussion also change position dramatically: at times they expand to embrace the entire period of German silent film, at others they shrink to include a mere handful of films (no more than half a dozen).

The uncertainty first surfaces in Siegfried Kracauer's and Lotte Eisner's classic studies on Weimar film production published after the war, and becomes steadily more acute with the ensuing publications, through to the (not numerous) more recent studies, which tend to balk when it comes to tackling the issue head-on in an organic way.[1]

This preamble does not intend to rehearse old issues. Important, decisive transformations of the debate have taken place in the past few years, such that to write about Expressionist film today is almost a completely new undertaking. A different concept of film archiving and a growing awareness of philological issues have given rise to a framework that was inconceivable a decade hence. New finds among the archives, reconstructions, restorations, new items – even in the question of color (to which the few stills included with this essay bear witness),[2] titles, and film music; greater attention to the sources as a whole (from the multiple copies of a single film, to the critical reception of a film upon its release): all these elements have not so much carried the study and analysis to a new pass, as generated a wholly new object of study.

It is no wonder, then, that a new inquiry into this field today will elicit many a reformulation of old issues, while making unexpected headway in new directions.

The history begins with the release in February 1920 of the film *The Cabinet of Doctor Caligari*, directed by Robert Wiene based on a screenplay by Hans Janowitz and Carl Mayer. Produced by Decla studios, the art directors were Walter Reimann, Walter Röhrig, and Hermann Warm; the cast included Werner Krauss (who starred in the Berlin stage productions of *Die Koralle*, and *Seeschlacht*, 1918), and Conrad Veidt (who had acted in the same plays). The grisly and haunting tale, the use of scenery with an overtly Expressionist pictorial style, and, in particular, the adoption of the kind of set-design that was typical of Expressionist theater, plus the performance of actors borrowed from the new stage current – all this left an enormous impression on the audience of the time, and heralded one of the most intense and rich periods in German silent film production.

While this outline may seem to vary little from the traditional analysis of film history, some of the implications allow for a new and original assessment. The new direction taken was not a chance, one-off venture undertaken by a group of young artists. Quite the opposite, it was the upshot of a precise agenda that was pondered by the German film industry. The resounding success of "Caligari" was neither accidental nor just lucky; it was piloted by a concerted promotional campaign that focused on its novelty and the surprise pairing of the film medium with the Expressionist movement.

The producers' goal was to give a new impulse to the film industry, grafting on its thematic repertoire, its stylistic resources, and its communicative basis the potential of the avantgarde movement. The operation was launched to break the stalemate in the industry, which had seen a rapid drying up of ideas, hackneyed repetition of themes, and the growing ennui of the audiences, who were tired of the traditional film genres, and of the "Sensationsfilm" in particular. The industry's new gamble involved drawing in a new class of figures from the art world (directors, actors, authors, stage designers, painters) who had no prior experience of the new medium, and were required to bring about a leap in quality, to shepherd the medium toward a new standard.

The phenomenon had had an important precedent in Germany in the form of the "Autorenfilm," a new genre of *auteur* productions. In the two years 1912 and 1913 the German film industry had undergone a crucial shift in scale which had completely transformed it at various levels (from the narrative and linguistic level, to those of production and presentation), through the collaboration of certain leading literary and theater figures (including Schnitzler, Hofmannsthal, Hauptmann, Reinhardt, Moissi, Bassermann).[3] In this context, marked by the transition of film production from the small company setup to an industry proper, also an important contribution of Expressionism took place. Kurt Pinthus had assembled a number of authors (Else Lasker-Schüler, Walter Hasenclever, Albert Ehrenstein, Ludwig Rubiner, *et al.*), who put together a *Kinobuch* of new

Hans Heinz von Twardowski
Lil Dagover, Friedrich Fehér
in *The Cabinet of Doctor Caligari*
Bologna, Cineteca Comunale

Conrad Veidt and Werner Krauß
in *The Cabinet of Doctor Caligari*
Bologna, Cineteca Comunale

The Cabinet of Doctor Caligari
Bologna, Cineteca Comunale

screenplays, only one of which,[4] however, ever got beyond the project stage. After the success of "Caligari," the attempts increased, also from the smaller studios, to reorient the production in the same direction. Many critical assessments of the years in question speak of a "Caligari mania," confirming the extent of the phenomenon. Even the organization of public viewing adapted to the craze, spawning "Expressionist" movie theaters, and the restructuring of existing theaters on the basis of the same criteria.[5] Advertising also received an overhaul. For months the graphics of the film publicity went Expressionist, even when the film being advertised had nothing to do with the new trend. The entire film sector (reacting either positively or negatively, as discussed further on) reacted to the new situation as the beginning of a new era.

That same year saw the announcement of the release of *Von morgens bis mitternachts*,[6] from the stage work by Georg Kaiser, directed by Karl Heinz Martin (who had already directed the stage version at the Thalia Theater in Hamburg in September 1918), with sets designed by Robert Neppach, and starring Ernst Deutsch (the lead in the 1916 stage production of *Der Sohn* in Dresden). The same director (together with Rudolf Leonhard for the screenplay) filmed *Das Haus zum Mond* (1923, since lost), once again with sets by Robert Neppach, and the participation on-screen of Fritz Kortner (another of the up-and-coming stars of Expressionist theater). Robert Wiene filmed *Genuine*, with sets by César Klein. Taking advantage of the contribution of the Expressionist architect Hans Poelzig, who unlike those before him built fully three-dimensional sets for the film, recreating a medieval ghetto, Paul Wegener filmed the second version of *The Golem*. Walter Reimann employed his imagination also in the realization of *Algol*, directed by Hans Werckmeister, based on an original idea of the "union of Expressionist-Cubist sets in a naturalistic environment."[7] The film *Masken* (lost) by William Wauer was hailed, with negative assessments, by the critics as another contribution to the new trend. In 1921 we find Neppach once more among the credits of *Brandherd* (1921), scripted by Carl Mayer and directed by Hans Kobe. Ensuing films resumed the "programmatic" framework of these first works, *Raskolnikow* (*Crime and Punishment*, 1923, again by Wiene, sets by Andreev), *Wachsfigurenkabinett* (Waxworks, 1924, by Paul Leni, costumes by Ernst Stern).

There are also many films, either lost or destroyed, which are mentioned in the press reviews of the period for their adoption (albeit partial) of a similar aesthetic outlook. These include *Toteninsel* by Carl Froelich (sets by Warm, Röhrig, and Robert Herlth); *Der zeugende Tod* by Heinz Sarnow, released in 1920; *Das zweite Leben* by Alfred Halm; *Zirkus des Lebens* by Johannes Guter (screenplay by Janowitz, for the acting of W. Krauß), presented in 1921. Others include *Zwischen Abend und Morgen* by Arthur Robison; *Der Puppenmacher von Kiang-Ning* by Robert Wiene (again with the collaboration of César Klein), all released in 1923. In the meantime, the after-effects of "Caligari" can also be noted, either directly or indirectly, in some of the most progressive films of German production, such as F. W. Murnau's *Nosferatu* (*idem*, 1922); *Schatten* (*Warning Shadows*, 1923) by Arthur Robison; *Der Schatz* (*The Treasure*, 1923) by G. W. Pabst; *Faust* (*idem*, 1926), also by Murnau. Moreover in "Kammerspielfilme" (or in the *Hintertreppe*, 1921, by Leopold Jessner; *Der letzte Mann/The Last Laugh*, 1924, by Murnau), whose intimistic and psychological framework is something of an antithesis to the Expressionist one, though in iconographic terms – particularly in the way the cityscape is represented – utilize and even vaunt the same models. Or in the "Straßenfilme" (*Die Straße/The Street*, 1923, by Karl Grune, working alongside the Expressionist painter Ludwig Meidner). The list ends with *Metropolis* (1927) by Fritz Lang, the most eclectic in its range of materials and references, but the work which is the one that on dramatic, iconographic, and thematic level represents a sort of recapitulation of "Expressionist cinema so far," and a threshold of this field.

The Expressionist components find their source in figurative field (from easel painting to scenery painting), architecture (the aforementioned Poelzig; but the utopian visions of the Gläserne Kette also fired the imagination), and in terms of subject matter: from the visionary realm of prose and poetry (*Die andere Seite/The Other Side* by Alfred Kubin; the poetry of Georg Heym, van Hoddis, and others), to the motifs of rebellion that emerged in new theater works. In the latter, far greater, arena (but also for many films of the former group), the new forms were grafted onto material of a highly heterogeneous nature and cohabited with different principles and styles. From Romanticism to Symbolism, from Naturalism to Heimatkunst; or, more simply and frequently, they were interwoven with characters, themes and settings, imagery typical of the literary subculture (adventure stories, exotic tales, melodrama, and detective stories) that under-

Friedrich Fehér
in *The Cabinet of Doctor Caligari*
Bologna, Cineteca Comunale

The director Paul Wegener
in *Der Bettle*
litograph by Bruno Paul, 1917
Munich, Theater Museum

The Golem (Union, 1920)
by Paul Wegener and Carl Boese
sets by Hans Poelzig
Bologna, Cineteca Comunale

pinned the storyline and the imagery of the films of the period. In some cases – particularly in 1920–21, when the trend issued from a precise program – we find the Expressionist style in a more "dominant" position and function, such that the other components are reshuffled into a new hierarchy. In other contexts, Expressionism as such becomes a kind of "value-added" feature, a stylistic label to enliven the film's texture and ensure greater operativeness.

Within a wider process, set off by the Expressionist chapter, German cinema in the 1920s became a melting pot for arts of diverse nature, albeit within the terms imposed by the movement. The heavily distorted sets and backdrops, the sharp angles and tilted perspectives, the tendency to make inanimate objects biomorphic, were the result of a translation to film of features inferred from painting, theater, and architecture. Other ideas plundered from the realm of theater include the lighting techniques, which build a dramatic space through studied chiaroscuro effects and angled lighting. In this respect, architecture provided a further source of inspiration. But the heavy shadows, the stark contrast of black and white, are also a feature of Expressionist painting, and particularly of drawings and other graphic media used by the movement's artists. Some scenes of "Caligari" are reminiscent of *Der Sohn* (in the Kiel version, 1919); at the time were noticed visual affinities with the paintings of Lyonel Feininger.[8] The scenes of *Von morgens bis mitternachts* were created by Neppach as an explicit two-dimensional development using simplified visuals typical of woodcut. Some of the buildings in *Algol* take their form from the architecture of Bruno Taut and the Gläserne Kette group.[9] César Klein infused *Genuine* with the more typical features of his painterly style. Similarly, films such as *Der Golem, Lebende Buddhas* (Wegener, 1925), *Zur Chronik von Grieshuus* (Arthur von Gerlach, 1925), make direct references to Poelzig's researches – such as the overloaded gothic and baroque forms, and the modulation of elements of archaic and sacred grandeur – to the extent that in some periods it is impossible to determine whether some of the sketches of the artist were for a film or stage, or for some architectural project.[10] Also starting with the film collaborations of certain leading figures whose work focused on such imagery (Karl Heinz Martin, Leopold Jessner), interiors such as prisons, the world of machinery, stairways, street scenes, the settings of Expressionist stage productions, are all used and reused to the point that they have virtually become icons of German silent film.

Further to this, the Expressionist aesthetic also provided the ingredient of subjective experience, which the film medium picks up, warping interior space to resemble exteriors, but also by developing new ideas that transformed the camera into an original factor in organizing space and a protagonist of the action. "The camera is no longer simply an eye that sees, but a kind of alien presence… that moves with startling acquisitive urgency and penetration. A presence that does not contemplate, but violates… ceasing to be an eye, the camera has become a far more complex and active device by which 'showing' is just one of the various functions, and not the most important," wrote the Italian historian and art critic G.C. Argan.[11] Through its movement and shooting angles, the movie camera becomes a decisive factor in subjectivizing both the perception and the filmic space. In this respect, "Caligari" was still a film of the past, so to speak, but in certain later productions (from *Sylvester;* 1923 by Lupu Pick, to *Varieté/Variety*, 1926 by E.A. Dupont) managed to acquire a mode of expression that would be one of the most significant acquisitions of the silent period. These observations leave no doubt that there is still a great deal of study to be made into the cross-fertilization and reciprocal effects of other arts on the film medium. With the exception of Rudolf Kurtz's eminent assessment (*Expressionismus und Film*,[12] 1926), and Eisner's careful analysis of the influence of theater on Expressionist cinema, film historians have so far been rather vague and reluctant to deal with the issue. Some have even considered such links merely relative, but in an ingenuous conjecture, as when links were sought and analyzed between film and other systems of expression *excluding levels of mediation with diverse materials*, from "Trivialliteratur" to public entertainment, which film had engendered,[13] thereby overlooking a link that had been immediately evident to Pinthus in his compilation of the *Kinobuch*. "We have to get used to the fact that kitsch cannot be eliminated from the human world."[14] We are unlikely to get any satisfaction from drawing parallels between the formal framework of one of Kirchner's paintings and a German film from the early 1920s, but this is not the point. Film should be assessed as a medium in which the figuration, even of Kirchner's kind, encounters different models, namely, those of popular figuration and entertainment. Moreover, the circumstance should be interpreted as part of a process that was by no means alien to the Expressionist aesthetic. An underlying feature of the movement was the need for direct contact be-

Fern Andra in *Genuine*
(Decla, 1920) by Robert Wiene
sets by César Klein
Bologna, Cineteca Comunale

Fern Andra and Harald Paulen
in *Genuine*
Bologna, Cineteca Comunale

Fern Andra in *Genuine*
Bologna, Cineteca Comunale

Der Golem wie er in die Welt kam
Bologna, Cineteca Comunale

tween the poet and masses at large (and the utopian idea of a "total" art can be set in this framework), German Expressionist film can be seen as a logical and singularly "effective" outcome of this path. Furthermore, the moment this impulse produces an original merger of avant-garde elements and popular culture, film takes its place as an important chapter in German avant-garde (from Berlin Dada to Neue Sachlichkeit), in which its particular field of action is translated to the realm of forms and systems of mass communication.

In this movement film is an "angewandte Kunst," an applied art, by which the Expressionist aesthetic gradually extended its influence after World War I. Rudolf Arnheim reached this same conclusion in 1925, notwithstanding his critical and restrictive outlook. "The success that accompanied ["Caligari"] depended less on the suggestive force of the storyline or the acting as on the 'Expressionist' ornaments… But once the procedure of using oblique lines, bunching the houses together, and creating jagged outlines has become routine in set design for cabaret, theater, and cinema, and once the walls of even the most squalid little café boast the traits of the new fashion, then visual devices of this type become more conventional than progressive, and we realize that in this case (together with a lot of what has been touted at the art exhibitions) has nothing to do with Expressionism, meaning, the exposure of the 'essence of things'; what is actually happening is that the surfaces of objects have been reworked from a purely ornamental standpoint."[15] The film's style is at this point defined as an "entzückende[r] Tapetenstil" and its proposals superseded by advertising strategies. "When the Dr. Caligari's obsession is expressed in the form of the exhortation 'Become Caligari!' projected onto walls and against the sky – now, in the year 1925, the fact that we are familiar with illuminated signs and slogans ehxorting us to 'Smoke Velascos!' tends to dampen the impact of this scene."

This "negative" observation (which is due to a misconceived idea of "avant-garde" that overlooks one of its fundamental aspects, namely, the very urge to exceed and go beyond itself, to penetrate the field of popular narrative and figuration and the culture industry and compete with their more typical forms of expression) testifies to the crucial role played by German film in this respect in the early 1920s. Another somewhat overlooked and underestimated factor is the role of cinema as a form of stimulus and frame of reference for Expressionist aesthetics, and the advances it fostered in other artistic spheres. The spheres most affected were theater and literature, but even painting (cf. the abstract components of Expressionism and the developments of "absoluter Film"). Although these questions have in fact been investigated (albeit relative to specific areas), a more global and detailed assessment has yet to be made.[16]

Such a study could prove fruitful for the historian of literature, theater, and art, though the finds would most likely lead back to the realm of cinema. In the case of *Von morgens bis mitternachts*, for example, such the study starts usually with a comparative analysis of the film with the original script, and then with preceding or almost coeval productions. Less frequent is the analysis of the specifically cinematographic aspects of Kaiser's original script.[17]

Regarding the aforementioned "program" behind a work like "Caligari," it is the kind of program that spawned a lot of outcomes, most of which have been generally overlooked.

We have already cited the effects "Caligari" had on the basic procedures of the film industry, including the adoption of a more coherent organization of the screening spaces; but the consequences can also be seen in the reaction of certain sectors of the industry, concerned about the changes under way in terms of standards of expression, and even on production methods.

Although the film was rated favorably, the comments tend to see it as a unique case and fear that it could spawn a "school" as such. The movie industry was actually wary of the growing avant-garde weight, and some feared that the film's influence might steer the industry's evolution away from the popular, mass distribution formula, or force changes in the sector's production methods and genre structure, and so forth. They were concerned that the cinema might become an elitist environment, a possibility presaged especially by the film *Genuine*. "Cinema must remain a thing of the masses; our films, for economical reasons, must be created with the masses in mind; but if they are steered off course by a Kunstfilm, then this Filmkunst has taken the wrong direction altogether."[18] But the project was accompanied by an astonishingly high estimation of the impact of the new trend at theoretical level. Expressionism was reckoned to be a vital catalyst for the industry in a global sense, a factor that would moreover enable the art form to exploit its most typical and original facets, and to correspond better with the "technical" nature of the film medium. Expressionist cinema was seen as a natural step in the "organic development" of the film in-

Ernst Deutsch in *Von morgens bis mitternachts* (Ilag-Film, 1920)
by Karl Heinz Martin
sets by Robert Neppach
Bologna, Cineteca Comunale

Portrait photo
of F.W. Murnau

Von morgens bis mitternachts
Bologna, Cineteca Comunale

The director Fritz Lang

dustry (Jhering).[19] Stated in even clearer terms, it was suddenly declared that the film medium was "expressionistic" per se. The cinema was not appraised for its dramatic potential, but for its visual qualities: "The eruptive nature of the imagery, the use of rapid sequences that manage to lend visual expression to the most fleeting mood, this is expressionism."[20] The film medium's inherent technical aspects, together with what was considered to be its authentic potential (the possibility to show the unreal, the supernatural, to project dreams: terrain that all the early film theoreticians held to be the medium's prerogatives), was paired with Expressionism and considered perfectly homologous: "The film medium," observed Robert Wiene, "lends itself naturally to the expression of the unreal, to representing it precisely in the Expressionist sense."[21] Wiene added that film allows a use of colors ("cinema is not, as most people like to believe, a black and white art; it has plenty to do with color"[22]) as Stimmungswerte. At the same time – and this is an interesting point – it was deemed capable of conveying the Expressionist "cry" by means of the technique of titles.

Other commentators underscore the affinities between the characteristics of the motion picture scenario and the choices of the new poet, the screenwriter: the screenplay embodied a kind of "compressed" style; it was no longer the essential phrase that counted, but words with *visual* impact. "A substantive, a verbal substantive stands for a sentence. One proceeds via sketches, eliminating the secondary elements. This kind of writing makes for a concentrated result, for clarity, ruling out vagueness."[23] As for the question of fantasy and dream-states, not only did the theorists stress (along with Wiene) the inherent syntony between the characteristics of film and Expressionism, they moreover pointed out the latter's contribution toward opening new possibilities for film, fostering the transition from the regime of "Vision" to that of "Visionäre."[24]

Another point in its favor was the cinema's ability to construct a coherent spatial system and weave a narrative thread through it: "What was particularly interesting about ["Caligari"] was not so much the plot (which could have been better), nor the actors' performance… but first and foremost the utterly novel concept of space."[25] As regards the process of subjectivization mentioned earlier, the discussion made altogether new inroads. What characterized Expressionist cinema, according to Alfred Polgar, was not merely the "skewed sets and Cubist-style landscapes;" what really distinguished it was its power to "project interior events toward the outside… this amazing opportunity to construct a universe from the distinct perspective of a given individual."[26] The commentators eventually reached an exact perception of the function assumed in this context by the "enfesselte Kamera."[27] For Jhering, the medium made it possible to break out of the dead-end of Naturalism, thanks to a new generation of stage actors ("cinema exists because new actors exist.")[28] Meanwhile, Balázs had begun to formulate a theory of film that took its cue from the characteristics of Expressionism: if this new medium could reveal the "latent physiognomy of things." "There was surely no other art form more capable of showing this hidden face of reality… Certainly, he conjectured, cinema is the most peculiar field for Expressionism, and perhaps its only legitimate homeland. Modern films all tend toward this mode of expression, even without wishing to, and sometimes without even realizing it."[29]

But the most surprising aspect that arose in the debate at the time was that cinematic Expressionism was ascribed a canon of its own, assigned the status of a cinematographic genre. From the time of the release of "Caligari", in most of the contributions to the debate (even those that manifest doubts or reservations) the term "Expressionist film" is used in an extensive sense, and not only to refer to individual films. The phase in question is characterized by new mechanisms of codification and categorization at production level. The industry passed from being a system that was still strongly "reproductive" (by which a successful film could be cloned to create a series of similar products) to being a system that comprised models or film genres with a production cycle of their own and solid mechanisms of reproduction. This process played a crucial role in the German film industry, as evidenced by the fact that in the ensuing years commentators increasingly indicated the industry's difficulty to properly develop this system of channeling and streamlining as one of the principal causes of its weakness. Expressionist film took its place in this framework, introducing an ulterior, strong element of novelty and transformation: by establishing a film category no longer on the basis of themes (as had largely been the case in the realm of "Kinodrama" and "Detektivfilm," etc.), but on a stylistic basis, in reference to a set of precise figurative, plastic and architectural ingredients. The transition brought sweeping changes at both production and theoretical level. The changes under way were punctually recorded and com-

Nosferatu (Prana-Film, 1922)
by F. W. Murnau
sets by Albin Grau
Bologna, Cineteca Comunale

Max Schreck in *Nosferatu*
Bologna, Cineteca Comunale

Greta Schröder in *Nosferatu*
Bologna, Cineteca Comunale

Nosferatu
Bologna, Cineteca Comunale

mented upon by the critics of the day, who on the one hand acknowledged the multiplicity of new models (not films) that were trying to get a foothold on the market; on the other, they contributed to the definition of the stylistic originality of the various new canons. In the post-Expressionist frenzy, various genres vied for position, including "Infantilismus," "Ballade," "Filmnovelle," "Stilfilm," and even "Kammerspielfilm."

The notion of style (anchored at various levels, from the sets to the camera technique) would play a fundamental role in the Weimar cinema, overruling other principles (such as author, in turn linked to various functions) but also breaking free of them and acquiring a new independence and highly mobile vitality. In this sense too, "Caligari" should not be viewed as an "isolated incident," without history or issue.

[1] The landmark studies by Siegfried Kracauer, *From Caligari to Hitler: A Psychological History of German Film* (Princeton: Princeton University Press, 1947) and Lotte Eisner's *The Haunted Screen* (*L'Ecran démoniaque*, Paris: André Bonne, 1952; 2nd ed. *Le Terrain Vague*, Paris, 1965) are complemented by Umberto Barbaro's work *Cinema tedesco* (Roma: Editori Riuniti, 1973), which was published posthumously, and the most restrictive as regards our object. Among the following studies, see Mario Verdone, ed., *Carl Mayer e l'espressionismo* (Roma: Edizioni di Bianco e Nero, 1969); Michael Henry, *Le cinéma expressioniste allemand: un langage métaphorique* (Fribourg: Editions du Signe, 1971); John Barlow, German *Expressionist Film* (Boston: Twayne, 1982); Francis Courtade, *Cinéma expressioniste* (Paris: Henry Veyrier, 1984); Jürgen Kasten, *Der expressionistische Film* (Münster: MAkS, 1990); Paul Coates, *The Gorgon's Gaze. German Cinema, Expressonism, and the Image of Horror* (Cambridge: Cambridge University Press, 1991); Leonardo Quaresima, "Der Expressionismus als Filmgattung," in Uli Jung, Walter Schatzberg, eds., *Filmkultur zur Zeit der Weimarer Republik* (München-London-New York-Paris: Saur, 1992). More specifically on "Caligari," worth noting among recent publications are Mike Budd, ed., *The Cabinet of Dr. Caligari. Texts, Contexts, Histories* (New Brunswick-London: Rutgers University Press, 1990); Uli Jung, Walter Schatzberg, Robert Wiene: *Der Caligari Regisseur* (Berlin:Henschel, 1995); and the publication of the screenplay (text + kritik, München 1995).

[2] All the images (taken straight from frames) are from restored copies of the films cited, in which the original color has also been restored. Worth noting is *Von morgens bis mitternachts* originally released in black and white for expressive reasons. *Faust* also seems to have been released exclusively in black and white. The restored copies are archived at the Cineteca Comunale, Bologna, for whom my deepest thanks.

[3] It also saw the launch of a national German cinema. The fact that this was undertaken largely by outside firms (the Danish company Nordisk, in particular), for whom Germany offered a fundamental market for the film industry's products, is due to an interesting paradox that I have discussed elsewhere in "L'Autorenfilm allemand. Un cinéma national produit par des sociétés étrangères," in Roland Cosandey, François Albera, eds., *Cinéma sans frontières. 1896-1918/Images Across Borders* (Québec-Lausanne: Nuit Blanche/Payot, 1995).

[4] The text that was effectively put on film was the one by Lautensack, *Zwischen Himmel und Erde* (*Between Heaven and Earth*), produced by Continental Kunstfilm, for whom the artist worked as "Dramaturg" and "Reklame-Chef" (*Lichtbild-Bühne*, no. 23, 7 June 1913, p. 162).

[5] Cases include Decla-Lichtspiele's "Unter den Linden" theater; a Decla movie theater at Weißensee; and one in Hamburg-Altona. For sources, see *Der Expressionismus als Filmgattung*, p. 194 (nos. 77-79).

[6] The film never went on general release, however. Cf. Inge Degenhardt, "Nuove forme contro vecchie formule? 'Von morgens bis mitternachts', in *Cinegrafie*, no. 7, 1994. The same writer is responsbile for an important study on the use of black and white in this same film, a choice made deliberately against the accepted use of color for films of the period: "On the Absence and Presence of Colour in Film," in Monica Dall'Asta, Guglielmo Pescatore, Leonardo Quaresima, eds., *Il colore nel cinema muto* (Bologna-Udine: Mano/Università di Udine, 1996). An Italian version of the text appeared in *Fotogenia*, no. 1, 1994. On the same film, see also the essays in Claudine Amiard-Chevrel, ed., *Théâtre et cinéma années Vingt*, vol. 1, *L'Age d'Homme* (Lausanne, 1990).

[7] F. O. [Fritz Olimsky], "Algol," in *Berliner Börsen-Zeitung*, 5 September 1920.

[8] "Der kubistische Film," in *Deutsche Allgemeine Zeitung*, 29 February 1920. *Die Stadt am Ende der Welt* (The City at the End of the World, 1911) is the work at issue.

[9] Cf. the figurative devices of Taut's *Alpine Architektur*, or those of Hermann Finsterlin; the latter's designs have close affinities to Reimann's sketches reproduced in "W. Reimann, Filmarchitektur - Filmarchitektur?!," in *Gebrauchsgraphik*, no. 26, p. 24.; this parallel was also pointed out in Dietrich Neumann ,ed., *Filmarchitektur. Von Metropolis bis Blade Runner* (München-New York: Prestel, 1996, p. 64). The question of possible influences from motifs of Paul Scheerbart, inspirer of the Gläserne Kette group, is discussed in "H[einrich] de Fries: Raumgestaltung im Film," in *Wasmuths Monatshefte für Baukunst*, nos. 3-4, 1920-21, p. 79.

[10] "About 1920 those borders disappear completely; each area of creativity spills into its neighbor; it is virtually impossible to consider each area as a separate entity. There are sketches for interiors for Golem that could easily be preparatory sketches for stage designs of the same period, and vice versa; at the same time, however, these drawings envision 'real' works of architecture, like so many preparatory plans. Part of the sketches can be 'confidently' attributed both to film/theater activity and to the preliminary drawings for the Festspielhaus in Salzburg." Gerhard Storck, "Architektur zur 'Erhöhung' des Lebensgefühles," in *Der dramatische Raum: Hans Poelzig - Malerei, Theater, Film* (Krefeld: Museen Haus Lange und Haus Esters, 1986, p. 31).

[11] Giulio Carlo Argan, "Espressionismo: pittura e cinema," in M. Verdone, ed., *Carl Mayer e l'espressionismo*, p. 70 and 67.

[12] Verlag der Lichtbildbühne, Berlin 1926 (Anastatic reprint, Zürich: Hans Rohr, 1965)

[13] The reference here is to the aforementioned and excellently researched study by J. Kasten, which also shows keen attention to the influences of popular literature and Schauerromantik on Expressionist film; the study's interpretation is, however, conditioned by overlooking this transition. If references to Expressionist paintings (and to Kirchner among the others), are here "questioned," a painting by Kirchner (*Der Rote Turm in Halle*, 1915) was actually indicated as a source for *Nosferatu*'s first frame by Angela Dalle Vacche, *Cinema and Painting*. Austin: University of Texas Press 1996, p.175. On Lang's Expressionist sources see Heide Schönemann, *Fritz Lang. Filmbilder*, Vorbilder. Berlin: Hentrich, 1992.

[14] Kurt Pinthus, "Das Kinostück," in *Das Kinobuch* (Kurt Wolff Verlag, Leipzig 1914), a work that has been reprinted several times.

[15] Rudolf Arnheim, "Dr. Caligari redivivus," in *Das Stachelschwein*, no. 19, 1925 (also in *Kritiken und Aufsätze zum Film*, Helmut H. Diederichs, ed., München: Hanser, 1977, p. 177).

[16] Among the few works bearing these characteristics: Mara Isaks Ubans, *Expressionist Drama and Film: Filmic Elements in Dramas and Film Scripts by Selected Expressionist Authors* (Ph. D. thesis, University of Southern California, 1975). A vital reference source is of course the work *Hätte ich das Kino! Die Schriftsteller und der Stummfilm*, edited by Ludwig Greve, Margot Pehle, Heidi Westhoff (Marbach a.N.-München: Schiller-Nationalmuseum/Kösel Verlag,1976).

[17] For an inquiry into this question, see Helga Vormus, "Autour de la pièce 'De l'aube à minuit' de Georg Kaiser. Structure expressioniste et infléchissement cinématographique de l'écriture théâtrale," in C. Amiard-Chevrel, *Théâtre et cinéma*.

[18] Fritz Olimsky, in *Berliner Börsen-Zeitung*, 5 September 1920.

[19] Herbert Jhering, "Ein expressionistischer Film," in *Berliner Börsen-Courier*, 29 February 1920 (now in *Von Reinhardt bis Brecht*, vol. 1, Berlin/DDR: Aufbau, 1961, p. 374).

[20] H.A.F., "Filmkunst und Expressionismus," in *Münchner Neueste Nachrichten*, 3 April 1920.

[21] Robert Wiene, "Expressionismus und Film," in *Berliner Börsen-Courier*, 30 July 1922. The article is reprinted in the appendixes to the screenplay of "Caligari."

[22] Wiene is not referring to the systems of colorization, but to the use of color in the design stage of the sets and costumes, so as to obtain specific lighting effects.

[23] F. Podehl, "Ein Film von Walter Hasenclever," in *Der Film*, no. 37, 1920 (a review of the text *Die Pest. Ein Film*). The author, however, denies the screenplay's status as an autonomous art form.

[24] Rolf Merkel, "Das Visionäre im Film," in *Der Film*, no. 6, 1923.

[25] *Heinrich de Fries.*, p. 68.

[26] Alfred Polgar, "Film," in *Berliner Tageblatt*, 1 September 1921.

[27] Cf. the text by Lotar Holland, "Die Evolution des Filmbildes," in *Der Bildwart*, no. 7, 1927.

[28] Herbert Jhering, "Der Schauspieler im Film," in *Berliner Börsen-Courier*, 31 October 1920 (now in *Von Reinhardt bis Brecht*, p. 378-79.). The article is the first in a series that ran through to 16 October 1921. (Now reprinted in *Von Reinhardt bis Brecht,* p. 378-414).

[29] Béla Balázs, *Der sichtbare Mensch, oder Die Kultur des Films* (Wien-Leipzig: Deutsch-Österreichischer Verlag, 1924). (Now in *Schriften zum Film*, vol. 1, *Der sichtbare Mensch. Kritiken und Aufsätze, 1922-1926*. München: Hanser, 1982, p. 93).

The complex and often convulsive history of Expressionist architecture has lasted the whole of this century. At its dawn there were the pioneers: Hans Poelzig, Peter Behrens and, above all, Antoni Gaudí. The protagonists of the golden age were Bruno Taut, in a promotional role, and Erich Mendelsohn, Hugo Haring and Herman Finsterlin in creative capacities. Expressionism was pronounced dead in 1924, but, in reality, it was in hibernation, interrupted with increasing intensity from the forties to the sixties. Abstract Expressionism, which emerged in painting in the United States, was matched by a similar phenomenon in architecture. But a truly astonishing, unexpected event has occurred in the nineties, when the revival of Expressionism – or "action-architecture" – has led to a linguistic revolution. This involves the achievement of an age-old objective that had been set in the Stone Age and again in Late Antiquity and the age of the catacombs, re-emerged in the Middle Ages, counter – Renaissance, and Baroque, and was revived for the duration of the Modern Movement. Essentially it is spatial architecture, freed from academic and formalistic preconceptions, proportions, symmetry, axiality, parallelism, right angles, rhythms and assonances and such taboos. It is, in other words, a democratic approach to architecture, able to transform each crisis into a value and make poetry of everyday affairs. It is humble art in a desolate landscape that has revived dialects and kitsch without indulging in the vernacular or populism. In short, it is the anti-authoritarian "zero degree" described by Roland Barthes. The history of Expressionism can, therefore, be reinterpreted afresh: its outcome at the end of the second millennium is epoch-making. It has been said that dodecaphony has changed music and the way we listen to it. In its metamorphosis, Expressionism has done the same thing in architecture. Only very few are aware of this, but in reality we read, write and speak about architecture in a totally different manner. Expressionism is famed for the explosive force with which it destroys the classicistic idolatry. It distorts and breaks up faces and images, tears apart the representation of bodies and souls, extracts and throws out crimes and monstrosities hidden behind portraits that are apparently meek, trustworthy and conformist.

Antoni Gaudí (1852-1926)

Chapel of the Güell community
at Santa Saloma near Barcelona
1908-13

Güell Park in Barcelona, detail
1900-14
Casa Batló, Barcelona, 1905-7
An airshaft in Casa Batló

Antoni Gaudí (1852-1926)

The roof-line of Casa Batló
Casa Milá, Barcelona, 1905-10
Güell Park in Barcelona
Church of the Sagrada Familia
Barcelona, 1884-1926

Casa Batló, Barcelona, detail

Casa Milá, Barcelona
Casa Batló, interior

Rudolf Steiner (1861-1925)

Goetheanum I, Dornach, 1913   Goetheanum II, detail
watercolor by Hermann Linde   Goetheanum II, partial view
Goetheanum II, Dornach, 1923   Goetheanum, side view

But if this subversive tendency is the glory of Expressionism, we should not forget the way it has resisted the attempt to dissipate and annihilate architectural language. This is a burning question: the defence of the third dimension, depth, which is a fundamental tectonic characteristic. This point needs to be clarified immediately.

The problem of the third dimension
The ethical and stylistic dilemma was – and still is – between "finished" completed, the perfectly executed work (nothing can be added to, or taken away from, it) and "unfinished" incompleted, characterized by growth, continuity and change.

The concept of finished has the approval of the masses of professionals who think and design in terms of types, rules and regulations, order and the orders, and also the great managers of architecture such as Leon Battista Alberti, Bramante, the Sangallo sect, Bernini and Gropius. In opposition to them are the minority of rebels, the enemies of idols and dogmas: Arnolfo di Cambio, Brunelleschi, Michelangelo, Borromini, Frank Lloyd Wright and Erich Mendelsohn. The finished constitutes the ideal and the method of classicism and academicism. The unfinished characterizes the behavior of the genius. The finished embodies the myth of equality; the unfinished is congenial to diversity and dissension.

In the late twenties and early thirties, two personalities occupied the opposite poles of European architectural culture. The first was the Dutch artist and intellectual Theo van Doesburg, founder of the De Stijl movement, who elaborated a grammar and syntax for the language of Cubism that constantly risked relapsing into classicism – in other words, in static structures even if on *pilotis*. The other was Erich Mendelsohn, who appreciated De Stijl more than its rival, the pseudo-Expressionist School of Amsterdam, but could not accept the mechanical operation of decomposing the building volume into two-dimensional slabs, only to reassemble them to produce a four-dimensional object. Evidently, the dispute regarded the fate of the third dimension, depth. The advocates of the finished claimed that it had to be destroyed because it derived from Renaissance perspective, a static vision from a fixed observation point.

Peter Behrens (1868-1940)

Courtyard of the Höchster Farbwerke offices
Frankfurt am Main
1920-24

Hans Poelzig (1869-1936)

Chemical factory
Luban, 1911-12
Sketch of Festspielhaus
Salzburg, 1919-20
Festspielhaus, auditorium
Fair district in Berlin
1927

Cubism had discovered that the viewpoint could be dynamic, that a person could move around, over, under, inside, and through the building. The third dimension could and should, therefore, be eliminated. The opposite side, although not very articulately, said no. The Expressionists agreed about dynamism and movement, and even about space-time, but criticized the fact that the new revolutionary approach was limited to the visitor, the person walking around or inside the buildings, and did not concern the true nature, the genetic structure of the building itself. The proposal to avoid the problem of the third dimension by abolishing it was unacceptable.

At the most dramatic stage of the search for a new architectural language, an important meeting was held in Paris in 1914, shortly before the outbreak of war. The French Cubists, the German Expressionists, and the Italian Futurists took part. Umberto Boccioni proposed an alliance in order to promote common action by the European avant-garde in the United States. An agreement was reached between the groups, which published a manifesto signed by the leading personalities, starting with Guillaume Apollinaire. But the results were negligible, and this cannot only be ascribed to the war and the death of Boccioni.

Three concepts of space-time were competing: the Cubist one, based on the changing viewpoint; the Futurist one, which attempted to apply kinetic elements, such as elevators and moving sidewalk, both inside and outside the buildings; and, lastly, the Expressionist one, which required that movement (the fourth dimension) belonged to, and emanated from, the walls, the "skeleton" and the 'skin' of the building. The Cubist thesis negated the third dimension. The Futurists, especially Antonio Sant'Elia, were more or less indifferent to it. The Expressionists, on the other hand, accepted the box-like structure, but distorted and tormented it, as in the sketches by Finsterlin and Mendelsohn, and the Einstein tower. Thus we have come to a central question regarding the language of architecture. What is the reason for shaping walls, ceilings and floors as if they were elastic, of a plastic able to take any form?

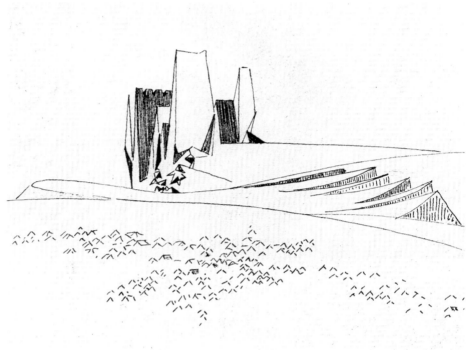

Bruno Taut (1880-1938)　　　Max Taut (1884-1967)

The Crystal Mountain, 1919　　Architectural drawing, 1921
The Valley as a Flower, 1919　　Watercolor and tempera, 1921

Hugo Haring (1882-1958)   The model farm of Gut Garkau
                          near Lubeck, 1924-25
                          Another view of the Gut Garkau farm

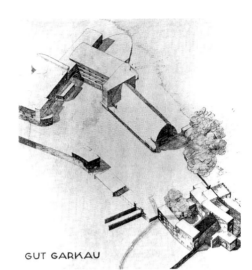

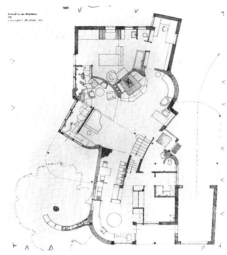

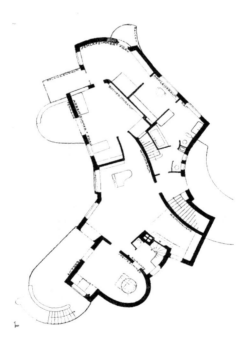

Sketch of the Gut Garkau buildings
House plan, 1923

Three house plans, 1923
House plan, 1941

Hermann Finsterlin (1887-1973)   Sketch of a house, 1919   Architectural drawing, undated
Architectural drawing, 1920
Small bathroom, 1927   Mountain landscape, 1922

The answer is obvious. In a box-shaped building there are box-shaped spaces, insignificant and devoid of fluxes. But in a volume in which walls, floors and ceilings can be fashioned at will, the cavities are all different; rather than deriving from their shell, they shape it. In other words, they become what they ought to be: protagonists of architecture.

There is no doubt that space could be magnificently handled using Van Doesburg's De Stijl vocabulary and syntax: think, for example, of Mies van der Rohe's delightfully ethereal Barcelona Pavilion or, in a different idiom, Le Corbusier's Villa Savoye at Poissy. But, in order to create genuinely human spaces in their full, articulate significance, the design philosophy of the Expressionists was necessary.

While Cubism and its derivative, the International Style, presumed to provide a universally valid aesthetic principle, Expressionism was a rare art, practiced by the few. Between the two world wars it was given concrete form by Gaudí, Häring, Mendelsohn and Hans Scharoun; and only Gaudí and Mendelsohn were fully aware of the incandescent values of their materials.

Second Expressionism

After the Second World War and the demise of the International Style, Le Corbusier produced his most revolutionary works, the Ronchamp Chapel and the Philips Pavilion at the Brussels World's Fair: these were incredibly courageous disavowals of the Cubist and Purist principles enunciated in 1921. The influence of these buildings is evident in Eero Saarinen's TWA Terminal at Kennedy Airport, New York; Giovanni Michelucci's Autostrada del Sole church near Florence; and John Johansen's Oklahoma Theater Center, Oklahoma City, which decomposes the whole structure so as immerse to it in the landscape. These personalities are overshadowed by the greatest architectural genius of the century, Frank Lloyd Wright, who was pre-Expressionist, Expressionist, and post-Expressionist in his organic mission addressed to three generations. In this respect, the letter that Mendelsohn sent to his wife, Louise, from Chicago on 5 November 1924 is particularly significant.

MENDELSOHN

232-233. «Dopo un'ora di sonno, sono colto da un nuovo accesso di febbre disegnativa che produce una massa di schizzi. Oggetti, per la maggior parte, tellurici e planetari, freundlichiani...», scrive dal fronte nel '17.

Turgide, ribollenti, appena esplose da profondità remote, aggressive fino all'anatema, non-finite, anzi rappresentate nel vortice del loro farsi, del loro trovare una forma, le immagini, segnate di regola su minuscoli pezzi di carta, spesso rovesciati per fermare un'altra visione, dicono la metodologia progettuale di Mendelsohn. Empito gestuale, calato nella polivalenza dell'azione architettonica vissuta nelle fasi del suo sviluppo, nella realtà di un divenire sempre consapevole delle possibili alternative, non metamente pensata e poi comunicata in un disegno. Questo il messaggio dei 1500 schizzi mendelsohniani.

La teoria della relatività sollecita un nuovo sentimento del mondo. Questo significa «freundlichiani...». Erwin Finley Freundlich era un giovane fisico, collaboratore di Albert Einstein. Fu lui a suggerire il nome di Mendelsohn per l'**Osservatorio a Potsdam**, sognato nelle veglie di guerra sin dal '17 e modellato al vero nel 1920-24.

Erich Mendelsohn (1887-1953)   Sketches of the Einstein Tower, Potsdam
Einstein Tower, Potsdam
Base of the Einstein Tower

Erich Mendelsohn (1887-1953)   Schocken department store, Stuttgart
                                      1926-28, sketch, view, and view from above
                                      Universum movie house, Berlin, 1926-28

Walter Gropius (1883-1969)

Monument in the Weimar cemetery
1920-22, sketch
View of the Weimar monument

He wrote: "I have spent two days with Frank Lloyd Wright at Taliesin, two wonderful days in the marvellous current, tense and relaxed... We immediately became friends, inebriated by space, moving our hands toward each other in space.
The same path, the same objective, the same life, I believe... We were at Taliesin, high up, on the top of the hill... Wright says that, for the first time in history, the architecture of the future will be totally architecture, space in itself, without any prescribed models – movement in three or four dimensions... A Joie de vivre expressed in space... This is his genius. And nobody else is anything like him".

Expressionism in the nineties
We thus come to the epic that still involves us. Architects whose conversion to Expressionism is not merely short-lived have appeared on the stage of world architecture. Reima Pietilä, Jörn Utzon, Jean Renaudie, Günther Behnisch, Zvi Hecker, Daniel Libeskind, Frank O. Gehry (and others could be added, such as Bruce Goff, Günther Domenig and Peter Eisenman), constitute a new Expressionist generation, "born of itself" and hence difficult for many critics to decipher. It is the nemesis after the scandal of post-Modernism, the deleterious attempt to obstruct the development of the Modern Movement.
It is the end of the mannerism that has lasted for five centuries: it is no longer a question of attacking and overthrowing classicism, which implies the need to revive it continually in order to subsequently demolish it.
Architecture has won a five thousand-years-long battle; it has freed itself from the canons of the past and has not sought to replace them.
And it has rediscovered the history of architecture in Paleolithic caves, in the decomposition of the Late Antique, the asymmetry of Arnolfo di Cambio, and the outstanding creativity of Brunelleschi, Bernardo Buontalenti, Michelangelo, Galeazzo Alessi, Borromini, and Giuseppe Terragni – that is, all those who, over the centuries, have flouted the rules and favored transgression.
This is the final objective of Expressionism in architecture.

Ludwig Mies van der Rohe (1886-1969)   Plan for a skyscraper, 1920-21
Monument to Karl Liebknecht
and Rosa Luxemburg, Berlin, 1926

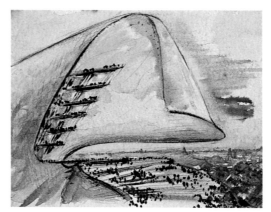

Hans Scharoun (1893-1972)

Project
Project
Philarmonie Hall, Berlin, 1963, exterior view
Philarmonie Hall, Berlin, side view

Hans Scharoun (1893-1972)   Philarmonie Hall, Berlin, staircase
                                   The area around
                                   the Philarmonie Hall, Berlin
                                   Philarmonie Hall, Berlin, interior

Alvar Aalto (1898-1976)   Ceiling of the Viipuri library
                          auditorium, 1934
                          Finnish pavilion at the New York
                          World's Fair, 1939

The first period of Expressionism, which ended in 1924, was the art of Sturm und Drang and Symbolism, a messianic, spasmodic revolutionary desire, with a chaotic, desperate revolt against the vision of man as a naked, one-dimensional being, slave to industry, bureaucracy and militarism. "Woe betide the land that needs heroes," says Brecht's Galileo, but, since his story is devised by heroes, he has to add: "I don't believe that the practice of science can be separated from courage... if men of science do not react against the intimidation of the powerful egoists, and are satisfied with accumulating knowledge, science will be forever enfeebled, and every new machine will be the cause of new suffering."

It is usually said that architecture is not a "pure" art. Since it has to meet practical requirements, it cannot express states of mind or sentiments such as love, fear, sadness, bewilderment or nostalgia. Certainly, for those who are incapable of interpreting it – that is, the majority of architects and art historians – architecture is silent. Hence Expressionism appears to be a deviant movement, an unrealizable, deranged vision, or a formalistic caprice. Its tenets are countered with the advocacy of teamwork and supposedly Rationalist objectivity – which is undermined by the principles of relativity and indeterminacy. The experience of liberty – by no means an easy matter – has been countered by the re-emergence of the mortifying academic system.

Those who know how to interpret architecture, however, are able to recognize the entire gamut of inner feelings, even in the most delicate and secret recesses: and these features are all the more evident because they are systematically seen in relation to reality and in conflict with it. A tendency to protest, a break with the past, and unconventionality are the hallmarks of Expressionism.

And since transgression is a typical feature of all art, especially the modern variety, the Expressionist experience involves all genuinely creative architects. Expressionism may be youthful, as in the cases of Walter Gropius and Mies van der Rohe; elderly, as in the case of Le Corbusier; and lifelong, as in the cases of Gaudí, Mendelsohn, and Scharoun.

Alvar Aalto (1898-1976)

Students' dormitory at the MIT
Cambridge, Mass., 1947

Oil painting, detail, 1955
Sketches of projects

Acoustic diagram of the Helsinki
Auditorium, 1962

Otaniemi University, 1965
Wood relief, 1968

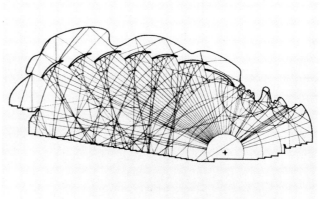

Le Corbusier (1887-1965)

Model of urban planning scheme
for Algiers, 1930

Le Corbusier (1887-1965)   Ronchamp Chapel, near Belfort   The Philips pavilion, Brussels   View of the Philips pavilion
                            1950-53   Exhibition, 1958, view of the interior
                            Ronchamp Chapel, interior   The Philips pavilion, exterior view

Frederick Kiesler (1890-1965) Surrealist hall of the Art of This The book sanctuary in Jerusalem, 1965
Century Gallery, New York, 1942 Endless House, interior, 1959

In order to overcome Rationalist hibernation, and the resulting regression to classicism, it is necessary to draw on Expressionism. Various currents which appeared in the sixties and seventies – Brutalism and spontaneous architecture, for instance – are simply equivocal, evasive and distorted substitutes for this persistent demand, which is so often suppressed or thwarted.

Action-architecture: crisis-free
Any attempt to establish a super-historic category of Expressionism to historical architecture would simply be the repetition of an old mistake. Nonetheless, this approach has opened up new critical perspectives even with regard to the past. For example, the revolutionary significance of the sketches for the fortifications of Florence made by Michelangelo in 1529 has not been fully comprehended by historians whose sensibility is tuned to the Renaissance, Mannerism, and Baroque. In order to perceive their remarkable stylistic innovations, it was necessary to study them from the standpoint of Expressionism and its extreme informal tendencies.
Why did Expressionism have a crisis and collapse, only to re-emerge later? There are two main reasons for this. First of all, people – artists, even leading architects – grow weary. The period of protest does not last long.
Few are able to resist when they become prosperous, since it is easy to yield to the temptations of the easy life, professional success and corrosive self-indulgence. This happened to Galileo, although he continued with his research; to Michelangelo, after he had designed the fortifications, even if he continued to elaborate the unfinished; to Mies van der Rohe, when he designed the Seagram Building, New York; to Gropius with the American Embassy in Athens and the Pan Am Building, New York. And it even happened to Alvar Aalto: his Expressionist impetus was at its height in the Finnish Pavilion at the 1939 New York World's Fair and the Senior Students' Dormitory at the Massachusetts Institute of Technology in Cambridge, Mass.; the decline is evident in the Enso-Gutzeit Building in Helsinki. Success is enervating, power corrupts: this is the rule that was confirmed by Victor Horta and J. J. P. Oud.

Eero Saarinen (1911-1961)

TWA Terminal, John F. Kennedy
Airport, New York, 1961
TWA Terminal, exterior view

TWA Terminal, exterior view
Dulles International Airport
near Washington, 1960-62

TWA Terminal, John F. Kennedy
Airport, New York, interior

Giovanni Michelucci (1891-1991)

Church of San Giovanni Battista
on the Autostrada del Sole (highway)
near Florence, 1961, exterior

Church on the Autostrada near
Florence, interior
View of the church structure
Sketch of a church, 1962

There are few exceptions: the most outstanding is that of Wright, the genius of modern architecture, while Le Corbusier is also remarkable for his ingenuity and perception.

The second reason for the recurring crises of Expressionism is that it is difficult to maintain a protestatory stance when the battle has been won. The revolutionaries on the barricades are more numerous than those who are able to govern. Expressionist architecture has not been able to formulate a convincing aesthetic doctrine, or an anti-classical canon, and thus effective didactics. It has been content with abusing academic aesthetic doctrines and didactics, whether they be traditional or modern. The most serious omission, however, is that it has not evolved its own approach to city planning, or rather anti-city planning. Its liberative impetus, which is aggressive at an individual level, is often defensive with regard to social problems. In other words, both the first and second periods of Expressionism used only part of their potential.

Present-day action-architecture rejects the heroic, apocalyptic stance of the first period of Expressionism – Sturm und Drang, existential anguish, and its symbols.

With regard to the second, it exposes its evasive behavior, which uses Expressionism only to fill the gap created by the crisis of Rationalism.

However, as far as architects like Libeskind or Gehry are concerned, the positive legacy of Expressionism consists in the call to dismantle the box-like structure of the building – the static shell that imprisons and paralyzes human functions. This is, in other words, a declaration of independence from the T-square, the drafting machine, the computer, and elementary geometry and stereometry. It is, above all, an approach that values the contents rather than the containers.

Thus, new spaces are created; these are linked through dissonant fluxes and faced without formal preconceptions, and their organicity remains intact.

Expressionism meets the present demands of technology: shell-like – or membrane-like – structures, molded plastic products, and advanced engineering techniques are hardly compatible with the aesthetics of Cubism.

John Johansen (1916)   Oklahoma Theater Center   Interior of the theater   Another view of the theater
                             Oklahoma City, 1971, foyer   View of the theater

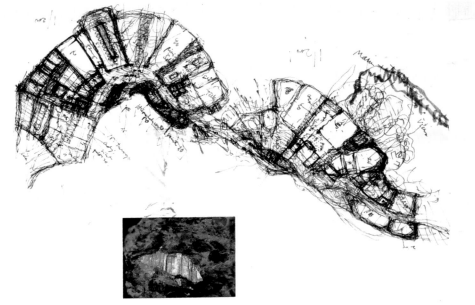

Reima Pietilä (1923-1993)

The Dipoli students' residence
at Otaniemi University, 1964-66
seen from above
View of the students' residence
View of the president's residence
in Helsinki, 1966
The president's residence
two details
The president's residence, sketch plan
View of the president's residence

Jörn Utzon (1918)

Opera House, Sidney, 1957
seen from above
Opera House, Sidney
Opera House's "sails" seen against
the sky

Opera House, Sidney, stair
Interior of the Opera Hous

The term "sculptural engineering" has been applied to the work of Felix Candela and, on occasion, to that of Pier Luigi Nervi. Now, if this engineering is to become architecture, it certainly cannot espouse Purism or the Neo-plasticism of De Stijl, or, even less, ignominious Neo-neo-classicism. It must meditate on the work of Häring, Mendelsohn, and Scharoun; or even better, on Michelangelo's fortifications in Florence, molded by internal spaces and the landscape.

On a territorial scale, the action-architects have paid due attention to Roland Barthes's proposition that – in architecture and city planning, too – the "un-marked" elements are infinitely more important than the "marked" ones. The powerful creation of spaces – whether they be refined or wild, agitated or retarded, bursting forth or swallowing up, traumatized or calm and joyful – lies at the root of all their designs.

Insofar as it is a non-style, Expressionism continues to stimulate at an ethical and formal level. If it no longer limits itself to being a consolatory art of solitary protest, it is able to address the problems of today with defiant optimism.

The language of action-architecture is organic, anti-authoritarian, and intrinsically democratic: rather than being read or written, it is spoken.

Transgression is foreign to it for the simple reason that it lacks rules. Individuals and groups express themselves spontaneously, without checks.

Instead of the utopian ideals of the Enlightenment, everyday events apply. Approved in December 1977, forty-five years after the promulgation of the Athens Charter by Le Corbusier and the CIAM (Congrès Internationaux d'Architecture Moderne), the Machu Picchu Charter outlines the suitable climate and context for action-architecture, which is no longer Eurocentric. "Athens 1933. Machu Picchu 1977. Places matter.

Athens is the cradle of Western civilization. Machu Picchu symbolizes the cultural contribution of another world. Athens meant the rationality and enlightenment of Plato and Aristotle. Machu Picchu represented everything that has escaped the categorical mentality of the Enlightenment and cannot be classified in its logic.

Jean Renaudie (1925-1981)

The new town center of Ivry
1975-76
The renewal of Ivry, detail
Municipal housing at Givors
1974-81
Municipal housing at Villetaneuse
1976-83

Günther Behnisch (1922)

Olympic stadium, Munich, 1972
detail of the roof
Hysolar Institute, Stuttgart, 1986-87
The Albert Schweitzer School
of Bad Rappenau, 1987-91, interior
Nursery school
at Stuttgart-Luginsland, 1987-90

Zvi Hecker (1931)   Municipal housing near Jerusalem

Jewish school, Berlin, 1996
seen from above

View of the Jewish school, Berlin

Elicoidal building, Jerusalem

Daniel Libeskind (1946)

Internal view of the Museum of Berlin, 1997
The Museum's Jewish wing, 1997, model

Plan for extending London's
Victoria & Albert Museum, 1997
the front façade
Plan for extending the museum
cross-section

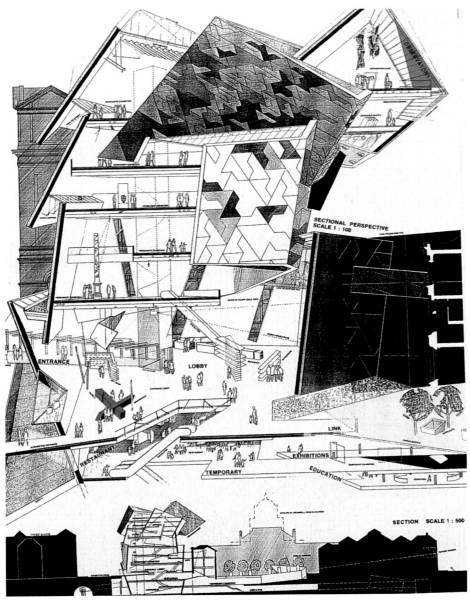

Our questions are infinitely more numerous and complex than those addressed by the authors of the Athens Charter". And, with regard to architecture: "In recent decades, the Modern Movement has developed. Its principal problem is no longer the masterly interplay of pure volumes in the light, but the creation of social spaces in which to live. Now the accent is not on the isolated building, however beautiful and sophisticated it may be, but on the continuity of the urban fabric... The aim in 1933 was to disintegrate the building and the city into their components. In 1977 an attempt was made to reassemble these components, which, when not related to each other, lose vitality and meaning... The new approach to city planning requires continuity of building, and this means that each element in the continuum must communicate with the other elements in order to complete its image." And it refers to the principle of the unfinished: "The experience of art has demonstrated that artists do not produce finished objects; they stop halfway, or three-quarterway, through the creative process, so that the observer is not in a state of passive contemplation, but becomes an active factor in its multivalent message. In the field of building, the participation of the users is even more important and concrete. People must participate creatively at each stage of the design process." On the threshold of the third millennium, therefore, architecture is looking ahead.

Frank Owen Gehry (1929)

Aerospace Museum, Los Angeles
1982-84
View of the interior, 1987

The seat of the Nationale
Nederlande, Prague, 1996
Design Museum "Vitra"
Weil-am-Rhein, 1988-89

American Center, Paris, 1994

The Works

Otto Dix, *Selbstbildnis als Soldat*, 1914
Self-Portrait as Soldier
oil on paper, 68x53.5 cm
Stuttgart, Galerie der Stadt
cat. 1

Erich Heckel, *Selbstbildnis*, 1919
Self-Portrait
oil on canvas, 80x70.5 cm
Berlin, Nationalgalerie
Staatliche Museen zu Berlin
cat. 2

Alexej Jawlensky, *Selbstbildnis*, ca. 1912
Self-Portrait
oil on paper on canvas
65.5x44.5 cm
Vienna, Museum moderner Kunst
Stiftung Ludwig
on loan from Österreichische Galerie
cat. 3

Ernst Ludwig Kirchner
Selbstbildnis mit Mädchen, 1914
Self-Portrait with Girl
oil on canvas, 60x49 cm
Berlin, Nationalgalerie
Staatliche Museen zu Berlin
cat. 4

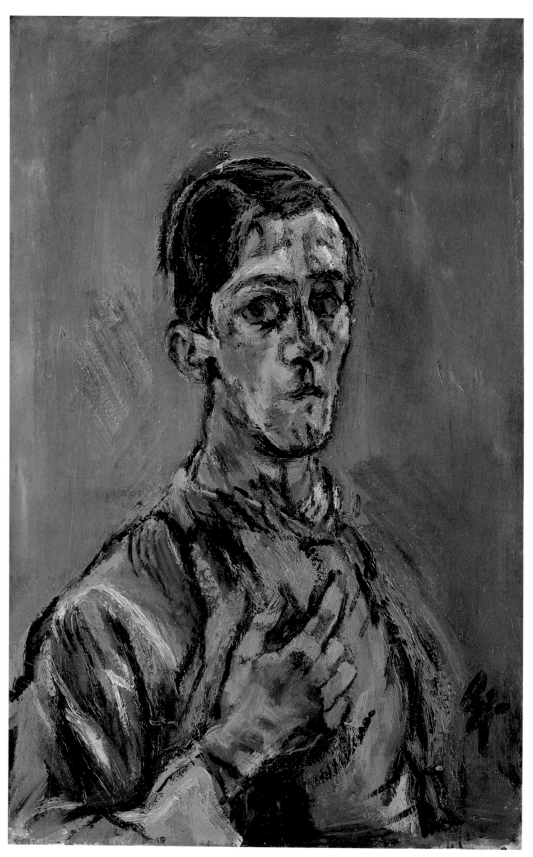

Oskar Kokoschka, *Selbstbildnis*, 1913
Self-Portrait
oil on canvas, 81.6x49.5 cm
New York
The Museum of Modern Art
cat. 5

Ludwig Meidner, *Selbstbildnis (Mein Nachtgesicht)*, 1913
Self-Portrait (My Nocturnal Visage)
oil on canvas, 66.7x48.9 cm
Milwaukee, The Marvin
and Janet Fishman Collection
cat. 6

Karl Schmidt-Rottluff
Selbstbildnis, 1920
Self-Portrait
oil on canvas, 91x75.5 cm
Berlin, Nationalgalerie
Staatliche Museen zu Berlin
cat. 7

Otto Müller, *Selbstbildnis*, 1918–19
Self-Portrait
oil on canvas, 71x54,7 cm
Munich, Bayerische Staatsgemäldesammlungen
Staatsgalerie moderner Kunst
cat. 8

Erich Heckel
Badende am Teich, 1911–12
Bathers in the Pond
oil on canvas, 95x120.5
Winterthur, Kunstmuseum
cat. 9

Alexej Jawlensky, *Die Fabrik*, 1910
The Factory
oil on cardboard, 72x85.7 cm
Switzerland, private collection
cat. 10

Wassily Kandinsky
Berglandschaft mit Kirche, 1910
Mountain Landscape with Church
oil on cardboard, 32.7x44.8 cm
Munich, Städtische Galerie
im Lenbachhaus
cat. 11

162

Wassily Kandinsky
Murnau mit Kirche I, 1910
Murnau with Church I
oil and watercolor on cardboard
64.9x50.2 cm
Munich, Städtische Galerie
im Lenbachhaus
cat. 12

Otto Müller
Badende im Schilfgraben, ca. 1922
Bathers in the Thicket of Reeds
glue color on jute, 92x79 cm
Berlin, Nationalgalerie
Staatliche Museen zu Berlin
cat. 13

Max Pechstein
Im Wald bei Moritzburg, 1909
In the Moritzburg Wood
oil on canvas, 68x78 cm
Berlin, Brücke-Museum
cat. 14

Max Pechstein
Am Strand von Nidden, 1911
Beach at Nidden
oil on canvas, 50x65 cm
Berlin, Nationalgalerie
Staatliche Museen zu Berlin
cat. 15

Max Pechstein
Sommer in den Dünen, 1911
Summer in the Dunes
oil on canvas, 75x100 cm
Berlin, Nationalgalerie
Staatliche Museen zu Berlin
cat. 16

Erich Heckel
Hafen von Flensburg, 1913
Flensburg Harbor
oil on canvas, 83x96.5 cm
Hamburg, private collection
cat. 17

Ernst Ludwig Kirchner
Ins Meer Schreitende, 1912
Striding into the Sea
oil on canvas, 146.4x200 cm
Stuttgart, Staatsgalerie
cat. 18

Ernst Ludwig Kirchner
Drei Badende, 1913
Three Bathers
oil on canvas, 197.5x147.5 cm
Sydney, The Art Gallery
of New South Wales
Art Gallery of New South Wales
Foundation Purchase, 1984
cat. 19

Franz Marc, *Die Hirten*, 1912
The Shepherds
oil on canvas, 100x135 cm
Private Collection
on loan to Bayerische
Staatsgemäldesammlungen Munich
cat. 20

Karl Schmidt-Rottluff
Häuser am Kanal, 1912
Houses by the Canal
oil on canvas, 74x101 cm
Berlin, Nationalgalerie
Staatliche Museen zu Berlin
cat. 21

Karl Schmidt-Rottluff, *Drei Akte
(Dünenbild aus Nidden)*, 1913
*Three Nudes (Picture of Dunes
by Nidden)*
oil on canvas, 106.5x98 cm
Berlin, Nationalgalerie
Staatliche Museen zu Berlin
cat. 22

Ernst Ludwig Kirchner
Drei Akte im Wald, 1908–20
Three Nudes in the Woods
oil on canvas, 76x100 cm
Amsterdam, Stedelijk Museum
cat. 23

Erich Heckel, *Weiße Pferde*, 1912
White Horses
woodcut, 30.8x31.3 cm
Berlin, Kupferstichkabinett
cat. 24

Ernst Ludwig Kirchner
Badeszene unter überhängenden
Baumzweigen, 1913
Bathing Scene under Overhanging
Branches
engraving, 49.5x32 cm
Berlin, Kupferstichkabinett
cat. 25

Otto Müller
Badeszene mit vier Figuren
Haus und Boot, ca. 1914
Bathing Scene with Four Figures
House and Boat
lithograph, 33x43.7 cm
Berlin, Kupferstichkabinett
cat. 26

Erich Heckel, *Parksee*, 1914
Lake in a Park
engraving, 24.8x19.8 cm
Berlin, Brücke-Museum
cat. 27

Ernst Ludwig Kirchner
Paar im Zimmer, 1912
Couple in a Room
oil on canvas, 95x85x3 cm
Private Collection
cat. 28

Ernst Ludwig Kirchner
Fünf Frauen auf der Straße, 1913
Five Women on the Street
oil on canvas, 120x90 cm
Cologne, Museum Ludwig
Stiftung Haubrich
cat. 29

Ernst Ludwig Kirchner
Zwei Frauen mit Waschbecken, 1913
Two Women with Washbasin
oil on canvas, 121x90.5 cm
Frankfurt am Main, Städelsches Kunstinstitut
property of Städelscher Museums Verein e. V.
cat. 30

Ernst Ludwig Kirchner
Berliner Straßenszene, 1913–14
Berlin Street Scene
oil on canvas, 121x95 cm
Berlin, Brücke-Museum
cat. 31

Ernst Ludwig Kirchner
Im Cafegarten, 1914
In the Café Garden
oil on canvas, 70.5x76 cm
Berlin, Brücke-Museum
cat. 32

Ernst Ludwig Kirchner
Zwei Frauen auf der Straße, 1914
Two Women in the Street
oil on canvas, 120.5x91 cm
Düsseldorf, Kunstsammlung
Nordrhein-Westfalen
cat. 33

Ernst Ludwig Kirchner
Das Zelt, 1914
The Tent
oil on canvas, 100x74.3 cm
Munich, Bayerische
Staatsgemäldesammlungen
Staatsgalerie moderner Kunst
cat. 34

Ernst Ludwig Kirchner
Tanzpaar, 1914
Dancing Couple
oil on canvas, 91x65 cm
Essen, Museum Folkwang
cat. 35

Ernst Ludwig Kirchner
Rheinbrücke in Köln, 1914
Bridge on the Rhine in Cologne
oil on canvas, 120.5x91 cm
Berlin, Nationalgalerie
Staatliche Museen zu Berlin
cat. 36

Ernst Ludwig Kirchner
Der Belle-Alliance-Platz in Berlin, 1914
Belle-Alliance-Square in Berlin
distemper on canvas, 96x85 cm
Berlin, Nationalgalerie
Staatliche Museen zu Berlin
cat. 37

Ernst Ludwig Kirchner
Stadtbahnbogen, 1915
Tramway Arch
color lithograph, 51x60 cm
Frankfurt am Main
Städtische Galerie
im Städelsches Kunstinstitut
cat. 38

Ernst Ludwig Kirchner
Der Mörder, 1913
The Murderer
color lithograph, 50.1x65.2 cm
New York, Museum of Modern Art
cat. 39

Ernst Ludwig Kirchner
Kokotten auf dem Kurfürstendamm
1914
Coquettes on Kurfürstendamm
lithograph on yellow paper
59.5x50.5 cm
Berlin, Kupferstichkabinett
cat. 40

Ernst Ludwig Kirchner
Frauen am Potsdamer Platz, 1914
Women at Potsdamer Platz
woodcut, 52x37.5 cm
Berlin, Kupferstichkabinett
cat. 41

Ernst Ludwig Kirchner
Straßenszene, am Schaufenster, 1914
Street Scene, at the Window
woodcut, 29.2x18.2 cm
Berlin, Kupferstichkabinett
cat. 42

Ernst Ludwig Kirchner
Fünf Kokotten, 1914
Five Coquettes
woodcut, 49.5x37.8 cm
Frankfurt am Main, Graphische
Sammlung, Städelsches Kunstinstitut
cat. 43

Ernst Ludwig Kirchner
Drei Kokotten bei Nacht, 1914
Three Coquettes by Night
etching on zinc plate
25.4x17.4 cm
Berlin, Kupferstichkabinett
cat. 44

Wilhelm Lehmbruck
Emporsteigender Jüngling, 1913
Ascending Youth
bronze, 228x76x62 cm
Duisburg
Wilhelm Lehmbruck Museum
cat. 45

Wilhelm Lehmbruck
Der Gestürzte, 1915–16
The Fallen Man
bronze, 72x239x83 cm
Berlin, Nationalgalerie
Staatliche Museen zu Berlin
cat. 46

Erich Heckel
Laute spielendes Mädchen, 1913
Girl Playing the Lute
oil on canvas, 72x79 cm
Berlin, Brücke-Museum
cat. 47

Erich Heckel
Unterhaltung (Beim Vorlesen), 1914
Discourse (Reading aloud)
oil on canvas, 94.4x81 cm
Halle, Staatliche Galerie Moritzburg
Landeskunstmuseum Sachsen-Anhalt
cat. 48

Alexej Jawlensky
Sinnende Frau, 1913
Meditating Woman
oil on cardboard, 53.5x50 cm
Bern, Kunstmuseum, Stiftung
Othmar Huber
cat. 49

Alexej Jawlensky
Spanierin, 1913
Spanish Woman
oil on cardboard, 67x48.5 cm
Munich, Städtische Galerie
im Lenbachhaus
cat. 50

Ernst Ludwig Kirchner
Porträt Erna Schilling, 1913
Portrait of Erna Schilling
oil on canvas, 71.5x60.5 cm
Berlin, Nationalgalerie, purchased
with funds of the Verein
der Freunde der Nationalgalerie
und des Bundes
cat. 51

Karl Schmidt-Rottluff
Bildnis Feininger, 1915
Portrait of Feininger
oil on canvas, 92x77 cm
Nuremberg, Germanisches
Nationalmuseum
on loan from a private collection
cat. 52

Karl Schmidt-Rottluff
Grünes Mädchen, 1915
The Green Girl
oil on canvas, 85x76 cm
Berlin, Nationalgalerie Staatliche
Museen zu Berlin
cat. 53

Erich Heckel
Zwei Männer am Tisch, 1913
Two Men at a Table
woodcut, 23.8x26.2 cm
Berlin, Kupferstichkabinett
cat. 54

Erich Heckel, *Geschwister*, 1913
The Brothers
woodcut, 41.7x31 cm
Berlin, Brücke-Museum
cat. 55

Erich Heckel, *Müde*, 1913
Tired
woodcut, 46.3x33.4 cm
Berlin, Kupferstichkabinett
cat. 56

Erich Heckel, *Die Tote*, 1912
The Dead Woman
engraving, 25x29.8 cm
Portland, Portland Art Museum
Vivian and Gordon Gilkey
Graphic Arts Collection
cat. 57

Erich Heckel, *Parksee*, 1914
Lake in a Park
oil on canvas, 120x96.5 cm
Private Collection
on loan from Bayerische
Staatsgemäldesammlungen, Munich
cat. 58

Ludwig Meidner, *Das Eckhaus*
(Villa Kochmann, Dresden), 1913
The Corner House (Villa Kochmann in Dresden)

oil on canvas on board, 97x78 cm
Madrid, Thyssen-Bornemisza Collection Foundation
cat. 59

Karl Schmidt-Rottluff
Zwei Frauen, 1914
Two Women
oil on canvas, 107x87 cm
Wuppertal, Von der Heydt-Museum
cat. 60

Karl Schmidt-Rottluff
Mädchen vor dem Spiegel, 1915
Girl in front of a Mirror
oil on canvas, 101x87 cm
Berlin, Nationalgalerie
Staatliche Museen zu Berlin
cat. 61

214

Karl Schmidt-Rottluff
Freundinnen, 1914
Friends
oil on canvas, 87.8x101.5 cm
Emden, Kunsthalle
Stiftung Henri und Eske Nannen
cat. 62

Karl Schmidt-Rottluff
Frau in den Dünen, 1914
Woman in the Dunes
woodcut, 39.4x50.1 cm
Berlin, Kupferstichkabinett
cat. 63

216

Karl Schmidt-Rottluff
Trauernde am Strand, 1914
Mourners on the Beach
woodcut, 39.5x49.7 cm
Berlin, Kupferstichkabinett
cat. 64

Karl Schmidt-Rottluff
Die Sonne, 1914
The Sun
woodcut, 39.8x49.7 cm
Berlin, Kupferstichkabinett
cat. 65

Karl Schmidt-Rottluff
Bei den Netzen, 1914
By the Nets
woodcut, 40x49.5 cm
Berlin, Kupferstichkabinett
cat. 66

Karl Schmidt-Rottluff
Die Schwestern, 1914
Sisters
woodcut, 40.1x50 cm
Berlin, Kupferstichkabinett
cat. 67

Karl Schmidt-Rottluff
Frau unter Bäumen, 1914
Woman under the Trees
woodcut, 49.5x40 cm
Berlin, Kupferstichkabinett
cat. 68

Wassily Kandinsky
Improvisation 30 (Kanonen), 1913
Improvisation 30 (Cannons)
oil on canvas, 109.2x109.9 cm
Chicago, The Art Institute of Chicago
Arthur Jerome Eddy Memorial
Collection
cat. 69

222

Franz Marc, *Das arme Land Tirol*, 1913
The Unfortunate Land of Tyrol
oil on canvas, 131.5x200 cm
New York, The Solomon
R. Guggenheim Museum
cat. 70

Ludwig Meidner
Apokaliptische Landschaft, 1913
Apocalyptic Landscape
oil on canvas, 67.3x80 cm
Milwaukee, The Marvin
and Janet Fishman Collection
cat. 71

Ludwig Meidner
Apokaliptische Vision, 1913
Apocalyptic Vision
indian ink and pencil on paper
54.9x43.6 cm
Milwaukee, The Marvin
and Janet Fishman Collection
cat. 72

Ludwig Meidner
Straße in Wilmersdorf, 1913
Street in Wilmersdorf
engraving, ca. 25.9x16.5 cm
Los Angeles, The Grunwald Center
for the Graphic Arts, UCLA
gift of Mr. and Mrs. Stanley I. Talpis
cat. 73

Ernst Ludwig Kirchner
Absalom, 1918
Absalom
frontispiece, color woodcut
76.5x60 cm
Kassel, Staatliche Museen
Graphische Sammlung
cat. 74I

Ernst Ludwig Kirchner
David ermahnt seinen Sohn Absalom
1918
David admonishes his son Absalom
woodcut, 76.5x60 cm
Kassel, Staatliche Museen
Graphische Sammlung
cat. 74II

Ernst Ludwig Kirchner, *Absalom
entzweit sich mit seinem Vater*, 1918
Absalom's estrangement
from his father
woodcut, 76.5x60 cm
Kassel, Staatliche Museen
Graphische Sammlung
cat. 74III

Ernst Ludwig Kirchner
Absalom mit seinen Ratgebern, 1918
Absalom with his advisor
woodcut, 76.5x60 cm
Kassel, Staatliche Museen
Graphische Sammlung
cat. 74IV

Ernst Ludwig Kirchner, *Absalom schändet*
die Kebsweiber seines Vaters, 1918
Absalom dishonors his father's concubine
woodcut, 76.5x60 cm
Kassel, Staatliche Museen, Graphische Sammlung
cat. 74V

Ernst Ludwig Kirchner, *Absalom spricht Recht*
an seines Vaters Statt, 1918
Absalom speaks correctly on behalf of his father
woodcut, 76.5x60 cm
Kassel, Staatliche Museen, Graphische Sammlung
cat. 74VI

Ernst Ludwig Kirchner
Tod Absaloms, 1918
Absalom's death
woodcut, 76.5x60 cm
Kassel, Staatliche Museen, Graphische Sammlung
cat. 74VII

Ernst Ludwig Kirchner
David klagt um Absalom, 1918
David laments over Absalom
woodcut, 76.5x60 cm
Kassel, Staatliche Museen
Graphische Sammlung
cat. 74VIII

Ernst Ludwig Kirchner
"Peter Schlemihls wundersame
Geschichte" von Adelbert
von Chamisso, 1915
"The Amazing Tale of Peter
Schlemihl" by Adelbert von Chamisso
cover, lithograph, 26.9x21.5 cm
Berlin, Brücke-Museum, Karl
und Emy Schmidt-Rottluff Stiftung
cat. 75

Ernst Ludwig Kirchner
Peter Schlemihls wundersame
Geschichte, 1915
The Amazing Tale of Peter Schlemihl
frontispiece, color woodcut
29.3x26.3 cm
Berlin, Brücke-Museum, Karl
und Emy Schmidt-Rottluff Stiftung
cat. 75I

Ernst Ludwig Kirchner
Der Verkauf des Schattens, 1915
Selling the Shadow
color woodcut, 32.3x22 cm
Berlin, Brücke-Museum, Karl
und Emy Schmidt-Rottluff Stiftung
cat. 75 II

Ernst Ludwig Kirchner
Die Geliebte, 1915
The Loved One
color woodcut, 28.8x23.6 cm
Berlin, Brücke-Museum, Karl
und Emy Schmidt-Rottluff Stiftung
cat. 75 III

Ernst Ludwig Kirchner
Kämpfe (Qualen der Liebe), 1915
Troubles (Tribulations of love)
color woodcut, 33.6x21.7 cm
Berlin, Brücke-Museum, Karl
und Emy Schmidt-Rottluff Stiftung
cat. 75IV

Ernst Ludwig Kirchner, *Schlemihl
in der Einsamkeit des Zimmers*, 1915
Schlemihl alone in his room
color woodcut, 33.3x23.8 cm
Berlin, Brücke-Museum, Karl
und Emy Schmidt-Rottluff Stiftung
cat. 75V

Ernst Ludwig Kirchner, *Begegnung Schlemihls mit dem grauen Männlein auf der Straße*, 1915
Schlemihl meets the little gray man on the road
color woodcut, 30.5x31 cm
Berlin, Brücke-Museum, Karl und Emy Schmidt-Rottluff Stiftung
cat. 75VI

Ernst Ludwig Kirchner, *Schlemihls Begegnung mit dem Schatten*, 1915
Schlemihl's meeting with the Shadow
color woodcut, 30.5x29.3 cm
Berlin, Brücke-Museum, Karl und Emy Schmidt-Rottluff Stiftung
cat. 75VII

Max Pechstein, *Das Vater Unser*, 1921
The Lord's Prayer
portfolio with 12 woodcuts
Berlin, Kupferstichkabinett
cat. 76

Max Pechstein
Das Vater Unser I, 1921
The Lord's Prayer I
woodcut from *Das Vater Unser*
Berlin, Kupferstichkabinett
cat. 76I

Max Pechstein, *Vater Unser*
Der Du bist im Himmel, 1921
Our Father, who art in Heaven
woodcut from *Das Vater Unser*
Berlin, Kupferstichkabinett
cat. 76II

Max Pechstein
Geheiliget werde Dein Name, 1921
Holy be Thy Name
woodcut from *Das Vater Unser*
Berlin, Kupferstichkabinett
cat. 76III

Max Pechstein, *Dein Reich Komme Dein Wille geschehe Wie im Himmel also auch auf Erden*, 1921
Thy Kingdom come, Thy Will be done, in Heaven as it is on Earth
woodcut from *Das Vater Unser*
Berlin, Kupferstichkabinett
cat. 76IV

Max Pechstein, *Unser täglich Brot gieb uns heute*, 1921
Give us this day our daily bread
woodcut from *Das Vater Unser*
Berlin, Kupferstichkabinett
cat. 76V

Max Pechstein
Und vergieb uns Unsre Schuld, 1921
And forgive us our trespasses
woodcut from *Das Vater Unser*
Berlin, Kupferstichkabinett
cat. 76VI

Max Pechstein, *Wie wir vergeben unsern Schuldigern*, 1921
We forgive those who trespass against us
woodcut from *Das Vater Unser*
Berlin, Kupferstichkabinett
cat. 76VII

Max Pechstein, *Und führe uns nicht in Versuchung*, 1921
And lead us not into temptation
woodcut from *Das Vater Unser*
Berlin, Kupferstichkabinett
cat. 76VIII

Max Pechstein, *Sondern erlöse uns von dem Übel*, 1921
Deliver us from evil
woodcut from *Das Vater Unser*
Berlin, Kupferstichkabinett
cat. 76IX

Max Pechstein
Denn Dein ist das Reich, 1921
For thine is the Kingdom
woodcut from *Das Vater Unser*
Berlin, Kupferstichkabinett
cat. 76X

Max Pechstein, *Und die Kraft
und Die Herrlichkeit*, 1921
The Power and the Glory
woodcut from *Das Vater Unser*
Berlin, Kupferstichkabinett
cat. 76XI

Max Pechstein, *Von Ewigkeit
zu Ewigkeit, Amen!*, 1921
Forever and ever, Amen!
woodcut from *Das Vater Unser*
Berlin, Kupferstichkabinett
cat. 76XII

Karl Schmidt-Rottluff, *Kuß der Liebe*
from *Neun Holzschnitten*, 1918
Loving Kiss, from *Nine Woodcuts*
Berlin, Kupferstichkabinett
cat. 771

Karl Schmidt-Rottluff, *Kristus*
from *Neun Holzschnitten*, 1918
Christ, from *Nine Woodcuts*
Berlin, Kupferstichkabinett
cat. 77 II

Karl Schmidt-Rottluff, *Jünger*
from *Neun Holzschnitten*, 1918
Apostle, from *Nine Woodcuts*
Berlin, Kupferstichkabinett
cat. 77 III

Karl Schmidt-Rottluff
Gang nach Emmaus
from *Neun Holzschnitten*, 1918
Road to Emmaus
from *Nine Woodcuts*
Berlin, Kupferstichkabinett
cat. 77 IV

Karl Schmidt-Rottluff
Kristus flucht dem Feigenbaum
from *Neun Holzschnitten*, 1918
Christ curses the fig-tree
from *Nine Woodcuts*
Berlin, Kupferstichkabinett
cat. 77 V

Karl Schmidt-Rottluff
Petri Fischzug
from *Neun Holzschnitten*, 1918
Draft of the Fishes
from *Nine Woodcuts*
Berlin, Kupferstichkabinett
cat. 77VI

Karl Schmidt-Rottluff
Kristus und die Ehebrecherin
from *Neun Holzschnitten*, 1918
Christ and the adulteress
from *Nine Woodcuts*
Berlin, Kupferstichkabinett
cat. 77VII

Karl Schmidt-Rottluff, *Maria*
from *Neun Holzschnitten*, 1918
The Virgin Mary
from *Nine Woodcuts*
Berlin, Kupferstichkabinett
cat. 77VIII

Karl Schmidt-Rottluff, *Kristus*
und Judas, from *Neun Holzschnitten*
1918
Christ and Judas
from *Nine Woodcuts*
Berlin, Kupferstichkabinett
cat. 77IX

Ernst Barlach, *Der Rächer*
The Avenger
bronze, after a 1914 model
44x22x58 cm
Ludwigshafen am Rhein
Wilhelm Hack Museum
cat. 78

Ernst Barlach, *Der Ekstatiker*
The Ecstatic One
wood, 52x16x35 cm
Zurich, Kunsthaus
cat. 79

Käthe Kollwitz
Liebespaar (Lovers), 1913
casting after a 1954 bronze
71x47x49 cm
Beverly Hills
The Robert Gore Rifkind Collection
cat. 80

Heinrich Maria Davringhausen
Der Irre, 1916
The Fool
oil on canvas, 198.5x119.5 cm
Münster
Westfälisches Landesmuseum
cat. 81

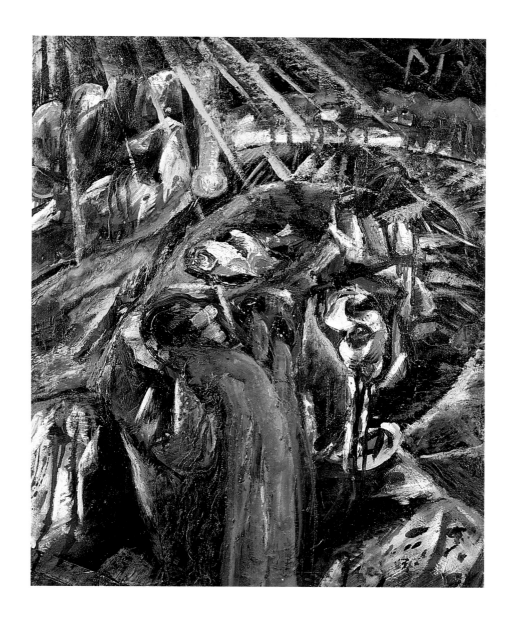

Otto Dix, *Sterbender Krieger*, 1915
Dying Warrior
oil on cardboard on board
68.5x54.4 cm
Schaffhausen
Museum zu Allerheiligen
Sturzenegger-Stiftung
cat. 82

Otto Dix, *Schützengraben*, 1918
Trench
gouache, 39x41 cm
Private Collection
cat. 83

August Macke, *Der Abschied*, 1914
The Farewell
oil on canvas, 100.5x130.5 cm
Cologne, Museum Ludwig
Stiftung Haubrich
cat. 84

Max Beckmann, *Die Granate*, 1915
The Grenade
drypoint, 43.6x28.9 cm
Frankfurt am Main
Städtische Galerie
im Städelsches Kunstinstitut
cat. 85

Max Beckmann
Die große Operation, 1914
The Big Operation
drypoint, 30x44.8 cm
Frankfurt am Main
Städtische Galerie
im Städelsches Kunstinstitut
cat. 86

Max Beckmann, *Leichenhaus*, 1915
Morgue
drypoint, 25.9x35.9 cm
Frankfurt am Main
Städtische Galerie
im Städelsches Kunstinstitut
cat. 87

Max Beckmann, *Sturmangriff*, 1916
Assault
drypoint etching, 17.7x25.5 cm
Hannover, Sprengel Museum
cat. 88

from left, from top to bottom
Otto Dix, *Soldatengrab zwischen den Linien*, 1924
Soldiers' grave between the lines
from the portfolio *Der Krieg (War)*, with 50
etchings with aquatint on copperplate paper
19.3x28.9 cm
published by Karl Nierendorf, Berlin, 1924
Berlin, Kupferstichkabinett
cat. 89I

Otto Dix, *Verschüttete; Januar 1916
Champagne*, 1924
Buried alive; January 1916, Champagne
from the portfolio *Der Krieg*
etching with aquatint on copperplate paper
14x19.7 cm
Berlin, Kupferstichkabinett
cat. 89II

Otto Dix, *Gastote; Templeux-La-Fosse, August 1916*, 1924
Gas victims; Templeux-La-Fosse, August 1916
from the portfolio *Der Krieg*
etching with aquatint on copperplate paper
19.4x28.9 cm
Berlin, Kupferstichkabinett
cat. 89III

Otto Dix, *Trichterfeld bei Dontrien von Leuchtkugeln
erhellt*, 1924
Crater field near Dontrien lit by flares
from the portfolio *Der Krieg*
etching with aquatint on copperplate paper
19.5x26 cm
Berlin, Kupferstichkabinett
cat. 89IV

Otto Dix, *Pferdekadaver*, 1924
Horse cadaver
from the portfolio *Der Krieg*
etching with aquatint on copperplate paper
14.5x19.7
Berlin, Kupferstichkabinett
cat. 89V

Otto Dix, *Verwundeter, Herbst 1916
Bapaume*, 1924
Wounded man, autumn 1916, Bapaume
from the portfolio *Der Krieg*
etching with aquatint on copperplate paper
19.7x29 cm
Berlin, Kupferstichkabinett
cat. 89VI

from left, from top to bottom
Otto Dix, *Bei Langemarck, Februar 1918*, 1924
Near Langemarck, February 1918
from the portfolio *Der Krieg*
etching with aquatint on copperplate paper
24.7x29.3 cm
Berlin, Kupferstichkabinett
cat. 89VII

Otto Dix, *Relaisposten, Herbstschlacht
in der Champagne*, 1924
Relay post, autumn battle in Champagne
from the portfolio *Der Krieg*
etching with aquatint on copperplate paper
14.8x19.8 cm
Berlin, Kupferstichkabinett
cat. 89VIII

Otto Dix, *Zerfallenden Kampfgraben*, 1924
Disintegrating trench
from the portfolio *Der Krieg*
etching with aquatint on copperplate paper
30x24.4 cm
Berlin, Kupferstichkabinett
cat. 89IX

Otto Dix, *Fliehender Verwundeter
Sommerschlacht 1916*, 1924
Wounded man fleeing summer battle 1916
from the portfolio *Der Krieg*
etching with aquatint on copperplate paper
19.7x14 cm
Berlin, Kupferstichkabinett
cat. 89X

Otto Dix, *Verlassene Stellung bei Neuville*, 1924
Abandoned position near Neuville
from the portfolio *Der Krieg*
etching with aquatint on copperplate paper
19.7x14.6 cm
Berlin, Kupferstichkabinett
cat. 89XI

Otto Dix, *Sturmtruppe geht unter Gas vor*, 1924
Shock troops advance under gas
from the portfolio *Der Krieg*
etching with aquatint on copperplate paper
19.6x29.1 cm
Berlin, Kupferstichkabinett
cat. 89XII

from left, from top to bottom
Otto Dix, *Mahlzeit in der Sappe, Lorettohohe*, 1924
Mealtime in the trench, Loretto heights
from the portfolio *Der Krieg*
etching with aquatint on copperplate paper
19.6x29 cm
Berlin, Kupferstichkabinett
cat. 89XIII

Otto Dix, *Ruhende Kompanie*, 1924
Resting company
from the portfolio *Der Krieg*
etching with aquatint on copperplate paper
26x19.8 cm
Berlin, Kupferstichkabinett
cat. 89XIV

Otto Dix, *Verlassene Stellung bei Vis-en-Artois*, 1924
Abandoned position near Vis-en-Artois
from the portfolio *Der Krieg*
etching with aquatint on copperplate paper
19.6x26 cm
Berlin, Kupferstichkabinett
cat. 89XV

Otto Dix, *Leiche im Drahtverhau Flandern*, 1924
Corpse in barbed wire, Flanders
from the portfolio *Der Krieg*
etching with aquatint on copperplate paper
30x24.3 cm
Berlin, Kupferstichkabinett
cat. 89XVI

from left, from top to bottom
Otto Dix, *Leuchtkugel erhellt die Monacuferme*, 1924
Flare illuminates the Monacuferme
from the portfolio *Der Krieg*
etching with aquatint on copperplate paper
14.8x19.8 cm
Berlin, Kupferstichkabinett
cat. 89XVII

Otto Dix, *Toter Sappenposter*, 1924
Dead sentry in the trench
from the portfolio *Der Krieg*
etching with aquatint on copperplate paper
19.8x14.7 cm
Berlin, Kupferstichkabinett
cat. 89XVIII

Otto Dix, *Totentanz anno 17, Höhe toter Mann*, 1924
Dance of death 1917, Dead Man's Hill
from the portfolio *Der Krieg*
etching with aquatint on copperplate paper
24.5x30 cm
Berlin, Kupferstichkabinett
cat. 89XIX

Otto Dix, *Die zweite Kompanie wird heute Nacht abgelöst*, 1924
The second company will be relieved tonight
from the portfolio *Der Krieg*
etching with aquatint on copperplate paper
19.8x25.8 cm
Berlin, Kupferstichkabinett
cat. 89XX

Otto Dix, *Abgekämpfte Truppe geht zurück, Sommeschlacht*, 1924
Battle-weary troops retreat, Battle of the Somme
from the portfolio *Der Krieg*
etching with aquatint on copperplate paper
19.8x28.9 cm
Berlin, Kupferstichkabinett
cat. 89XXI

Otto Dix, *Nächtliche Begegnung mit einem Irrsinigen*, 1924
Nocturnal encounter with a lunatic
from the portfolio *Der Krieg*
etching with aquatint on copperplate paper
26.2x19.7 cm
Berlin, Kupferstichkabinett
cat. 89XXII

from left, from top to bottom
Otto Dix, *Toter im Schlamm*, 1924
Dead man in the mud
from the portfolio *Der Krieg*
etching with aquatint on copperplate
paper, 19.5x25.8 cm
Berlin, Kupferstichkabinett
cat. 89XXIII

Otto Dix, *Granattrichter mit Blumen
Frühling 1916*, 1924
Shell-crater with flowers, spring
1916, from the portfolio *Der Krieg*
etching with aquatint on copperplate
paper, 14.8x19.8 cm
Berlin, Kupferstichkabinett
cat. 89XXIV

Otto Dix
Die Trümmer von Langemarck, 1924
The ruins of Langemarck
from the portfolio *Der Krieg*
etching with aquatint on copperplate
paper, 30x24.6 cm
Berlin, Kupferstichkabinett
cat. 89XXV

Otto Dix, *Sterbender Soldat*, 1924
Dying soldier
from the portfolio *Der Krieg*
etching with aquatint on copperplate
paper, 19.8x14.8 cm
Berlin, Kupferstichkabinett
cat. 89XXVI

from left, from top to bottom
Otto Dix, *Abend in der Wijtschaete-Ebene,
November 1917*, 1924
Evening on the Wijtschaete plain, November 1917
from the portfolio *Der Krieg*
etching with aquatint on copperplate paper
24.6x30 cm
Berlin, Kupferstichkabinett
cat. 89XXVII

Otto Dix, *Gesehen am Steilhang von Cléry-sur-Somme*, 1924
Seen on the escarpment at Cléry-sur-Somme
from the portfolio *Der Krieg*
etching with aquatint on copperplate paper
26x19.6 cm
Berlin, Kupferstichkabinett
cat. 89XXVIII

Otto Dix, *Gefunden beim Grabendurchstich,
Auberive*, 1924
Found while digging a trench, Auberive
from the portfolio *Der Krieg*
etching with aquatint on copperplate paper
19.5x29 cm
Berlin, Kupferstichkabinett
cat. 89XXIX

Otto Dix, *Drahtverhau vor dem Kampfgraben*, 1924
Tangled barbed wire before the trench
from the portfolio *Der Krieg*
etching with aquatint on copperplate paper
26x19.5
Berlin, Kupferstichkabinett
cat. 89XXX

Otto Dix, *Schädel*, 1924
Skull
from the portfolio *Der Krieg*
etching with aquatint on copperplate paper
25.7x19.5 cm
Berlin, Kupferstichkabinett
cat. 89XXXI

Otto Dix, *Matrosen in Antwerpen*, 1924
Sailors in Antwerp
from the portfolio *Der Krieg*
etching with aquatint on copperplate paper
24.5x30 cm
Berlin, Kupferstichkabinett
cat. 89XXXII

from left, from top to bottom
Otto Dix, *Lens wird mit Bomben belegt*, 1924
Lens being bombed
from the portfolio *Der Krieg*
etching with aquatint on copperplate paper
29.8x24.6 cm
Berlin, Kupferstichkabinett
cat. 89XXXIII

Otto Dix, *Frontsoldat in Brüssel*, 1924
Front-line soldier in Brussels
from the portfolio *Der Krieg*
etching with aquatint on copperplate paper
28.8x19.8 cm
Berlin, Kupferstichkabinett
cat. 89XXXIV

Otto Dix, *Die Irrsinnige von Sainte-Marie-à-Py*, 1924
The madwoman of Sainte-Marie-à-Py
from the portfolio *Der Krieg*
etching with aquatint on copperplate paper
28.8x19.8 cm
Berlin, Kupferstichkabinett
cat. 89XXXV

Otto Dix, *Besuch bei Madame Germaine in Méricourt*, 1924
Visit to Madame Germaine's in Méricourt
from the portfolio *Der Krieg*
etching with aquatint on copperplate paper
26,1x19.8 cm
Berlin, Kupferstichkabinett
cat. 89XXXVI

Otto Dix, *Kantine in Haplincourt*, 1924
Canteen in Haplincourt
from the portfolio *Der Krieg*
etching with aquatint on copperplate paper
19.8x25.9 cm
Berlin, Kupferstichkabinett
cat. 89XXXVII

Otto Dix, *Zerschossene*, 1924
Shot to pieces
from the portfolio *Der Krieg*
etching with aquatint on copperplate paper
14.9x20.1
Berlin, Kupferstichkabinett
cat. 89XXXVIII

from left, from top to bottom
Otto Dix, *Durch Fliegerbomben zerstörtes Haus*, 1924
House destroyed by aerial bombs
from the portfolio *Der Krieg*
etching with aquatint on copperplate paper
29.8x24.4 cm
Berlin, Kupferstichkabinett
cat. 89XXXIX

Otto Dix, *Transplantation*, 1924
Skin graft
from the portfolio *Der Krieg*
etching with aquatint on copperplate paper
19.8x14.9 cm
Berlin, Kupferstichkabinett
cat. 89XL

Otto Dix, *Maschinengewehrzug geht vor, Somme, November 1916*, 1924
Machine-gun squad advances, Somme, November 1916
from the portfolio *Der Krieg*
etching with aquatint on copperplate paper
24.5x30 cm
Berlin, Kupferstichkabinett
cat. 89XLI

Otto Dix, *Toter, Saint-Clément*, 1924
Dead man, Saint-Clément
from the portfolio *Der Krieg*
etching with aquatint on copperplate paper
29.9x25.9 cm
Berlin, Kupferstichkabinett
cat. 89XLII

Otto Dix, *Essenholer bei Pilkem*, 1924
Ration carriers near Pilkem
from the portfolio *Der Krieg*
etching with aquatint on copperplate paper
24.5x29.8 cm
Berlin, Kupferstichkabinett
cat. 89XLIII

Otto Dix
Überfall einer Schleichpatrouille, 1924
Surprise attack
from the portfolio *Der Krieg*
etching with aquatint on copperplate paper
20x15 cm
Berlin, Kupferstichkabinett
cat. 89XLIV

Otto Dix, *Unterstand*, 1924
Foxhole
from the portfolio *Der Krieg*
etching with aquatint on copperplate
paper, 19.8x29 cm
Berlin, Kupferstichkabinett
cat. 89XLV

Otto Dix, *Die Schlafenden*
von Fort Vaux; Gastote, 1924
The sleepers of Fort Vaux
gas victims
from the portfolio *Der Krieg*
etching with aquatint on copperplate
paper, 24.8x29.8 cm
Berlin, Kupferstichkabinett
cat. 89XLVI

Otto Dix, *Verwundetentransport*
im Houthulster Wald, 1924
Transporting the wounded
in Houthulster Forest
from the portfolio *Der Krieg*
etching with aquatint on copperplate
paper, 19.8x25.4 cm
Berlin, Kupferstichkabinett
cat. 89XLVII

Otto Dix, *Die Sappenposten haben*
nachts das Feuer zu unterhalten, 1924
The outposts in the trenches must
mantain the bombardment at night
from the portfolio *Der Krieg*
etching with aquatint on copperplate
paper, 24.7x30 cm
Berlin, Kupferstichkabinett
cat. 89XLVIII

Otto Dix
Appell der Zurückgekehrten, 1924
Roll call of returning troops
from the portfolio *Der Krieg*
etching with aquatint on copperplate
paper, 19.8x28.8 cm
Berlin, Kupferstichkabinett
cat. 89XLIX

Otto Dix
Tote vor der Stellung bei Tahure, 1924
Dead men before the position
near Tahure
from the portfolio *Der Krieg*
etching with aquatint on copperplate
paper, 19.7x25.8 cm
Berlin, Kupferstichkabinett
cat. 89L

Heinrich Ehmsen
Geiselerschießung (Revolution I), 1924
The Firing Squad (Revolution I)
oil on canvas, 135x105.5 cm
Berlin, Nationalgalerie
Staatliche Museen zu Berlin
cat. 90

Conrad Felixmüller
Otto Dix malt, 1920
Otto Dix paints
oil on canvas, 120.5x95.5 cm
Berlin, Nationalgalerie
Staatliche Museen zu Berlin
cat. 91

Conrad Felixmüller
Der Agitator, 1920
The Agitator
oil on canvas, 125x93 cm
Berlin, Nationalgalerie
Staatliche Museen zu Berlin
cat. 92

George Grosz, *Explosion*, 1917
oil on board, 47.8x68.2 cm
New York
The Museum of Modern Art
gift of Mr. and Mrs. Irving
Moscovitz, 1963
cat. 93

Walter Jacob
Das Jüngste Gericht, 1920
The Last Judgment
oil on canvas, 115.3x120.7 cm
Beverly Hills, The Robert Gore
Rifkind Foundation
cat. 94

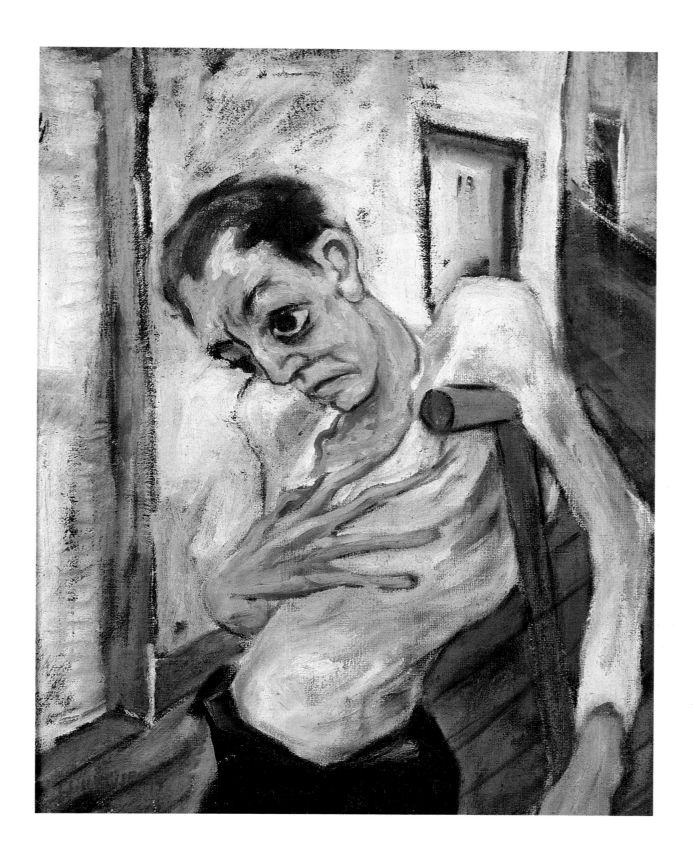

Will Küpper, *Nach dem Krieg*, 1919
After the War
oil on canvas, 70x55 cm
Düsseldorf, Stadtmuseum
cat. 95

Georg Scholz, *Nächtlicher Lärm*
(Nightly Noise), 1919
oil on canvas, 56.8x50.9 cm
Milwaukee, The Marvin
and Janet Fishman Collection
cat. 96

Gert Wollheim
Der Verwundete, 1919
The Wounded One
oil on canvas, 156x178 cm
Private Collection
cat. 97

from left, from top to bottom
Otto Dix, *Straße*, 1919
Street
woodcut, 24x17.7 cm
from *Neun Holzschnitte*, 1919–21
Nine Woodcuts
portfolio with 9 woodcuts, 43x35 cm
Berlin, Kupferstichkabinett
cat. 98I

Otto Dix, *Elektrische*, 1920
Streetcar
woodcut, 28x23.8 cm
from *Neun Holzschnitte*, 1919–21
portfolio with 9 woodcuts, 43x35 cm
Berlin, Kupferstichkabinett
cat. 98II

Otto Dix, *Die Prominenten
(Konstellation)*, 1920
(The celebrities: constellation)
woodcut, 25,1x20 cm
from *Neun Holzschnitte*, 1919–21
portfolio with 9 woodcuts, 43x35 cm
Berlin, Kupferstichkabinett
cat. 98III

Otto Dix, *Lärm der Straße*, 1920
Street noise
woodcut, 27.9x23.5 cm
from *Neun Holzschnitte*, 1919–21
portfolio with 9 woodcuts, 43x35 cm
Berlin, Kupferstichkabinett
cat. 98IV

Otto Dix, *Liebespaar*, 1921
Lovers
woodcut, 25.2x19.9 cm
from *Neun Holzschnitte*, 1919–21
portfolio with 9 woodcuts, 43x35 cm
Berlin, Kupferstichkabinett
cat. 98V

Otto Dix, *Katzen*, 1920
Cats
woodcut, 24x17.5 cm
from *Neun Holzschnitte*, 1919–21
portfolio with 9 woodcuts, 43x35 cm
Berlin, Kupferstichkabinett
cat. 98VI

Otto Dix, *Nächtliche Szene*, 1920
Nocturnal scene
woodcut, 25x15.8 cm
from *Neun Holzschnitte*, 1919–21
portfolio with 9 woodcuts, 43x35 cm
Berlin, Kupferstichkabinett
cat. 98VII

Otto Dix, *Apotheose*, 1919
Apotheosis
woodcut, 28,1x19.8 cm
from *Neun Holzschnitte*, 1919–21
portfolio with 9 woodcuts, 43x35 cm
Berlin, Kupferstichkabinett
cat. 98VIII

Otto Dix, *Scherzo*, 1920
woodcut, 24x17.6 cm
from *Neun Holzschnitte*, 1919–21
portfolio with 9 woodcuts, 43x35 cm
Berlin, Kupferstichkabinett
cat. 98IX

29/30   Lärm der Straße   DIX 20

29/30   Nächtlich Scene   DIX 20

29/30   Liebespaar   DIX 21

29/30   Apotheose   DIX M

29/30   Katzen   DIX 20

29/30   Scherzo   DIX 20

GEORGE GROSZ

„GOTT MIT UNS"

George Grosz, "*Gott mit uns*", 1920
God with us
portfolio with 10 photolithographs
frontispiece
Berlin, Kupferstichkabinett
cat. 99

George Grosz, *Gott mit uns*, 1920
God with us
photolithograph from the portfolio
Gott mit uns
30.2x42.9 cm
Berlin, Kupferstichkabinett
cat. 991

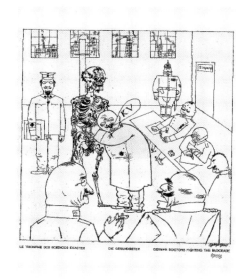

from left, from top to bottom
George Grosz, *Für Deutsches Recht und Deutsche Sitte*, 1920
For German right and custom
photolithograph from the portfolio
Gott mit uns
38x31.3 cm
Berlin, Kupferstichkabinett
cat. 99II

George Grosz, *Feierabend*, 1920
Evening rest
photolithograph from the portfolio
Gott mit uns
38.7x39.9 cm
Berlin, Kupferstichkabinett
cat. 99III

George Grosz
Licht und Luft dem Proletariat, 1920
Light and air for the proletariat
photolithograph from the portfolio
Gott mit uns
34.9x29.7 cm
Berlin, Kupferstichkabinett
cat. 99IV

George Grosz
Die Gesundbeter, 1920
The healers
photolithograph from the portfolio
Gott mit uns
31.6x29.6 cm
Berlin, Kupferstichkabinett
cat. 99V

George Grosz
Zuhälter des Todes, 1920
The pimp of death
photolithograph from the portfolio
Gott mit uns
38.4x30.1 cm
Berlin, Kupferstichkabinett
cat. 99VI

George Grosz
Die vollendete Demokratie, 1920
Perfect democracy
photolithograph from the portfolio
Gott mit uns
44.5x30.3 cm
Berlin, Kupferstichkabinett
cat. 99VII

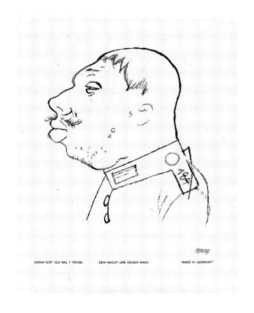

George Grosz, *Die Kommunisten
fallen – und die Devisen steigen*, 1920
The communists fall
The banners rise
photolithograph from the portfolio
Gott mit uns
30.5x45.2 cm
Berlin, Kupferstichkabinett
cat. 99VIII

George Grosz
Den Macht uns keiner Nach, 1920
We are the strongest
photolithograph from the portfolio
Gott mit uns
28.4x24.7 cm
Berlin, Kupferstichkabinett
cat. 99IX

Max Beckmann
Adam und Eva, 1917
oil on canvas, 79.8x56.7 cm
Berlin, Nationalgalerie
Staatliche Museen zu Berlin
purchased thanks to the
Ernst von Siemens-Kunstfond
cat. 100

Max Beckmann, *Frauenbad*, 1919
The Women's Bath
oil on canvas, 97 x 65 cm
Berlin, Nationalgalerie
Staatliche Museen zu Berlin
cat. 101

front page
Max Beckmann, *Das Trapez*, 1923
The Trapeze
oil on canvas, 196.5x84 cm
Toledo, The Toledo Museum of Art
purchased with funds from
the Libbey Endowment
gift of Edward Drummond Libbey
cat. 102

Max Beckmann, *Die Hölle*, 1918–19
The Hell
portfolio with 11 autographical
lithographs, cover with self-portrait
Berlin, Kupferstichkabinett
cat. 103

Max Beckmann
Der Nachhauseweg, 1918–19
The return
lithograph from the portfolio
Die Hölle
Berlin, Kupferstichkabinett
cat. 103I

Max Beckmann, *Die Straße*, 1918–19
The street
lithograph from the portfolio
Die Hölle
Berlin, Kupferstichkabinett
cat. 103II

Max Beckmann
Das Martyrium, 1918–19
Martyrdom
lithograph from the portfolio
Die Hölle
Berlin, Kupferstichkabinett
cat. 103III

Max Beckmann
Der Hunger, 1918–19
Hunger
lithograph from the portfolio
Die Hölle
Berlin, Kupferstichkabinett
cat. 103IV

Max Beckmann
Die Ideologen, 1918–19
The ideologues
lithograph from the portfolio
Die Hölle
Berlin, Kupferstichkabinett
cat. 103 V

Max Beckmann, *Die Nacht*, 1918–19
The night
lithograph from the portfolio
Die Hölle
Berlin, Kupferstichkabinett
cat. 103 VI

Max Beckmann, *Malepartus*, 1918–19
lithograph from the portfolio
Die Hölle
Berlin, Kupferstichkabinett
cat. 103 VII

Max Beckmann
Das patriotische Lied, 1918–19
Patriotic song
lithograph from the portfolio
Die Hölle
Berlin, Kupferstichkabinett
cat. 103 VIII

Max Beckmann, *Die Letzten*, 1918–19
The last
lithograph from the portfolio
Die Hölle
Berlin, Kupferstichkabinett
cat. 103 IX

Max Beckmann, *Die Familie*, 1918–19
The family
lithograph from the portfolio
Die Hölle
Berlin, Kupferstichkabinett
cat. 103 X

Oskar Kokoschka
Die Verkündigung, ca. 1911
The Annunciation
oil on canvas, 83x122.5 cm
Dortmund, Museum am Ostwall
cat. 104

Oskar Kokoschka
Dresden, Neustadt V, 1918–22
oil on canvas, 71x111 cm
Jerusalem, The Israel Museum
Sam Spiegel Collection
cat. 105

Oskar Kokoschka, *Die Heiden*, 1914
The Heathen
oil on canvas, 75.5x126 cm
Cologne, Museum Ludwig
Stiftung Haubrich
cat. 106

Oskar Kokoschka, *Die Jagd*, 1918
The Hunt
oil on canvas, 100x150.5 cm
Berlin, Nationalgalerie
Staatliche Museen zu Berlin
cat. 107

Oskar Kokoschka
Mann mit Puppe, 1922
Man with Doll
oil on canvas, 80x120 cm
Berlin, Nationalgalerie
Staatliche Museen zu Berlin
cat. 108

front page
Oskar Kokoschka
Bildnis William Wauer, 1910
Portrait of William Wauer
oil on canvas, 94x54.5 cm
Amsterdam, Stedelijk Museum
cat. 109

from left, from top to bottom
Oskar Kokoschka
Selbstbildnis, Brustbild mit Zeichenstift
Bust-length self-portrait
with drawing pencil
lithograph, 45.5x30.5 cm
from *"O Ewigkeit, du Donnerwort"*
Bachkantate, 1914
portfolio with 11 lithographs
Los Angeles County Museum of Art
The Robert Gore Rifkind Center
for German Expressionist Studies
cat. 110I

Oskar Kokoschka
Drachen über einer Flamme
Dragons over a flame
lithograph, 26.5x18.5 cm
from *"O Ewigkeit, du Donnerwort"*
Bachkantate, 1914
portfolio with 11 lithographs
Los Angeles County Museum of Art
The Robert Gore Rifkind Center
for German Expressionist Studies
cat. 110II

Oskar Kokoschka
Der Wanderer im Gewitter
Traveler in a thunderstorm
lithograph, 43x29.8 cm
from *"O Ewigkeit, du Donnerwort"*
Bachkantate, 1914
portfolio with 11 lithographs
Los Angeles County Museum of Art
The Robert Gore Rifkind Center
for German Expressionist Studies
cat. 110III

Oskar Kokoschka
Das Weib führt den Mann
The woman leads the man
lithograph, 39.2x31.3 cm
from *"O Ewigkeit, du Donnerwort"*
Bachkantate, 1914
portfolio with 11 lithographs
Los Angeles County Museum of Art
The Robert Gore Rifkind Center
for German Expressionist Studies
cat. 110IV

from left, from top to bottom
Oskar Kokoschka, *Die Flehende*
The supplicant
lithograph, 41,1x27.7 cm
from *"O Ewigkeit, du Donnerwort"*
Bachkantate, 1914
portfolio with 11 lithographs
Los Angeles County Museum of Art
The Robert Gore Rifkind Center
for German Expressionist Studies
cat. 110V

Oskar Kokoschka, *Das letzte Lager*
The last camp
lithograph, 41,1x30.7 cm
from *"O Ewigkeit, du Donnerwort"*
Bachkantate, 1914
portfolio with 11 lithographs
Los Angeles County Museum of Art
The Robert Gore Rifkind Center
for German Expressionist Studies
cat. 110VI

Oskar Kokoschka, *Furcht und*
Hoffnung: Der Mann tröstet das Weib
Fear and hope: the man comforts
the woman
lithograph, 38.5x30.3 cm
from *"O Ewigkeit, du Donnerwort"*
Bachkantate, 1914
portfolio with 11 lithographs
Los Angeles County Museum of Art
The Robert Gore Rifkind Center
for German Expressionist Studies
cat. 110VII

Oskar Kokoschka, *Mann und W...*
auf dem Sterbeweg
Man and woman on the road to death
lithograph, 38.1x30 cm
from *"O Ewigkeit, du Donnerwort"*
Bachkantate, 1914
portfolio with 11 lithographs
Los Angeles County Museum of Art
The Robert Gore Rifkind Center
for German Expressionist Studies
cat. 110VIII

Oskar Kokoschka
Der Adler: "Selig sind die Toten"
The eagle: "Blessed are the dead"
lithograph, 35.3x29.1 cm
from *"O Ewigkeit, du Donnerwort"*
Bachkantate, 1914
portfolio with 11 lithographs
Los Angeles County Museum of Art
The Robert Gore Rifkind Center
for German Expressionist Studies
cat. 110IX

Oskar Kokoschka, *Der Mann erhebt*
seinen Kopf aus dem Grabe
The man raises his head
from the grave
lithograph, 44.4x33.7 cm
from *"O Ewigkeit, du Donnerwort"*
Bachkantate, 1914
portfolio with 11 lithographs
Los Angeles County Museum of Art
The Robert Gore Rifkind Center
for German Expressionist Studies
cat. 110X

Oskar Kokoschka
Pieta: "Es ist genug"
Pietà: "It is enough"
lithograph, 29.2x33.7 cm
from *"O Ewigkeit, du Donnerwort"*
Bachkantate, 1914
portfolio with 11 lithographs
Los Angeles County Museum of Art
The Robert Gore Rifkind Center
for German Expressionist Studies
cat. 110XI

Erich Heckel
Varieté (Vorstadtkabarett), 1919
Variety (Suburban Cabaret)
oil on canvas, 96x81.8 cm
Munich, Bayerische
Staatsgemäldesammlungen
Staatsgalerie moderner Kunst
cat. 111

Erich Heckel, *Am Strand*, 1921
On the Beach
oil on canvas, 80.5x70.5 cm
Essen, Museum Folkwang
cat. 112

Ernst Ludwig Kirchner
Wintermondnacht, 1919
Winter Landscape in Moonlight
oil on canvas, 120.7 x 120.7 cm
Detroit, The Detroit Institute of Arts
Gift of Curt Valentin
cat. 113

Ernst Ludwig Kirchner
Rückkehr der Tiere, Stafelalp, 1919
Return of the Animals, Alpine Pasture
oil on canvas, 120.5x168 cm
Bern-Davos, E. W. K.
Collection
cat. 114

Otto Müller, *Sommertag*, 1921
Summer Day
oil on canvas, 80x98 cm
Berlin, Nationalgalerie
Staatliche Museen zu Berlin
cat. 115

Karl Schmidt-Rottluff
Heide und Mond, 1920
Moor and Moon
oil on canvas, 76.5x90 cm
Hannover, Sprengel Museum
cat. 116

Karl Schmidt-Rottluff
Blauer Mond, 1920
Blue Moon
oil on canvas, 75.5x89 cm
Berlin, Brücke-Museum
cat. 117

Karl Schmidt-Rottluff
Gespräch über den Tod, 1920
Conversation about Death
oil on canvas, 123 x 110 cm
Munich, Bayerische
Staatsgemäldesammlungen
Staatsgalerie moderner Kunst
cat. 118

Otto Dix, *Prager Straße*, 1920
oil on canvas, 100x80 cm
Stuttgart, Galerie der Stadt
cat. 119

Otto Dix, *Die Skatspieler*, 1920
Skat Players
oil on canvas and collage, 110x87 cm
Berlin, Nationalgalerie Staatliche Museen zu Berlin purchased with funds
of the Verein der Freunde der Nationalgalerie und des Bundes
cat. 120

Otto Dix, *Salon I*, 1921
oil on canvas, 86x120.5 cm
Stuttgart, Galerie der Stadt
cat. 121

front page
George Grosz, *Grauer Tag*, 1921
Gray Day
oil on canvas, 115x80 cm
Berlin, Nationalgalerie
Staatliche Museen zu Berlin
cat. 122

George Grosz
Stützen der Gesellschaft, 1926
The Pillars of Society
oil on canvas, 200x108 cm
Berlin, Nationalgalerie
Staatliche Museen zu Berlin
cat. 123

Max Beckmann
Tanz in Baden-Baden, 1923
Dance in Baden-Baden
oil on canvas, 108x66 cm
Munich, Bayerische
Staatsgemäldesammlungen
Staatsgalerie moderner Kunst
cat. 124

George Grosz, *Ich will alles um mich her ausrotten*, 1922
photolitograph from *Die Räuber*
I want everything to annihilate myself
from *The Robbers*, act I, 1 Scene
Berlin, Kupferstichkabinett
cat. 125I

George Grosz, *In meinem Gebiet soll's soweit kommen ...*, 1922
May it happen in my own land
photolitograph from *Die Räuber*
act II, 2 Scene
Berlin, Kupferstichkabinett
cat. 125II

George Grosz, *Es ist doch eine jämmerliche Rolle ...*, 1922
The poor man's lot
photolitograph from *Die Räuber*
act I, 1 Scene
Berlin, Kupferstichkabinett
cat. 125III

from left, from top to bottom
George Grosz, *Ich habe das Meine getan ...*, 1922
I have done my part
photolitograph from *Die Räuber*
act II, 3 Scene
Berlin, Kupferstichkabinett
cat. 125IV

George Grosz, *Da donnern
sie Sanftmut und Duldung aus ihren Wolken ...*, 1922
Meekness and tolerance have returned
photolitograph from *Die Räuber*
act II, 3 Scene
Berlin, Kupferstichkabinett
cat. 125V

George Grosz, *Löwen und Leoparden
füttern ihre Jungen ...*, 1922
Lions and leopards feed their young
photolitograph from *Die Räuber*
act I, 2 Scene
Berlin, Kupferstichkabinett
cat. 125VI

George Grosz, *Schwimme
wer schwimmen kann ...*, 1922
Sink or swam
photolitograph from *Die Räuber*
act I, 1 Scene
Berlin, Kupferstichkabinett
cat. 125VII

George Grosz, *Gottes sichtbarer
Segen ist bei mir*, 1922
God's blessing is with me
photolitograph from *Die Räuber*
act II, 3 Scene
Berlin, Kupferstichkabinett
cat. 125VIII

George Grosz, *Das Recht wohnet
beim Überwältiger*, 1922
Might is right
photolithograph from *Die Räuber*
act I, 1 Scene
Berlin, Kupferstichkabinett
cat. 125IX

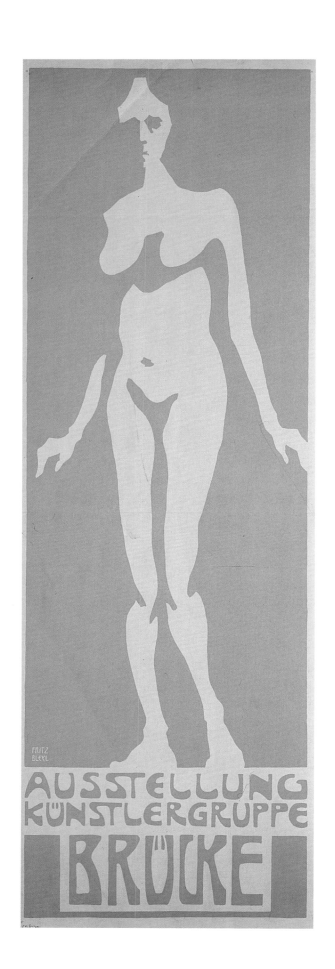

Hilmar Friedrich Wilhelm (Fritz) Bleyl,
*Ausstellung Künstlergruppe
Brücke*, Dresden 1906
Brücke group exhibition
poster, color lithograph
cat. 126

Max Pechstein, *Kunstausstellung III. Austellung Neue Secession Galerie M. Macht*, Berlin 1911
Art Exhibition III. New Secession Exhibition, Galerie M. Macht
poster, color lithograph
cat. 127

Ernst Ludwig Kirchner, *KG Brücke in Galerie Arnold*, 1910
KG Brücke at the Galerie Arnold
poster, woodcut
cat. 128

Oskar Kokoschka
Oskar Kokoschka, 1921
poster for
the exhibition
at Fritz Gurlitt
lithograph
cat. 129

Wassily Kandinsky
Phalanx 1. Ausstellung
Munich 1901
Phalanx 1. Exhibition
poster
color lithograph
cat. 130

Rudolf Bauer
Sonderausstellung
Der Sturm
Expressionisten
Futuristen - Kubisten
Galerie Arnold
Dresden 1918
Special Exhibition
of the Der Sturm
Expressionists -
Futurists - Cubists
Galerie Arnold
poster, lithograph
cat. 131

Erich Heckel
Kaiser Wilhelm
Museum Crefeld I.
Ausstellung
Neuzeitlicher Deutscher
Kunst, 1920
Kaiser Wilhelm
Museum (Crefeld) I.
Modern German Art
Exhibition
poster, woodcut
cat. 132

Wassily Kandinsky
Neue Künstler
Vereinigung München
Ausstellung I
Munich 1909
I Exhibition
of the Neue Künstler
Vereinigung (New
Artists' Union)
of Munich
poster
color lithograph
cat. 133

Erich Heckel and
Ernst Ludwig
Kirchner
Der Neue Kunstsalon
München, 1912
New Art Salon
Munich
poster, woodcut
cat. 134

Richter-Berlin, *3 Worte: Ungestörte Demobildmachung Aufbau der Republik Frieden*, 1918–19
3 Words: Untroubled Demobilization Construction of the Peace Republic
poster, color lithograph
cat. 135

Max Pechstein, *Erwürgt nicht die junge Freiheit durch Unordnung und Brudermord Sonst verhungern Eure Kinder*, 1919
Do not smother this new freedom with turmoil and fratricidal warring Or your children will die of hunger
poster, color lithograph
cat. 136

Max Pechstein, *Die National Versammlung der Grundstein der Deutschen Sozialistischen Republik*, 1919
National Assembly of the German Socialist Republic Cornerstone
poster, color lithograph
cat. 137

Laszlo Peri, *Bündnis Moskau Berlin bringt Rettung*, 1921
The Moscow-Berlin alliance comes to the rescue
poster, color lithograph
cat. 138

César Klein, *Wer nicht arbeitet ist der Totengräber seiner Kinder*, 1919
Those who do not work dig their children's graves
poster, color lithograph
cat. 139

Heinrich Vogeler, *Konsumenten! Vereinigt euch der Konsumgenossenschaft Vorwärts-Bremen Gemeinwirtschaft Socialismus*, Bremen ca. 1920
Consumers! Join the Vorwärts-Bremen (Forward-Bremen) Socialist Producers' Collective
poster, color lithograph
cat. 140

Heinz Fuchs, *Arbeiter Hunger Tod naht Streik*
zerstört, Arbeit ernährt Tut eure
Pflicht arbeitet, 1919
Worker Hunger Death approaches Strikes destroy
Work nourishes Do your duty work
poster, color lithograph
cat. 141

César Klein, *Arbeiter Bürger Bauern Soldaten aller*
Stamme Deutschlands
vereinigt euch zur Nationalversammlung, 1919
Workers citizens farmers soldiers
all groups of Germany join the National Assembly
poster, color lithograph
cat. 142

Max Pechstein, *An die Laterne*, 1919
poster for the magazine
lithograph
cat. 143

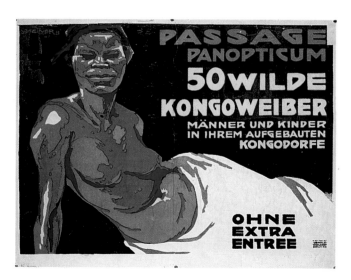

Erich Deutsch(-Dryden)
Richard's Grill Room, Berlin 1913
poster, color lithograph
cat. 144

Jo Steiner, *Bier Cabaret Senta Söneland*
Berlin, 1912
poster, color lithograph
cat. 145

Jo Steiner, *Passage Panopticum
50 wilde Kongoweiber*, Berlin 1913
Panoptic Passage 50 wild women
of the Congo
poster, color lithograph
cat. 146

Hans Poelzig, *Der Golem wie er
in die Welt kam Paul Wegener
UFA Union*, 1919–20
The Golem how it came into
the world, Paul Wegener-UFA Union
poster, color lithograph
cat. 147

Josef Fenneker, *Pogrom mit Ulka
Grüning Marmorhaus*, Berlin 1919
Pogrom with Ulka Grüning
Marmorhaus
poster, color lithograph
cat. 148

Josef Fenneker, *Der geheimnisvolle
Juwelendieb Abenteurer Geschichte
aus New Yorker Miliardarkreisen
Marmorhaus*, Berlin 1921
The mysterious jewel-thief Tale
of adventure of the New York circle
of Marmorhaus the millionaire
poster, color lithograph
cat. 149

Josef Fenneker, *Johannes Goth
Marmorhaus*, 1920
poster, lithograph
cat. 150

Ernst Ludwig Stahl, Otto Arpke
*Das Cabinet
des Dr. Caligari*, 1920
for the film *The Cabinet
of Dr. Caligari*
poster, color lithograph
cat. 151

Appendix

Programs, Manifestoes, Critical Writings
by Andrea Frey e Janni Müller-Hauck

Biographies of the Artists
by Wolf-Dieter Dube

Selected Chronology
by Janni Müller-Hauck
with the contribution of Massimo Cescon

Selected Bibliography
by Susan Trauger

Index of Names

Index of the Authors and the Works

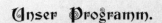

Unser Programm
manifesto of the Brücke group, 1906

Ernst Ludwig Kirchner
manifesto of the Brücke group, 1906

With faith in development and in a new generation of creators and appreciators we call together all youth. As youth, we carry the future and want to create for ourselves freedom of life and of movement against the long-established older forces. Everyone who with directness and authenticity conveys that which drives him to creation, belongs to us.

Ernst Ludwig Kirchner, "Gedrucktes Programm der Künstlergruppe 'Brücke'," 1906

In the year 1902 the painters Bleyl and Kirchner met in Dresden. Heckel came to them through his brother, a friend of Kirchner. Heckel brought Schmidt-Rottluff along, whom he knew from Chemnitz. They came together in Kirchner's studio to work there.
Here they found the opportunity to study the nude – the basis of all visual arts – in its natural freedom. From drawing on this basis resulted the desire, common to all, to derive inspiration for work from life itself, and to submit to direct experience. In a book *Odi profanum*, each individual drew and wrote down his ideas, and in this way they made it possible to compare their distinctive features.
So they grew, very naturally, into a group which came to be called "Brucke." One inspired the other. From southern Germany Kirchner brought the woodcut, which he had revived under the inspiration of the old prints in Nürnberg. Heckel carved wooden figures. Kirchner enriched this technique with polycromy and sought the rythm of closed form in pewter casting and in stone. The first exhibition of the group took place on its own premises in Dresden; it was given no recognition.
Dresden, however, yielded much inspiration through its scenic charm and old culture. Here "Brücke" also found its art-historical corroboration in Cranach, Beham and other medieval German masters. During an exhibit of Amiet in Dresden he was appointed to membership in the group. In 1905 Nolde followed, his fantastic style bringing a new feature to "Brücke." He enriched our exhibitions with his interesting etching technique and learned how we worked with the woodcut. On his invitation Schmidt-Rottluff went with him to Alsen, and later Schmidt-Rottluff and Heckel went to Dangast.
The brisk air of the North Sea brought forth a monumental Impressionism, especially in Schmidt-Rottluff. During this time, in Dresden, Kirchner continued to work in closed composition and in the ethnographic museum found in a parallel to his own creation in African negro sculpture and in Oceanic beam carvings. The desire to free himself from academic sterility led Pechstein to join "Brücke." Kirchner and Pech-

stein went to Gollverode, to work there together. An exhibition of "Brücke," including its new members, took place in the Salon Richter in Dresden and made a great impression on the young artists of Dresden. Heckel and Kirchner attempted to bring the new painting and its exhibition space into harmony. Kirchner furnished the rooms with murals and batiks, on which Heckel had worked with him.

In 1907 Nolde resigned from "Brücke"; Heckel and Kirchner went to the Moritzburg lakes, in order to study the nude in the open air; Schmidt-Rottluff worked in Dangast on the completion of his color rhythm; Heckel travelled to Italy and brought back with him the inspiration of Etruscan art; Pechstein went to Berlin to work on a commission for decorations. He attempted to bring the new painting into the "Sezession." In Dresden Kirchner studied tha hand printing of litography. Bleyl, who had gone into teaching, left "Brücke" in 1909. Pechstein went to Dangast to join Heckel. During the same year both of them came to Kirchner at Moritzburg in order to do studies of the nude in the lake environment.

In 1910 the "Neue Sezession" was organized after the rejection of younger German painters by the old "Sezession." In order to support Pechstein's position in the "Neue Sezession" Heckel, Kirchner and Schmidt-Rottluff also became members. In the first exhibition of the "Neue Sezession" they met Müller. In his studio they saw Cranach's "Venus," which they themselves had always esteemed very highly. The sensuous harmony of his life with his work made Müller a natural member of "Brücke." He introduced us to the fascination of distemper technique. In order to keep their endeavors pure the members of "Brücke" resignd from membership in the "Neue Sezession." Then followed an exhibit of "Brücke" in the entire gallery of the art salon, Gurlitt. Pechstein broke the confidence of the group by becoming a member of the "Sezession," and was expelled from "Brücke." The "Sonderbund" invited "Brücke" to join its Cologne exhibition of 1912, and commissioned Heckel and Kirchner to decorate and paint the chapel of the exhibition rooms.

The majority of the members of "Brücke" is now in Berlin. "Brücke" has retained here its intrinsic character. From its internal coherence it radiates the new values of artistic creation to the modern artistic production throughout Germany. Uninfluenced by contemporary movements of cubism, futurism, etc., it fights for a human culture, the soil of all real art. "Brücke" owes its present position in the art world to these goals.

Ernst Ludwig Kirchner, "Chronik der Künstergruppe 'Brücke'," 1913, transl. by Peter Selz

Ernst Ludwig Kirchner, *Chronik KG Brücke*, 1913
cover, woodcut
Berlin, Staatliche Museen zu Berlin

Ernst Ludwig Kirchner; Karl Schmidt-Rottluff
Erich Heckel, illustrations for *Chronik KG Brücke*
1913, pages 2, 3 and 4, woodcut
Berlin, Staatliche Museen zu Berlin

der Lithographie. Bleyl, der sich der Lehrtätigkeit zugewandt hatte, trat aus "Brücke" 1909 aus. Pechstein ging nach Dangast zu Heckel. Im selben Jahre kamen beide zu Kirchner nach Moritzburg, um an den Seen Akt zu malen. 1910 wurde durch die Zurückweisung der jüngeren deutschen Maler an alten Sezession die Gründung der "Neuen Sezession" hervorgerufen. Um die Stellung Pechsteins in der neuen Sezession zu stützen, wurden Heckel, Kirchner und Schmidt-Rottluff auch dort Mitglieder. In der ersten Ausstellung der N.S. lernten sie Mueller kennen. In seinem Atelier fanden sie die Cranachsche Venus, die sie selbst sehr schätzten, wieder. Die sinnliche Harmonie seines Lebens mit dem Werk machte Mueller zu einem selbstverständlichen Mitglied von "Brücke". Er brachte uns den Reiz der Leimfarbe. Um die Bestrebungen von "Brücke" rein zu erhalten, traten die Mitglieder der "Brücke" aus der neuen Sezession aus. Sie gaben sich gegenseitig das Versprechen, nur gemeinsam in der "Sezession" in Berlin auszustellen. Es folgte eine Ausstellung der "Brücke" in sämtlichen Räumen des Kunstsalons Gurlitt. Pechstein brach das Vertrauen der Gruppe, wurde Mitglied der Sezession und wurde ausgeschlossen. Der Sonderbund lud "Brücke" 1912 zu seiner Cölner Ausstellung ein und übertrug Heckel und Kirchner die Ausmalung der darin befindlichen Kapelle. Die Mehrzahl der Mitglieder der "Brücke" ist jetzt in Berlin. "Brücke" hat auch hier ihren internen Charakter beibehalten. Innerlich zusammengewachsen, strahlt sie die neuen Arbeitswerte an das moderne Kunstschaffen in Deutschland aus. Unbeeinflusst durch die heutigen Strömungen, Kubismus, Futurismus usw., kämpft sie für eine menschliche Kultur, die der Boden aller wirklichen Kunst ist. Diesen Bestrebungen verdankt "Brücke" ihre heutige Stellung im Kunstleben. E. L. Kirchner.

zum Mitglied von "Brücke" ernannt. Ihm folgte 1905 Nolde. Seine phantastische Eigenart gab eine neue Note in "Brücke", er bereicherte unsere Ausstellungen durch die interessante Technik seiner Radierung und lernte die unseres Holzschnittes kennen. Auf seine Einladung ging Schmidt-Rottluff zu ihm nach Alsen. Später gingen Schmidt-Rottluff und Heckel nach Dangast. Die harte Luft der Nordsee brachte besonders bei Schmidt-Rottluff einen monumentalen Impressionismus hervor. Währenddessen führte Kirchner in Dresden die geschlossene Komposition weiter; er fand im ethnographischen Museum in der Negerplastik und den Balkenschnitzereien der Südsee eine Parallele zu seinem eigenen Schaffen. Das Bestreben, von der akademischen Sterilität frei zu werden, führte Pechstein zu "Brücke". Kirchner und Pechstein gingen nach Gollverode, um gemeinsam zu arbeiten. Im Salon Richter in Dresden fand die Ausstellung der "Brücke" mit den neuen Mitgliedern statt. Die Ausstellung machte einen grossen Eindruck auf die jungen Künstler in Dresden. Heckel und Kirchner versuchten die neue Malerei mit dem Raum in Einklang zu bringen. Kirchner stattete seine Räume mit Wandmalereien und Batiks aus, an denen Heckel mitarbeitete. 1907 trat Nolde aus "Brücke" aus. Heckel und Kirchner gingen an die Moritzburger Seen, um den Akt im Freien zu studieren. Schmidt-Rottluff arbeitete in Dangast an der Vollendung seines Farbenrhythmus. Heckel ging nach Italien und brachte die Anregung der etruskischen Kunst. Pechstein ging in dekorativen Aufträgen nach Berlin. Er versuchte die neue Malerei in die Sezession zu bringen. Kirchner fand in Dresden den Handdruck

Im Jahre 1902 lernten sich die Maler Bleyl und Kirchner in Dresden kennen. Durch seinen Bruder, einen Freund von Kirchner, kam Heckel hinzu. Heckel brachte Schmidt-Rottluff mit, den er von Chemnitz her kannte. In Kirchners Atelier kam man zum Arbeiten zusammen. Man hatte hier die Möglichkeit, den Akt, die Grundlage aller bildenden Kunst, in freier Natürlichkeit zu studieren. Aus dem Zeichnen auf dieser Grundlage ergab sich das allen gemeinsame Gefühl, aus dem Leben die Anregung zum Schaffen zu nehmen und sich dem Erlebnis unterzuordnen. In einem Buch "Odi profanum" zeichneten und schrieben die einzelnen nebeneinander ihre Ideen nieder und verglichen dadurch ihre Eigenart. So wuchsen sie ganz von selbst zu einer Gruppe zusammen, die den Namen "Brücke" erhielt. Einer regte den andern an. Kirchner brachte den Holzschnitt aus Süddeutschland mit, den er, durch die alten Schnitte in Nürnberg angeregt, wieder aufgenommen hatte. Heckel schnitzte wieder Holzfiguren; Kirchner bereicherte diese Technik in den seinen durch die Bemalung und suchte in Stein und Zinnguss den Rhythmus der geschlossenen Form. Schmidt-Rottluff machte die ersten Lithos auf dem Stein. Die erste Ausstellung der Gruppe fand in eigenen Räumen in Dresden statt; sie fand keine Anerkennung. Dresden gab aber durch die landschaftlichen Reize seine alte Kultur viele Anregung. Hier fand "Brücke" auch die ersten kunstgeschichtlichen Stützpunkte in Cranach, Beham und andern deutschen Meistern des Mittelalters. Bei Gelegenheit einer Ausstellung von Amiet in Dresden wurde dieser

Wassily Kandinsky, design for the frontispiece
of *Der Blaue Reiter Almanac*, 1912
color woodcut
Berlin, Staatliche Museen zu Berlin

"Everything that comes into existence on earth can only be a beginning." This statement by Däubler could well be the motto for our work and our intentions. There will be a fulfillment sometime, in a new world, in another existence. On earth we can furnish only the theme. The first book is the opening note of a new theme. The alert listener must have sensed the meaning of the book in its disconnected, restlessly moving manner. He found himself near some headwaters where, at a hundred different places at once, there was mysterious bubbling, now hidden, now openly singing and murmuring. With a divining rod we searched through the art of the past and the present. We showed only what was alive, what was not touched by the tone of convention. We gave our ardent devotion to everything in art that was born out of itself, lived in itself, did not walk on crutches of habit. We pointed to each crack in the crust of convention only because we hoped to find there an underlying force that would one day come to light. Some of these cracks have closed again, our hope was in vain; out of others a lively spring is now gushing. But this is not the only reason for the book. It has always been the great consolation of history that nature continuously thrusts up new forces through outlived rubbish. If we saw our task as simply pointing out the natural spring of a new generation, we could calmly leave this to the course of time; there would be no need to conjure up the spirit of a great epoch of change with our cries.

We say No to the great centuries. We know that with this simple denial we cannot stop the serious methodical development of the sciences and triumphant "progress." Also we do not even dream of anticipating this development, but to the scornful amazement of our contemporaries, we take a side road, one that hardly seems to be a road, and we say: this is the main road of mankind's development.

We know that the great mass cannot follow us today; the path is too steep and too far from the beaten track for them. But a few already do want to walk with us. The fate of this first book taught us this. Now we let the book go forth again unchanged, while we ourselves are detached from it and involved in new projects. We do not know yet when we will get together for the second book. Perhaps only when we are entirely alone again, when the cult of modernity has stopped trying to industrialize the virgin forest of new ideas. Before the second book is completed, many things that fastened onto the movement in those years must be cast off or torn away, even by force. We know that everything could be destroyed if the beginnings of a spiritual discipline are not protected from the greed and dishonesty of the masses. We are struggling for pure ideas, for a world in which pure ideas can be thought and proclaimed without becoming impure. Only then will we or others who are more talented be able to show the other face of the Janus head, which today is still hidden and turns its gaze away from the times.

We admire the disciples of early Christianity who found the strength for inner stillness amid the roaring noise of their time. For this stillness we pray and strive every hour.

Franz Marc, "Der Blaue Reiter," March 1914.
The Blaue Reiter Almanac, Wassily Kandinsky and Franz Marc, eds. New York: The Viking Press, 1974, p. 258-59

Content and Form
The work of art consists of two elements: the *inner* and the *outer*. The inner element, taken by itself, is the emotion in the soul of the artist. This emotion is capable of calling forth what is, essentially, a corresponding emotion in the soul of the observer. As long as the soul is joined to the body, it can as a rule only receive vibrations via the medium of the feelings. Feelings are therefore a bridge from the nonmaterial (in the case of the artist) and from the material to the nonmaterial (in the case of the observer).

Emotion – feeelings – the work of art – feelings – emotion.

The inner element of the work of art is its content. Thus, there must be a vibration in the soul. Unless this is the case, a work of art cannot come into being. Or, that is to say, what is produced is a mere sham. The inner element, created by the soul's vibration, is the content of the work of art. Without inner content, no work of art can exist. For the content, which exists first of all only *"in abstracto,"* to become a work of art, the second element – the external – must serve as its embodiment. Thus content seeks a means of expression, a "material" form.

Thus the work of art is an inevitable, inseparable joining together of the internal and external elements, of the content and the form.

The determining element is the content. Just as the concept determines the word, and not the word the concept, so too the content detemines the form: *form is the material expression of abstract content.* Therefore, the choice of form is determined by *internal necessity,* which, essentially, is the only unalterable law of art.

A work of art which has come into being in the way described as "beautiful." Thus *a beautiful work of art is an ordered combination of the two elements, the internal and the external.* It is this combination that confers upon the work its unity. The work of art becomes a subject. A painting is a spiritual organism that, like every material organism, consists of many individual parts. In isolation, these individual parts are lifeless, like a chopped-off finger. The life of the finger, its effectiveness is determined by its ordered juxtaposistion with other parts of the body. This *ordered juxtaposition is called construction*. Like the work of nature, the work of art is subordinated to the same law, that of construction. The individual parts have life only by virtue of the whole. The infinite number of individual parts may, as regards painting, be divided into two groups:

linear form and

painterly form.

It is the planned and purposeful combination of the individual parts belonging to both groups that results in the picture.

Nature

If we apply these two categories (the constituent elements of the work of art, and in particular of the picture) to individual works, we come upon what appears to be the accidental presence of foreign elements within the picture. This is what is called *nature*. But nature has no place in either category. How does she come to be in the picture? The origins of painting are the same as those of every other art and of every human action. They are purely practical. If a primitive hunter hunts game for days on end, it is hunger that drives him to do so. If today a princely huntsman hunts game, it is pleasure that spurs him on. While hunger is a bodily quality, pleasure is here an aesthetic quality. When primitive man employs artificially produced noises as an accompaniment to his dance, it is the sexual drive that impels him. These artificial noises, out of which through millennia, present-day music developed, were for primitive man an incitement to the movement that today we call dance, which has its origin in the desire for the female. When modern man goes to a concert, he does so not for practical ends; rather, it is a pleasure that he seeks in the music. Here, also, the original bodily or practical impulse has become an aesthetic impulse. That is to say, what was originally a bodily need has become a spiritual need.

In the course of this process of *refinement* (or spiritualization) of the simplest practical (or bodily) needs, one consistently notices two consequences: the *separation* of the spiritual from the bodily element, and its further independent *development*, by means of which the various arts come into being. Here, gradually, but ever more precisely, the above-mentioned *laws* (of content and form) apply, eventually *creating out of each transitional art a pure art*. This process is one of tranquil, natural growth, like the growth of a tree.

Painting

The same process is to be seen in *painting*.

First period – *Origin*: the practical desire to fix the transitory *corporeal* element.

Second period – *Development*: the gradual departure from this practical goal and the gradual *predominance* of the *spiritual* element.

Third period – *Goal*: the attainement of the high level of *pure art*, whereby the remains of practical desires are eliminated. This art speaks in artistic language from spirit to spirit, is a realm of painterly-spiritual essences (subjects).

In the *state* in which painting finds itself today, all three characteristics can be observed in different combinations and in different degrees. It is, however, the characteristics of development (second period) that constitute the *determining* factor. That is:

First period: *Realistic painting* (realism is here understood in the sense in which it traditionally developed up to the nineteenth century): predominance of those characteristics one associates with the term origin – the practical desire to fix the transitory corporeal element (portraits, landscape, history-painting in the direct sense.

Second period: *Naturalistic painting* (in the form of Impressionism, Neo-Impressionism, and Expressionism – to which belong in part Cubism and Futurism): the departure from practical goals and the gradual predominance of the spiritual element (starting with Impressionism, an ever-increasing departure and an ever-greater predominance, by way of Neo-Impressionism to Expressionism).

In this period the inner desire to attribute exclusive significance to the spiritual element is so intense that even the impressionistic "credo" declares: "The essential art consists not of 'what' (by which is meant nature, not artistic content), but of 'how'." It would appear that so little importance is attached to the remains of the first period (origin) that no account whatsoever is taken of nature as such. It would appear that nature is regarded exclusively as a point of departure, a pretext for giving expression to spiritual content. At all events, these views are recognized and proclaimed even by the Impressionists as vital parts of the "credo." In reality, however, this "credo" is no more than a "*pium desiderium*" of painting of the second period.

If the choice of subject (nature) were indifferent to this kind of painting, then it would not be necessary to seek after "motifs." Here, on the contrary, it is the object which determines the manner of treatment, *the choice of form is not free*, but is dependent upon the object.

If, in looking at a picture of this period, we exclude the subject matter (nature), so that *only* the purely artistic element in the picture remains, we notice at once that the subject matter (nature) constitutes a kind of support without which the purely artistic structure (construction) collapses for lack of form. Or it transpires that, having excluded the subject matter, there remain on the canvas nothing but wholly inde-

terminate, accidental artistic forms (in an embryonic state), incapable of independent existence. Thus *nature* (which this painting regards as the "what") is by no means incidental in this kind of painting, but *essential*. This exclusion of the practical element, of subject matter (nature) is only possible if this essential element is replaced by another equally essential component. And this component is purely artistic form, which can confer upon the painting the strength necessary for independent life, and which is able to raise the picture to the level of a spiritual subject. It is clear that this essential component can only be – as described and defined above – construction.

Wassily Kandinsky, "Painting as Pure Art," *Der Sturm*, 1913, *Kandinsky. Complete Writings on Art*, Kenneth C. Lindasy and Peter Vergo, eds. Boston, Mass.: G.K. Hall and Co., 1982, p. 349-353

The disagreement begins on this point: who believes he is closer to the heart of nature, the Impressionists or today's moderns? There is no standard by which one could measure this; it stands, though, to substantiate the fact that we believe ourselves in our pictures to be at least as close to the heart of nature as Manet when he sought, in artful rendering, to reveal the outward form and color of the peach or the scent of the rose, and to make their inner secrets perceptible. ... Today we seek under the veil of appearances things hidden in nature that seem to us more important than the discoveries of the Impressionists, things that they simply passed over. We are looking for and painting the innermost, spiritual side of nature, not as a whim or because we are overcome by a desire to be different, but because we see this side, just as people used to "see" purple shadows and the aether settling over everything. It is as difficult to say why this is for them as why it is for us. It is the spirit of the age.

... Nature is everywhere, in us and outside us. However, there is something that is not wholly nature, but rather something that is more its domination and interpretation, whose strength emanates from a stronghold *unknown to us* : art. Art was and is in its make-up, in every period, the boldest departure from nature and "simplicity," the bridge into the realm of the spirit, the necromancy of mankind. We understand anxiety and incomprehension in the face of its continually new forms, but not criticism.

Franz Marc, "The New Painting," *Pan*, March 7, 1912, *German Expressionism*, Rose-Carol Washton Long, ed. New York: G.K. Hall and Co., 1993, p. 97-98

In this time of great struggle for a new art we fight like disorganized "savages" against an old, established power. The battle seems to be unequal, but spiritual matters are never decided by numbers, only by the power of ideas.

The dreaded weapons of the "savages" are their *new ideas*. New ideas kill better than steel and destroy what was thought to be indestructible.

Who are these "savages" in Germany?

For the most part they are both well known and widely disparaged: the Brücke in Dresden, the Neue Sezession in Berlin, and the Neue Vereinigung in Munich.

The oldest of the three, the Brücke, was inaugurated with great seriousness, but Dresden proved too infertile a soil for its ideas. The time was probably not yet ripe in Germany for a more significant effect. A few years had to pass before the exhibitions of the two other groups brought new, dangerous life to the country.

Originally, the Neue Sezession was recruited in part from members of the Brücke. It was actually formed, however, by unsatisfied members of the old Secession, which moved too slowly for them; courageously the New Secessionists jumped over the dark wall behind which the old Secessionists had hidden themselves, and suddenly they stood, dazzled, before the immense freedom of art.

They have no program and no restraint; they want only to proceed at any price, like a river that carries along everything, possible and impossible, trusting in its own purifying force.

Lack of historical perspective prevents us from attempting here to distinguish between the noble and the weak. Any criticism we might make would concern only trifles and would stand disarmed and ashamed before the defiant freedom of this movement, which we in Munich greet with a thousand cheers.

The genesis of the Neue Vereinigung is more obscure and complex.

In Munich the first and only serious representatives of the new ideas were two Russians who had lived there for many years and had worked quietly until some Germans joined them. Along with the founding of the association began those beautiful, strange exhibitions that drove critics to despair.

Characteristics of the artists in the association was their strong emphasis on the *program*. Artists learned from each other and competed among themselves as to who understood the new ideas best. Perhaps one heard the word "synthesis" too often.

Later the young Frenchmen and Russians who exhibited with them as guests proved a liberating influence.

They stimulated thought, and people came to understand that art was concerned with the most profound matters, that renewal must not be merely formal but in fact a rebirth of thinking. *Mysticism* was awakened in their souls and with it the most ancient elements of art.

It is impossible to explain the recent works of these "savages" as a formal development and new interpretation of impressionism (as B.W. Niemeyer tried to do in the statement of the Düsseldorf Sonderbund [Special Society]). The most beautiful prismatic colors and the celebrated cubism are now meaningless goals for these "savages".

Their thinking has a different aim: To create out of their work *symbols* for their own time, symbols that belong on the altars of a future spiritual religion, symbols behind which the technical heritage cannot be seen.

Scorn and stupidity will be like roses in their path. Not all the official "savages" in or out of Germany dream of this kind of art and of these aims. All the worse for them.

After easy successes they will perish from their own superficiality despite all the programs, cubist and otherwise.

But we believe – at least we hope we are justified in believing – that apart from all these "savage" groups in the forefront there are many quiet powers in Germany struggling with the same high, distant goals and that ideas are silently maturing unknown to the heralds of the battle.

In the dark, without knowing them, we give them our hand.

Franz Marc, "The 'savages' of Germany," *The Blaue Reiter Almanac*, Wassily Kandinsky and Franz Marc, eds. New York: The Viking Press, 1974, p. 61-64

... In general, therefore, color is a means of exerting a direct influence upon the soul. Color is the keyboard. The eye is the hammer. The soul is the piano, with its many strings.

The artist is the hand that purposefully sets the soul vibrating by means of this or that key.

Thus it is clear that harmony of colors can only be based upon the principle of purposefully touching the human soul.

... Clashing discords, loss of equilibrium, "principles" overthrown, unexpected drumbeats, great questionings, apparently purposeless strivings, stress and longing (apparently torn apart), chains and fetters broken (which had united many), opposites and contradictions – this is our harmony.

Composition on the basis of this harmony is the juxtaposition of coloristic and linear forms that have an independent existence as such, derived from internal necessity, which create within the common life arising from this source a whole that is called a picture.

... Our painting today is, however, in a different state: its emancipation from direct dependence upon "nature" is in its very earliest stages. If, up until now, color and form have been used as inner forces, this use has been largely unconscious. The subjugation of composition to geometrical form had been used already in ancient art (e.g., in the art of the Persians).

Construction upon a purely spiritual basis, however, is a lenghty process, which begins relatively blindly and at random. Thus it is essential that the painter should develop not only his eyes, but also his soul, so that it too may be capable of weighing colors in the balance, and active not only in receiving external impressions (also, admittedly, sometimes internal ones), but also as a determining force in the creation of works of art...

Wassily Kandinsky, "Über das Geistige in der Kunst," *Kandinsky. Complete Writings on Art*, Kenneth C. Lindsay and Peter Vergo, eds. Boston, Mass.: G.K. Hall and Co., 1982, p. 159-160, 193, 197

In my opinion there are two tendencies in art. One, which at this moment is in the ascendency again, is a flat and stylized decorative art. The other is an art with deep spacial effects.

It is Byzantine art and Giotto versus Rembrandt, Tintoretto, Goya, Courbet, and the early Cézanne. The former wants the whole effect on the surface and is consequently abstract and decorative while the latter wants to get as close to life as possible using spacial and sculptural qualities.

Sculptural mass and deep space in painting need not by any means be naturalistic in effect. It depends upon the vigor of presentation and the personal type.

Rembrandt, Goya, and the young Cézanne strove for important sculptural effects without succumbing to the danger of naturalism in the least. It makes me sad to have to emphasize this, but thanks to the current fad for flat paintings people have reached the point where they condemn a picture a priori as naturalistic simply because it is not flat, thin, and decorative. I certainly don't want to deprive decorative painting of its right to exist as art.

That would be absurdly narrowminded. But I am of the opinion that not one of the French followers of Cézanne has vindicated the principle of two-dimensionality which followed the inspired clumsiness of the late Cézanne, the holy simplicity of Giotto, and the religious folk cultures of Egypt and Byzantium. As for myself, I paint and try to develop my style exclusively in terms of deep spece, something which in contrast to superficially decorative art penetrates as far as possible into the very core of nature and the spirit of things. I know full well that many of my feelings were already part of my makeup. But I also know that there is within me what I sense as new, new from this age and its spirit. This I will and cannot define. It is in my pictures.

Max Beckmann, "The New Program," *Voices of German Expressionism*, Victor H. Miesel, ed., Englewood Cliffs, N.J.: Prentice-Hall, 1970, p. 106-107

People who are futurist in life:
1. Anyone who loves life, energy, joy, freedom, progress, courage, new things, expediency and speed.
2. Anyone who reacts rapidly and energetically and does not hold back in a cowardly fashion.
3. Anyone who, when faced with two possible decisions, chooses the more generous and bolder of the two, provided that it will contribute to greater perfection and to the development of individuals and the people.
4. Anyone who acts blithely, always looking to the future, without pangs of conscience, without pedantry, without false shame, without mysticism and without melancholy.
5. Anyone who is flexible and uninhibited enough to alternate serious work with joyful leisure.
6. Anyone who loves life in the open air, loves sport and gymnastics and takes daily care of the supple strength of his own body.
7. Anyone who knows how to strike a blow at time and give it a determined box on the ears, anyone who admires the bold and acts like the bold.

People who are futurist in politics:
1. Anyone who loves the future of Italy more than himself.
2. Anyone who wants to abolish the papacy, parliamentarianism, the senate and bureaucracy.
3. Anyone who wants to abolish national service and the conscripted army, in order to replace it with an army of volunteers, and anyone who wants to create a manly, strong, hard-working, completely free democracy, anyone who is equally capable of suddenly starting a war or purifying himself by revolution.
4. Anyone who want to abolish the present police force, in order to modernize and ennoble the whole of the public security service and to encourage state citizens to defend themselves.
5. Anyone who wants to put the government of Italy into the hands of all the young front-line soldiers who have gained our overwhelming victory.
6. Anyone who wants to confiscate land that is fallow or in bad condition, in order to prepare for land to be shared out among the workers.
7. Anyone who wants to abolish any kind of industrial or capitalist parasitic behaviour.

8. Anyone who wants every worker to reap the reward appropriate to his services.
9. Anyone who loves and longs for freedom in all things, except the freedom to be a coward, a parasite or anti-Italian.

People who are futurist in art:
1. Anyone who thinks and expresses himself originally, forcefully, vigorously, enthusiastically, clearly, simply, dextrously and synthetically.
2. Anyone who hates ruins, museums, cemeteries, libraries, educational assiduity, professors, academicism, imitation of the past, purism, verbosity and meticulous precision.
3. Anyone who would rather have cabaret, where the spectators smoke, laugh and work with the performers without gloomy solemnity and monotony than tragedies and dramas played in hushed theatres.
4. Anyone who wants to rejuvenate and strengthen Italian art and make it more relaxed by liberating it from having to imitate the past, from traditionalism and academicism, and anyone who encourages the young to be boldly creative.

F.T. Marinetti, Settimalli, Mario Carli, "Futurism. Basic Credo," 1920

Marinetti, Boccioni, Corrà, Russolo, "Futurism's political programme," 11 October 1913, Onista Baumgarth *Die Geschichte des Futurismus*, Hamburg, 1966, p. 156-57

This programme will be victorious

Over the clerical-moderate liberal program	*Over the democratic-republican-socialist program*
Monarchy and the Vatican	Republic
Hatred and contempt for the people	The sovereignty of the people
Traditional memorial-loving patriotism	Pacifistic internationalism
Intermittent militarism	Anti-militarism
Clericalism	Anti-clericalism
Petty protectionism and sloppy liberalism	Profit-greedy liberalism
Ancestor worship and scepticism	Dominance by the moderate and sceptical
Senescence and moralism	Senescence and moralism
Opportunism and dishonest business dealings	Opportunism and unfair business dealings
Rabble-rousing	Demagogy
The cult of museums, ruins and monuments	The cult of museums, ruins and monuments
The tourist industry	The tourist industry
Obsession with culture	Socialism in the style of election meetings
Academicism	Positivist rationalism
Ideal of an archaeological, hypocritical and palsied Italy	The ideal of a petit-bourgeois miserly and sentimental Italy
Quietism of the belly	Quietism of the belly
The cowardice of the blacks	The cowardice of the reds
"Trade-windism"	"Trade-windism"

Futurist voters! Try to cast your votes in such a way as to realize the following programme:
A completely sovereign Italy – the word Italy must stand above the word freedom.
Everything is permitted, except for being a coward, a pacifist or anti-Italian.
A larger fleet and a larger army; a people that is proud of being Italian, in favour of war, which is the only hygiene in the world, and in favour of a great Italy with intensive agriculture, industry and trade.
Economic protection and patriotic education for the proletariat.
A cynical, cunning and aggressive foreign policy – a policy of colonial expansion – a free economy.
Irredentism – pan-Italianism – Italian supremacy
Anti-clericalism and anti-socialism
A cult of progress and speed, of sport, of physical strength, that is for audacity, heroism and danger and against obsession with culture, humanist education, museums, libraries and ruins – academies and conservatories to be abolished.
Many technical schools for commerce, industry and agriculture – many physical training institutions – daily gymnastics instruction in schools – gymnastics to come before books.
A minimum of professors, very few lawyers, very few doctors, many farmers, engineers, chemists, mechanics and businessmen.
Power to be stripped from the dead, the old and opportunists in favour of bold youth.
Against the mania for monuments and governmental interference in questions of art.
Thorough modernization of the "trade-wind" cities (Rome, Venice, Florence etc.)
Abolition of the humiliating and dependent tourist industry, which is dependent on chance.

Marinetti, Boccioni, Corrà, Russolo, "Futurism's political programme," 11 October 1913, Onista Baumgarth *Die Geschichte des Futurismus*, Hamburg, 1966, p. 156-57

Dada wants nothing, Dada grows. Expressionism wanted inwardness, it conceived of itself as a reaction against the times, while Dadaism is nothing but an expression of the times. Dada is one with the times, it is a child of the present epoch which one may curse, but cannot deny. Dada has taken the mechanisation, the sterility, the rigidity and the tempo of these times into its broad lap, and in the last analysis it is nothing else and in no way different from them. Expressionism is not spontaneous action.
It is the gesture of tired people who wish to escape themselves and forget the present, the war and the misery.
To this end they invented "humanity," and walked versifying and psalmodysing along streets on which the escalators rise and descend and the telephones ring shrilly.
The Expressionists are tired people who have turned their backs on nature and do not dare look the cruelty of the epoch in the face. They have forgotten how to be daring.
Dada is daring *per se*, Dada exposes itself to the risk of its own death. Dada puts itself at the heart of things.
Expressionism wanted to forget itself, Dada wants to affirm itself. Expressionism was harmonious, mystic, angelic, Baaderish-Superdadaist – Dada is the scream of brakes and the bellowing of the brokers at the Chicago Stock Exchange. Vive Dada!

Richard Huelsenbeck, "What did Expressionism want?," *The Dada Almanac*, Eng. ed. by Malcom Green. London: Atlas Press, 1993, p. 44

Circular Letter of December 31, 1918
Potsdammerstrasse 113, Villa II

Most Honorable Sir!
The future of art and the gravity of the present hour force us revolutionaries of the spirit (Expressionists, Cubists, Futurists) to unification and close alliance.
We therefore direct an urgent call to all visual artists who have shattered the old forms in art to declare their membership in the "Novembergruppe." The formulation and the realization of a wide-ranging program that will be carried out by trusted people in various art centers should bring us the closest interaction between art and the people.
Renewed contact with the like-minded in all countries is our duty. The creative instinct united us as brothers years ago. A group exhibition is planned as the first sign that we have come together. It is to be shown in all large cities in Germany and later in Europe.
The working committee:
M. Pechstein, C.Klein, G. Tappert, Richter-Berlin,
M. Melzer, B. Krauskopf, R. Bauer, R. Belling, H. Steiner, W. Schmid
Guidelines of the "Novembergruppe" (January 1919)
I. The "Novembergruppe" is the (German) union of radical visual artists.
II. The "Novembergruppe" is not an association for economic protection, nor is it (merely) an exhibition society.
III. Through a broad alliance of the like-minded, the "Novembergruppe" seeks to give creative powers a decisive voice in all artistic questions.
IV. We demand influence and involvement:
1. on all occasions when architecture is a public matter, urban development – housing estates –

public administrative buildings, industry and public welfare – private building activities – monument preservation – abolition of artistically worthless show buildings

2. in redesigning art schools and their teaching and abolishing the authorities' right to impose their will – teachers to be chosen by artists' associations and students – grants to be abolished – amalgamation of schools of architecture, sculpture, painting and jewellery – establishment of workshops and experimental facilities

3. in transforming the museums, abolishing one-sided collecting policies – eliminating academic clutter – museums to be transformed into art-places for the people, where timeless laws are communicated without prejudice.

4. in allotting exhibition spaces, and abolishing privileges and capitalist influences.

5. in making laws about art

Equal social rights for artists as intellectual and spiritual creators – protection of artistic property – freedom from taxation on works of art (free import and export).

V. The "Novembergruppe" will provide proof of its unity and its achievements by continually issuing publications and with an exhibition that will take place every year in November.

The Central Working Committee will organize the flow of publications and exhibitions.

Members of the association are entitled to equal exhibition area and do not have to go before a selection committee. The Central Working Committee will decide about special exhibitions in the same way.

"We stand on the fertile ground of revolution.

Our motto is: LIBERTY, EQUALITY, FRATERNITY! Our union resulted from the identity between human and artistic conviction.

We consider it our noblest duty to dedicate our best energies to the moral reconstruction of a new, free Germany.

We plead for rectitude in everything, and we support this conviction with all the means at our disposal.

We insist on unlimited freedom of expression and a public statement about it.

We hold it as our special duty to gather all serious artistic talents and to turn them toward the public good.

We are neither party nor class itself, but people who tirelessly perform, in places assigned to them by nature, difficult tasks, which must, like any task that benefits all the people, take into account the general public interest and win the appreciation and recognition of the whole.

We hold achievements in every area and in every form in high esteem and believe that the most difficult problems will be given to the most capable people, who must consider the use and

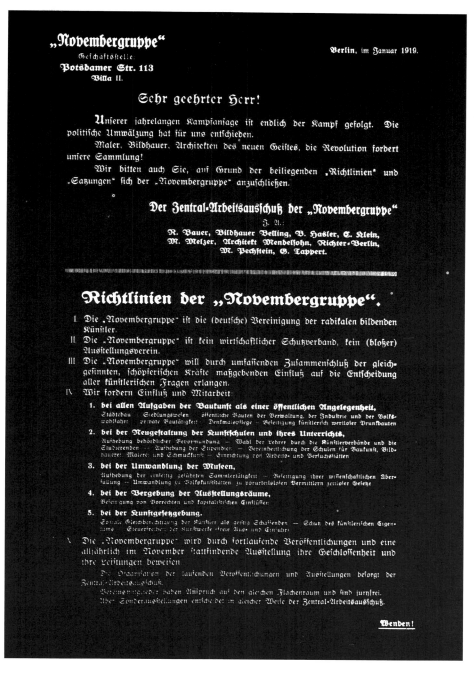

"*Novembergruppe*", manifesto of Novembergruppe, Berlin, January 1919

Esposizione Espressionisti Novembergruppe
(Exhibition of the Novembergruppe Expressionists)
brochure, Galleria della Casa d'arte italiana, 1920

benefit of the whole populace in finding solutions. Our goal is for each to work – hard and tirelessly – in his place, to build collectively.

Our struggle applies to all destroyers – our love to all reconstructive powers.

We feel young and free and pure.

Our immaculate love goes out to a young and free Germany, from which we intend to fight backwardness and reaction with all the powers at our disposal, courageously and without reservation.

In the hope that they will join us, we send our fraternal greeting to all Cubist, Futurist, and Expressionist artists who feel addressed and accountable."

"Manifest der Novembristen," *German Expressionism*, Rose-Carol Washton Long, ed. New York: G.K. Hall and Co., p. 212-14

Convinced that the recent political revolution must be used to free art from decades of domination, a circle of like-minded artists and art lovers has congregated in Berlin. This circle is striving to collect all scattered and splintered forces committed to moving beyond the preservation of one-sided occupational interests, in order to cooperate in rebuilding our entire art world. In close touch with the elected governments and with like-minded associations such as the Art Council in Munich, Dresden, etc., the Arbeitsrat für Kunst hopes to be able to succeed in its immediate goals in the near future. The goals are outlined in the following program excerpt.

Above all, this *slogan* guides us:

Art and people must form a unity. Art should no longer be the pleasure of a few but should bring joy and sustenance to the masses. The goal is the union of the arts under the wings of a great architecture.

From now on the artist, as shaper of the sensibilities of the people, is alone responsible for the external appearance of the new nation. He must determine the boundaries of form from statuary down to coins and stamps.

On this basis, we *currently* make *six demands*:

1. Recognition of the public nature of all building activity, an end to public and private privileges enjoyed by civil servants. Uniform management of whole city boroughs, streets and housing developments, without encroaching on individual freedom. New assignments: community centers as distribution points of all arts to the people. Permanent experimental grounds for testing and perfecting architectural effects.

2. Dissolution of the Royal Academy of Arts, the Royal Academy of Architecture, and the Royal Prussian State Art Commission in their present form, replacement of these bodies along with a narrowing of their field of activity, with others created out of the community of producing artists itself without state influence. Transformation of privileged art exhibitions into free ones.

3. Freedom for all education in architecture, sculpture, painting, and crafts from government domination. Transformation of arts and crafts education from the ground up. Allocation of government funds for this purpose and for masters' education in teaching workshops.

4. Vitalization of museums as places of education for the people. Establishment of constantly changing exhibitions, made accessible to all the people through lectures and guided tours. Withdrawal of scientific materials into buildings appropriate for them. Segregation of technically organized study collections for craftsmen working in artistic crafts. Fair distribution of government funds for acquisition of old and new works.

5. Elimination of all monuments without artistic value is disproportionate to the value of their materials, which might be made use of in other ways. Prevention of construction of hastily planned war monuments and immediate stoppage of work on the war museums planned in Berlin and elsewhere in the nation.

6. Organization of a government department to ensure promotion of art within the framework of future lawmaking.

Bruno Taut, "Arbeitsrat für Kunst Program," *German Expressionism*, Rose-Carol Washton Long, ed. New York: G.K. Hall and Co., p. 193-94

To all artists from all countries!

Art has been free of national shackles from time immemorial. We artists resident in Germany have always been aware of the great value of our contacts with comrades beyond our borders.

The war has not made us waver in this conviction. For over four years we stood alone. But now at last the ban is lifted and we are pleased to make contact with you all again.

Hands have already stretched out to us from east and west . . . and we will take those hands. At last we can greet our brothers again. For we have always been brothers. We feel that there was no time at which anything about this changed for us. Our passion was and is for art. No other passions can weaken or stifle this one. There is no more to be said. We understand each other.

We must all come together… from all countries, for an international congress. There is an immeasurable amount of work ahead of us. We should start a constant exchange of our work.

We should visit each other and make friends. We should persuade our governments to appoint artists from other countries to create and to teach. Exhibitions can be exchanged and tour throughout our countries. We could set up centres from which travelling comrades can acquire all the information they need.

But above all we want to create! It would be of great benefit to the cause if we were to propose constant mutual exchange of experiences.

Adolf Behne, "Aufruf des 'Arbeitstrates für Kunst' in Berlin" (Appeal from the "Arbeitstrat für Kunst" in Berlin), *Der Cicerone*, vol. XI, 1919, p. 264, quoted from *Expressionisten, Die Avantgarde in Deutschland 1905-1920*, exhibition catalogue, Berlin, 1986, p. 157 ff.

So that we no longer have to be ashamed before the heavens, we must finally get busy and help establish a just order in government and society. We artists and poets must join in the first ranks. There can be no more exploiters and exploited! It can no longer be the case that a huge majority must live in the most miserable, disgraceful, and degrading conditions, while a tiny minority eat like animals at an overflowing table. We must commit ourselves to socialism: to a general and unceasing socialization of the means of production, which gives each man work, leisure, bread, a home, and the intimation of a higher goal. Socialism must be our new creed!

It must rescue both: the poor out of the humiliation of servitude, oppression, brutality, and malice – and the rich it will deliver forever more from merciless egotism, from their greed and harshness.

Let a holy solidarity ally us painters and poets with the poor! Have not many among us also known misery and the shame of hunger and material dependence?! Do we have a much better and more secure position in society of the art-collecting bourgeoisie!

If we are still young and unknown, they throw us alms or leave us silently to die.

If we have a name, then they seek to divert us from the pure goals with money and vain desires. And when we are finally in the grave, then their ostentatiousness covers our undefiled works with mountains of gold coins – painters, poets, composers, be ashamed of your dependence and cowardice and join as a brother with the expelled; outcast, ill-paid menial!

We are not workers, no. Ecstasy, rapture – passion is our daily work. We are free and knowing and must, like guiding banners, wave before our strong brothers.

Painters, poets… who other than we should then fight for the just cause?! In us the world conscience still throbs powerfully.

Ever anew the voice of god breathes fire into our rebellious fists.

Let us be on our guard!

For will the bourgeoisie not seize power again, through putsches, bribery and unscrupulous election practices? Will this new Germany of the ruling bourgeoisie not exploit the human workforce even more shamelessly, and intimidate the poor even more brutally? Will it not desire to exult all the more arrogantly and impudently about spiritual things than ever was the case in Imperial Germany?!

For that Imperial Germany, dolled up in all the power of its cannons, barracks and iron ships, elementary schools, policemen and false priests, was too crude and idle and ignorant to be able to inflict any great or serious damage in the realms of the spiritual. But wherever the despotic bourgeoisie prevails – wherever they get their filthy paws on the noble heartlands of the spirit – there grass will never grow again.

Painters, poets! let us make common cause with our intimidated, defenseless brothers, for the sake if the spirit.

The worker respects the spirit. He strives with powerful zeal for knowledge and learning.

The bourgeois is irreverent. He loves only dalliance and aesthetically embellished stupidities and hates and fears the spirit – because he feels that he could be unmasked by it.

The bourgeois knows only one freedom, his own – namely to be able to exploit others. That is the pale terror that goes about silently, and millions collapse and wither early.

The bourgeois knows no love – only exploitation and fraud. Arise, arise to battle against the ugly of prey, the booty-hungry, thousand-headed emperor of tomorrow, the atheist and Anti-Christ!

Painters, architects, sculptors, you whom the bourgeois pays high wages for your work – out of vanity, snobbery, and boredom – listen: on this money sticks the sweat and blood and life juices of thousands of poor, overexerted people – listen: that is an unclean profit.

Ah, all we want is to be able to live and to do our work to the glory of God!

Painters, poets and all artists, comrades all: we must make ourselves strong: it is of Socialism that we speak. We want no more *bloodstained* wages. We want to be free, to flow towards our joy and the joy of mankind.

Comrades, hear more: we must be true Socialists – we must kindle the highest Socialist virtues within ourselves: the brotherhood of man. That means: goodness, friendship for each other and insight into things that we all need.

Listen further: we must take our conviction seriously, the new wondrous belief. We must join with the workers' party, the decisive, unequivocal party.

We may no longer tolerate windbags, gamblers, aesthetes and corrupt bourgeois collaborators within our circle.

Just as the true Christian shuns dealings with the Evil One – so we must keep ourselves clean from the unclean, from those who despise mankind and from story-telling idlers.

We must pin down the cynics in the filth of their own malice. Let us not be deterred by their poisonous speeches and threats.

O may the divine voice lead us, on this our day: justice and love.

We must work together, body and soul, with our own hands.

Socialism is at stake – that means: justice, freedom, and human love at stake – at stake, God's order in the world!

Ludwig Meidner, "To All Artists, Musicians, Poets," *Das Kunstblatt*, 1919, *German Expressionism*, Rose-Carol Washton Long, ed., New York: G.K. Hall and Co., p. 175-76

The association known as "Die Brücke" is a fundamentally very pleasing new phenomenon in the Dresden fine art world. This is a group of young and enthusiastic artists who want to go their own way independently and confidently, without being inhibited by a wise and thoughtful Dresden selection committee's ideas of what is and is not acceptable as art. They flourish out in the Löbtau, which alas is tantamount to being in hiding; these young people have made a home for themselves here in Max Seifert's studio. It remains to be seen whether that is a suitable place for them to occupy.

… the whole group has something very appealing about it, although there is still an element of immaturity. But their aim "as young people who are responsible for the future to create freedom for their arms and lives vis-à-vis older and more established forces", is a high and worthy one, and we can only wish that many young people who are striking out on their own will join the group, in order to find the counterweight that is so sorely needed in Dresden against a tendency to adopt a caste approach to art, which is evidenced by a sad existence in cliques.

Otto Sebaldt, "Dresdner Kunstschau II," *Sächsische Arbeiter-Zeitung*, 23 Oct. 1906, no. 246, supplement, p. 1, quoted from *Expressionisten, Die Avantgarde in Deutschland 1905-1920*, exhibition catalogue, Berlin, 1986, p. 79

… to show a public that is as interested in art as that of Dresden that we no longer need to import even the most audacious extremes of Impressionism in painting from abroad.

Max Pechstein, *Arbeitsrat für Kunst, Berlin*, March 1919, woodcut for a leaflet

No, no – this outrageous audacity, this loud appeal for absolute liberation from everything traditional, from anything with an academic background, is also alive here in Dresden today...

"Die Brücke" is a growing and emerging association of young people. It is a product of surging fermentation, a cry for the barriers to come down, a trembling anxiety to achieve everything that lies beyond the bounds of things that have hitherto been permitted, beyond things that have hitherto been artistically acceptable...

What we saw of "Die Brücke" at Richter's was astounding to say the least: it was impossible to get anything at all from some of the pictures. I mistook two children reading for a couple of cabbages first of all, and took a bouquet for an old greatcoat. But then again there were some fine effects in these patches of color, juxtaposed amazingly and without transition.

A bunch of roses by Nolde seemed to have strong color values, birches by K. Schmidt-Rottluff were refined and unique, a woman smoking by E.L. Kirchner had some especially effective color tones, and some strengths in terms of drawing as well. And what I saw here gave me heart, although I have just as much fun as most of the other visitors.

F.E. Köhler-Haussen, "'Die Brücke' in Kunstsalon Richter," *Dresdner Jahrbuch*, 1, 1908, p. 52 ff., quoted from *Expressionisten, Die Avantgarde in Deutschland 1905-1920*, exhibition catalogue, Berlin, 1986, p. 81

"A poster image like nothing the world has ever seen is to be found in the display windows of M. Macht's art gallery at 1 Rankestraße; it alarms and outrages passers-by, but it also amuses them. Such a wretched, scruffy piece of incompetent botching as this poster drawing has probably never ventured into the glare of publicity. A miserable dauber has painted a kneeling, fat, naked person incredibly roughly in broad outlines. This person has a completely shapeless face with a pair of thick, shockingly bright red Moor's lips bulging out of it, and she is pulling the string of a bow in order to fire off the arrow that has been fitted.

This unique poster invites passers-by to make their way to the top storey of the building, either by lift or on foot, where they will find Galerie Macht open. Here 27 gentlemen rejected by the Berlin Secession selection committee are exhibiting 56 of the 98 paintings that have met this fate. It must be considered amazing that a committee that admitted to its exhibition the gruesome daubings of an artist like Munch, and others that are scarcely more tolerable, was able to declare any artefact too bad to be accepted for exhibition. One wonders whether it is possible to paint stuff that is so much worse than these pictures that it can be declared unfit for such society? And then, when one enters the galleries containing these 56 paintings, one very quickly sees that even the expectations raised by this lovely image of a woman remain well beyond the horrifying reality."

Ludwig Pietsch, "Kunstausstellung Zurückgewiesener der Secession Berlin–Kunst Salon Maximiliam Macht," exhibition of art rejected by the Berlin Secession–Kunst Salon Maximilian Macht), *Vossische Zeitung*, quoted from Werner Doede, *Kunst und Künstler seit 1870. Anfänge und Entwicklung*, Recklinghausen, 1961.

Young artists are showing some of their work rejected by the Secession selection committee under the banner of the "Neue Secession" in Kunstsalon Maximilian Macht, whose galleries are now very well equipped. This event has been received with horror, as they fully intended; a particular comedy has been unfolding for decades on occasions of this kind, played out between defiantly provocative art revolutionaries and a morally outraged public, and this promptly started up on a small scale.

There was no particularly profound reason for this. None of the artists exhibited is so talented that he would be entitled to feel martyred about his fate, or for attacks on his work to be psychologically explicable. But on the other hand, despite the fact that all this revolution is heartily boring, it is not possible to speak of an absolute lack of talent.

Admittedly the exhibition does not contain what the good and tastefully prepared catalogue promises. Most of the pictures suffer from the fact that it is impossible to get far enough back from them because the galleries are so cramped. As they are without exception decorative paintings, this unfortunate state of affairs is very damaging to the exhibitors. When shown in this way, talents like Pechstein, Kirchner, Heckel, Schmidt-Rottluff etc. are unable to convince viewers how fine their ornamental coloring can be – admittedly experimental coloring of unsuitable subjects for the most part. It seems that the individuals who come out best among these savages are those who seem to be making compromises: Otto Müller for example, who is striking because of a certain *esprit*, Fritz Lederer or H. Richter, who was trained under the Kunowski system.

Karl Scheffler, "Kunstausstellung Zurückgewiesener der Secession Berlin–Kunst Salon Maximilian Macht," *Kunst und Künstler*, 1910, p. 524 quoted from *Berlin – Ort der Freiheit für die Kunst*, Berlin, 1960.

There are only two ways of explaining this absurd exhibition: either one assumes that the majority of the members and guests at this event are incurably insane, or that one is dealing with shameless bluffers who are well aware that this is an age that needs sensation and have worked out how to exploit this boom. For my own part, I incline, despite solemn assurances to the contrary, to the latter view, but I am prepared to accept the former in a spirit of goodwill and to devote a few words to the symptomatic features of this show. Our fathers – and this applies not just to the field of fine art – were subject to the fatal misfortune of having made a few particularly appalling errors in rapid succession when assessing large and powerful artistic talents… And now, to avoid being suspected of being a philistine, it is not just that any old nonsense is exhibited and then admired, but it is also bought, as example has shown, and at fantastic prices as well. The satyr play after the tragedy!… After saying this, I can probably deal with the exhibition quite briefly. It is enough, I think, for me to quote a few sentences from the introductions in the catalogue (there are five of them):… Anyone who writes such arrant nonsense is almost bound to paint rubbish as well. "Synthesis" is one of the key words for this Munich association of Eastern Europeans, and it is completely achieved here. Firstly, their exhibition, taken as a whole, is concentrated nonsense, but then one finds a synthesis of every possible inadequacy and mannerisms that could at best be called potentially productive from the art of all peoples and regions, from primitive cannibalistic tribes right down to the recent Parisian decadents. But there is one other point that I must address. This happens quite sporadically, but from time to time one comes across a few works in this exhibition whose creators are genuinely talented people with truly artistic sensibilities. Thus there is a marble head, "Diana", by *S. Soudbinine* that can be considered a masterpiece because of its fine treatment of materials and delicate modelling; *B. Hoetger's* sculptures also reveal a powerful talent, despite their abundant eclecticism, and pieces by artists like *Moyssey Kogan* and *A. Nieder* also show some quality. How have these people ended up among this band of bunglers (their crazed assertions of genius should surely be tempered by the fact that genius has never cropped up by the herd, like this)? – I cannot avoid the suspicion that we are dealing with opportunism of the worst kind here, and that they are exploiting the situation as a vehicle for getting themselves talked about rather more quickly. But it is precisely today, when lack of conviction is a trump card everywhere, that an artist who wants to be seen as a cultural leader should more than ever be a "perfect gentleman", and not get into bad company for the sake of per-

Max Pechstein, *An alle Künstler!*, 1919 manifesto of Arbeitsrat für Kunst Berlin, Staatliche Museen zu Berlin

Ernst Ludwig Kirchner, *Kuenstlervereinigung Bruecke*, 1905, woodcut, logo of the Brücke

Max Pechstein, *Kunstausstellung Zurückgewiesener der Secession Berlin 1910*, manifesto of the exhibition organized by the artists rejected from the Berlin Secession, Kunstsalon Maximilian Macht 15 May - 15 July 1910

sonal gain. When a man like *A. Kubin* exhibits in a show like this I am less surprised. Kubin's significance is to be found merely in the world of experience presented by his work, which although pathological is nevertheless original and powerful. However, I have always that technically he is a mere dilettante, and so he fits in effortlessly here. But let that be an end to the debate! Were I to find, and this is something that can by no means be ruled out in this day and age, that I am inadvertently giving publicity to this exhibition among sensation-seeking members of the public by my derogatory view of it, then I should be extremely sorry about this.

M.K. Rohe, "Zweite Ausstellung der Neuen Künstlervereinigung München," in H. Thannhausers Moderne Galerie in the Arco-Palais (September 1910) [Second exhibition by the Neue Künstlervereinigung München in H. Thannhausers Moderne Galerie in the Arco-Palais, September 1910]

Whatever one feels about this circle of powerful talents, it is no longer possible to deny the seriousness and the belief in artistic convictions with which these artists are trying to express the desire to create a new painting culture here. In order to understand this art, which still takes a strongly revolutionary stand, (even though the last few years have unmistakably led to more visible maturity), it is certainly necessary to revise the traditional view of artistic creation radically, and to empathize with the spirit of these innovators in painting as a visual experience of light and colors while completely rejecting the individual form, painting as rhythm and color. For here color is the last and only resource that can be used to express feelings, and if in individual cases the acrobats of this painting drawn from the soul try to leap a little too violently, it should also not be forgotten that these are personalities who have powerful talents and could eventually become the born precursors of a new monumental style. Ultimately the only question is whether there will be enough walls available in future decades in Germany to try out these young artists' experiments on a sufficiently large scale. Because even the pictures that are smaller if formats are huge in their conceptual scale, and the intoxicating frenzy of colors, rhythm and music, which sticks in the memory very strongly, can only make a full and compelling impact from some distance and on large surfaces.

Incidentally the history of this new movement can be explained quite logically from the work of artists like *Cézanne* and *Gauguin* on the one hand, and above all that of *Van Gogh* on the other. And I am quite happy to accept what is happening here on experimental byways as a quite

appropriate expressive form for our age. Painters in this association, which on this occasion has invited guests from Prague and Munich, though they are of absolutely no importance, include first and foremost *Moritz Melzer* and *Max Pechstein*, the former predominantly monumental, the latter working more to an effect in terms of coloring. As well as these, *Georg Tappert, Artur Segal, E.L. Kirchner, César Klein* and *Otto Müller* are artists who differ as individuals, but show the full maturity of their intentions; among the Munich artists the painters Bechtejeff, Erbslöh and Jawlensky should be noted, and they are joined as a proof of the paradoxical and impossible by W. Kandinsky as a deterrent example. But it is precisely in such extremes that the good work is striking, and while work of this kind is produced the movement cannot go wrong. The colorful quality of vigorous life, the glowing passion of the paintbrush, as demonstrated here, have future when the form as such regains its due rights and there is a possibility of realizing today's tentative experiments on a larger scale. Purely as a problem it seems to me that the Neue Sezession, which has to be addressed as a striking note in modern art life in Berlin, is one of the most interesting documents of our time.

G.B. (Georg Biermann), "Zur A. Ausstellung der 'Neuen Sezession'" (On the 4th "Neue Sezession" exhibition), *Der Cicerone*, vol. III 1911, p. 930 ff.

The most modern school has established itself under the collective name "Blauer Reiter",... The painter Kandinsky has tried to set down the principles of this new movement in a book called "Das Geistige in der Kunst." It would be going too far here to go into the mixture of extremes and a pinch of healthy perception, of foolish illusion and very spirited action... Kandinsky really pursues all the consequences of this view in his – all right, let's say – pictures. He paints abstract forms, or at least that's what he calls them, and invests the expression of his feelings in them. It's a pity – but the final effect is that absolutely nobody can make sense of any of this expression, as the changes that his feelings make in this chaotic convulsions of loops and lines cannot be grasped because it is impossible to know whether convulsive line number seven was perhaps proceeded by six others in which the looping was somehow different... Certainly it is possible to say: a strongly rising line symbolizes a life enhancing feeling, a feeling of joy and enthusiasm, and a strongly falling line expresses a feeling of unhappiness and lack of enthusiasm. But if the rising line is not rising from something, but is just hanging around somewhere or other, it can just as well be a falling one, and can mean precisely the opposite. But this "something" from which it is rising can absolutely never be abstract. But it is logically impossible to throw abstract and concrete forms together (in other words a floor, for example, from which a line as such rises as a line) in a single work. And so when Kandinsky asserts that there are never mistakes in the drawing, that is nonsense. There certainly are errors in drawing arising from incompetence, and this is just as painful as a situation in which deviation from a natural form dictated by a powerful feeling fails to satisfy our artistic needs. Incidentally, Kandinsky is good proof of what... has been said about art in artists' statements. He writes far too well about these questions to be able to be an artist himself – and his "works" show that as well.

Anton Mayer, "Malerei und Gefühlsausdruck" (Painting and the Expression of Feelings), *Der Blaue Reiter, Documente einer geistigen Bewegung*, Leipzig, 1989

The fundamental thing about Futurist painters is that in the most extreme principles and typical examples they are not content to synthesize one impression, they want to give several at the same time and thus create the possibility of representing a continued action, in other words the movement of the scene. And yet the individual moments still seem paralysed. The principle has not been fully thought through. Thus they have gone on where Impressionism left off, in step with their experimental technique, and a picture like Severini's "Pan-Pan-Tanz" (Pan-Pan-Dance) seems to combine the techniques of cinematography and the gramophone on the same canvas. This work could stand as a paradigm for the school; it is so at ease within itself that it would fulfil one purpose excellently: as a mosaic wall decoration in a dance-hall. Only a few Futurist works embody their intentions and thought as clearly and fully, as purposefully.

Rudof Klein, "Kleine Kunst-Nachrichten. Juni 1912," par. "Die Futuristen in 'Sturm'" (Futurists in the "Sturm"), *Deutsche Kunst und Dekoration*, vol. XXX, 1912, p. 276.

Ludwig Meidner may have made far too much use of Van Gogh's famous self-portrait in his own, but in the rest of his work he provides admirable demonstrations of an artistic struggle. The "Weltuntergang" (End of the World) and the "Landschaft mit verbranntem Haus" (Landscape with a Burnt-Out House), and the boundless loneliness in "Hiob" (Job) come closest to

the ideals of Expressionism. His drawings and Steinhardt's graphics, as well as a few paintings by Richard Janthur, follow the same paths in the search for a more profound intellect and spirituality in works of art. Here and there it might be reasonable to ask for a little more self-discipline, but the serious efforts made by these three Silesians make us glad to overlook what is still imperfect, and allows us to hope that a new beauty will arise from sober theories of these latest Expressionist endeavours.

Walter Georgi, "'Die Pathetiker' in 'Sturm'" ("Die Pathetiker" in the "Sturm"), *Deutsche Kunst und Dekoration*, vol. XXXI, 1912-13, p. 438

One of those unhappy monomaniacs who consider themselves to be prophets of a new art of painting has just held an exhibition at Louis Bock & Sohn's. We have more than once campaigned on good aesthetic grounds against these people's nonsensical theories and all their botching, and so we are able to deal with this Russian, Kandinsky, rapidly and without much ado. When... standing in front of these hideous scrawls of paint and babbling lines it is hard to know at first what to admire most: the larger-than-life-sized arrogance with which Mr Kandinsky claims that his botching should be taken seriously, the unappealing impudence with which the journeymen of "Sturm", the protectorate of this exhibition, are promoting this uncouth painting as the revelation of a new art with a big future, or the reprehensible sensation-seeking of the art dealer who has made his galleries available for all this lunatic color and form. But what finally comes out on top is regret about this crazy and thus irresponsible painter who, as a few earlier pictures show, was capable of creating beautiful and noble painterly forms before the darkness closed around him: at the same time one feels satisfied that this kind of art has now arrived at the point at which it reveals itself as precisely that -ism at which it had to land up and be stranded: idiot-ism.

Kurt Küchler, "Für Kandinsky" [The Journeyman of Idiot-ism (for Kandinsky)], *Hamburger Fremdenblatt*, 15.2.1913

Berlin – The magazine "Der Sturm" has arranged an international exhibition of pictures and sculptures by artists that have emerged recently, under the proud title "Erster Deutscher Herbstsalon" (First German Autumn Salon). It is impossible to assess this exhibition objectively because there is scarcely anything objective in it to asses, and it is hard

Wassily Kandinsky, *Der Blaue Reiter*, 1911-12
cover for the catalogue of the first exhibition
of the Blaue Reiter, woodcut
Berlin, Staatliche Museen zu Berlin

to remain in a mood to mock as the sight of a younger generation that generally seems so hopeless fills one with sadness. The bad thing is that intimate contact with this revolutionary monomaniac art gives the viewer a sensation of being put at a disadvantage.

This is not because of the revolutionary nature of this new will, and also not because of the incomplete nature of the experiments, nor the weakness of the forces that are showing their paces here; what is depressing is the absolute lack of youthful naturalness, and the symptoms of an infectious conceptual disease, the military hospital atmosphere in the exhibition galleries and the impurity of imagination in most of the works.

If one considers the groups into which these painters and sculptors fall, and if one also counts "Sturm's" rascally literary chappies, then it is like watching unhappy youth raging against itself. The organizer has done grave damage to modern art with this ill-judged exhibition. Even its committed friends are now clearly shifting away. The damage caused by an exhibition world with no limitations can be seen more dramatically than ever before.

It is possible to convey this kind of art in words. To use some terminology of Goethe's, the copy-ist, the sketcher, the fantasist, the skeleton-merchant, the undulist and the phantomist have come together in such a way that they have produced a caricature that calls itself "synthesist". A portrait of the Futurist leader Marinetti by Gino Severini is a good example of what this exhibition contains: the sleeves of the black habit have been made three-dimensional with outward-curving paper on which a strip of real velvet indicates where they would be turned up, the moustache is made of real hair and stuck on and real newspaper with Futurist manifestoes has been pasted in the background.

This jokey approach is called turning away from a banal imitation of nature, it is supposed to be psychological impression painting. It is a pity about one person in particular in this crazy exhibition and that is Franz Marc.

His is a genuine talent in which creative force is youthfully brewing. This would be a hopeful sign if he could detach himself from this proletarian intellectual atmosphere, if he could make a clean break at the right time with misshapen enthusiasts, vain fellow-travellers and success-crazed sans-culottes.

Karl Scheffler, "Erster Deutscher Herbstsalon," *Kunst und Künstler*, vol. XII, 1914, p. 119 ff.

Impressionists	*Expressionists*
tendency to merge	tendency to contrast
rhythm and harmony covered with nature	rhythm and harmony detached from nature
the cosmic	the individual
discovery, interpretation	charm and sound
psychological	decorative
individualizing	generalizing
ordering instinctively	building up consciously
abstraction in the face of nature	abstraction from nature
working according to views	working according to ideas and memories
naturalism	romanticism
receiving the law from the object	receiving the law from the subject
love of the real environment	preference for the exotic
prose	verse and rhyme
characterizing, intimate	summary, representative
flowing outline	contour
painterly	drawing-based
stress on value	stress on colouring
atmospheric colors	local colors
forms dissolved into movement	forms fixed for ornamental purposes
covering, thick-textured, primary painting	thin, varnished, dabbing painting
representation of space	dividing up the area
easel picture	wall picture
enhancing intention by ability	proceeding from intention to ability

Karl Scheffler, "Impressionismus-Expressionismus (Die Ausstellung der Freien Secession)" [Impressionism-Expressionism (The Freie Secession Exhibition)], *Kunst und Künstler*, vol. XIV, 1916, p. 327 ff.

Tiny symptoms are threatening a tragic end for art. Certainly masters are still working here and there, untroubled by the noises of the day. Do they have disciples who are capable of stanching the flow? The signs that speak against this are nothing against the six centuries spanned for which our art has existed. The frightening thing is the depressing quantity of negative signs. The vein of creativity seems to give out at the very moment at which we become aware of the failing social conditions for the existence of art. Even more threatening than the impudent shrieks of the pictures is the viewers' numb feeling that even the impressive art business of our day with its museums and countless collections cannot conceal, the unstoppable decline and dulling of the masses, the paralysis in which no spark glimmers.

Julius Meier-Graefe, "Wohin Treiben wir?", Julius Meier-Graefe, *Die doppelte Kurve*, essays, Berlin–Leipzig, 1924, p. 90 ff.

All the Expressionists' speeches tell us that what Expressionism is trying to do is unparalleled in the past: a new art is about to dawn. And anyone who sees an Expressionist picture, by Matisse or Picasso, by Pechstein or Kokoschka, by Kandinsky or Marc, by Italian or Bohemian Futurists, will agree: he really does find them unparalleled. But that is all that these groups have in common. The most recent painting consists of nothing but little sects denouncing each other. They have in common that they have turned away from Impressionism, indeed against it (for which reason I lump them all together as Expressionists, even if that is only the name of one sect, and the others will protest about it). They share the trait that when Impressionism insists on conveying the illusion of a piece of reality, when it is working toward an effect, they pour scorn on this. They share the trait of passionately resisting all the demands that we are used to making on a picture in order for it to be valid as a picture at all. Even if we do not know anything about any of these pictures we are certain of one thing: they violate reality, appearance, the sensual world. And this is the true reason for all the outrage: everything that hitherto, from the very beginning of painting, has made sense of all painting seems to be denied here, and something is being sought that has never been attempted before since the very beginning of painting. That is how it seems to the viewer and Expressionism itself will be in complete agreement with that. But the viewer asserts that something that is not authenticated by nature, indeed something that nature deliberately resists, can never be art, but Expressionism asserts that precisely this is art, is its art. And when the viewer violently retorts that the painter can paint nothing that we see, then the Expressionist assures us: we too do not paint anything but what we see. But they are not able to reach an agreement about this. They cannot reach an agreement about seeing.

Hermann Bahr, "Unparalleled," *Expressionism*, Munich, 1916, p. 54 ff., from *Expressionisten, Die Avantgarde in Deutschland 1905-1920*, exhibition catalogue, Berlin, 1986

Today we have indigenous and truly important artists in Germany again. Schmidt-Rottluff is probably the most spirited of them. It is the last word about Pechstein's talent to say that it is vital and decorative. However, I think we can assume that he will perhaps produce his best work when he reaches the peak of his development as a result of contracts for stained glass or mosaic work. Kirchner is one of the most genuine and spontaneous architects. Heckel is at his most intelligible in ghostly landscapes. Otto Müller is much gentler, and confronts us full of attractive tradition. Emil Nolde opened up a new, actually independent way to art. In a certain sense he is the antithesis of Matisse. Both have discovered the naturally painterly element in modern art: creating a picture purely and naturally from color. Nolde is a far more forceful and indeed raw temperament; Matisse a more refined and highly cultured artist. But he also shows to what extent natural qualities and culture have to be intertwined. Ludwig Meidner cannot be ignored. His explosive force, his rebellious temperament have made it possible to create genuine works of art. Georg Grosz should also be mentioned again: he is successful like no one else in presenting the metropolis in stratified layers of color. His characteristic feature is an ability to cause caricatures to walk in color, among ghosts or normal human beings. Actually a modern Hieronymus Bosch fantasy.

Theodor Däubler, *Im Kampf um die moderne Kunst*, 1919, p. 47 ff.

The problems that are dawning for art today are now well beyond the revolutionary approach of yesterday. I admit that today as well, despite the victorious revolution of Expressionism, despite the fact that its radical requirements were met after the spiritualization of art, there is still a set of problems that art has to confront. I further admit that this set of problems arises directly from that very spiritualization… The exciting feature about the history of Expressionism is that it was the first attempt that did not shrink back from any consequences in order to carry out an experiment of completely spiritualizing expression within the confines of our European, post-medieval art… Who knows whether later generations will not see Expressionism in this sense as a heroic final gesture by art, as the last great convulsion before its abdication. Perhaps in this way art reared up for the last time, searching for the last expressive possibilities with desperate gestures, for its last build-up of power, this moment at which art took a deep breath and resorted to the extremes of primitivism, that makes the whole thing seem so apocalyptic and so like the end of the world to us. For any apocalypse contains the first ominous signs of the end of an Empire of a Thousand Years.

Wilhelm Worringer, "Kritische Gedanken zur neuen Kunst", *Genius*, book 2, 1919, p. 221 ff.

Artists and art historians work… with writers, poets, musicians, decadent art enthusiasts, actors, theater directors, film-makers, film-stars, to "live their lives to the full" under the common flag of Expressionism or Dadaism. It should not be taken amiss that this draws them almost without exception into political radicalism, but academic endeavours can really not be promoted in this mixed propaganda society. And no one will dare to assert that their diligence is stimulated by this, and their morale strengthened. The objection will doubtless be made that "morality is a private matter": but for the state this is certainly not the case. Since the state has completely taken over theatre and music we have seen lasciviousness in plays and their production, have seen the nature of cinema shows degenerate into obscene or even perverse films, we have seen the discovery of dance, the most recent art, degenerating wildly into shameless exposure and even naked dancing, and all this has brought with it a sad brutalization of our people, and has produced a large class of "artists" who have become the "people's favourites," and modern youth rushes in to their society and lives life to the full. Do people believe that Germany's renewal can come from this swamp?

Wilhelm von Bode, "Die 'Not der geistigen Arbeiter' im Gebiet der Kunstforschung", *Kunst und Künstler*, vol. XVIII, 1920, p. 299 ff.

Under the old regime there were constant complaints that the Kaiser stopped art from developing freely by interfering personally. The Secessions were forced into a counter-position to the "state-sustaining" parties, which became a decisive factor for the way in which many people decided their own political position. There was a confusion – and not just here in Germany – between a revolutionary attitude in art and a revolutionary approach in politics, and this led to the combination of two elements that were entirely different in their nature, which was only made possible by the fact that artists are in many respects children in terms of politics, but politicians are absolute laymen in terms of art. The phenomenal intensification of the political struggle and the change in the parties' power relationships have now produced conditions for art that are starting to become menacing... Art and socialism are as alien to each other as art and any kind of politics. Or does anyone seriously believe that a communist is better able than a monarchist to empathize with the artistic achievements of his day?

Curt Glaser, "Kunst und Politike–Kunst und Sozialismus", *Kunstchronik und Kunstmarkt*, no. 19, 6 February 1920, p. 381 ff., from *Expressionisten, Die Avantgarde in Deutschland 1905-1920*, exhibition catalogue, Berlin, 1986, p. 168-69

Expressionism is dead. The individuals, who are distinct from each other and from the movement, even though they may derive from each other and from the movement – they are alive. The category has nothing left to say. It has served its purpose. It can go. Selection is being carried out. A remnant of the Expressionist populace is perishing; with full academic fuss and bother; boring in life and death.

Wilhelm Hausenstein, *Die Kunst in diesem Augenblick*, München 1920-1960, p. 265, from *Expressionisten, Die Avantgarde in Deutschland 1905-1920*, exhibition cat., Berlin, 1986, p. 167

The Novembergruppe in Berlin shows middle-of-the-road art, or if you wish: radical middle-of-the-road art. It is lacking in any values of its own that stand out above a certain level. The leaders of this movement are talents without independence who attract in particular all the second- and third-class forces from the more remote provinces that are remotely worthy of being exhibited. The association has been further reinforced by the group of artists who withdrew from the "Sturm" gallery when its members founded a so-called "International Association of Expressionists" last year. The main gallery is interesting to an extent in terms of principle. Here – and this is handled very skilfully in terms of exhibition technique – a series of artists are brought together who have taken up the program of abstract art. In principle these artists (rightly) reject framed pictures and free sculpture, in order – to fill whole walls her with nothing but framed pictures. This is a contradiction which I shall return to later, when there will be an opportunity to say something from this point of view about the works of the Section d'Or, to which Goll has committed himself. The experiments shown by the Novembergruppe use the same kind of architecture as their supporting base. It could be that this will produce possibilities of the kind that

dominated 9th, 10th and 11th century wall painting, where (according to Dehio) the aim of painting was to continue architecture, in other words "to divide areas, to create intermediate elements, to interpret the work of the architectural elements through ornamental symbols, in brief, to fill the still and silent masses with rhythmic life." These possibilities are not available to the exhibition picture that tends to be threatened rather than suggested as a solution because of this mania to keep producing masses of exhibition items.

Paul Westheim, "Novembergruppe," *Das Kunstblatt*, vol. IV, 1920, p. 223

The Neue Merkur has published a special issue called "Werden" (Becoming). In contradiction, perhaps in delight at the paradox of the contradiction, Hausenstein has provided a concluding essay for the issue: Art at the present moment is not very interested in becoming, it is proclaiming the end of something, and that is the end of Expressionism. A wittily informal essay, full of ideas and justifications, like everything that Hausenstein writes, disciplined, with an eye to the broader perspective and with the aim of taking a clear line. Hausenstein comes up with a definition of Expressionism, a formula that is no more wrong, but probably no more right, than the 375 formulas that have been constructed by German art historians in the last few years. He is at least aware of the limited nature of his construction, complains about "the fact that the concept cannot be grasped; the immeasurable span between Picasso and Nolde, Kandinsky and Rousseau, Klee and Meidner, Seewald and Kokoschka". He states that the great Impressionists: Renoir, Manet "are more than Impressionism". They stood above the school... Quite right. They were creative personalities of broad dimensions, strong, separate and unique creators, great despite the school with which they were connected and which they had grown out of. And the great Expressionists (for once to use the word that has generally been avoided in this magazine because of its ambiguity), the creative, separate creators of this moment, who cannot be reduced to a conceptual common denominator?! Hausenstein mentions a few who "are now walking down the path to freedom away from their own (sometimes bitter) freedom": Kokoschka, Meidner, Nolde, Heckel, Kirchner, Klee, Albiker, Lehmbruck, Fiori, Scharff, Kubin, and also mentions some that I would not have chosen: Beeh, Unold, Caspar, and overlooks Barlach, Feininger, Poelzig, and could have added quite a few from beyond the borders where those who are still not the least significant live. Are there many artists – able to create powerfully and uniquely – who are more than a

school, more than a tendency? I believe that a time that has six separate characterful artists to show for itself is not poor, is not at the end of the road, and if ever a time had a claim that it is developing and has a future then it is ours. And yet we still have the gesture of resignation? It seems to me that Hausenstein has mistaken the true direction of a tendency that has been perceptible since he went back to Munich. He thinks that he is fighting an issue and is fencing with a phantom. He picks out the few who stand out above the school, the only ones (today as always) that the movement is really about – and then prophesies an end for the others. Certainly quite right. One could even wish that this prophecy would come true. All the rest: the Expressionist academy, Expressionist fashion, Expressionist hangers-on, that smart catch-phrase Expressionism with which smart art-dealers and clever art writers use to turn out their propaganda, if only all that were already at an end! What should we not fight more keenly or more passionately that these freeloaders of Expressionism – though here I ask you please not to forget that these satellites were there on every occasion and knew how to thrust themselves into the foreground! What has the Kunstblatt been fighting in every issue for the past three and a half years with a decisiveness that has naturally been interpreted as our one-sidedness or preferably our prejudice? We have been fighting against this Expressionist pseudo-talent that has so many enthusiastic and tireless supporter behind it, against the school, against the trends, against these many mannerists who have nothing to say and who mean nothing, who will have a new programme and a new manner tomorrow if that happens to be the fashion. Unfortunately it cannot be assumed that this Expressionism is already at an end; but it does not mean anything, it does not matter, just as little as the "Scholle" mattered in its time. The others, the few of which Hausenstein himself recognizes quite a number, they are there, and today they are creating art, our art, which will probably still mean something tomorrow and the day after as well. Whether they fit in with a formula that is fixed in one way or another, whether they are Expressionists or non-Expressionists, what does that matter? As far as I am concerned each and every tendency can come to an end; so long as this one thing is still the case: that creative individuality that in its work synthetically encompasses nature and ego, world and spirit; if that is so, then we have no need to be worried about art.

Paul Westheim, "Das Ende des Expressionismus" (The End of Expressionism), *Das Kunstblatt*, vol. IV, 1920, p. 187, quoted from *Expressionisten, Die Avantgarde in Deutschland 1905-1920*, exhibition catalogue, Berlin, 1986, p. 174

Biographies of the Artists   *by Wolf-Deter Dube*

Ernst Barlach
Wedel, Holstein 2.1.1870 – Rostock 22.10.1938

Barlach went to the Arts and Crafts School in Hamburg in 1888, in 1891 to Dresden Academy and pursued his studies in 1895–1896 in the Académie Julian in Paris, to which he returned in 1897. He then lived in Hamburg and Wedel, became a teacher at the technical school for ceramics in Höhr (Westerwald) and settled in Berlin in 1905.

The experience which gave self-revelation to Barlach, was a journey to Russia in 1906 where he found an opportunity as a sculptor to develop form into self-contained substance which could convey vision and expression. Russian beggars and farmers, whom he saw as symbols of human existence, comprised Barlach's favourite themes after his return.

In them Barlach sought, as in his very last works, to embody the realization that the outer clothing of external reality must coincide at one point with the inner expression of its essence. The same motifs were frequently treated in the sculpture and graphic art of this period. After this trip he exhibited in 1907 and 1908 at the Sezession in Berlin, then in 1908 in Dresden. In 1907 Barlach signed a contract with the art dealer Paul Cassirer which relieved him from financial worry. In 1909 he was working in the Villa Romana in Florence. In 1912 Barlach's first play, *Der tote Tag* (The Dead Day), was published by Bruno Cassirer, together with a series of lithographs. Although Barlach sought for expression and synthesis in his work, he rejected the contemporaneous endeavours of modern art in a similar direction. In 1910 he withdrew to Güstrow in Mecklenburg where in the years that followed, he produced ever more variations on the same themes, both in form and content, until in the end he became a self-plagiarist.

In 1937, under the title of *The Bad Year of 1937* (*Das schlimme Jahr 1937*), he depicted the silhouette of a woman who, despite her suffering, is nevertheless upright, confronting barbarity. Endowed with an inspiration which is often mystical and religious, Barlach's art conforms to the expressionist aesthetic, through its inner *élan* which is the source of the form that he creates. But Barlach himself always remained on the fringe of particular movements. He managed to establish his own personality at the very time when Expressionism was emerging. Massive, heavy, his volumes are at the same time compact and concentrated, every detail attaining the most intense degree of expressiveness.

At the time of an exhibition in 1952, Brecht wrote: "I consider Barlach to be one of the greatest sculptors we Germans have had. The line, the significance of what he is expressing, the technical genius, the beauty without artifice, a grandeur which is not forced, a harmony which is not facile, a vigour without brutality, make his sculptures into masterpieces."

The biography of Ernst Barlach (as painter) is by Wolf-Dieter Dube
The biography of Ernst Barlach (as sculptor) is by Lionel Richard

Max Beckmann
Leipzig 12.2.1884 – New York 27.12.1950

For a long time, Beckmann remained opposed to the artistic problems of his generation; even in 1912 he carried on a polemic against modern art with Franz Marc in the journal *Pan*. He avoided the radical rejuvenation of form and sought instead to get to the root of nature and the soul of things; with a conscious continuation of tradition.

Beckmann went to the Weimar Academy in 1900 where he received a thorough education. In 1903 he left the Academy and went to Paris for six months where he was decisively influenced by Manet and the impressionists, but also discovered Cézanne for himself. From 1904 onward, he was resident in Berlin. He won the Villa Romana prize, and with it a period of study in Florence, with a large composition of figures shown in 1906 at an exhibition mounted by the artists' union in Weimar.

In Berlin Beckmann became a member of the Sezession and in 1910 was elected to their committee. He sought to express the drama of his time with the methods of history painting and portrayed battles and scenes from the Old and New Testaments on large canvas, but also drew on current events. He also provided landscapes and portraits in small format. By 1913 he was an artist known far and wide who had already had a monograph, with a catalogue of his works, devoted to him.

But Beckmann himself was well aware that his methods were not suited to express the spirit of things. On the outbreak of war in 1914, he volunteered for the medical service and went to Flanders where he met Heckel. In the proximity to horror and death, Beckmann found himself. In 1915 he suffered a physical and nervous breakdown, was discharged and moved from Berlin to Frankfurt. Beckmann now tried to exorcise fear, torment and loneliness. The immeasurable solitude in eternity: to experience the extremities of emotion is already to create form. Form is salvation.

The pictures he now produced were built up from the drawn line into angular shapes which fill the whole field of vision – color was reduced to local color. Beckmann could only bear life by conceiving of it as one scene in the theatre of eternity. He gained the objectivity to be able to depict the world as a grotesque, and joyless farce. Distance and a rigid arrangement in his paintings were the means by which Beckmann succeeded in controlling the pressures of emotion from 1922 onward, in going beyond the phase of his art which had been concerned purely with expression.

Heinrich Maria Davringhausen
Aachen 21.10.1894 – Niece 13.12.1970

Davringhausen was prevalently self-taught, but for a brief period in 1913–14 he attended the Academy at Düsseldorf. His training was largely obtained from his artist friends; his first Futurist paintings of 1914 germinated under the influence of Carlo Mense.

In 1915 Davringhausen moved to Berlin, where he met Meidner and Grosz, and became close friends with the Herzfelde brothers.

He was one of the first artists to realize that the experience of war and revolution could not be properly stated in Expressionism, and voiced a need for a new form of objectivity.

In 1918 he moved to Munich, where he worked until his return to Berlin in 1922. Davringhausen's paintings focus on isolated figures with rigid facial expressions.

Otto Dix
Untermhaus, Thuringia 2.12.1891 – Singen 25.7.1969

Dix began with an apprenticeship as an interior decorator in Gera from 1905–1909. In 1910 he went to Dresden, the centre of expressionism, to study at the art and craft school. He stayed there until 1914 and gained inspiration from the Brücke, the Blaue Reiter and futurism. In 1913 we was deeply impressed by a Van Gogh exhibition which was directly assimilated into his work. At the outbreak of war, Dix volunteered for military service. He wanted to witness the end of an epoch and the downfall of bourgeois society, which so many artists hoped from the war. He now painted soldiers in heightened, expressionist colors, and depicted himself as Mars. He captured these apocalyptic events in innumerable drawings and gouaches, not merely recording, but tranforming them into ecstatic, expressive visions. These forms, which seem to split asunder of their own accord, and the aggressive rhythms in the lines, are not formulations of an artistic problem, but rather the only possible means of simultaneously portraying these great and earth-shattering events that changed the world. It has therefore been rightly said that the aim of the futurists reached its climax in Dix's war paintings. In 1919 Dix continued his studies at Dresden Academy and became a founder-member of the 19 Group, whose goal was to "search for a new expression for the new world that surrounds us." Dix's work continued to revolve around his war experiences. However, heightened emotion evaporated when confronted by the knowledge that only evil and horror had triumphed. This was the new truth which had to be faced objectively and soberly. In order to overcome it, Dix turned to verisimilitude.

Heinrich Ehmsen
Kiel 9.8.1886 – East Berlin 1964
After working as a decorator, Ehmsen attended courses from 1906 to 1909 at the Kunstgewerbeschule in Düsseldorf with Jan Thorn-Prikker, Peter Behrens, and others. His connections with the art dealer Alfred Flechtheim drew him into the avant-garde movement, and in 1909 he left for Paris with Ernesto de Fiori, where he remained two years. There he met Jawlensky, Marc, and Klee, and was prompted to move to Munich.
After serving in the army from 1914 to 1918, he returned to Munich, where he became deeply involved in the events surrounding

the revolutionary soviets of the Bavarian Republic.
He established his reputation as a critical artist with a series of paintings on the November Revolution and the collapse of the soviets that had emerged in Bavaria in 1919.

Conrad Felixmüller
Dresden 21.5.1897 – Berlin 24.3.1977
Encouraged by his family, Felixmüller took up music studies at the Dresden conservatory while also attending courses at the Kunstgewerbeschule.
At 15 he began studying painting at the academy, but quit in 1915 to work as an independent artist. During his term in Berlin, thanks to the mediation of Meidner, he mixed with the new generation of writers. It was principally through Raoul Hausmann that Felixmüller found himself in an antimilitary group that occupied itself not so much with artistic matters as questions of social politics. As a consequence of this involvement, in 1917 Felixmüller refused to enlist. With Otto Dix he jointly founded the secessionist movement known as the Dresdner Sezession Gruppe 1919, whose members saw themselves as prophets ushering in a new world. He joined the Communist Party, and was also in the Novembergruppe. When in 1920 he was awarded the Rome prize, he decided not to leave for Italy, but for the Ruhr district to study the miserable life led by the miners. "Given the problems of the subject – namely, the task of representing the world of the uneducated proletariat – I was forced to paint in a concise style, knowing full well I was reproducing in simplistic but organic form the things of nature, humanity, and social content." After the rise of the bourgeois republic, Felixmüller changed his mode of expressionism, preferring landscapes and intimately personal portraits.

George Grosz
Berlin 26.7.1893 – 6.7.1959
The son of an antiques restorer, from a very early age Grosz showed great skill in draftsmanship. In 1908 he was expelled from the Oberrealschule for returning a slap dealt him by one of the teachers. In 1909 he entered the Dresden Academy, where his teachers were Richard Müller and Robert Sterl. In 1912 he resettled in Berlin and, thanks to a state grant, was able to attend courses at the Kunstgewerbeschule until 1917. In his second year he met Franz Jung, the publisher of the brothers Wieland Herzfelde and John Heartfield, with whom he created his collages and experimental photomontage works. In 1914 he enlisted as a volunteer, but the following year he was declared unfit for service.
Grosz meanwhile worked on his first portfolios, and co-founded the Dada magazine *Neue Jugend*.
In 1917 he was called up for service again, but was certified mentally unstable. Imputed in 1918 for desertion, he narrowly escaped execution through the intervention of Harry Graf Kessler.
In 1919 he founded with Herzfelde the journal *Die Pleite*; with Franz Jung *Jedermann sein eigener Fußball*; and with Carl Einstein *Der blutige Ernst*.
In 1920 he took part in the First International Dada Exhibition held in Berlin; co-wrote with Heartfield the satirical opera *Schall und Rauch* (Smoke); and produced the sets for G. B. Shaw's *Ceasar and Cleopatra* staged by Max Reinhardt.
He was brought before the law courts three times from 1920 to 1928 for his comments in *Angriff auf die Reichswehr* (Assault on the Armed Forces of the Third Reich), and his book of satirical drawings *Gott mit uns* (God with us); in 1924 for *Angriff auf die öffentliche Moral* (Assault on public morals); for *Ecce Homo*; and again in 1928 for

Gotteslästerung (Blasphemy) and *Hintergrund* (Background).
In 1922 he left Germany for the United States with Martin Andersen Nexö.
In 1923 he designed the sets for the stage version of the satire on war, *The Good Soldier Schweik* by the Czech writer Jaroslav Hasek. In 1924 he was elected president of the Roten Gruppe, an association of Communist artists.
In time, the marked Futurist and Dadaist bent of Grosz's satirical works gravitated toward an increasingly insistent "objective realism" that lampooned contemporary society.

Erich Heckel
Döbeln, Saxony 31.7.1883 – Hemmenhofen on Lake Constance 27.1.1970
Heckel and Schmidt-Rottluff had become friends in 1901 at secondary school in Chemnitz, and began to draw and paint together. In 1904 Heckel went to Dresden to study architecture. He met Kirchner and Bleyl, and in 1905 founded the Brücke circle with them and Schmidt-Rottluff. At the same time he abandoned his studies in order to devote himself entirely to painting. Heckel, who had an almost fanatical conception of friendship and artistic partnership, became the cohesive element in the group, and as their manager, its practical organizer. This work with his friends, whom Nolde and Pechstein had joined in 1906, also meant, above all, a close examination of Van Gogh, which expressed itself in a vigorous painting style.
However, Heckel very soon realized that for him, painting born from instinct alone could not lead to the discovery of form.
In the summer of 1907 he had gone with Schmidt-Rottluff to Dangast on the North Sea for the first time. The experience of nature in its original state, linked with his own

intellectual discipline, led him in 1908 to a grandiose style. In Spring 1909 he travelled in Italy; he spent the summer with Kirchner at the Moritzburg Lakes and in the autumn went to stay with Schmidt-Rottluff. His journey to Italy brought about a clarification of his forms. He was especially impressed by Etruscan art, which confirmed him in his striving after rigour, simplification and increased spirituality. By 1910 the typically flat style of the Brücke had become perfected by Heckel as well. Areas of color, delineated with jagged, angular contours are intertwined to form a completely compact and immutable composition. Yet Heckel's intensity remained austere, barren and curiously harsh. Landscape followed in close succesion at the Moritzburg Lakes and in Dangast, as well as urban views, nudes, bathing figures and music hall scenes. In 1911 Heckel painted at Prerow on the Baltic where Jawlensky was also working.

In the Autumn of that year he moved to Berlin like his friends, where he took over Otto Müller's studio. This change represents no break in his artistic aims. He was not concerned, as was Kirchner, with the dynamism of the city; from now on he was interested in trends which were not subject to the moment. He directed his attention toward the variety in landscape and the passing of the seasons, and also the behaviour of men in their longings, joys and sufferings. His paintings originated in human compassion.

The year 1912 brought numerous meetings for Heckel, with Macke and Marc, for example and the start of his friendship with Feininger. The high point was the exhibition of the Sezession in Cologne, when Heckel and Kirchner decorated the chapel. In 1913 the Brücke broke up. Heckel mounted his first solo exhibition the same year. He progressed toward ordering objects in his pictures into a stable equilibrium. From now on he transformed his findings from cubism into an angular, as it were, disjointed structure which enabled him to portray light in a character-

istic way. He represented reflections as crystalline shapes so that, with the aid of this 'visible' atmosphere, the heavens, the earth, water and man fused into a single mode of expression.

In 1914 Here volunteered for military service and in 1915 was appointed to nurse the wounded in Flanders. Here he met Beckmann and made friends with Ensor. Heckel and Beckmann were, with other artists, under the command of the art historian Walter Kaesbach, who so detailed their duties, that every other day was left free for artistic work. In 1918 Heckel returned to Berlin. He evolved his art within the framework of themes he had already elaborated and strove to portray in his pictures what is permanent and universal.

Walter Jacob
Altenburg 21.10.1893 – Hindenlang 13.7.1964
Jacob's training as an artist began in 1910 in Dresden as a private student, but by 1912 he staged his first show at Leipzig.

After serving in the army, he became a pupil of Robert Sterl at the Dresden Academy, where, until 1921, he worked alongside Dix and Kokoschka, one of his closest friends. Jacob did not pursue the characteristic exasperated style of Expressionism for long, however; in 1925, after meeting Lovis Corinth, he turned toward that artist's harsh brand of pictorial realism.

Alexej Jawlensky
Kuslovo 13.3.1864 – Wiesbaden 15.3.1941
Born the son of a Russian colonel, Jawlensky seemed destined auto-

matically for a military career. In 1877 he entered Cadet School in Moscow and in 1882 the Alexander Military Academy. In 1884 he became a lieutenant in a Moscow infantry regiment.

He associated with painters and began to copy paintings in the Tretyakov Gallery. In 1887 he applied for acceptance by the Academy in St Petersburg. Since he could not leave the services for financial reasons, he had to be transferred to St Petersburg, which he managed in 1889.

In 1890 he met Ilya Repin, then the most important artist in Russia. He brought Jawlensky and Marianne von Werefkin together. She was his private pupil and already well-known as a painter.

In 1896 Jawlensky, now a captain, left the army and moved with Werefkin to Munich. They attended the Azbe School, where they met Kandinsky.

It soon became clear to Jawlensky that color was the only means of expression that suited him; he aimed to achieve harmonic effects in his use of it. In 1903 he travelled in Normandy and to Paris, and took part in the exhibitions mounted by the Munich and Berlin Sezession. In his work with the medium of colors in motion, Van Gogh was his model and in 1904 he purchased a picture of the Dutchman.

In Brittany in 1905 Jawlensky painted brilliantly colored, crudely pointillist pictures which he exhibited the same year with the fauves in the Salon d'Automne. He realized that color was not intended to depict an object, but that the object was the occasion for a structure of color in which the emotions of the artist and the 'essence of things' was revealed.

The colors must unite into a harmony shot through with dissonances in "order to reproduce the things which exist without being." (Jawlensky) This conviction corresponded exactly to the aim of the fauves, of whom Jawlensky knew through his meeting with Matisse. In 1906 Jawlensky exhibited again the Salon d'Automne and in 1907 returned to Paris, to work in Matisse's studio.

In Munich the same year he renewed his friendship with Kandinsky. In the summer of 1908 they went together to paint at Murnau. That summer, Jawlensky created grandiose landscapes out of a rigorous composition. Brilliant areas of color, darkly outlined produce a two-dimensional structure.

These paintings are without dimension and without a story, as are the still-lifes he painted at the same time. The themes are interchangeable and barely have any meaning in themselves any more. Form emerged from a synthesis between impressions of the external world and the experiences of the artist's inner world.

Jawlensky required more time for perfecting his portraits, but from 1911 on he succeeded in simplifying the object in his paintings of figures too. Attention was concentrated more and more on the head, where the eyes became the dominant motif.

Form was thus made monumental and symbolic. In 1909 Jawlensky was one of the founder members of the New Artists' Association in Munich and remained a member after the departure of Kandinsky and Marc.

He did not therefore take part in the exhibitions of the Blaue Reiter in Munich, although this did not indicate a rupture either on a personal or an artistic level.

In 1911 Jawlensky travelled to Paris for the last time and met Matisse and Van Dongen. He had spent the summer of that year at Prerow on the Baltic where Heckel was painting.

Here he created landscapes from an inner ecstasy that were similar to Nolde's work in expression, something which Jawlensky himself felt. A further heightening of the paintings of the senses was not possible for Jawlensky.

In 1914 he had to leave Germany, when he moved to St Prex on Lake Geneva. Henceforth he painted meditative pictures on a small scale, formal, endless variations on a landscape theme, and the human face, thereby evolving a tranquil expression of religious feeling and intensity.

Wassily Kandinsky
Moscow 4.12.1866 – Neuilly sur Seine 13.12.1944

Kandinsky had begun studying law and political economy in Moscow in 1886 which he completed in 1892 before entering a university career. As a school-boy he had already painted on the side, and also been deeply interested in art as a student. At an exhibition of French impressionists in 1895 he discovered Monet's *Haystacks* which fascinated him because he could not at first detect any object in them. The problem of an art without objects preoccupied him from then on.

In 1896 therefore he did not take up an appointment to a chair in jurisprudence in Dorpat University, but instead devoted himself entirely to painting and moved to Munich. Munich had become one of the most important places for artistic training in the last decades of the nineteenth century, and particularly attracted young artists from Eastern and Northern Europe. The town was the same time the centre of art nouveau. In 1895 the journals *Jugend* (Youth) and *Simplicissimus* had been founded. Artists like Herman Obrist, Henry van der Velde, August Endell and Adolf Hoelzel were preparing the ground for an art that was to "signify nothing, depict nothing and remind us of nothing." So Kandinsky found tendecies which coincided with his own vague ideas. He entered Anton Azbe's school and here he met his fellow countrymen Jawlensky and Werefkin. In 1900 he transferred to the Academy and became Stück's pupil. He had scarcely left the academy when he became a teacher at the college of the artistic circle, Phalanx whose president he was from 1902–1904. His first pupil was Gabriele Münter, his companion until 1916. The Phalanx group also organized exhibitions, amongst which was one of French neo-impressionists, which

was important for Kandinsky since art nouveau and neo-impressionism were the starting point for his work in the year that followed.

Kandinsky painted landscapes in a crude pointillist manner, and scenes containing many figures from a fairy world, drawn from history or folklore. At the same time, he was deeply interested in art nouveau woodcuts. In order to widen his range of vision he went on several journeys. In 1905 he was in Venice, Odessa and Moscow; in 1904–1905 in Tunis for several months. In 1905–1906 he worked for four months in Rapallo; in 1906–1907 at Sèvres near Paris; in 1907–1908 in Berlin. Despite his travels, Kandinsky constantly participated in exhibitions, for example, from 1902 in those of the Berlin Sezession from 1904 in the Salon d'Automne, to whose jury he was elected. He also took part in the second exhibition of the Brücke in Dresden in 1906. In 1908 he returned to Munich. He spent the summer in Murnau together with Jawlensky, Münter and Werefkin. He now assimilated numerous influences, in particular Cézanne, Matisse and Picasso. The elementary power of color was released in his many landscapes. His encounter with Bavarian folk art provided additional methods of simplification. Areas of red, blue, green and yellow emerged from hastily applied patches and short strokes; they form stark contrasts, and only serve to a limited extent to describe the subject matter. Kandinsky was on the way toward a synthesis between external reality and the inner world experienced by the artist.

In 1909 he was a founder-member of the New Artists' Association in Munich, which elevated this synthesis to the status of a programme. In 1910 he met Franz Marc, and the Burliuk brothers on a journey to Odessa. That year Kandinsky was able to complete his manuscript *On the Spiritual in Art*, which had been written over a period of several years. He now had all he required to take the decisive step. His paintings admittedly still began with a subject, but he subordinated natural shapes to a process of 'rhythmification', so

that they now only had the function of building up the picture. These paintings could no longer be understood in terms of an analysis of the object, with the result that it became discordant and superfluous.

Since only Jawlensky and Marc had the power to pursue these developments, a break occurred in the New Artists' Association. Kandinsky and Marc left them and organized the 1911 and 1912 exhibitions of the *Der Blaue Reiter*. In 1912, they, as editors, published the almanach of the same name. Kandinsky had published *On the Spiritual in Art*, followed by *A Retrospective Look* and *Tones* in 1913. Because Kandinsky was seeking a mode of expression for the sensations stored within us, it was not possible for him to move away gradually from the closeness of nature with 'imaginary forms'. He could only use such shapes as formed by themselves in his inner imagination so that he merely needed to copy them down. As a consequence, pictures which referred to some subject were being produced for a time alongside abstract paintings, until Kandinsky succeeded in 1913-1914 in concentrating his imaginative powers in such a way that the last traces of an object could be eliminated. Kandinsky had reached the climax of abstract expressionism.

The outbreak of war forced him to leave Germany and return to Moscow. When he again became active in Germany in 1922 as a teacher in the Bauhaus, after some years of full cultural and political commitment, his art had also changed and was striving towards new goals.

Ernst Ludwig Kirchner
Aschaffenburg 6.5.1880 – Frauenkirch, near Davos 15.6.1938

Kirchner began as an architecture student in 1901 at the tecnical college in Dresden. After a preliminary examination which he took in 1903

he went to Munich for two semesters at Debschitz and Obrist's studio for the theory and practice of the pure and applied arts. He thus came into contact with the centre of art nouveau in Munich, whose findings wer not confined to formal considerations. Obrist's belief in conveying a deepened expressiveness instead of fleeting impressions, and in conceiving of art not as a heightened and intensified form of life, had an effect on Kirchner.

His great ideal which took shape in Munich was the desire to rejuvenate German art. He saw that academic studio painting had nothing in common with real life. He set himself the task of grasping life in motion and uniting it with art. Rembrandt's drawings showed a way to him. He began to take notes of what he saw with bold, rapid strokes whenever and wherever possible; a method to which he remained faithful for the rest of his life. In the haste and excitement of work, new forms of expression emerged which were then brought under control, simplified, and preserved, in his studio, in drawings taken from the imagination and in woodcuts. The latter, which has central importance in Kirchner's work, was first used in Munich and evolved under the influence of Valloton and Munch in the years that followed into one of the most fundamental media of German expressionism. Through an exhibition of French neo-impressionists organized by the Phalanx group, over which Kandinsky presided, Kirchner was made aware of the problems of pure color. In 1904 he returned to Dresden and got to know Erich Heckel. However, he concentrated at first on his architectural studies, which he completed in 1905 with a diploma.

Now he could devote himself entirely to painting and in 1905 he founded the Brücke with Fritz Bleyl, Erich Heckel and Karl Schmidt-Rottluff. In 1906 Pechstein and Nolde joined them. They worked feverishly in joint studies, taking their themes from the environment they saw around them: views of city life, landscapes, portraits of friends and later, also circus and music hall scenes, and, above all, nudes. He learnt from Seurat, Gauguin, Van Gogh and Munch; this is clearly evident in the structure and rhythm of his application of paint in the years up to 1908. In 1908, he went for the first time to the Baltic island of Fehmarn. From this encounter with nature he evolved his particular drawing style, which he later called hieroglyphic: "Hieroglyphic in the sense that it reduced the forms of nature to simple, surface forms to suggest their significance to the spectator. Emotion creates even more hieroglyphics which become separated from the mass of lines that seemed so random intially and become almost geometric characters." Thus, simplified and when necessary distorted, he let shapes emerge from his desire for expression, in order to be able to put across what he thought more forcibly and clearly. In 1910 he evolved a consistently flat picture composition, like the style his friend used, which is known as the Brücke style; it is created from simple, clear contours and pure colors applied over a large area.

At the same time, Kirchner had discovered sculptures from the South Seas in the Museum of Ethnology in Dresden; these were important to him because of their lapidary form and as expressions of 'primitive state.' In order to portray the simple and primitive elements, Kirchner used to go to the Moritzburg Lakes, accompanied by Erich Heckel, during the summer months from 1909 to 1911. There he painted nudes set in the landscape; they were an expression of his longing for the natural harmony between man and nature. Kirchner now developed his particular coloring, which is characterized by the frequent use of pink and violet. In 1910, Kirchner joined the Neue Sezession in Berlin and made friends with Otto Müller, with whom he travelled to Bohemia in 1911. In October 1911 he moved to Berlin and founded an art college with Pechstein, which did not, however, meet wich success. In the summers from 1912 to 1914, he again painted at

Fehmarn, and pursued the themes of his stays in Moritzburg. In these, he saw man as a part of creation. In sharp contrast to this was his experience of modern city life: on the one hand, a natural liberty and yearning for the 'new man;' on the other, existential constraint, rejection and the loneliness of modern man. Kirchner reacted violently. He drew his mode of expression from the dynamic, bustling, artificial world of the city, to create a hectic, nervous drawing style and fragmented shapes. He depicted evil and harshness, and laid bare its abnormality with allegorical force in his street scenes of 1914. In this way, he achieved a portrayal of modern life that remains unique in the art world. He fulfilled the task he had set himself, "to create a picture out of the chaos of the age."

After his rupture with the Brücke in 1913, Kirchner became dependent on himself alone. The tension which he strove to endure provoked an existential crisis. In 1914 he volunteered for military service. But while still training he suffered a complete mental and physical breakdown. Van Gogh's fate seemed to be coming to pass in Kirchner, who sought in his art to bear witness to his love for men, without inhibiting them. However, friends brought the semi-paralysed artist to Davos in 1917, where he recovered enough to be able to endure life for a while longer, before ending it himself in 1938.

Oskar Kokoschka
Pöchlarn, near Vienna 1.3.1886 – Montreux 22.2.1980
Although Kokoschka was the son of a goldsmith and had tried his hand at painting at a very early stage, he wanted to become a chemist. But since he was entitled to a grant to study at the School of Arts and Crafts in Vienna, he went to study there with the intention of

becoming a teacher. Kokoschka learnt a great variety of artistic techniques, but not painting, which he acquired by teaching himself. In 1906 he was deeply impressed by a Van Gogh exhibition. He was interested in Far Eastern Art and studied Klimt.

In 1907 he became a contributor to the Wiener Werkstätten (Vienna Workshop) which published his book, *The Dreaming Youth*, in 1908. His one act play, *Murderer. The Hope of Women*, was first performed amid tumultuous scenes at the Wiener Kunstschau in 1909. He came to the notice of Adolf Loos, the architect, who introduced him to Karl Kraus.

Both of them gave him commissions for their portraits, with the result that Kokoschka left the school of arts and crafts and the Vienna Workshop and hoped to earn his living as a portrait painter.

However, his method of projecting his own torments and sufferings on to the model, in order to be able to express their soul, and his 'distorting' glaze, thwarted any success.

In 1900 he went to Berlin and became a contributor to the Sturm, which admittedly did not relieve his Sezession in Berlin, in Cologne, and the Neue Sezession in Munich. In 1913 the first monograph appeared in Leipzig; *Oskar Kokoschka - Plays and Paintings*.

From now on he painted predominantly figure compositions, amongst them religious subjects. He overlaid his pictures with a prismatic net of colored lines, and patches of color, thus introducing color as a sensual expressive element. In 1912 he went to Italy, with Alma Mahler-Werfel, and studied principally Venetian painting.

In 1914 he volunteered for military service and was severely wounded in 1915. In 1917 he returned to Dresden to convalesce.

His painting now was constructed out of tense, rapid brushstrokes which, combined with softened coloring, reveal how hard Kokoschka had to combat his mental and physical state. In 1919 he was appointed to the Academy in Dresden; and he returned to thickly applied and brilliant colors.

Käthe Kollwitz
Königsberg 8.7.1867 – Moritzburg 22.4.1945
Kollwitz took her first drawings lessons in 1881 in Königsberg. From 1884 to 1885 she attended the Künstlerinnenschule in Berlin under Stauffer-Bern; in 1888–89 she studied in Munich under Ludwig Herterich, where she learnt etching and decided to devote herself to graphics. In 1891 she married a doctor and moved back to Berlin. In 1893 she began her masterpiece, *Weavers' Uprising*, a work that marks her artistic maturity.

From 1898 to 1903 she held a teaching post at the Berlin Künstlerinnenschule. In 1904 she made a trip to Paris, where she met Rodin and began to take an interest in sculpture. In 1907 she won the Villa Romana award and traveled to Italy. Shortly after she had completed the second great cycle of graphic works, *Peasants' War* (1908), Kollwitz turned to sculpture.

After the death of her son in Flanders in 1914 she became intensely pacifist, and was politically involved in the struggle against poverty and hunger, as well as war. In 1919 she was the first woman to be admitted to the Prussian Academy. Even through the 1920s her work continued to contain anti-war slogans (*No More War!*, 1924).

Will Küpper
Brühn, near Cologne 11.6.1893 – Düsseldorf 26.3.1972
In 1906 he took his first art lessons together with Max Ernst from the latter's father Philipp Ernst. From 1907 to 1913 he attended the Kunstgewerbeschule in Cologne. In 1912 he worked alongside Ernst, and in

1913 with Kirchner. From 1915 to 1919 he served in the army and was wounded numerous times. From 1921 to 1926 he studied at the academies of Munich and Düsseldorf. The upheavals and horrors of war were expressed by Küpper in a heightened brand of Expression, which evolved into a classical Surrealism in the 1920s.

Wilhelm Lehmbruck

Duisburg-Meiderich 4.1.1881 – Berlin 25.3.1919

He studied decorative art at Düsseldorf, from 1895 to 1899. Then he attended the Fine Arts Academy until 1907. A stay in Paris, in 1910, led to his meeting Matisse, Brancusi and Archipenko. Called up during the Great War, the experience marked him for life. He gassed himself in Berlin. In his sculpture, he was influenced by Rodin and by Gothic art: the forms appear as if rising out of an inner tension, as if enhanced by this very tension. Their movement seems to emanate from their depths. The body is cast aside to allow the full radiance of the soul to emerge. This aspect is perceptible in his *Kneeling Woman* (1919), which is the embodiment of humility and piety. His art owes so much to the symbolist tradition.

The biography of W. Lehmbruck is by Lionel Richard For E. Barlach, M. Beckmann, O. Dix, E. Heckel, A. Jawlensky, W. Kandinsky, O. Kokoschka, W. Lehmbruck, A. Macke, F. Marc, L. Meidner, M. Pechstein, K. Schmidt-Rottluff © Somogy Editions d'Art, *Petite Encyclopédie de l'expressionnisme*, Paris, 1993

August Macke

Meschede 3.1.1887 – Perthes-les-Hurlus 26.9.1914

August Macke was a close friend of Franz Marc and participated in the activities of the Blaue Reiter. Nevertheless, he was fully aware that his talents placed him in direct opposition to the Munich circle. He was a temperament completely bound up with the temporal world, and far removed from the hereafter. Rather, he considered reflections on metaphysical problems to be a waste of time. The little time that he had was used to satisfy his insatiable curiosity about life.

From 1904 to 1906 he had attended the Academy in Düsseldorf and designed costumes and décor for the theatre there. In 1907 he went to Paris to study the impressionists. Monet and Degas made the strongest impression on him. He experimented with pure color and seized every opportunity to increase his knowledge and capacities.

In 1907 he went to Berlin for six months and was Corinth's pupil. In the summer of 1908 he was again in Paris and studied Seurat, Cézanne and Gauguin in depth. In 1909 he settled for a year at Lake Tegern in Upper Bavaria. During this period he produced about two hundred pictures, and realized what his goal was: "for me, work is a complete rejoicing in nature." For Macke, the ordering of his impressions of the visible world included the feelings of the heart, the sense of something mysterious and a wonderment at nature. However much he let himself be influenced by Matisse's 'plastic' use of pure color, and however much he had adopted views of the Blaue Reiter, and above all of cubism, Picasso, La Fauconnier and Delaunay regarding formal composition, he was never in danger of being an imitator. His starting point was his experience of reality and whilst painting, he intuitively adapted the formal elements which were useful to him. He thus avoided the danger of which he warned Marc and Kandinsky, that is, that form would become too important and emotion be inadequate to fill it.

In 1910 he had made friends with Marc and established a loose connection with the New Artists' Association in Munich. In 1911 he collaborated in the preparation of *Blaue Reiter Almanach*, to which he contributed an essay. In 1912 he and Marc visited Delaunay in Paris. A friendship developed – Delaunay and Apollinaire visited Macke in Bonn in 1913 – and Macke gained important insights regarding spatial values and movement in color. In the autumn of 1913, he went to Lake Thun in Switzerland for eight months. He now possessed the means to express all the beauty of the world, its joy and the fullness of life, to portray the world as visual poetry. At Lake Thun he conceived the idea of travelling to Tunis with Klee and Moilliet. This famous stay in Tunis in April only lasted two weeks and yielded spontaneous water-colors and hundreds of drawings. There was no time left to Macke to elaborate this rich material. He was called up for military service on August 8th – six weeks later he was dead.

Franz Marc

Munich 8.2.1880 – Verdun 4.3.1916

Marc began his studies with theology, then philosophy, and suddenly decided in 1900 to follow his father's example and become a painter. He lamented the general loss of religious unity, and chose art as a means of creating a new one. He was convinced that no great art had ever existed, or could exist, without religion. He attended the academy in Munich until 1903 and travelled to Paris for the first time; here was greatly influenced by impressionism, though this scarcely showed in his paintings. He reacted similarly in 1907. He was enthusiastic about the impressionists, but Van Gogh alone exercised a lasting influence on him, and this was only put into practice in 1909.

Marc already knew that it was necessary to express "the inner truth of things," and that neither theory nor the study of nature were of use for this. The way could only be found through the imagination. In the years that followed, therefore, he concerned himself with deepening his imaginative powers by learning nature by heart. He studied nature's laws through animal anatomy, in order to be in a position to let new creatures emerge in his imagination, that nevertheless could be genuine because they were constructed according to the laws of nature. He thus hoped to simplify form in order to express the symbolism, the pathos and the mystery of nature. Up until 1910 this problem was only successfully solved as regards structure. Color which remained bound to the object, retained its arbitrary randomness and hindered expression. In 1910 Marc had his first one-man exhibition, bringing favourable reviews, in which he exhibited *plein-air*-like pictures still with an overall light base. At the same time, he made the acquaintance of August Macke, who made him aware of the independent power of expression in pure color. Marc now pursued the problems of color with the same intensity as he had examined structure before, and developed his own theory about the potential for expressionism in color. He met Kandinsky in 1911 and joined the New Artists' Association.

The contact with the more advanced endeavours of his friends who were striving in the same direction, enabled Marc to make rapid progress. He concentrated more and more on animal paintings. Admittedly, he did turn his attention to nude portraits, but they did not provide a satisfying solution. "The ungodly human beings who surrounded me (the men above all) did not arouse my true emotions, whereas the inherent feel for life in animals made all that was good in me come out." (Marc). He thus defined his goal to be "an animalization of art," i.e. so to unite the characteristic forms of animals and landscapes into a continuous organic shape, that a cosmic rhythm emerges, held in balance by the pure color of expression. Marc's experience of cubism was important for fostering the inter-penetration of subject and surroundings. For the process of rhythmification he adapted what he had learnt from futurism. In 1911 Kandinsky and

Marc left the New Artists' Association, organized the Blaue Reiter exhibition and published the almanach of the same name. In 1912 he went with Macke to Paris and visited Delaunay. In 1913 he played a vital part in the selection and hanging of the first German autumn salon in Berlin. What he had learnt in Paris and Berlin strengthened his realization that he had not yet succeeded in achieving a synthesis of the outer and inner world. Now aware that all forms are memories, he abandoned the object in 1914, and created abstract pictures from his inner imagination alone. In 1914 he was called up; he fell at Verdun in 1916.

Ludwig Meidner
Bernstadt, Silesia 18.4.1884 – Darmstadt 14.5.1966
In 1912, Herwarth Walden mounted an exhibition in the Sturm gallery in Berlin of a short-lived group who called themselves the Pathetiker. Their most gifted member was Ludwig Meidner. He had attended the Imperial Art School in Breslau from 1903 to 1905. In 1906 he lived as a fashion designer in Berlin and went the same year to study at the Académie Julian. Although he made friends with Modigliani, he remained aloof from the concerns of contemporary artists. In 1908 he returned to Berlin and lived there in very harsh circumstances. He was encouraged to give free rein to his passionate nature by the exhibitions of the futurists and Delaunay. He now gave utterance to his cries and his ectasy. Without restraint, nor concern for formal problems, he produced inner visions of apocalyptic landscapes and burning cities using agitated brush- and pencil-work. His distorted portraits were also full of emotion, which appeared in an almost incalculable number of paintings of writers, actors and painters; angry visions full of un-

ease and bitterness; *September Cry: Hymns, Prayers, Blasphemies* for example, is the title of one of Meidner's poems, which he produced alongside his drawings and paintings to describe his inner state. Meidner knew no limits in his endeavour to lay bear his soul.
His visions paled when from 1916 to 1918 he had to do military service and his paintings lost their power of conviction. Confronted with the hideous nature of reality he realized that his previous path had been mistaken and returned to the Jewish faith ten years after his first artistic awakening. In 1923 he disavowed his previous work, which he called an intolerable expression of 'lunacy and indecency.'

Otto Müller
Liebau, Slesia 16.10.1874 – Breslau 24.9.1930
After four years as an apprentice lithographer in Görlitz, Müller came to the Dresden Academy where he worked until 1896. In 1896 and 1897 he travelled with the writer, Gerhart Hauptmann, to whom he was related, to Italy and Switzerland. In 1898–1899 he continued his studies with Stuck at the Munich Academy. Then he returned to Dresden where the Hauptmanns had furnished a studio for him. Until moving to Berlin in 1908 Müller withdrewever more frequently to small villages in the Riesen Gebirge, painted in Bohemia, and the area round Dresden. No paintings exist from this period, for the painter destroyed them.
He received a vital impetus from Böcklin whose work gave him important ideas concerning the mythical element in nature and the possibilities of composition from blocks of color. On the other hand, he remained uninfluenced by all those models which owed their expressivity to intensifying contrasted, pure color. His use of color aims rather toward tranquillity,

does not go beyond the object and achieves unity within the picture through similarity of color tone.
What linked him with his contemporaries was his yearning for a simple and natural way of life: "The chief goal of my endeavour is to express my feelings for landscapes and for men with the greatest possible simplicity." The essential theme of Müller's work, which was already decided when he met the Brücke painters in 1910, was to portray the harmony of man and nature. Kirchner, Heckel and Pechstein were pursuing similar goals so that Müller became a member of the group as a matter of course. He had already evolved his largescale two-dimensional nudes, but they were still outlines with rounded, gentle, mellifluous contours. Under the influence of his friends – he went with Kirchner to Bohemia in 1911 – his outlines became more angular and taut and the organization of the surface area clearer. Once he had found the motif of the nude in a landscape, it became decisive for his work. It was followed in the twenties by pure landscape, and a few portraits and paintings of gypsies. Müller continued to re-work these themes in a self-satisfied manner without any noticeable stylistic change. In 1919 he was appointed to teach at Breslau Academy.

Max Pechstein
Zwickau, Saxony 31.12.1881 – Berlin 19.6.1955
Pechstein had a versatile talent. After a four-year apprenticeship with an interior decorator in Zwickau he came to Dresden in 1900 to study at the School of Arts and Crafts. As early as 1902 he took part in the school's competition in all six subjects, and won five first prizes and one second. He was immediately asked to become a teacher at the school, but he decided to transfer to the Academy where he remained as

star pupil until 1906. The same year he won the State prize in Saxony.
He met Heckel and became a member of the Brücke. In the autumn of 1907 he set out for Italy and returned to Paris in 1908 – where he stayed for six months – settling in Berlin a short while later. His close collaboration with his Brücke friends thus lasted only a year. He skilfully adapted the discoveries of his friends without having to catch up with their developments in laborious work.
His stay in Paris had resulted in a meeting with Van Dongen – who became a member of the Brücke in 1908 – and also a knowledge of Matisse's work, which exercised a direct influence on Pechstein's pictures in 1911–1912.
The violent, strong colors which he juxtaposed in large areas to emphasize structure are the expression of a powerful and primitive temperament. He intensifies the colorful splendour of the world, without however, wishing to move into symbolism or myth.
His best pictures were produced in the summer of 1910, when he painted with Kirchner and Heckel the Moritzburg Lakes, and then travelled with Heckel to Schmidt-Rottluff in Dangast.
The works of the following years, the numerous pictures of bathing figures amongst the dunes, which were created at Nidden in the Baltic, where Pechstein had painted in the summer since 1909, impress principally by their beautifully decorative and rhythmic lines. In 1910 Pechstein was one of the founders of the Neue Sezession in Berlin, whose Chairman he became; when he returned in 1912 to the old Sezession, he was excluded from the Brücke.
In 1914 he went to Palau in the South Seas. He found here the harmony between nature and man which he had sought in remote Nidden and in 1913 in a fishing village near Genoa.
The outbreak of war soon put an end to his light-hearted way of life, and Pechstein was taken prisoner by the Japanese. In 1915 he succeeded in returning to Germany after many adventures.

Karl Schmidt-Rottluff
Rottluff, near Chemnitz 1.12.1884 –
Berlin 10.8.1976
After finishing secondary school in
Chemnitz, Schmidt-Rottluff had at
first chosen, like Franz Marc, to
study theology, but then followed
the example of his friend Heckel
and went to study architecture in
Dresden. They soon discovered
their common love for painting as
well as for poetry, and began to
paint and draw together. When
Schmidt-Rottluff came to Dresden
in 1905 he immediately joined the
circle of Kirchner, Bleyl and Heckel
and formed the Brücke group
with them. Schmidt-Rottluff suggested the name. This fervent admirer of Nietzsche had been stimulated by the fourth prologue of
Zarathustra, "what is noble in man
is that he is a bridge and not a goal;
what can be loved in an man is that
he is a crossing over and a going
under." Schmidt-Rottluff persuad-
ed Nolde, whom he had visited in
Alsen in 1906, to join the group
and corresponded with Munch
concerning his joining the Brücke.
It was he who introduced lithography into the group.
Nevertheless, amid all this activity
on behalf of the group, he always
held himself a little aloof. He visited and shared studios less frequently and also did not take part
in the work trips to the Moritzburg
lakes near Dresden.
Instead, he went to Dangast in Oldenburg during the summer months
from 1907 to 1912; Heckel followed him there. He was the only
one of the friends to exhibit in
Braunschweig in 1907, and in one-
man exhibitions in Hamburg in
1910; the rest only appeared as a
group until the dissolution of the
Brücke in 1913.
Schmidt-Rottluff's temperament
was reserved and introverted, but
this was necessary to be able to sus-
tain the almost one-sided consis-
tency of his work. Thematically,

this meant restricting himself to
landscapes, thus avoiding the depiction of city life and, until 1912,
he only occasionally used the human figures, which held the attention of his friends so much.
"The harsh air of the North Sea
yielded, particulary in Schmidt-
Rottluff, a monumental impressionism," Kirchner wrote in 1913
in the *Die Brücke* chronicle.
Thus he described that vigorous
brushwork, expressive of great
force of will, with which Schmidt-
Rottluff produces unity in his
paintings. However, the extrava-
gant gesture, still inspired by Van
Gogh, gave way in 1910 to a structure of large areas of color that was
also employed as a means of achieving greater monumentality and
greater simplification.
The paintings that resulted from
his journey to Norway in 1911
mark a climax.
In 1911 Schmidt-Rottluff moved
(as did his friends at the same time)
from Dresden to Berlin, where he
lived for the rest of his life. Here he
came across diverse artistic stimuli
which stirred him to investigate
them. However, his approaches to
the emphatic expressiveness of abstract art, as well as cubist method,
remained experiments limited to a
few pictures. He preferred to use
figures and still life to find a more
exact definition of the object that
would encompass space and volume but would not disturb his two-
dimensional style.
He found the solution in 1913 in
Nidden on the Courland penninsu-
la with what is known as 'a
heraldic-symbolic style.' Human
figures and the elements of landscape are reduced to images of
equal importance in the picture,
and promote a symbolic unity.
In 1914 Schmidt-Rottluff again
changed his surroundings and
went to Hohwacht on the Baltic
coast of Holstein. The paintings
that he produced here could not
maintain the harmony between
man and nature. For the first time
the figures show a spiritual opres-
sion in his work. From 1915 to
1918 he was called up for military
service in Russia. Even though the
war left no trace on his work as re-

gards themes – which always reflected the universal and never topical events – nevertheless, the
shock could not be hidden. He felt
more and more clearly the 'tension
between this world and the next,'
as he himself wrote. In the years after 1918 he sought to revitalize reality by incorporating the subject
into objective existence.

Georg Scholz
Wolfenbüttel 19.10.1890 – Wald-
kirch, Baden 27.11.1945
He began studying painting at the
Karlsruhe Academy in 1908 with
Ludwig Dill, Hans Thoma, and
Wilhelm Trübner. After four years
of service and a war wound, Scholz
started working as an industrial designer and illustrator. Like many of
his generation, in 1919 he joined
the Communist Party, and was a
member of the Novembergruppe.
Together with Karl Hubbuch and
Rudolf Schlichter he founded the
Rih group at Karlsruhe, and his
work evinces Futurist aspects with
the starkly contrasting colors of Expressionism, as part of his progres-
sion toward a new form of objectivity in art. In 1924 he was appointed
director of the beginners' courses
at the Karlsruhe Academy.

Gert Wollheim
Loschwitz, near Dresden 11.9.1894
– New York 1974
In 1911 he began studying at the
Weimar Kunsthochschule; his fel-
low students included Otto Pankok
and Carl Lohse.
In 1914 he followed his teacher Eg-
ger-Lienz to the new Kunst-
hochschule at Klausen in the Tyrol.
Called up for military service, he
fought on both eastern and western

fronts, and suffered the horrors of
trench warfare. In 1917 he was
badly wounded.
In 1918 he met up once more with
Pankok in Berlin, who had had the
same experiences, and they worked
together for several years.
In 1919 he moved to Düsseldorf,
where until 1925 he played an important role in the Ey and Junges
Rheinland groups.
Wollheim's large-scale paintings of
ecstatic decomposition of forms are
a searing and heartfelt statement
against the ignominy of war.

1900

Death of Friedrich Wilhelm Nietzsche (b. 1844), one of the most influential thinkers of contemporary Europe.

Sigmund Freud (1856-1939) published *Die Traumdeutung* (*The Interpretation of Dreams*), which marked the birth of psychoanalysis and perhaps better than any other interpred the spirit of the new century.
Max Planck (1858-1947) formulated the "quantum theory," a crucial discovery for physics in the twentieth century.

After the assassination of Umberto I, his son Vittorio Emanuele III became king (he abdicated in 1946). Publication of *Il fuoco* (*The Flame of Life*), a novel by Gabriele D'Annunzio (1863-1938).

In Paris, the inauguration of the Metro, the Universal Exhibition, the second Olympiad of the modern era, the first large-scale retrospective of the painting of Van Gogh.

First flight of a rigid airship built by Ferdinand von Zeppelin (1838-1917).

1901

Death of Queen Victoria, who had been queen since 1837.

Thomas Mann (1875-1955) published *Buddenbrooks*, a novel which describes the rise and fall of a bourgeois merchant family in nineteenth-century Lübeck.

Nobel Prize for physics awarded to Wilhelm Konrad Röntgen (1845-1923) for his discovery of x-rays.

Death of Giuseppe Verdi (b. 1813).

Guglielmo Marconi (1874-1937) made the first wireless telegraph transmission across the Atlantic from Poldhu, in Cornwall, to St. John's, in Newfoundland.

1902

Benedetto Croce (1866-1952) published *L'estetica come scienza dell'espressione e linguistica generale* (*Aesthetics*), a work which for some forty years was to have a great influence on criticism of literature and the other arts.

Edvard Munch (1863-1944) painted *Kinder des Dr Linde* (Dr Linde's Children) and *Bewachsenes Haus* (The Big House), his first Expressionistic works.

First performance of *Pelléas et Mélisande*, the only opera by Claude Debussy (1862-1918), based on the play of the same name by Maurice Maeterlinck (1892).

Leon Trotsky (1879-1940) fled from internal exile in Siberia and took refuge in London. In 1905 he became president of the Soviet of St. Petersburg, before again fleeing abroad.

Opening of the first line of the Berlin underground (begun in 1896).

1903

Giovanni Giolitti (1842-1928), a Liberal, Prime Minister in 1892-93, became Prime Minister for the second time; he held the post almost continuously until 1914 (and then again in 1920-21), having a reformist influence on Italian politics in the first fifteen years of the century.

At the Second Party Congress, opposing the centralist movement of Lenin, the Russian socialists split into Bolshevics (the revolutionary majority) and Menshevics (the moderate minority).
Lenin wrote *What is to be done?*

Death in Polynesia of Paul Gauguin (b. 1848).

Nobel Prize for physics awarded to Henri Becquerel (1852-1908), Marie Sklodowska-Curie (1867-1934), and Pierre Curie (1859-1906), for their research on radioactivity.

In USA the brothers Orville (1871-1948) and Wilbur Wright (1867-1912) carried out the first flight (12 seconds, 50 metres) in a heavier-than-air motor-driven aircraft.
Henry Ford founded the automobile company of the same name with capital of 100,000 dollars.

Opening of the Panama canal.
First cycling Tour de France (won by Maurice Garin).

1904

"Entente cordiale" between Great Britain and France: the former confirmed the French protectorate of Morocco, the latter renounced her influence over Egypt and recognized Spanish authority in North Africa.

Frank Wedekind (1864-1918) published the play *Die Büchse der Pandora* (*Pandora's Box*).

Alfred Messel (1853-1909) completed the building of the big Wertheim stores in Berlin.

Ernest Rutherford, Baron Rutherford of Nelson (1871-1937), and Sir Frederick Soddy (1877-1956) discovered that the radio-active process leads to the transformation of the original atoms into different atoms.

Death of Anton Pavlovich Chekhov (b. 1860).

Luigi Pirandello (1867-1936) published the novel *Il fu Mattia Pascal*, (*The Late Mattia Pascal*).

First performances of the opera *Tosca* by Giacomo Puccini (1858-1924) and the play *La figlia di Iorio* (*The Daughter of Iorio*) by Gabriele D'Annunzio.

1905

The Emperor of Germany, Wilhelm II, landed at Tangiers declaring that he guaranteed Morocco's independence, an act which was to lead to the first Moroccan crisis the following year.
Germany and Russia signed a pact of mutual military assistance.

Revolutionary uprisings in Russia (the army fired on the crowd in front of the Winter Palace in St. Petersburg) achieved a partial success: the Czsar published the Manifesto of Liberties and allowed a constitutional government.

Erich Heckel (1883-1970), Ernst Ludwig Kirchner (1880-1938), and Karl Schmidt-Rottluff (1884-1976) founded the association of Expressionist artists Die Brücke (The Bridge) in Dresden. Future members included Emil Nolde (1867-1956), Max Pechstein (1881-1955), and Otto Müller (1874-1930).

At the Salon d'Automne in Paris the case of the Fauves (Wild Beasts) exploded, the leading figures being Henri Matisse (1869-1954), André Derain (1880-1954), and Maurice de Vlaminck (1876-1958).
Nobel Prize for medicine awarded to Robert Koch (1843-1910) for his research on tuberculosis.

Albert Einstein (1879-1955) formulated the theory of restricted relativity: the speed of light in a vacuum is a constant independent of that of the light source.

1906

The British workers' party, founded in 1900, took the name The Labour Party (in 1904 it had joined the Second International).

Alfred Dreyfus (1859-1935) was released and rehabilitated: a French official, in 1894 he had been accused of high treason in favour of Germany and deported to Devil's Island.

Nobel Prize for literature awarded to Giosuè Carducci (1835-1907).

Publication of the novel *Die Verwirrungen des Zöglings Törless* (*Young Törless*) by Robert Musil (1880-1943).

Deaths of Paul Cézanne (b. 1839) and Henrik Ibsen (b. 1828).

Roald Amundsen (1872-1928) travelled all the way along the northwest passage (he had left three years earlier on a cutter from which he had studied the magnetic pole, confirming its displacement).

An earthquake destroyed San Francisco.

1907

Second peace conference at The Hague, promoted on the initiative of the American President Theodore Roosevelt and on the invitation of Czar Nicholas II: the right to neutrality is redefined and the Triple Alliance is formed between Great Britain, France, and Russia.

Oskar Kokoschka (1886-1973) wrote *Mörder-Hoffnung der Frauen* (*Murderer, Hope of Women*), an Expressionist play which would be set to music by Paul Hindemith in 1921.

Pablo Picasso (1881-1973) painted *Les demoiselles d'Avignon*, the work which opened the way toward the great season of Cubism.

Ludwig Mies van der Rohe (1886-1969) built the Riehl House in Neubabelsberg.

Stefan George (1868-1933) published *Der siebente Ring* (*The Seventh Ring*).
In the cinema subtitles replaced the commentator.
First experiments with phototelegraphy: Arthur Korn (1870-1945) made a transmission of images between Munich, Berlin, Paris, and London.

1908

Austria-Hungary, with German support and despite the protests of Great Britain, Serbia, and Russia, annexed Bosnia and Herzegovina (under Austrian administration since 1878).

Posthumous publication of *Ecce Homo*, by Friedrich Wilhelm Nietzsche.

Rainer Maria Rilke (1875-1926) published *Der Neuen Gedichte Anderer Teil (Second Part of New Poems)*.

Publication of *A lume spento*, first book of poems by Ezra Pound (1885-1972).

First publication of the journal *La Voce*, which assembled the best of the new Italian intellectual energies.

Foundation in Detroit of the General Motors Company (in 1916 it was to be renamed General Motors Corporation).

Messina was destroyed by an earthquake in which 84,000 people die.

1909

Filippo Tommaso Marinetti (1876-1944) published the Manifesto of Futurism in *Le Figaro*.

Sergej Diaghilev (1872-1929) created the company of the Ballets Russes in Paris.

First performance of *Elektra*, by Richard Strauss (1864-1949), to a libretto by Hugo von Hofmannsthal (1864-1929).

Arnold Schönberg (1874-1951) wrote *Fünfzehn Gedichte aus Das Buch der hängenden Gärten von Stefan George (Fifteen Poems from the Book of the Hanging Gardens by Stefan George)* op. 15.

Henri Matisse (1869-1954) paints *La danse*.

Louis Blériot (1872-1936) makes the first flight across the English Channel.

First cycling Giro d'Italia (won by Luigi Ganna).

1910

Czar Nicholas II at Potsdam: Germany and Russia declared their opposition to the politics of alliances.

Sigmund Freud (1856-1939) published *Über Psychoanalyse (Origin and Development of Psychoanalysis)*.

Herwarth Walden (1878-missing in Russia from 1930) founded *Der Sturm*, closely linked with Expressionism (publication continued until 1932).

Wassily Kandinsky (1866-1944) painted the first abstract water-color.

The painters Giacomo Balla (1871-1958), Umberto Boccioni (1882-1916), Carlo Carrà (1881-1966), Luigi Russolo (1885-1947), and Gino Severini (1883-1966) signed the Manifesto of Futurist Painters.

Death of Leo Tolstoy (b. 1828).

Alban Berg (1885-1935) published *Streichquartett (String Quartet)* op. 3.

Gustav Mahler (1860-1911) composed his *Ninth* and *Tenth Symphonies*; the latter was left unfinished.

In Paris Diaghilev's Ballets Russes performed *L'oiseau de feu (The Firebird)*, by Igor F. Stravinsky (1882-1971).

Foundation of the International Psychoanalytic Association.

Rainer Maria Rilke published *Die Aufzeichnungen des Malte Laurids Brigge (The Notebooks of Malte Laurids Brigge)*.

Georges Claude (1870-1960) made the first neon tubes.

First diesel motor for automobiles.

1911

Second Moroccan crisis: Germany renounced its influence over Morocco in favor of France and obtained in exchange territorial compensation in Cameroon.

Outbreak of the Italo-Turkish war over the annexation to Italy of Tripoli and Cirenaica.

Publication of the first issues of the journal *Die Aktion* ("in favour of the great German left").

Foundation in Munich of the Expressionistic movement Der Blaue Reiter (The Blue Rider); members included Wassily Kandinsky (1866-1944), Paul Klee (1879-1940), August Macke (1887-1914), and Franz Marc (1880-1916).

In Vienna Adolf Loos (1870-1933) built the Steiner House and the house on the Michaelerplatz.

Death of Gustav Mahler, conductor of the Vienna Hofoper from 1897 to 1907.

Arnold Schönberg published *Harmonielehre* (*Manual of Harmony*).

First performance of *Der Rosenkavalier*, by Richard Strauss, to a libretto by Hugo von Hofmannsthal (1874-1929).

Ernest Rutherford, Baron Rutherford of Nelson, described the model of the atom as comprising a positive nucleus and distant peripheric electrons.

Leonardo da Vinci's *Mona Lisa* was stolen from the Louvre (it was found in Italy in 1913).

1912

Renewal of the Triple Alliance, formed in 1882, between Germany, Austria-Hungary, and Italy.
The Congress of the Socialist International published an anti-war document in Basel.
Balkan War (until 1913): Bulgaria, Serbia, Greece, and Montenegro defeated Turkey.
Universal male suffrage in Italy.

Deaths of August Strindberg (b. 1849) and Giovanni Pascoli (b. 1855).

Franz Kafka (1883-1924) published *Betrachtung* (*Meditation*) and wrote the stories *Das Urteil* (*The Judgement*) and *Die Verwandlung* (*The Metamorphosis*).

Thomas Mann (1875-1955) published *Der Tod in Venedig* (*Death in Venice*).

Umberto Boccioni painted *Elasticità* (*Elasticity*).
Exhibition of the Futurist painters in Paris.

Arnold Schönberg (1874-1951) composes *Pierrot lunaire*, one of the masterpieces of musical Expressionism.

Rediscovery of the painted bust of the Egyptian queen Nefertiti.
Sinking of the *Titanic* off Newfoundland after a collision with an iceberg.

1913

Second Balkan War: Europe, riddled with local conflicts, was a powder-keg waiting to explode.

Ernst Ludwig Kirchner (1880-1938) dissolved Die Brücke (The Bridge), the group which since 1905 had united the leading Expressionist artists.

Kasimir Malevich (1878-1935) painted *Black Square on White Background*, a monochromatic work with which Russian Suprematism superseded Futurism.

In New York a great exhibition at the Armory Show introduced post-Impressionist European art: it raised scandal.

Marcel Duchamp (1887-1968) produced his first ready-made.

Marcel Proust (1871-1922) published *Du côté de chez Swann*, the first volume of *A la recherche du temps perdu* (*Remembrance of Things Past*).

Publication of *Gedichte* (*Poems*) by Georg Trakl (1887-1914).

Because of the innovatory means of expression used in the work, the first performance of Stravinsky's *Le sacre du printemps* (*The Rite of Spring*) is a total fiasco.

1914

In Sarajevo, the assassination of Archduke Francis Ferdinand of Austria (b. 1863), heir to the Habsburg throne, by the Serb nationalist Gavrilo Princip, led within the brief space of a month to the outbreak of the First World War: the Central Empires (Germany and Austria-Hungary) against the Triple Alliance (Great Britain, France, and Russia). End of the *Belle Epoque*; the world will never be the same again. Death of Georg Trakl (b. 1887).

Franz Kafka (1883-1924) wrote the novel *Der Prozess* (*The Trial*).

James Joyce (1882-1941) published the short-story collection *Dubliners*.

Publication of the novel *Les caves du Vatican* (*The Vatican Caves*) by André Gide (1869-1951).

At Alfeld an der Leine, Walter Gropius (1883-1969) built the Fagus factory, a classic prototype of the modern industrial building.

Charlie Chaplin (1889-1977) made no less than thirty-five films in the space of one year.

1915

Italy, changing alliance at the last moment, after the territorial promises obtained by the Treaty of London, declared war on Austria. First bloody attacks, with slight advances on the Isonzo front.

On the western front Germany unleashed the first large-scale attack with toxic chlorine gas.

Posthumous publication of *Sebastian im Traum* (*Sebastian in a Dream*), by Georg Trakl (1887-1914).

The director David Griffith (1875-1948) made the film *The Birth of a Nation*, one of the greatest masterpieces in cinema history.

Golden age of classical jazz in New Orleans.

1916

In France, the battle of the Somme, despite the deployment of 104 French and British divisions supported by artillery and aircraft, produced minimal gains: it was a war of position and attrition.
Italy declared war on Germany.
The steel helmet and the gas-mask were introduced in the German army. A peace proposal by the German Emperor Wilhelm II was rejected.

Death of Emperor Franz Josef after a reign of 68 years.

Giuseppe Ungaretti (1888-1970) published *Il porto sepolto* (*The Buried Harbor*).

Albert Einstein (1879-1955) set out the theory of general relativity.

At the Cabaret Voltaire in Zurich, Tristan Tzara (1896-1963) founded the Dada movement, based on the concept of absolute arbitrariness in art and literature.

Franz Marc died in the battle of Verdun.

1917

Famine in Germany (*Kohlrübenwinter*, the Winter of Turnips). German submarine warfare.
The United States entered the war against Germany, having a crucial influence on the final outcome of the conflict.
The Italian army suffered a disastrous defeat at Caporetto and was forced to pull back from the Isonzo to the Piave.

Revolution in Russia: Lenin, Trotsky, Zinovyev, and the other Bolshevik leaders formed the Republic of Soviets. It was the outbreak of a bloody civil war which was to continue until 1921.

In Paris the Dutch ballerina Margaretha Geertruida Zelle, known as Mata Hari (b. 1876), was arrested on suspicion of spying and shot.

Sigmund Freud published *Vorlesungen zur Einführung in die Psychoanalyse* (*A General Introduction to Psychoanalysis*).

Gottfried Benn (1886-1959) published the poems of *Söhne* (*Sons*).

In Ferrara, Giorgio de Chirico (1888-1978), together with Carlo Carrà (1881-1966), launched metaphysical painting, which was to have a significant influence, in particular, on the Surrealist movement.

In Paris, performance of the ballet *Parade*, with music by Erik Satie (1866-1925); scenery and costumes by Pablo Picasso (1881-1973).

Death of Edgar Degas (b. 1834).

1918

The First World War ended with the defeat of the Central Empires: the Austro-Hungarian empire, together with the Turkish empire, broke up.
In Germany, revolutionary unrest in Berlin and Munich. Mutiny of sailors at Kiel.
Emperor Wilhelm II abdicated and went into exile in Holland, where he died in 1941.
Birth of the German communist party (Spartakusbund, the Spartacus League). Karl Liebknecht (1871-1919) proclaimed the German Republic of Soviets.
Despite the revolutionary ferment, power in Germany remained in the hands of the conservatives (the military, the bureaucrats, the judges).

In Russia, Czar Nicholas II was assassinated, together with his wife and five children.

An epidemic of "Spanish flu" caused thousands of deaths all over Europe: among these were the poet Guillaume Apollinaire (b. 1880) and the painter Egon Schiele (b. 1890).

Thomas Mann published *Betrachtungen eines Unpolitischen* (*Reflections of an Unpolitical Man*).
Publication of *Der Untertan* (*The Patrioteer*) by Heinrich Mann (1871-1950), a novel (banned in 1914) attacking the Wilhelmine spirit.

Igor F. Stravinsky (1882-1971) composed the chamber opera *L'histoire du soldat*, and *Rag-time* for eleven instruments.

Nobel Prize for physics awarded to Max Planck (1858-1947) for the discovery of quantums.

Otto Hahn (1879-1968) and Lise Meitner (1878-1968) discovered protoactinium, a radioactive element.

Deaths of Claude Debussy (b. 1862) and of Gustav Klimt (b. 1862).

1919

Rosa Luxemburg (b. 1870) and Karl Liebknecht (b. 1871) were assassinated by officers of the radical right for their role in the Spartacist movement.
In Weimar the National Assembly launched the Constitution of the German Reich in the form of a strongly centralized democratic parliamentary and federal republic. Friedrich Ebert was elected the first President.
Signing of the Treaty of Versailles: Germany was forced to accept extremely harsh conditions, which were later to fuel the nationalist spirit of revenge.
Birth of the Deutsche Arbeiterpartei (German Workers' Party), later renamed NSDAP (Nationalsozialistische Deutsche Arbeitspartei, the National Socialist Workers' Party), of which Adolf Hitler had membership card no. 7.
Separation of State and Church in Germany.
The South Tyrol, with Bolzano and Merano, was annexed to Italy.

In Milan Benito Mussolini, a socialist until 1914, formed the Fasci di combattimento.

In Weimar Walter Gropius (1883-1969), with Lyonel Feininger (1871-1956) and others, founded the Staatliches Bauhaus (Institute of Arts and Crafts).

Bertolt Brecht (1898-1956) wrote *Trommeln in der Nacht* (*Drums in the Night*).
Development, with the productions of Erwin Piscator (1893-1966), of a new theatre of strong political and propagandist commitment.

1920

Communist uprisings in the Ruhr were suppressed by the Reichswehr (Army of the Reich).

In a Munich beer-hall Adolf Hitler announced his 25-point programme.

Robert Wiene (1881-1938) made *Das Kabinett des Dr Caligari* (*The Cabinet of Doctor Caligari*), the film-manifesto of cinematic Expressionism.

Paul Wegener (1874-1948) directed and starred in the film *Golem*.

Birth of the artistic movement opposed to Expressionism, Die Neue Sachlichkeit (The New Objectivity), influenced in part by the Italian Metaphysical school.

Jazz arrives in Germany.

Claude Monet (1840-1926) continued to paint his series *Les Nymphéas* (*Water-lilies*), a supreme synthesis and surpassing of Impressionism.

In Paris Piet Mondrian (1872-1944) publishes *Le néoplasticisme* (*Neoplasticism*).

1921

First appearance of the storm troops (SA, Sturmabteilungen) to terrorize political opponents.

The United States rejected the Treaty of Versailles and signed a special peace treaty with Germany.

Robert Musil (1880-1943) wrote the play *Die Schwärmer* (*The Fanatics*).

The first performance of Luigi Pirandello (1867-1936) *Sei personaggi in cerca d'autore* (*Six Characters in Search of an Author*) was greeted by scandal and uproar.

Ludwig Wittgenstein (1889-1951) published his *Tractatus logico-philosophicus*.

Charlie Chaplin made *The Kid*.

Nobel Prize for physics awarded to Albert Einstein for the discovery of light quantums (photons).

1922

Walther Rathenau (b. 1867), economist and German Minister for Foreign Affairs, was assassinated by the nationalists.

In Italy, the march on Rome by the Fascists: Benito Mussolini, with a mandate from King Vittorio Emanuele III, formed the new government and became Prime Minister.

Official formation of the USSR (Union of Soviet Socialist Republics), with its capital in Moscow.

Publication of *Charmes* (*Odes*) by Paul Valéry (1871-1945), *The Waste Land* by T.S. Eliot (1888-1965), and *Siddharta* by Hermann Hesse (1877-1962).

James Joyce (1882-1941) published *Ulysses* in Paris.

Death of Marcel Proust (b. 1871).

Oswald Spengler (1880-1936) published *Der Untergang des Abendlandes* (*The Decline of the West*).

Charles-Edouard Jeanneret, known as Le Corbusier (1887-1965), presented his ideal town-plan for a "city of the present" with three million inhabitants.
Ludwig Mies van der Rohe (1886-1969) designed glass skyscrapers.

Nosferatu, by Friedrich Wilhelm Plumpe, known as Murnau (1888-1931), and *Dr Mabuse*, by Fritz Lang (1890-1976), two classics of Expressionist cinema.

Howard Carter (1873-1939) discovered the tomb of the Egyptian pharaoh Tutankhamen.
The fad of Egyptology exploded.

1923

In Germany inflation reached a peak: one dollar was worth 4.2 billion Marks. The debts of those with real assets were written off; poverty principally hit the middle class. Toward the end of the year the currency was stabilized by the introduction of the *Rentenmark*. The government headed by Gustav Stresemann nipped in the bud attempts at revolt. The *coup d'état* planned in Munich by Adolf Hitler and Erich Ludendorff failed; Hitler was condemned to confinement in a fortified prison.

Publication of *Duineser Elegien* (*Duino Elegies*) and *Sonette an Orpheus* (*Sonnets to Orpheus*) by Rainer Maria Rilke (1875-1926).
György Lukács published *Geschichte und Klassenbewusstsein* (*History and Class-Consciousness*).

Publication of *Das Ich und das Es* (*The Ego and the Id*), the most important theoretical text of Freud's maturity.

Italo Svevo published *La coscienza di Zeno* (*The Confessions of Zeno*).

An earthquake in Tokyo causes 100,000 deaths and destroys 650,000 buildings.

1924

The Dawes plan for deciding on war reparations was applied, but without any specification of its duration and the final sum: Germany must pay 5.4 billion Marks by 1928 and from the following year 2.5 billion a year, with an annual increase of between 1.2 and 1.77 billion gold Marks according to the prosperity index of the German economy.
Adolf Hitler was released before the end of his prison term; during his imprisonment he wrote *Mein Kampf* (*My Struggle*), which set out precisely all the projects which he was to put into effect when he achieved power.

Assassination of the Socialist deputy Giacomo Matteotti (b. 1885) by the Fascists; most of the non-Fascist deputies abandoned the Parliament (on the Aventine).

Great Britain, France, and Italy recognized the USSR.

Death of Lenin (pseudonym of Vladimir Ilich Ulyanov, b. 1870), the founder of Bolshevism and of the Soviet Union. After his death, following internal struggles, Joseph Vissarionovich Dzugashvili, known as Stalin, gained power.

Death of Thomas Woodrow Wilson, President of the United States from 1913 to 1920, promoter of the League of Nations, winner of the Nobel Peace Prize in 1919.

Thomas Mann published *Der Zauberberg* (*The Magic Mountain*).

André Breton (1896-1966) signed the Manifesto of Surrealism.
Filippo Tommaso Marinetti published *Futurismo e fascismo* (Futurism and Fascism), a programmatic text proclaiming Futurism as the artistic style of Fascism.

Lyonel Feininger (1871-1956), Alexej Jawlensky (1864-1941), Wassily Kandinsky (1866-1944), and Paul Klee (1879-1940) founded the Expressionist group Die Blauen Vier (*The Blue Four*).

Fritz Lang (1890-1976) made the *Nibelungen* (The Nibelungs). René Clair (pseudonym of René Chomette, 1898-1981) made *Entr'acte*. Fernand Léger (1881-1955) made the short film *Le ballet mécanique* (The Mechanical Ballet).

Alban Berg (1885-1935) composed *Kammerkonzert* (*Chamber Concerto*) for piano, violin, and thirteen wind instruments for the fiftieth birthday of Arnold Schönberg.
First performance of *Rhapsody in Blue*, for piano and orchestra, by George Gershwin (1898-1937).
Arthur Honegger (1892-1955) composed *Pacific 231*, a symphonic poem imitating the sounds made by a locomotive in motion.

Deaths of Ferruccio Busoni (b. 1866), Franz Kafka (b. 1883), and Giacomo Puccini (b. 1858).

Selected Bibliography
by Susan Trauger

The bibliography is a listing
of monographic sources selected
with regard
to the period under consideration.
Periodical literature,
with few exceptions, is not cited
but is referred to in suggested
reference bibliographies

EXPRESSIONISM

Reference Bibliographies

GORDON, DONALD E. *Expressionism: Art and Idea*. New Haven, CT/London: Yale University Press, 1987, p. 245-57

MÄRZ, ROLAND, and ANITA KÜHNEL, eds. *Expressionisten: Die Avantgarde in Deutschland 1905–1920*. Exhibition catalogue. Berlin: Henschelverlag, 1986, p. 456-68

Books

ANZ, THOMAS, and MICHAEL STARK, eds. *Expressionismus, Manifeste und Dokumente zur deutschen Literatur 1910–1920*. Stuttgart: Metzler, 1981

ANZ, THOMAS, and MICHAEL STARK, eds. *Die Modernität des Expressionismus*. (Metzler Studienausgabe). Stuttgart: Metzler, 1996

BAHR, HERMANN. *Der Expressionismus*. München: Delphin, 1916; *Expressionism*. London: F. Henderson, 1925

BEHNE, ADOLF. *Zur neuen Kunst*. Berlin: Verlag der Sturm, 1915

BONNER, STEPHEN ERIC, and DOUGLAS KELLNER, eds. *Passion and Rebellion: The Expressionist Heritage*. New York: Universe Books, 1983

BRINKMANN, RICHARD. *Expressionismus: Internationale Forschung zu einem internationalen Phänomen*. Stuttgart: Metzler, 1980

BUCHHEIM, LOTHAR-GÜNTHER. *Graphik des deutschen Expressionismus*. Feldafing: Buchheim, 1958; *The Graphic Art of German Expressionism*. New York: Universe Books, 1960

CAREY, FRANCES, and ANTONY GRIFFITHS. *The Print in Germany 1880–1933: The Age of Expressionism*. London: British Museum, 1984; 2nd ed. 1993

DAVIS, BRUCE, and STEPHANIE BARRON, eds. *German Expressionist Prints and Drawings: The Robert Gore Rifkind Center for German Expressionist Studies*. 2 vols. Los Angeles: Los Angeles County Museum of Art; Munich: Prestel, 1989

DUBE, WOLF-DIETER. *The Expressionists*. London: Thames and Hudson, 1972; *Expressionism*. New York: Praeger, 1973; *Die Expressionisten*. Frankfurt am Main: Ullstein, 1973

DUBE, WOLF-DIETER. *Der Expressionismus in Wort und Bild*. Genf: Skira, 1983; *Expressionists and Expressionism*. Genf, 1983

EDSCHMID, KASIMIR, ed. *Briefe der Expressionisten*. (Ullstein Buch, Nr. 471). Frankfurt am Main: Ullstein, 1964

EDSCHMID, KASIMIR. *Über den Expressionismus in der Literatur und die neue Dichtung*. Berlin: E. Reiss, 1919

ELGER, DIETMAR. *Expressionismus: Eine deutsche Kunstrevolution*. Köln: B. Taschen, 1988

EYKMAN, CHRISTOPH. *Denk- und Stilformender Expressionismus*. München: Francke, 1974

FECHTER, PAUL. *Der Expressionismus*. München: R. Piper, 1914

FRÖHLICH, JÜRGEN. *Liebe im Expressionismus: Eine Untersuchung der Lyrik in den Zeitschriften Die Aktion und Der Sturm von 1910–1914*. (Studies in Modern German Literature, vol. 38). New York: P. Lang, 1990

GORDON, DONALD E. *Expressionism: Art and Idea*. New Haven, CT/London: Yale University Press, 1987

GRINTEN, HANS VAN DER, and RON MANHEIM. *Holzschnitte des deutschen Expressionismus: Aus den Beständen der Stiftung Museum Schloss Moyland, Sammlung van der Grinten*. Bedburg-Hau: Förderverein Museum Schloss Moyland, 1996

HAMANN, RICHARD, and JOST HERMAND. *Expressionismus*. Berlin: Akademie-Verlag, 1975

HAPPEL, REINHOLD, and BIRGIT SCHULTE, eds. *Druckgraphik des Expressionismus: Aus der Sammlung des Karl Ernst Osthaus-Museums Hagen*. Hagen: Neuer Folkwang-Verlag im Karl Ernst Osthaus-Museum, 1993

HARTLAUB, G. F. *Die Graphik des Expressionismus in Deutschland*. Stuttgart: G. Hatje, 1947

HOFMANN, WERNER. *Aquarelle des Expressionismus 1905–1920*. Köln: DuMont Schauberg, 1966

JANDA, ANNEGRET, and JÖRN GRABOWSKI. *Kunst in Deutschland 1905–1937: Die verlorene Sammlung der Nationalgalerie im ehemaligen Kronprinzen-Palais: Dokumentation*. (Bilderheft der Staatlichen Museen zu Berlin, Heft 70/72.) Berlin: Gebr. Mann, 1992

JANDA, ANNEGRET. *Das Schicksal einer Sammlung: Die neue Abteilung der Nationalgalerie im ehemaligen Kronprinzen-Palais*. Berlin: Staatliche Museen zu Berlin, Nationalgalerie, 1986

KENNERT, CHRISTIAN. *Paul Cassirer und sein Kreis: Ein Berliner Wegbereiter der Moderne*. (Gesellschaften und Staaten im Epochenwandel, Nr. 4). Bern: Lang, 1996

LANG, LOTHAR. *Expressionistische Buchillustration in Deutschland 1907–1927*. Leipzig: C.J. Bucher, 1975

LANGUI, EMILE. *Het expressionisme in België*. Brussel: Laconti, 1970; *Expressionism in Belgium*, Brussel, 1971

LLOYD, JILL. *German Expressionism: Primitivism and Modernity*. New Haven, CT/London: Yale University Press, 1991

MÄRZ, ROLAND. *Kunst in Deutschland 1905–1937: Gemälde und Skulpturen aus der Sammlung der Nationalgalerie*. (Bilderheft der Staatlichen Museen zu Berlin, Heft 67-69.) Berlin: Gebr. Mann, 1992

MYERS, BERNARD S. *The German Expressionists: A Generation in Revolt*. New York: Praeger, 1957; *Expressionism*. London: Thames & Hudson, 1957; *Die Malerei des Expressionismus*. Köln: DuMont, 1957

PERKINS, GEOFFREY C. *Contemporary Theory of Expressionism*. (Britische und Irische Studien zur deutschen Sprache und Literatur, nr. 1). Bern/Frankfurt am Main: H. Lang, 1974

PERKINS, GEOFFREY C. *Expressionismus: Eine Bibliographie zeitgenössischer Dokumente 1910–1925*. Zürich: Verlag für Bibliographie, 1971

PIPER, REINHARD. *Nachmittag: Erinnerungen eines Verlegers*. München: R. Piper, 1950

RAABE, PAUL. *Die Autoren und Bücher des literarischen Expressionismus*. 2nd rev. and enlarged ed. with supplement and appendix 1985–1990. Stuttgart: Metzler, 1992.

RAABE, PAUL, ed. *Expressionismus: Aufzeichnungen und Erinnerungen der Zeitgenossen*. Olten: Walter, 1965; *The Era of German Expressionism*. London: Calder & Boyars, 1974

RAABE, PAUL, ed. *Expressionismus: Der Kampf um eine literarische Bewegung*. (Sonderreihe DTV, 41). München: Deutscher Taschenbuch Verlag, 1965

RAABE, PAUL. *Die Zeitschriften und Sammlungen des literarischen Expressionismus: Repertorium der Zeitschriften, Jahrbücher, Anthologien, Sammelwerke, Schriftenreihen und Almanache 1910–1921*. Stuttgart: Metzler, 1964

REMSZHARDT, GODO, ed. *Deutsche Expressionisten der Privatsammlung Hanna Bekker vom Rath*. Frankfurt am Main: G. Remszhardt, 1968

RICHARD, LIONEL. *Phaidon Encyclopedia of Expressionism: Painting and the Graphic Arts, Sculpture, Architecture, Literature, Drama, the Expressionist Stage, Cinema, Music*. Oxford: Phaidon, 1978

SCHMIDT, DIETER. *Ich war, ich bin, ich werde sein! Selbstbildnisse deutscher Künstler des 20. Jahrhunderts*. Berlin: Henschel, 1968

SCHMIDT, PAUL F. *Geschichte der modernen Malerei*. Stuttgart: W. Kohlhammer, 1952

SCHMIDT, PAUL F. *Von neuer deutscher Kunst: Abbildungen neuer Malerei, Plastik und Baukunst*. Dresden: R. Kaemmerer, 1920

Schöperische Konfession. (Tribune der Kunst und Zeit, 13). Berlin: E. Reisz, 1920

SELZ, PETER. *German Expressionist Painting*. Berkeley: University of California Press, 1957

SHAPIRO, THEDA. *Painters and Politics: The European Avant-Garde and Society 1900–1925*. New York: Elsevier, 1976

SPIELMANN, HEINZ. *Stiftung und Sammlung Rolf Horn: Gemälde, Aquarelle, Zeichnungen, Werke der Bildhauerei, Druckgraphik*. 2nd ed. Schleswig: Schleswig-Holsteinisches Landesmuseum, 1995

STARK, MICHAEL. *Für und wider den Expressionismus: Die Entstehung der Intellektuellendebatte in der deutschen Literaturgeschichte*. Stuttgart: Metzler, 1982

SYDOW, ECKARDT VON. *Die deutsche expressionistische Kultur und Malerei*. Berlin: Furche, 1920

THOENE, PETER. *Modern German Art*. Harmondsworth, England: Penguin, 1938

VOGT, PAUL. *Expressionismus: Deutsche Malerei zwischen 1905–1920*. Köln: DuMont, 1979; *Expressionism: German Painting between 1905 and 1920*. Köln, 1979; *Deutscher Expressionismus 1905–1920*. Enlarged ed. München: Prestel, 1981

WERENSKIOLD, MARIT. *The Concept of Expressionism: Origin and Metamorphoses*. Oslo: Universitetsforlaget, 1984

WESTHEIM, PAUL, ed. *Künstlerbekenntnisse: Briefe, Tagebuchblätter, Betrachtungen heutiger Künstler*. Berlin: Propyläen, 1925

WHITFORD, FRANK. *Expressionism*. London: Hamlyn, 1970

WIESE, STEPHAN VON. *Graphik des Expressionismus*. Stuttgart: G. Hatje, 1976

WILLETT, JOHN. *Expressionism*. London: Weidenfeld and Nicolson, 1970

WORRINGER, WILHELM. *Abstraktion und Einfühlung: Beitrag zur Stilpsychologie*. München: R. Piper, 1908; New ed. München, 1976; *Abstraction and Empathy: A Contribution to the Psychology of Style*. Michael Bullock, trans. New York: International Universities Press, 1963

Exibition Catalogues
1960 Marbach, Schiller-Nationalmuseum. *Expressionismus: Literatur und Kunst 1920–1923: Eine Ausstellung des Deutschen Literaturarchivs*. Paul Raabe, and H.L. Greve
1960 Schleswig-Holsteinisches Landesmuseum, Schloß Gottorf; Hamburg, Altonaer Museum. *Plastik und Kunsthandwerk von Malern des deutschen Expressionismus*
1963 Berkeley, University Art Gallery; Pasadena Art Museum. *Viennese Expressionism 1910–1924: The Work of Egon Schiele, with Work by Gustav Klimt and Oskar Kokoschka*
1964 Firenze, Palazzo Strozzi. *L'espressionismo: pittura, scultura, architettura*. Marisa Volpi, and Giovanni Klaus König
1969 Wien, Museum des 20. Jahrhunderts. *Expressionisten: Sammlung Morton D. May*. Otto Graf
1970 Berlin, Galerie Nierendorf. *Die zwanziger Jahre: Deutsche Kunst von 1914 bis 1923: Gemälde, Plastiken, Zeichnungen, Druckgraphiken*. (Kunstblätter der Galerie Nierendorf, 18/19). Hans Kinkel
1976–1977 Köln, Wallraf-Richartz-Museum und Museum Ludwig. *Unmittelbar und unverfälscht: Frühe Graphik des Expressionismus*. Hella Robels
1977 Houston, Sarah Campbell Blaffer Gallery, University of Houston. *Deutscher Expressionismus: Toward a New Humanism*. Peter W. Guenther
1977 Kiel, Kunsthalle; Schleswig-Holsteinischer Kunstverein. *Deutsche Expressionisten aus dem Besitz der Kunsthalle zu Kiel*. Johann Schlick
1977 Los Angeles, Frederick S. Wight Gallery, University of California at Los Angeles. *German Expressionist Art: The Robert Gore Rifkind Collection*. Orrel P. Reed Jr
1978 Chicago, Museum of Contemporary Art. *German and Austrian Expressionism: Art in a Turbulent Era*. Peter Selz, essay

1980–1981 New York, Solomon R. Guggenheim Museum; San Francisco Museum of Modern Art. *Expressionism: A German Intuition 1905–1920*
1983 Philadelphia, Port of History Museum at Penn's Landing; Madison, Elvehjem Museum of Art, University of Wisconsin; Minneapolis Institute of Arts. *Expressionism: The Buchheim Collection*. Wolf-Dieter Dübe, and Herbert Pée, essays; Norbert Messler, and William Walker, trans.
1983–1984 Los Angeles County Museum of Art; Washington D.C., Hirschhorn Museum and Sculpture Garden. *German Expressionist Sculpture*; Köln, Josef-Haubrich-Kunsthalle. *Skulptur des Expressionismus*. Stephanie Barron, ed.
1984 Milano, Palazzo Reale. *Espressionisti dal Museo Sprengel di Hannover*. Nadine Bortolotti, and Toni Ebner
1985 Halle, Staatliche Galerie Moritzburg. *Im Kampf um die moderne Kunst: Das Schicksal einer Sammlung in der 1. Hälfte des 20. Jahrhunderts*. Peter Romanus
1985–1986 Bielefeld, Kunsthalle. *O meine Zeit! So namenlos zerrissen ...* Jutta Hülsewig-Johnen, ed.
1986 Berlin, Staatliche Museen zu Berlin, Nationalgalerie und Kupferstichkabinett. *Expressionisten: Die Avantgarde in Deutschland 1905–1920: 125 Jahre Sammlungen der Nationalgalerie 1861–1986*. Roland März, and Anita Kühnel, eds.
1987 Berlin, Martin-Gropius-Bau. *Ich und die Stadt: Mensch und Grosstadt in der deutschen Kunst des 20. Jahrhunderts*. Eberhard Roters, and Bernhard Schulz
1988 Berlin, Martin-Gropius-Bau. *Stationen der Moderne: Die bedeutenden Kunstausstellungen des 20. Jahrhunderts in Deutschland*. Eberhard Roters, and Bernhard Schulz, eds.
1988–1989 Apeldoorn, Van Reekum Museum. *Houtsneden van het Duitse Expressionisme: 1905–1930*. Marcella and Hans van der Grinten
1989 Roslyn, NY, Nassau County Museum of Art. *From Kandinsky to Dix: Paintings of the German Expressionists*. Serge Sabarsky
1989–1990 Berlin, Käthe Kollwitz-Museum; Firenze; Siena; Bolzano; Bruxelles. *Illustrierte Bücher des deutschen Expressionismus*. Ralph Jentsch
1990 Frankfurt am Main, Jüdisches Museum. *Expressionismus und Exil:*

Die Sammlung Ludwig und Rosy Fischer. Georg Heuberger, ed.
1991 Frankfurt am Main, Städtische Galerie im Städelschen Kunstinstitut. *ReVision: Die Moderne im Städel 1906–1937*. Klaus Gallwitz, and Beatrice von Bismarck
1992 Paris, Musée d'art moderne de la ville de Paris. *Figures du moderne: l'espressionnisme en Allemagne 1905–1914: Dresde, Munich, Berlin*. Suzanne Pagé, and Annie Pérez
1992–1993 Bielefeld, Kunsthalle. *O Mensch! Das Bildnis des Expressionismus*. Jutta Hülsewig-Johnen, ed.
1993–1997 Berlin, Käthe Kollwitz-Museum; München, Städtische Galerie im Lenbachhaus; Duisburg, Wilhelm-Lehmbruck-Museum; Frankfurt am Main, Schirn Kunsthalle; Emden, Kunsthalle in Emden, Stiftung Henri Nannen; Bielefeld, Kunsthalle; Nürnberg, Germanisches Nationalmuseum. *Expressionistische Bilder: Sammlung Firmengruppe Ahlers*. Jutta Hülsewig-Johnen
1995 Dortmund, Museum am Ostwall. *Meisterwerke des Expressionismus und der Klassischen Moderne*. Ingo Bartsch, and Tayfun Belgin, eds.
1995 Frankfurt am Main, Schirn Kunsthalle. *Sehnsucht nach Glück; Wiens Aufbruch in die Moderne: Klimt, Kokoschka, Schiele*. Sabine Schulze
1995 Schleswig-Holsteinisches Landesmuseum, Schloss Gottorf. *Das Erbe des Expressionismus*
1995–1996 Hagen, Karl Ernst Osthaus-Museum. *Druckgraphik des Expressionismus*
1996 Köln, Museum Ludwig. *Die Expressionisten: Vom Aufbruch bis zur Verfemung*. Gerhard Kolberg
1996 Ligornetto, Museo Vela; Chiasso, Sala Diego Chiesa; Mendrisio, Museo d'arte Mendrisio. *L'espressionismo "Rot-Blau" nel Mendrisiotto*. Domenico Lucchini, and Gianna A. Mina Zeni
1996–1997 Hannover, Sprengel Museum; Wuppertal, Von der Heydt-Museum. *Garten der Frauen: Wegbereiterinnen der Moderne in Deutschland 1900–1914*

Die Brücke

Reference Bibliographies
BUCHHEIM, LOTHAR-GÜNTHER. *Die Künstlergemeinschaft Brücke: Gemälde, Zeichnungen, Graphik, Plastik, Dokumente*. Feldafing: Buchheim, 1956, p. 375-393

MOELLER, MAGDALENA M. *Die "Brücke": Gemälde, Zeichnungen, Aquarelle und Druckgraphik*. München: Hirmer, 1995, p. 220-223

Books
APOLLONIO, UMBRO. *"Die Brücke" e la cultura dell'espressionismo*. Venezia: Alfieri, 1952
BUCHHEIM, LOTHAR-GÜNTHER. *Die Künstlergemeinschaft Brücke: Gemälde, Zeichnungen, Graphik, Plastik, Documente*. Feldafing: Buchheim, 1956
DÜCKERS, ALEXANDER. *Graphik der "Brücke" im Berliner Kupferstichkabinett*. (Bilderheft der Staatlichen Museen Preussischer Kulturbesitz, Heft 48-50). Berlin: Staatlichen Museen Preussischer Kulturbesitz, 1984
JÄHNER, HORST. *Künstlergruppe Brücke: Geschichte, Leben und Werk ihrer Maler*. Stuttgart: W. Kohlhammer, 1984; 5th corrected and enlarged ed. Berlin: Henschelverlag, 1996
MOELLER, MAGDALENA M. *Die Brücke: Gemälde, Zeichnungen, Aquarelle und Druckgraphik...: Aus der Sammlung des Brücke-Museums Berlin*. München: Hirmer, 1995
MOELLER, MAGDALENA M. *Die "Brücke": Zeichnungen, Aquarelle, Druckgraphik*. Stuttgart: G. Hatje, 1992
MOELLER, MAGDALENA M. *Meisterwerke des Expressionismus: Gemälde, Aquarelle, Zeichnungen und Druckgraphik aus dem Brücke-Museum Berlin*. Stuttgart: G. Hatje, 1990
REIDEMEISTER, LEOPOLD. *The Brücke Museum*. Fort Lee, N.J.: Penshurst Books, 1981
REINHARDT, GEORG. "Die fruhe 'Brücke': Beiträge zur Geschichte und zum Werk der Dresdner Künstlergruppe 'Brücke' der Jahre 1905 bis 1908". In: *Brücke-Archiv*, Heft 9/10. Berlin: Brücke-Museum, 1977
TOBIEN, FELICITAS. *Die Künstlergruppe Brücke*. Kirchdorf-Inn: Berghaus, 1987
WENTZEL, HANS. *Bildnisse der Brücke-Künstler*. (Werkmonograhien zur bildenden Kunst, Nr. 63). Stuttgart: P. Reclam, 1961
WINGLER, HANS MARIA. *Die Brücke: Kunst im Aufbruch: Holzschnitte von Erich Heckel, Ernst Ludwig Kirchner, Karl Schmidt-Rottluff, Otto Müller, Emil Nolde, Max Pechstein*. Feldafing: Buchheim, 1954

Exhibition Catalogues

1960 Bremen, Kunsthalle; Hannover, Kunstverein; Köln, Wallraf-Richartz-Museum. *Meisterwerke des deutschen Expressionismus: E.L. Kirchner, E. Heckel, Schmidt-Rottluff, M. Pechstein, Otto Müller*

1962 Schleswig-Holsteinisches Landesmuseum; Lübeck, Overbeck-Gesellschaft. *Die Maler der Brücke in Schleswig-Holstein.* Martin Urban

1964 London, Tate Gallery. *Painters of the Brücke.* Arts Council of Great Britain

1965? Essen, Museum Folkwang. *Ausgewählte Graphik des deutschen Expressionismus 1905–1920: E. Heckel, E.L. Kirchner, K. Schmidt-Rottluff, M. Pechstein, O. Müller, Chr. Rohlfs.* Paul Vogt

1970 Berlin, Brücke-Museum. *Künstler der Brücke an den Moritzburger Seen 1909–1911: Ein Beitrag zur Geschichte der Künstlergruppe Brücke.* Leopold Reidemeister

1971 Köln, Wallraf-Richartz-Museum. *Maler suchen Freunde: Jahresmappen, Plakate und andere werbende Graphik der Künstlergruppe Brücke.* Hans Albert Peters

1972 Berlin, Brücke-Museum. *Künstler der Brücke in Berlin 1908–1914.* Leopold Reidemeister

1972–1973 Wetzlar, Kulturamt; Reinickendorf, Kunstamt. *Grafik des Expressionismus in Berlin: Lithographien, Holzschnitte, Radierungen.* Rudolf Pfefferkorn, ed.

1973 Städtische Galerie im Lenbachhaus. *Die Künstlergruppe Brücke und der deutsche Expressionismus: Sammlung Buchheim.* 2 vols. Wolf-Dieter Dube, et al.

1977 Roma, Galleria nazionale d'arte moderna. *Espressionismo tedesco: "Die Brücke".* Wolf-Dieter Dube

1980 Halle, Staatliche Galerie Moritzburg. *Expressionistische Graphik: Aquarelle, Handzeichnungen und Druckgraphik von Künstlern der "Brücke" und des "Blauen Reiter" aus den Beständen der Graphischen Sammlung.* Irma G. Weber

1980 Saarbrücken, Saarland-Museum, Moderne Galerie. *Künstler der Brücke: Heckel, Kirchner, Müller, Pechstein, Schmidt-Rottluff: Gemälde, Aquarelle, Zeichnungen, Druckgraphik 1909–1930.* Georg W. Költzsch, and Lorenz Dittmann, eds.

1982 Hannover, Kunstmuseum Hannover mit Sammlung Sprengel. *Die Künstlergruppe "Brücke": Ernst Ludwig Kirchner, Erich Heckel, Karl Schmidt-Rottluff, Max Pechstein, Otto Müller: Gemälde, Aquarelle, Zeichnungen und Druckgraphik: Verzeichnis der Bestände.* Bernhard Holeczek, ed.

1984 New York, Helen Serger/La Boetie. *Max Pechstein: Brücke Period Works by Heckel, Nolde, Kirchner, Schmidt-Rottluff in Collaboration with Kunsthandel Wolfgang Werner.* Wolfgang Werner

1988 Evanston, Ill., Mary and Leigh Block Gallery. *Brücke: German Expressionist Prints from the Granvil and Marcia Specks Collection* Reinhold Heller

1990–1991 Vernon, Musée Alphonse-Georges Poulin; Rouen, Hôtel de la Région; Oldenburg, Landesmuseum. *Le groupe d'artistes Brücke: gravures, dessins et aquarelles du Musée Oldenburg = Die Künstlergruppe Brücke: Druckgraphik, Zeichnungen, und Aquarelle aus dem Niedersächsischen Landesmuseum Oldenburg.* G. Reindl-Scheffer

1991 Berlin, Brücke-Museum; München, Städtische Galerie im Lenbachhaus; Saabrücken, Saarland Museum. *Expressionistische Grüsse: Künstlerpostkarten der "Brücke" und des "Blauen Reiter".* Magdalena M. Moeller

1992 Dortmund, Galerie Utermann. *Erich Heckel, Ernst Ludwig Kirchner, Max Pechstein, Karl Schmidt-Rottluff: Arbeiten der Sommermonate 1908–1914.* Ute Eggeling, and Petra Utermann

1995 Moritzburg, Museum Schloss. *Künstler der Brücke in Moritzburg: Malerei, Zeichnung, Graphik, Plastik von Heckel, Kirchner, Pechstein, Bleyl.* Volkmar Billig

1995 Schleswig-Holsteinisches Landesmuseum, Schloss Gottorf. *Die Maler der Brücke: Sammlung Hermann Gerlinger.* Heinz Spielmann

1996 Berlin, Brücke-Museum. *Aquarelle der "Brücke".* Magdalena M. Moeller

1996 Bietigheim-Bissingen, Stadtmuseum. *Künstlergruppe "Brücke": Graphik und Handzeichnungen aus der Coninx-Stiftung Zürich*

1996 Dortmund, Museum am Ostwall. *Von der Brücke bis zum Blauen Reiter: Farbe, Form und Ausdruck in der deutschen Malerei von 1905–1914.* Tayfun Belgin

1996–1997 Davos, Kirchner Museum; Wuppertal, Von der Heydt-Museum. *Sammlung Etta und Wolfgang Stangl: Brücke und Blauer Reiter*

Der Blaue Reiter

Reference Bibliographies

BUCHHEIM, LOTHAR-GÜNTHER. *Der Blaue Reiter und die "Neue Künstlervereinigung München".* Feldafing: Buchheim, 1959, p. 334-40

HÜNEKE, ANDREAS, ed. *Der Blaue Reiter: Dokumente einer geistigen Bewegung.* 3rd ed. (Reclam-Bibliothek, Bd. 1122). Leipzig: P. Reclam, 1991, p. 602-607

TAVEL, HANS CHRISTIAN VON, ed. *Der Blaue Reiter.* Bern: Kunstmuseum Bern, 1989, p. 285-291

Books

BUCHHEIM, LOTHAR-GÜNTHER. *Der Blaue Reiter und die "Neue Künstlervereinigung München".* Feldafing: Buchheim, 1959

FISCHER, OTTO. *Das neue Bild: Veröffentlichung der neuen Künstler-Vereinigung München.* München: Delphin, 1912

GOLLEK, ROSEL. *Der Blaue Reiter im Lenbachhaus München: Katalog der Sammlung in der Städtischen Galerie.* München: Prestel, 1974; 2nd enlarged and corrected ed. München, 1982; 3rd enlarged ed., München, 1985

HOLZINGER, HANS. *Der Blaue Reiter in der Städtischen Galerie im Lenbachhaus München.* München: Städtische Galerie im Lenbachhaus, 1963

HÜNEKE, ANDREAS. *Der Blaue Reiter: Dokumente einer geistigen Bewegung.* (Kunstwissenschaften; Reclams Universal-Bibliothek, Bd. 1122). Leipzig: P. Reclam, 1986

KANDINSKY, WASSILY, and FRANZ MARC, eds. *Der Blaue Reiter.* 2nd ed. München: Piper, 1914

KLUMPP, HERMANN. *Abstraktion in der Malerei: Kandinsky, Feininger, Klee.* Berlin: Deutscher Kunstverlag, 1932

LANKHEIT, KLAUS, WASSILY KANDINSKY, and FRANZ MARC, eds. *Der Blaue Reiter.* New documentary ed. München: Piper, 1965; *The Blaue Reiter Almanac.* New documentary ed. New York: Viking, 1974

MOELLER, MAGDALENA M. *Der Blaue Reiter.* Köln: DuMont, 1987

ROETHEL, HANS K. *The Blue Rider: With a Catalog of the Works by Kandinsky, Klee, Macke, Marc, and other Blue Rider Artists in the Municipal Gallery, Munich.* New York: Praeger, 1971

TOBIEN, FELICITAS. *Der Blaue Reiter.* Kirchdorf-Inn: Berghaus, 1986

VERGO, PETER. *The Blue Rider.* Oxford: Phaidon, 1977

VEZIN, ANNETTE and LUC. *Kandinsky und der Blaue Reiter.* Paris: Terrail, 1991

VOGT, PAUL. *Der Blaue Reiter.* Köln: DuMont, 1977; *The Blue Rider.* Woodbury, NY: Barron's, 1980

VOLPI ORLANDINI, MARISA. *Kandinsky und der Blaue Reiter.* Brigitte Hannecke, trans. München: Schuler Verlagsgesellschaft, 1973

WINGLER, HANS MARIA. *Der Blaue Reiter: Zeichnungen und Graphik von Marc, Kandinsky, Klee, Macke, Jawlensky, Campendonk, Kubin.* Feldafing: Buchheim, 1954

ZWEITE, ARMIN, and ANNEGRET HOBERG. *The Blue Rider in the Lenbachhaus, Munich: Masterpieces by Franz Marc, Vassily Kandinsky, Gabriele Münter, Alexei Jawlensky, August Macke, Paul Klee.* Munich/New York: Prestel, 1989; *Der Blaue Reiter im Lenbachhaus München.* München, 1991

Exhibition Catalogues

1960 London, Tate Gallery. *The Blue Rider Group: An Exhibition Organized with the Edinburgh Festival Society by the Arts Council of Great Britain.* Hans K. Roethel

1961 Winterthur. Kunstverein/Kunstmuseum; Wien, Österreichische Galerie im Oberen Belvedere; Linz, Neue Galerie der Stadt. *Der Blaue Reiter und sein Kreis.* Walter Kasten

1962 München, Galerie Stangl. *Vor 50 Jahren: Ausstellung Neue Künstlervereinigung, Der Blaue Reiter.* Klaus Lankheit, introduction

1962 Paris, Galerie Aimé Maeght. *Der Blaue Reiter*

1963 New York, Leonard Hutton Galleries. *Der Blaue Reiter*

1971 München, Städtische Galerie im Lenbachhaus. *Der Blaue Reiter: Sonderausstellung der Städtischen Galerie München.* Johannes Segieth

1971 Torino, Galleria civica d'arte moderna. *Il Cavaliere azzurro = Der blaue Reiter.* Luigi Carluccio

1974 Berlin, Nationalgalerie. *Hommage à Schönberg: Der Blaue Reiter und das Musikalische in der Malerei der Zeit.* Lucius Grisebach, et al.

1975 Schwenningen, Beethovenhaus. *Der Blaue Reiter und sein Kreis: Der Blaue Reiter und die Neue Künstlervereinigung München: Gemälde, Aquarelle, Zeichnungen, Graphik.* (24. Kunstausstellung Villingen-Schwenningen). Margarete Willmann.

1977 New York, Leonard Hutton Galleries. *Der Blaue Reiter und sein Kreis*

1980 Halle, Staatliche Galerie Moritzburg. *Expressionistische Graphik: Aquarelle, Handzeichnungen und Druckgraphik von Künstlern der "Brücke" und des "Blauen Reiters" aus den Beständen der Graphischen Sammlung der Staatlichen Galerie Moritzburg.* Irma C. Weber
1986–1987 Bern, Kunstmuseum. *Der Blaue Reiter.* Hans Christoph von Tavel
1987–1988 München, Staatsgalerie Moderner Kunst. *Franz Marc, Else Laker-Schüler, "Der Blaue Reiter präsentiert eurer Hoheit sein blaues Pferd": Karten und Briefe; Franz Marc: Postcards to Prince Jussuf.* Abridged ed. Munich/New York: Prestel, 1988
1989–1990 Hannover, Sprengel Museum. *Der Blaue Reiter: Kandinsky, Marc und ihre Freunde: Wassily Kandinsky, Franz Marc, August Macke, Alexej Jawlensky, Gabriele Münter, Marianne von Werefkin: Gemälde, Aquarelle, Zeichnungen, Druckgraphik und Buchpublikationen: Verzeichnis der Bestände des Sprengel Museum Hannover.* Perdita Lottner, and Norbert Nobis
1991 Berlin, Brücke-Museum; München, Städtische Galerie im Lenbachhaus; Saarbrücken, Saarland Museum. *Expressionistische Grüsse: Künstlerpostkarten der "Brücke" und des "Blauen Reiter".* Magdalena M. Moeller
1993 München, Galerie Thomas. *Künstler des Blauen Reiter: Gemälde, Aquarelle, Zeichnungen, Graphiken.* Gabriele Karpf, and Giannina Spargnapani
1996 Dortmund, Museum am Ostwall. *Von der Brücke zum Blauen Reiter: Farbe, Form und Ausdruck in der deutschen Malerei von 1905–1914.* Tayfun Belgin
1996–1997 Davos, Kirchner Museum; Wuppertal, Von der Heydt-Museum. *Sammlung Etta und Wolfgang Stangl: Brücke und Blauer Reiter*

Der Sturm

Reference Bibliographies
PIRSICH, VOLKER. *Der Sturm: Eine Monographie.* Herzberg: T.Bautz, 1985, p. 655-806
WALDEN, NELL, and LOTHAR SCHREYER. *Der Sturm: Ein Gedenkbuch an Herwarth Walden und die Künstler des Sturmkreises.* Baden-Baden: W. Klein, 1954, p. 257-270

Books
BEHNE, ADOLF. *Zur neuen Kunst.* (Sturm-Bücher, VII). Berlin: Der Sturm, 1915
BOORMAN, HELEN. *Herwarth Walden and Der Sturm 1910–1930: German Cultural Idealism and the Commercialization of Art.* 2 vols. Ph.D. diss. Norwich, University of East Anglia, 1987
BRÜHL, GEORG. *Herwarth Walden und "Der Sturm".* Köln: DuMont, 1983
FRÖHLICH, JÜRGEN. *Liebe im Expressionismus: Eine Untersuchung der Lyrik in den Zeitschriften Die Aktion und Der Sturm von 1910–1914.* (Studies in Modern German Literature, vol. 38). New York: P. Lang, 1990
GODÉ, MAURICE. *Der Sturm de Herwarth Walden: l'utopie d'un art autonome.* (Collection Diagonales). Nancy: Presses Universitaires de Nancy, 1990
GODÉ, MAURICE. *Les théories utopiques dans les revues expressionnistes allemandes: 'Der Sturm', 'Die Aktion', 'Die Weissen Blätter': théories et réalisations.* Ph. D. diss. Aix-en-Provence, Université de Provence, 1986
JONES, M.S. *Der Sturm: A Focus of Expressionism.* Columbia, SC: Camden House, 1984
MÜLHAUPT, FREYA. *Herwarth Walden 1878–1941: Wegbereiter der Moderne.* Berlin: Berlinische Galerie, 1991
PIRSICH, VOLKER. *Der Sturm: Eine Monographie.* Herzberg: T. Bautz, 1985
PIRSICH, VOLKER. *Der "Sturm" und seine Beziehungen zu Hamburg und zu Hamburger Künstlern.* Göttingen: T. Bautz, 1981
SCHREYER, LOTHAR. *Erinnerungen an Sturm und Bauhaus: Was ist des Menschen Bild?* München: Langen-Müller, 1956
VOERMANEK, WILDERICH. *Untersuchungen zur Kunsttheorie des "Sturm"-Kreises.* Ph.D. diss. Freie Universität Berlin, 1970
WALDEN, HERWARTH. *Einblick in Kunst: Expressionismus, Futurismus, Kubismus.* Berlin: Der Sturm, 1917
WALDEN, HERWARTH. *Gesammelte Schriften. Bd.1: Kunstkritiker und Kunstmaler.* Berlin: Der Sturm, 1916
WALDEN, HERWARTH. *Die neue Malerei.* Berlin: Der Sturm, 1919
WALDEN, HERWARTH. *Der Sturm: Eine Einführung.* Berlin: Der Sturm, 1919

WALDEN, NELL. *Herwarth Walden: Ein Lebensbild.* Berlin/Mainz: Kupferberg, 1963
WALDEN, NELL, and LOTHAR SCHREYER, eds. *Der Sturm: Ein Erinnerungsbuch an Herwarth Walden und die Künstler aus dem Sturmkreis.* Baden-Baden: W. Klein, 1954
WINGLER, HANS MARIA, ed. *Künstler und Poeten: Bildniszeichnungen: Literarische Porträtskizzen von Herwarth Walden, Else Lasker-Schüler und anderen Schriftstellern aus dem Künstlerkreis "Der Sturm".* Feldafing: Buchheim, 1954
WINGLER, HANS MARIA. *Der Sturm: Zeichnungen und Graphiken: Kokoschka, Klee, Chagall, Campendonk, Kandinsky u.a.* Feldafing: Buchheim, 1955

Exhibition Catalogues
1961 Berlin, Schloss Charlottenburg. *Der Sturm: Herwarth Walden und die europäische Avantgarde: Berlin 1912–1932*
1967 Bern, Kunstmuseum. *Schenkung Nell Walden*
1979 New York, Matignon Gallery. *Art of the Twenties: Selections of Der Sturm and Bauhaus related East-European Artists.* Paul K. Kovesdy
1981 New York, Helen Serger/La Boetie. *Herwarth Walden and Der Sturm: Artists and Publications*
1982 New York, Matignon Gallery. *East-European Artists of Herwarth Walden's "Der Sturm" in Berlin 1920–1932: Expressionist, Constructivist, Cubist, Futurist*
1987–1988 Köln, Galerie Stolz. *Herwarth Walden und Der Sturm: Konstruktivisten, Abstrakte, eine Auswahl*

Second Generation

Reference Bibliographies
HOFFMEISTER, CHRISTINE, and CHRISTIAN SUCKOW, eds. *Revolution und Realismus: Revolutionäre Kunst in Deutschland 1917 bis 1933.* Berlin: Staatliche Museen zu Berlin, 1978, p. 99-105
WEINSTEIN, JOAN. *The End of Expressionism: Art and the November Revolution in Germany 1918–1919.* Chicago/London: University of Chicago Press, 1989, p. 307-23

Books
An alle Künstler! Berlin: Fackelträger-Verlag, 1919
BEHNE, ADOLF, PAUL LANDAU, and HERBERT LÖWING. *Das politische Plakat.* Berlin: Verlag "Das Plakat", 1919

BEHNE, ADOLF. *Die Wiederkehr der Kunst.* Leipzig: K. Wolff, 1919
BIERMANN, G. *Jahrbuch der Jungen Kunst.* Leipzig: Klinkhardt und Biermann, 1920–1924
BISCHOFF, WILLIAM. *Artists, Intellectuals, and Revolution 1918–1919.* Ph.D. diss. Cambridge, MA, Harvard University, 1970
BOHNEN, ULI. *Das Gesetz der Welt ist die Änderung der Welt: Die rheinische Gruppe Progressiver Künstler 1918–1933.* Berlin: Kramer, 1976
BUDERER, HANS-JÜRGEN. *Neue Sachlichkeit: Bilder auf der Suche nach der Wirklichkeit: Figurative Malerei der zwanziger Jahre.* München / New York: Prestel, 1994
EBERLE, MATTHIAS. *Der Weltkrieg und die Künstler der Weimarer Republik: Dix, Grosz, Beckmann, Schlemmer.* Stuttgart / Zürich: Belser, 1989
FRIEDRICH, OTTO. *Before the Deluge: A Portrait of Berlin in the 1920's.* New York: Harper & Row, 1972
FRITTON, MICHAEL HUGH. *Literatur und Politik in der Novemberrevolution 1918–19: Theorie und Praxis revolutionärer Schriftsteller in Stuttgart und München.* (Europäische Hochschulschriften. Reihe I, Deutsche Sprache und Literatur, Bd. 926). Frankfurt am Main: P. Lang, 1986
GAY, PETER. *Die Republik der Aussenseiter: Geist und Kultur in der Weimarer Zeit 1918–1933.* Frankfurt am Main: S. Fischer, 1970
GAY, PETER. *Weimar Culture: The Outsider as Insider.* New York: Harper & Row, 1968
GEHRIG, OSKAR. *Plakatkunst und Revolution.* Berlin: E. Wasmuth, 1919
GERSTL, MAX. *Die Münchner Räterepublik.* München: Verlag der "Politischen Zeitfragen", 1919
GRAUTOFF, OTTO. *Die neue Kunst.* Berlin: K. Siegismund, 1921
GREENBERG, ALLAN C. *Artists and Revolution: Dada and the Bauhaus 1917–1925.* (University Studies in the Fine Arts: The Avant-garde, no. 4). Ann Arbor, MI: UMI Research Press, 1979
GROHMANN, WILL. "Zehn Jahre Novembergruppe." *Kunst der Zeit,* 3. Sonderheft., Nr 1-3, 1928
HAUSENSTEIN, WILHELM. *Bild und Gemeinschaft: Entwurf einer Soziologie der Kunst.* München: K. Wolff, 1920
HIRSCHBACH, FRANK D., et al., eds. *Germany in the Twenties: The Artist*

as Social Critic. New York: Holmes and Meier, 1980

KAES, ANTON, MARTIN JAY, and EDWARD DIMENDBERG, eds. *The Weimar Sourcebook*. Berkeley: University of California Press, 1994

KANE, MARTIN. *Weimar Germany and the Limits of Political Art: A Study of the Work of Georg Grosz and Ernst Toller*. Tayport, Scotland: Hutton Press, 1987

KLAPHECK, ANNA. *Mutter Ey: Eine Düsseldorfer Künstlerlegende*. Düsseldorf: Droste, 1958; 3rd. ed. Düsseldorf, 1978

KLIEMANN, HELGA. *Die Novembergruppe*. (Bildende Kunst in Berlin, Bd. 3). Berlin: Mann, 1969

KOLB, EBERHARD, EBERHARD ROTERS, and WIELAND SCHMIED. *Kritische Grafik in der Weimarer Zeit*. Stuttgart: Klett-Cotta, 1985

KOLINSKY, EVA. *Engagierter Expressionismus: Politik und Literatur zwischen Weltkrieg und Weimarer Republik*. Stuttgart: Metzler, 1970

KUTSCHERA, JOHANNA. *Aufbruch und Engagement: Aspekte deutscher Kunst nach dem Ersten Weltkrieg 1918–1920*. (Europäische Hochschulschriften. Reihe XXVIII, Kunstgeschichte, Bd. 208). Frankfurt am Main: P. Lang, 1994

LAQUER, WALTER. *Weimar: A Cultural History 1918–1933*. New York: Perigree, 1980

LONG, ROSE-CAROL WASHTON. *German Expressionism: Documents from the End of the Wilhelmine Empire to the Rise of National Socialism*. New York: G.K. Hall, 1993

LUDEWIG, PETER. *Schrei in die Welt: Expressionismus in Dresden*. Berlin: Buchverlag der Morgen, 1988

MESKIMMON, MARSHA, and SHEARER WEST, eds. *Visions of the "Neue Frau": Women and the Visual Arts in Weimar Germany*. Aldershot, England: Scolar Press, and Brookfield, VT: Ashgate, 1995

MOTHERWELL, ROBERT, ed. *The Dada Painters and Poets: An Anthology*. 2nd ed. Boston: G.K. Hall, 1981; reprint, Cambridge, MA: Belknap Press of Harvard University Press, 1989

PAULSEN, WOLFGANG. *Expressionismus und Aktivismus*. Strassburg: Heitz, 1934

PIRSICH, VOLKER. *Der späte Expressionismus 1918–1925*. (Pfälzische Arbeiten zum Buch- und Bibliothekswesen und zur Bibliographie, Heft 12). Speyer: Pfälzische Landesbibliothek, 1985

ROH, FRANZ. *Nach-Expressionismus, magischer Realismus: Probleme der neuesten europäischen Malerei*. Leipzig: Klinkhardt & Biermann, 1925

SCHMIDT, ANNALISE, ed. *Der Bolschewismus und die deutschen Intellektuellen: Äusserungen auf eine Umfrage des Bundes deutscher Gelehrter und Künstler*. Leipzig: Deutsche Verlagsgesellschaft für Politik und Geschichte, 1920

SCHMIDT, DIETER. *Manifeste, Manifeste 1905–1933*. Dresden: VEB Verlag der Kunst, 1964

SCHMIED, WIELAND. *Neue Sachlichkeit und magischer Realismus in Deutschland 1918–1933*. Hannover: Fackelträger-Verlag, 1969

SCHNEEDE, UWE M., ed. *Die zwanziger Jahre: Manifeste und Dokumente deutscher Künstler*. Köln: DuMont, 1979

STENZEL, BURKHARD. *Harry Graf Kessler: Ein Leben zwischen Kultur und Politik*. Weimar: Böhlau, 1995

UTITZ, EMIL. *Die Überwindung des Expressionismus*. Stuttgart: F. Enke, 1927

WALDEN, HERWARTH, ed. *Expressionismus: Die Kunstwende*. Berlin: Der Sturm, 1918

WEINSTEIN, JOAN. *The End of Expressionism: Art and the November Revolution in Germany 1918–1919*. Chicago / London: University of Chicago Press, 1990

WILLETT, JOHN. *Art and Politics in the Weimar Period: The New Sobriety 1917–1933*. New York: Pantheon, 1978

WILLETT, JOHN. *The Weimar Years: A Culture Cut Short*. New York: Abbeville Press, and London: Thames & Hudson, 1984

WINGLER, HANS MARIA. *Das Bauhaus 1919–1933: Weimar, Dessau, Berlin und die Nachfolge in Chicago seit 1937*. 3rd ed. Bramsche: Gebr. Rasch, 1975; *The Bauhaus: Weimar, Dessau, Berlin, Chicago*. 3rd rev. ed. Joseph Stein, ed.; Wolfgang Jabs, and Basil Gilbert, trans. Cambridge, MA: MIT Press, 1976

WOLLHEIM, GERT, GERTH SCHREINER, and FRANZ STÖFFHASE, ed. *Buch Eins-, Buch Zwei-, and Buch Drei des Aktivisten-Bundes 1919*. Düsseldorf: Aktivistenbund, 1920

Exhibition Catalogues
1962 Hannover, Kunstverein. *Die zwanziger Jahre in Hannover 1916–1933*
1964 Berlin, Staatliche Museen zu Berlin, Nationalgalerie. *Anklage und Aufruf: Deutsche Kunst zwischen den Kriegen: Malerei, Graphik, Plastik*
1966 Biberach an der Riss, Kleine Galerie. *Der Späte Expressionismus 1918–1922: Bücher, Bilder, Zeitschriften, Dokumente*. Paul Raabe
1967 Wuppertal, Kunst- und Museumsverein, 1967. *Magischer Realismus in Deutschland 1920–1923*
1968–1969 Berlin, Staatliche Museen zu Berlin, Nationalgalerie. Kupferstichkabinett und Sammlung der Zeichnungen. *Vor 50 Jahren: Erster Weltkrieg, Novemberrevolution, Nachkriegszeit: Druckgraphik und Zeichnungen deutscher Künstler 1914–1924 aus eigenen Beständen*
1970 Düsseldorf, Städtische Kunsthalle. *Avantgarde gestern: Das Junge Rheinland und seine Freunde 1919-29*
1970–1971 Berlin, Galerie Nierendorf. *Die zwanziger Jahre 1914–1923*
1971 Stuttgart, Württembergischer Kunstverein. *Realismus zwischen Revolution und Machtergreifung 1919–1933*. Uwe M. Schneede
1976 Bonn, Rheinisches Landesmuseum. *Die zwanziger Jahre im Porträt: Porträts in Deutschland 1918–1933: Malerei, Graphik, Fotografie, Plastik*. Joachim Heusinger von Waldegg
1976 Frankfurt am Main, Historisches Museum. *Ein Krieg wird ausgestellt*
1977 Berlin, Kunstamt Wedding. *Die Novembergruppe*. (Tendenzen der zwanziger Jahre. Teil 1: Die Maler). Peter Hopf
1977 Berlin, Staatliche Kunsthalle. *Wem gehört die Welt?: Kunst und Gesellschaft in der Weimarer Republik*. Jürgen Kleindienst
1977 München, Gallerie del Levante. *Dresdner Sezession 1919–1923*. Emilio Bertonati, Fritz Löffler, and Joachim Heusinger von Waldegg
1978–1979 Berlin, Altes Museum. *Revolution und Realismus: Revolutionäre Kunst in Deutschland 1917 bis 1933*. Christine Hoffmeister, and Christian Suckow
1979 Münchner Stadtmuseum. *Die zwanziger Jahre in München*. Christoph Stölzl, ed.
1980 Berlin, Akademie der Künste. *Arbeitsrat für Kunst, Berlin 1918–1921*. Manfred Schlösser
1980–1981 Dresden, Staatliche Kunstsammlungen Dresden, Gemäldegalerie Neue Meister. *Kunst im Aufbruch, Dresden 1918–1933*. Joachim Uhlitzsch, et al.

1983–1984 San Diego State University, University Gallery; Detroit Institute of Arts; Chicago, David and Alfred Smart Gallery. *An alle Künstler!* Ida Katherine Rigby
1985 Berlin, Galerie Nierendorf. *Künstler der Novembergruppe*
1985 Berlin, Otto-Nagel-Haus. *Wählt Links!: Das politische Plakat in Deutschland 1918–1933*. Jörn Grabowski
1985 Düsseldorf, Städtische Kunsthalle. *Am Anfang: Das Junge Rheinland: Zur Kunst und Zeitgeschichte einer Region 1918–1945*. Ulrich Krempel, ed.
1985–1986 Halle, Staatliche Galerie Moritzburg. *Kunst im Klassenkampf: Proletarisch-revolutionäre und antifaschistische Malerei, Grafik und Plastik*. Peter Romanus, and Axel Wendelberger
1986 Norwich, Sainsbury Centre for Visual Arts, University of East Anglia. *Icon and Revolution: Political and Social Themes in German Art 1918–1933*. Willi Guttsman
1988–1989 Los Angeles County Museum of Art; Fort Worth, Modern Art Museum. *German Expressionism 1915–1925: The Second Generation*; Düsseldorf, Kunstmuseum; Halle, Staatliche Galerie Moritzburg. *Expressionismus: Die zweite Generation 1915–1925*. Stephanie Barron, ed.
1990 Bielefeld, Kunsthalle. *Neue Sachlichkeit, magischer Realismus*. Jutta Hülsewig-Johnen
1991–1992 Los Angeles County Museum of Art; Chicago, Art Institute; Washington D.C., Smithsonian Institution, International Gallery. *Degenerate Art: the Fate of the Avant-garde in Nazi Germany*; Berlin, Altes Museum. *Entartete Kunst: Das Schicksal der Avantgarde im Nazi-Deutschland*. Stephanie Barron, ed.
1992–1993 Kiel, Stadtgalerie im Sophienhof. *Kunstwende: Der Kieler Impuls des Expressionismus 1915–1922*. Knut Nievers, and Bärbel Manitz
1993 Evanston, IL, Mary and Leigh Block Gallery; Hanover, NH, Hood Museum of Art; Austin, TX, Archer M. Huntington Art Gallery. *Stark Impressions: Graphic Production in Germany 1918–1933*. Reinhold Heller
1993 Los Angeles County Museum of Art. *Expressionist Utopias: Paradise, Metropolis, Architectural Fantasy*. Timothy O. Benson
1993–1994 Berlin, Galerie Bodo Niemann. *Novembergruppe*

1993–1994 München, Städtische Galerie im Lenbachhaus. *Süddeutsche Freiheit: Kunst der Revolution in München 1919*. Justin Hoffmann, and Helmut Friedel

1994 Berlin, Altes Museum. *Die letzten Tage der Menschheit: Bilder des Ersten Weltkrieges*. Rainer Rother, ed.

1995 Darmstadt, Galerie Netuschil. *Die Graphik des Darmstädter Expressionismus 1915–1925*. Claus K. Netuschil, ed.

ARTISTS

Ernst Barlach

Reference Bibliographies

DOPPELSTEIN, JÜRGEN. *Ernst Barlach: beeldhouwer, tekenaar, graficus, schrijver ... 1870–1938*. Leizig: E.A. Seemann, 1994, p. 459-468

SCHULT, FRIEDRICH. *Ernst Barlach: Das plastische Werk*. Hamburg: E. Hauswedell, 1960, p. 270-284

SCHULT, FRIEDRICH. *Ernst Barlach: Werkkatalog der Zeichnungen*. Hamburg: E. Hauswedell, 1971, p. 14-15

Written Works and Correspondence

Die Briefe I, 1888–1924. Friedrich Dross, ed. München: R. Piper, 1968

Die Briefe II, 1925–1938. Friedrich Dross, ed. München, R. Piper, 1969

Das dichterische Werk. Bd. 1, Die Dramen; Bd. 2, Die Prosa I; Bd. 3, Die Prosa II. Friedrich Dross, ed. München: R. Piper, 1956–1959

Güstrower Tagebuch im Auszug 1914–1917. Wolfgang Theopold, ed [S.l.: s.n.], 1938

Ein selbsterzähltes Leben. Berlin: P. Cassirer, 1928; A Selftold Life. Naomi Jackson Groves, trans. Waterloo, Ontario: Penumbra, 1990

Oeuvre Catalogues

SCHULT, FRIEDRICH. *Ernst Barlach: Das graphische Werk*. Hamburg: E. Hauswedell, 1958

SCHULT, FRIEDRICH. *Ernst Barlach: Das plastische Werk*. Hamburg: E. Hauswedell, 1960

SCHULT, FRIEDRICH. *Ernst Barlach: Werkkatalog der Zeichnungen*. Hamburg: E. Hauswedell, 1971

Books

ALBRECHT, DIETMAR. *Literaturreisen: Barlach in Wedel, Hamburg, Ratzeburg und Güstrow*. (Literaturreisen: Wege, Orte, Texte). Stuttgart: Klett-Verlag, 1990

BELOUBEK-HAMMER, ANITA. *Ernst Barlach: Plastische Meisterwerke.*

Leipzig: E.A. Seemann, 1996

CARLS, CARL DIETRICH. *Ernst Barlach*. Berlin: Rembrandt, 1931; New enlarged and supplemented ed. Berlin, 1968; English ed. New York: Praeger, 1969

CREPON, TOM. *Leben und Leiden des Ernst Barlach*. Rostock: Hinstorff, 1988

DOPPELSTEIN, JÜRGEN. *Ernst Barlach: beeldhouwer, tekenaar, graficus, schrijver = Sculpteur, dessinateur, graveur, écrivain = Bildhauer, Zeichner, Graphiker, Schriftsteller, 1870–1938*. Leipzig: E.A. Seemann, 1994

FECHTER, PAUL. *Ernst Barlach*. Gütersloh: C. Bertelsmann Verlag, 1957

FLEMMING, WILLI. *Ernst Barlach: Wesen und Werk*. Bern: Francke, 1958

FÜHMANN, FRANZ. *Das Wirkliche und Wahrhaftige: Briefe, Grafik, Plastik, Dokumente*. 2nd ed. Wiesbaden: R. Löwit, 1974

GLOEDE, GÜNTER. *Barlach: Gestalt und Gleichnis*. Hamburg: Furche-Verlag, 1966

GOSEBRUCH, MARTIN, KLAUS LAZAROWICZ, and HARALD SEILER, eds. *Zugang zu Ernst Barlach: Einführung in sein künstlerisches und dichterisches Schaffen*. Göttingen: Vandenhoeck & Ruprecht, 1961

GROVES, NAOMI JACKSON. *Ernst Barlach: The Development of a Versatile Genius*. Ph.D. diss. Cambridge, MA, Harvard University, 1950

GROVES, NAOMI JACKSON. *Ernst Barlach, Leben und Werk: Plastiken, Zeichnungen und Graphiken, Dramen, Prosawerke und Briefe (Die blauen Bücher); Ernst Barlach, Life in Work: Sculpture, Drawings, and Graphics, Dramas, Prose Works and Letters in Translation*. Königstein im Taunus: K.R. Langewiesche Nachfolger H. Köster, 1972.

HOOPER, KENT W. *Ernst Barlach's Literary and Visual Art: The Issue of Multiple Talent*. (Studies in Fine Arts. Art Theory, no. 15). Ann Arbor, MI: U.M.I.. Research Press, 1987

JANSEN, ELMAR. *Ernst Barlach*. 4th ed. Berlin: Henschelverlag, 1993

KLINGE, EKKART. *Ernst Barlach: Porzellan*. Hans Barlach, ed. Leipzig: E.A. Seemann, 1995

KRAHMER, CATHERINE. *Ernst Barlach: Mit Selbstzeugnissen und Bilddokumenten*. (Rowohlts Monographien, 335). Reinbek bei Hamburg: Rowohlt, 1990

KRAHMER, CATHERINE. *Ernst Barlach:*

un sculpteur-écrivain: les années 1906–1912. (Les Dossiers du Musée d'Orsay, no. 19). Paris: Éditions de la Réunion des musées nationaux, 1988

PROBST, VOLKER, and JOACHIM FISCHER. *Der Ernst Barlach Nachlass in Güstrow*. Güstrow: Ernst Barlach Stiftung, 1995

SCHILLING, JÜRGEN, ed. *Ernst Barlach: Plastiken, Entwurfszeichnungen*. Ratzeburg: E. and H. Barlach, 1986

SCHULZ, ILONA. *Stationen der Begegnung in Thüringen*. Berlin: Akademie der Künste zu Berlin, 1991

SCHUREK, PAUL. *Begegnungen mit Barlach: Ein Erlebnisbericht*. Gütersloh: Rufer-Verlag, 1954

STUBBE, WOLF. *Ernst Barlach: Plastik*. München: R. Piper, 1959; 6th ed. München, 1985

TILLE, PETER. *Ernst Barlach: Eine Skizze seines Lebens und Schaffens*. (Hefte aus Burgscheidungen, 251). Berlin: Sekretariat des Hauptvorstandes der Christlich-Demokratischen Union Deutschlands, 1988

WALTER, REINHOLD VON. *Ernst Barlach: Eine Einführung in sein plastisches und graphisches Werk*. Berlin: Furche-Kunstverlag, 1929

WERNER, ALFRED. *Ernst Barlach*. New York: McGraw-Hill, 1966

Exhibition Catalogues

1961 London, Arts Council of Great Britain. *Ernst Barlach 1870–1938: Sculpture and Drawings*. Wolf Stubbe

1962 New York, Galerie St. Etienne. *Ernst Barlach 1870–1938: Sculptures and Drawings*

1962 Ottawa, National Gallery of Canada. *The Graphic Art of = l'oeuvre graphique de Ernst Barlach*. Naomi Jackson Groves

1962–1963 Washington, D.C., Smithsonian Institution. *Work by Ernst Barlach*. Wolf Stubbe, and Armgard Hardt

1965 Hamburg, Kunsthalle. *Ernst Barlach: Zeichnungen aus dem Hause des Künstlers auf dem Heidberg bei Güstrow*

1966 Hamburg, Ernst Barlach Haus. *Ernst Barlach*. Kurt Sternelle, and Gerhard Schack

1968 Bremen, Kunsthalle. *Ernst Barlach: Das druckgraphische Werk, Dore und Kurt Reutti-Stiftung*. Henning Bock, ed.

1970 Hamburg, Ernst Barlach Haus, 1970. *Ernst Barlach: Holzplastiken: Jubiläumsausstellung zum 100. Geburtsjahr des Künstlers*. Isa Lohmann-Siems, ed.

1975 Köln, Kunsthalle Köln. *Ernst Barlach: Plastik, Zeichnungen, Druckgraphik*. 2nd. ed. Manfred Schneckenburger

1981 Berlin, Akademie der Künste der DDR. *Ernst Barlach: Werke und Werkentwürfe aus fünf Jahrzehnten*. (Katalog 1: Plastik 1894–1937, Elmar Jansen; Katalog 2: Zeichnungen und Skizzenhefte 1891–1938, Maria Rüger; Katalog 3: Druckgraphik 1910–1930, Tanja Frank).

1981 München, Museum Villa Stuck. *Ernst Barlach: Plastik, Zeichnungen, Graphik*. Ralph Jentsch, ed

1984 Wien, Künstlerhaus. *Ernst Barlach 1870–1938: Werke, Meinungen*. Elmar Jansen, ed.

1988 Berlin, Akademie der Künste der DDR. *Ernst Barlach: Denkzeichen*. Ilona Schulz.

1988 Unna, Kreisverwaltung Unna. *Ernst Barlach: Plastik, Zeichnung, Druckgraphik, 1906–1937*. Jürgen Schilling

1991 Köln, Käthe Kollwitz Museum. *Ernst Barlach: Skulpturen, Handzeichnungen, Druckgraphik aus den Beständen der Barlach-Museen in Ratzeburg und Güstrow*. Hannelore Fischer.

1995 Güstrow, Ernst Barlach Stiftung. *Ernst Barlach: Berlin, Florenz, 1909: Skulpturen, Zeichnungen, Handschriften*. Inge Tessenow

1995 Güstrow, Ernst Barlach Stiftung. *Nachlass Marga Böhmer*.

1996 Güstrow, Ernst Barlach Stiftung. *Ernst Barlach, Der Dramatiker: Plastiken, Lithographien, Holzschnitte, Handschriften*

1996 Hannover, Sprengel Museum. *Ernst Barlach und Käthe Kollwitz: Verzeichnis der Bestände: Originale auf Papier und Druckgraphik*

Max Beckmann

Reference Bibliographies

GÖPEL, ERHARD and BARBARA. *Max Beckmann: Katalog der Gemälde*. Bern: Kornfeld, 1976, vol. 2: p. 1-129. [1906–1970]

SCHULZ-HOFFMANN, CARLA, and JUDITH C. WEISS. *Max Beckmann Retrospective*. München/New York: Prestel, 1984, p. 475-477. [1911–1984]

WESTHEIDER, ORTRUD. *Die Farbe Schwarz in der Malerei Max Beckmanns*. Berlin: Reimer, 1995, p. 219-252. [1920's–1994]

Written Works and Correspondence

BECKMANN, PETER, and JOACHIM SCHAFFER, eds. *Die Bibliothek Max*

Beckmanns: Unterstreichungen, Kommentare, Notizen und Skizzen in seinen Büchern. Worms: Werner'sche Verlagsgesellschaft, 1992
Briefe im Kriege. Gesammelt von Minna Tube. Berlin: B. Cassirer, 1916; reprint, (Langen-Müller's kleine Geschenkbücher, 36). München: Langen-Müller, 1955; München: Piper, 1984
BUENGER, BARBARA COPELAND, ed. *Max Beckmann: Self-Portrait in Words: Collected Writings and Statements 1903–1950.* Chicago/London: University of Chicago Press, 1997
GALLWITZ, KLAUS, UWE M. SCHNEEDE, and STEPHAN VON WIESE, eds. *Max Beckmann: Briefe: Bd. 1 1899–1925.* München: Piper, 1993
KINKEL, HANS, ed. *Max Beckmann, Leben in Berlin: Tagebuch 1908–1909.* (Piper-Bücherei, 216). München: R. Piper, 1966; 2nd ed. (Serie Piper, vol. 325). München, 1983
PILLEP, RUDOLF, ed. *Die Realität der Träume in den Bildern: Schriften und Gespräche 1911 bis 1950.* (Serie Piper, 814). München: R. Piper, 1990
SCHMIDT, DORIS, ed. *Max Beckmann: Frühe Tagebücher 1903-04 und 1912-13.* Mit Erinnerungen von Minna Beckmann-Tube. München: R. Piper, 1985

Oeuvre Catalogues
GALLWITZ, KLAUS. *Max Beckmann: Die Druckgraphik: Radierungen, Lithographien, Holzschnitte.* Exhibition catalogue. 2nd rev. ed. Karlsruhe: Badischer Kunstverein, 1962
GÖPEL, ERHARD, and BARBARA GÖPEL. *Max Beckmann: Katalog der Gemälde.* (Schriften der Max Beckmann Gesellschaft, 3). 2 vols. Bern: Kornfeld, 1976
HOFMAIER, JAMES. *Max Beckmann: Catalogue raisonné of his Prints.* 2 vols. Bern: Gallery Kornfeld, 1990
WIESE, STEPHAN VON. *Max Beckmanns zeichnerisches Werk 1903–1925.* Düsseldorf: Droste, 1978

Books
BECKMANN, PETER. *Max Beckmann.* (Nürnberger Liebhaberausgaben, 4). Nürnberg: Glock und Lutz, 1955
BECKMANN, PETER, ed. *Max Beckmann: Sichtbares und Unsichtbares.* (Bibliothek der Kunst). Stuttgart: Belser, 1965
BELTING, HANS. *Max Beckmann: Die Tradition als Problem in der Kunst der Moderne.* Berlin: Deut-

scher Kunstverlag, 1984; *Max Beckmann: Tradition as a Problem in Modern Art.* New York: Timken, 1989
BUCHHEIM, LOTHAR-GÜNTHER. *Max Beckmann.* Feldafing: Buchheim, 1959
BUENGER, BARBARA COPELAND. *Max Beckmann's Artistic Sources: The Artist's Relation to Older and Modern Traditions.* Ph.D. diss. New York, Columbia University, 1979
BILLETER, FELIX, et al., *Max Beckmann: Bibliographie 1971–1993.* (Hefte der Max Beckmann Archivs, 1). München: Max Beckmann Archiv, 1994
BUSCH, GÜNTER. *Max Beckmann: Eine Einführung.* München: R. Piper, 1960; rev. ed. 1989
EBERLE, MATTHIAS. *Max Beckmann, Die Nacht: Passion ohne Erlösung.* Frankfurt am Main: Fischer Taschenbuch, 1984
ERFFA, HANS MARTIN, and ERHARD GÖPEL. *Blick auf Beckmann: Dokumente und Vorträge.* (Schriften der Max Beckmann Gesellschaft, 2). München: R. Piper, 1962
ERPEL, FRITZ. *Max Beckmann.* (Welt der Kunst). Berlin: Henschelverlag, 1981
ERPEL, FRITZ. *Max Beckmann: Leben im Werk, die Selbstbildnisse.* Berlin: Henschelverlag, 1985
FISCHER, FRIEDHELM W. *Der Maler Max Beckmann.* Köln: DuMont Schauberg, 1972; *Max Beckmann.* P.S. Falla, trans. London: Phaidon, and New York: Praeger, 1973
FISCHER, FRIEDHELM W. *Max Beckmann, Symbol und Weltbild: Grundriss zu einer Deutung des Gesamtwerkes.* München: W. Fink, 1972
GÄSSLER, EWALD. *Studien zum Frühwerk Max Beckmanns: Eine motivkundliche und ikonographische Untersuchung zur Kunst der Jahrhundertwende.* Ph.D. diss. Göttingen Universität, 1974
GLASER, CURT, JULIUS MEIER-GRAEFE, WILHELM FRAENGER, and WILHELM HAUSENSTEIN. *Max Beckmann.* München: R. Piper, 1924
GÖPEL, ERHARD. *Max Beckmann: Der Zeichner.* München: R. Piper, 1954; 2nd ed. München, 1958
GÖPEL, ERHARD. *Max Beckmann: Der Maler.* (Piper-Bucherei, 116) München: R. Piper, 1957
GÜSE, ERNST-GERHARD. *Das Frühwerk Max Beckmanns: Zur Thematik seiner Bilder aus den Jahren 1904–1914.*(Kunstwissenschaft-

liche Studien, vol. 6). Frankfurt am Main: P. Lang, 1977
JÄHNER, HORST. *Max Beckmann.* Dresden: VEB Verlag der Kunst, 1973
KAISER, HANS. *Max Beckmann.* (Kunst unserer Zeit, 1). Berlin: P. Cassirer, 1913
LACKNER, STEPHAN. *Ich erinnere mich gut an Max Beckmann.* Mainz: Kupferberg, 1967; *Max Beckmann: Memories of a Friendship.* Coral Gables, FL: University of Miami Press, 1969
LACKNER, STEPHAN. *Max Beckmann.* (The Library of Great Painters). New York: H. Abrams, 1977; German ed. (DuMont's Bibliothek grosser Maler). Köln: DuMont, 1978
LENZ, CHRISTIAN. *Max Beckmann und Italien.* Frankfurt am Main: Deutsch-Italienische Vereinigung, 1976
NAGEL, W.A., ed. *Max Beckmann: Die Frankfurter Jahre.* (Die silberne Reihe. Kunst und Künstler). Hanau: Peters, 1991
NEUMANN, J.B., and GUENTHER FRANKE, eds. *Max Beckmann.* (The Art Lover Library, 5). New York/München: J.B. Neumann, 1931
REIFENBERG, BENNO, and WILHELM HAUSENSTEIN. *Max Beckmann.* München: R. Piper, 1949
REIMERTZ, STEPHAN. *Max Beckmann.* (Rowohlts Monographien, 558). Reinbek bei Hamburg: Rowohlt, 1995
REIMERTZ, STEPHAN. *Max Beckmann und Minna Tube: Eine Liebe im Porträt.* (Paare). Berlin: Rowohlt, 1996
ROTHER, SUSANNE. *Beckmann als Landschafsmaler.* (Beiträge zur Kunstwissenschaft, vol. 34). München: Scaneg, 1990
SCHUBERT, DIETRICH. *Max Beckmann: Auferstehung und Erscheinung der Toten.* Worms: Werner'sche Verlagsgesellschaft, 1985.
SCHULZ-HOFFMANN, CARLA. *Max Beckmann: Der Maler.* München: Bruckmann, 1991
SCHWARZ, BIRGIT. *Dix und Beckmann: Stil als Option und Schicksal.* Mainz: P. von Zabern, 1995
SELZ, PETER. *Max Beckmann: The Self-Portraits.* New York: Gagosian Gallery and Rizzoli, 1992
SIMON, HEINRICH. *Max Beckmann.* (Junge Kunst, Bd. 56). Berlin: Klinkhardt & Biermann, 1930
SPIELER, REINHARD. *Max Beckmann: Der Weg zum Mythos.* Köln: B. Taschen, 1994; *Max Beckmann:*

The Path to Myth. Köln, 1995
WESTHEIDER, ORTRUD. *Die Farbe Schwarz in der Malerei Max Beckmanns: Zwischen Figuration und Abstraktion.* Berlin: Reimer, 1995.
ZENSER, HILDEGARD, ed. *Max Beckmann: Selbstbildnisse.* München: Schirmer/Mosel, 1984

Exhibition Catalogues
1962 Karlsruhe, Badischer Kunstverein. *Max Beckmann, die Druckgraphik: Radierungen, Lithographien, Holzschnitte.* Klaus Gallwitz
1963 Karlsruhe, Badischer Kunstverein. *Max Beckmann, das Pörträt: Gemälde, Aquarelle, Zeichnungen.* Klaus Gallwitz
1964 Boston, Museum of Fine Arts; New York, Museum of Modern Art; Chicago, The Art Insititute. *Max Beckmann.* Peter Selz
1964 München, Galerie Günther Franke. *Max Beckmann: Bildnisse aus den Jahren 1905–1950: Gemälde, Aquarelle, Pastelle und Zeichnungen*
1965 London, Tate Gallery. *Max Beckmann 1884–1950: Paintings, Drawings, and Graphic Work.* Organized by the International Council of the Museum of Modern Art, New York
1966–1967 Berlin, Akademie der Künste. *Max Beckmann: Gemälde und Aquarelle der Sammlung Stephan Lackner, USA: Und Druckgraphik aus dem Besitz der Kunsthalle Bremen.* Henning Bock, and Johann Heinrich Müller
1968–1969 Paris, Musée national d'art moderne; München, Haus der Kunst; Bruxelles, Palais des beaux-arts. *Max Beckmann.* Günter Busch, and Sabine Helms
1970–1971 Amsterdam, Stedelijk Museum, Prentenkabinet. *Max Beckmann: Grafiek*
1974 Bremen, Kunsthalle. *Max Beckmann in der Sammlung Piper: Handzeichnungen, Druckgraphik, Dokumente 1910–1923.* Anne Röver, and Bernhard Schnackenburg
1975 Bielefeld, Kunsthalle. *Max Beckmann.* 2 vols. Ulrich Weisner, and Rüdiger Jörn
1975 München, Galerie Günther Franke. *Max Beckmann: 180 Zeichnungen und Aquarelle aus deutschem und amerikanischem Besitz*
1976 Zürich, Kunsthaus. *Max Beckmann: Das druckgraphische Werk.* Ursula Perucchi-Petri
1977–1978 Bielefeld, Kunsthalle; Tübingen, Kunsthalle; Frankfurt am Main, Städtische Galerie im

Städelschen Kunstinstitut. *Max Beckmann: Aquarelle und Zeichnungen 1903–1950.* Ulrich Weisner
1979 Hamburg, Kunstverein. *Der Zeichner und Grafiker Max Beckmann.* Uwe M. Schneede
1982 Bielefeld, Kunsthalle; Frankfurt am Main, Städtische Galerie im Städelschen Kunstinstitut. *Max Beckmann: Die frühen Bilder.* Ulrich Weisner, and Klaus Gallwitz, eds.
1983 Berlin, Staatliche Museen Preussischer Kulturbesitz, Kupferstichkabinett. *Max Beckmann: Die Hölle 1919.* Alexander Dückers
1983–1984 Frankfurt am Main, Städtische Galerie im Städelschen Kunstinstitut. *Max Beckmann: Frankfurt 1915–1933: Eine Ausstellung zum 100. Geburtstag*
1983–1984 Hannover, Kunstmuseum Hannover mit Sammlung Sprengel. *Max Beckmann: Werke aus der Sammlung des Kunstmuseum Hannover mit Sammlung Sprengel.* Norbert Nobis, and Ernest W. Uthemann
1984 Bremen, Kunsthalle. *Max Beckmann, seine Themen, seine Zeit: Zum 100. Geburtstag des Künstlers.* Gerhard Gerkens, and Jürgen Schultze
1984 Esslingen, Galerie der Stadt. *Max Beckmann: Graphik zum 100. Geburtstag.* Christian Lenz
1984 Köln, Josef-Haubrich-Kunsthalle. *Max Beckmann.* Siegfried Gohr
1984 Leipzig, Museum der Bildenden Künste. *Max Beckmann: Graphik, Malerei, Zeichnung*
1984–1985 München, Haus der Kunst; Berlin, Nationalgalerie; Saint Louis Art Museum; Los Angeles County Museum of Art. *Max Beckmann: Retrospektive.* Carla Schulz-Hoffmann, and Judith C. Weiss
1990 Leipzig, Museum der Bildenden Künste; Frankfurt am Main, Städtische Galerie im Städelschen Kunstinstitut. *Max Beckmann: Gemälde 1905–1950.* 2nd rev. ed. Klaus Gallwitz
1992 Fort Worth, TX, Modern Art Museum; Miami, Center for the Fine Arts; Toledo, OH, Museum of Art; San Francisco Museum of Modern Art; Calgary, Alberta, Glenbow Museum; Williamstown, MA., Williams College Museum of Art; Oklahoma City Art Museum. *Max Beckmann: Prints from the Museum of Modern Art*
1992 Zürich, Thomas Ammann Fine Art. *Max Beckamnn: Ausgewählte Werke*

1993 München, Villa Stuck. *Max Beckmann: Welt-Theater.* Jo-Anne Birnie Danzker, and Amélie Ziersch, eds.
1993 Hamburg, Kunsthalle; München, Staatsgalerie Moderner Kunst. *Max Beckmann: Selbstbildnisse.* Uwe M. Schneede, et al.
1994 Albstadt, Städtische Galerie. *Max Beckmann, Weltbild und Existenz: Druckgraphik.* Adolf Smitmans, and Anne Peters
1994 München, Staatsgalerie Moderner Kunst. *Max Beckmann: Briefe an Reinhard Piper.* (Patrimonia, 95). Christian Lenz
1994 New York, Michael Werner Gallery. *Max Beckmann.* Siegfried Gohr
1994 Sables d'Olonne, Musée de l'Abbaye Sainte-Croix. *Max Beckmann: gravures 1911–1946.* Lydie Joubert
1994–1995 Stuttgart, Staatsgalerie. *Max Beckmann: Meisterwerke aus Saint Louis 1907–1950.* Karin von Maur
1996 Roma, Galleria nazionale d'arte moderna. *Max Beckmann.* Klaus Gallwitz, et al.

Otto Dix
Reference Bibliographies
BARTON, BRIGID. *Otto Dix und die Neue Sachlichkeit 1918–1925.* Ann Arbor, MI: University Microfilms International, 1981, p. 253-70
LÖFFLER, FRITZ. *Otto Dix: Leben und Werk.* Dresden: VEB Verlag der Kunst, 1982, p. 399-412; *Otto Dix: Life and Work.* New York/London: Holmes and Meier, 1982, p. 392-405
PFÄFFLE, SUSE. *Werkverzeichnis der Aquarelle und Gouachen.* Stuttgart: G. Hatje, 1991, p. 290-294

Oeuvre Catalogues
KARSCH, FLORIAN. *Otto Dix: Das graphische Werk.* Hannover: Schmidt-Küster, 1970
LÖFFLER, FRITZ. *Otto Dix 1891–1969: Oeuvre der Gemälde.* Recklinghausen: A. Bongers, 1981
PFÄFFLE, SUSE. *Otto Dix: Werkverzeichnis der Aquarelle und Gouachen.* Stuttgart: G. Hatje, 1991

Books
BARTON, BRIGID S. *Otto Dix und die Neue Sachlichkeit 1918–1925.* Ann Arbor, MI: University Microfilms International, 1981
BECK, RAINER. *Otto Dix 1891–1969: Zeit, Leben, Werk.* (Schriftenreihe der Akademie der Bilden-

den Künste in Nürenberg, Bd. 6). Konstanz: Stadler, 1993
CONZELMANN, OTTO. *Der andere Dix: Sein Bild vom Menschen und vom Krieg.* Stuttgart: Klett-Cotta, 1983
CONZELMANN, OTTO. *Otto Dix.* Hannover: Fackelträger-Verlag, 1959
CONZELMANN, OTTO. *Otto Dix: Die Handzeichnungen.* Hannover: Fackelträger-Verlag, 1968
CONZELMANN, OTTO. *Zur Dix-Sammlung der Galerie der Stadt Stuttgart: Sonderdruck.* Stuttgart: Galerie der Stadt Stuttgart, 1978
FISCHER, LOTHAR. *Otto Dix: Ein Malerleben in Deutschland.* Berlin: Nicolai, 1981
HARTMANN, CHRISTINE. *Untersuchungen zum Kinderbild bei Otto Dix.* Münster: Lit, 1989
KARCHER, EVA. *Otto Dix 1891–1969: Leben und Werk.* Köln: B. Taschen, 1988
KIM, JUNG-HEE. *Frauenbilder von Otto Dix: Wirklichkeit und Selbstbekenntnis.* (Form und Interesse, Bd. 44 [i.e. 45]). Münster: Lit, 1994
KINKEL, HANS. *Die Toten und die Nackten: Beiträge zu Dix.* Berlin: H. Kinkel, 1991
LEHMANN, HANS-ULRICH. *Otto Dix: Die Zeichnungen im Dresdner Kupferstich-Kabinett: Katalog des Bestandes.* Dresden: Kupferstich-Kabinett des Staatlichen Kunstsammlungen, 1991
LÖFFLER, FRITZ. *Otto Dix: Bilder zur Bibel und zu Legenden, zu Vergänglichkeit und Tod.* Stuttgart: Belser, 1987
LÖFFLER, FRITZ. *Otto Dix: Leben und Werk.* Dresden: VEB Verlag der Kunst, 1960; Wien/München: Schroll, 1967; *Otto Dix: Life and Work.* New York/London: Holmes and Meier, 1982
LÖFFLER, FRITZ. *Otto Dix und der Krieg.* (Reclams Universal-Bibliothek, Bd. 1166). Leipzig: P. Reclam, 1986
LÜDECKE, HEINZ. *Otto Dix.* (Künstler der Gegenwart, Bd. 3). Dresden: VEB Verlag der Kunst, 1958
MCGREEVY, LINDA F. *The Life and Works of Otto Dix: German Critical Realist.* Ann Arbor, MI: UMI Research Press, 1981
MOSER, EVA, ed. *Otto Dix: Landschaften.* Friedrichshafen: R. Gessler, 1984
SCHMIDT, DIETHER. *Otto Dix im Selbstbildnis: ... und einer Sammlung von Schriften, Briefen und Gesprächen.* Berlin: Henschelverlag, 1978

SCHMIDT, JOHANN-KARL, ed. *Otto Dix: Bestandskatalog: Gemälde, Aquarelle, Pastelle, Zeichnungen, Holzschnitte, Radierungen, Lithographien.* Stuttgart: Galerie der Stadt Stuttgart, 1989
SCHMIDT, PAUL FERDINAND. *Otto Dix.* Köln: K. Nierendorf, 1923
SCHUBERT, DIETRICH. *Otto Dix in Selbstzeugnissen und Bilddokumenten.* (Rowohlts Monographien, Nr. 287). Reinbek bei Hamburg: Rowohlt, 1980
SCHULT, FRIEDRICH. *Barlach im Gespräch.* Elmar Jansen, ed. 3rd ed. Leipzig: Insel, 1989
SCHWARZ, BIRGIT. *Otto Dix: Grossstadt.* (Insel Taschenbuch, Nr. 1486). Frankfurt am Main: Insel, 1993
STROBEL, ANDREAS. *Otto Dix: Eine Malerkarriere der zwanziger Jahre.* Berlin: Reimer, 1996
TITTEL, LUTZ, ed. *Otto Dix: Die Friedrichshafener Sammlung: Bestandskatalog.* Friedrichshafen: Zeppelin-Museum. 1992
WOLFRAT, WILLI. *Otto Dix.* (Junge Kunst, Bd. 41). Leipzig: Klinkhardt & Biermann, 1924

Exhibition Catalogues
1960 Düsseldorf, Kunstmuseum. *Otto Dix: Gemälde, Aquarelle, Zeichnungen, Druckgraphik.* Heinz Peters, and Ernst Bickel
1961–1962 St. Gallen, Galerie "Im Erker". *Otto Dix: Der Krieg*
1966 Berlin, Galerie Nierendorf. *Otto Dix.* (Kunstblätter der Galerie Nierendorf; Nr. 10/11)
1966 Köln: Baukunst-Galerie. *Otto Dix: Ölgemälde, Aquarelle, Handzeichnungen, Radierungen, Lithographien: Retrospektiv-Ausstellung anlässlich des 75. Geburtsjahres*
1966 Stuttgart, Galerie der Stadt. *Otto Dix zum 75. Geburtstag: Gemälde, Zeichnungen und Druckgraphik aus Stuttgarter Museums- und Privatbesitz.* Eugen Keuerleber
1966–1967 Hamburg, Kunstverein; Frankfurt am Main, Kunstverein. *Otto Dix: Gemälde, Aquarelle, Zeichnungen, Graphik*
1966–1967 Wien, Graphische Sammlung Albertina. *Otto Dix zum 75. Geburtstag: Graphik*
1970 Aachen, Suermondt-Museum. *Otto Dix: Handzeichnungen, Graphik und Gemälde der Sammlung Fritz Niescher, Aachen*
1970 Paris, Centre culturel allemand, Goethe-Institut. *Otto Dix 1891–1969: aquarelles, dessins*
1971 Paris, Musée d'art moderne de la ville de Paris. *Otto Dix*

1971 Stuttgart, Galerie der Stadt. *Dix ... zum 80. Geburtstag: Gemälde, Aquarelle, Gouachen, Zeichnungen, Radierfolge Der Krieg*. 2nd enlarged ed. Stuttgart, 1972. Eugen Keuerleben
1972 Essen, Museum Folkwang; Frankfurt am Main, Kunstverein; Bielefeld, Kunsthalle. *Otto Dix: Aquarelle, Zeichnungen, Radierfolge "Der Krieg"*. Dieter Honisch, ed.
1976 Albstadt, Städtische Galerie. *Otto Dix: Handzeichnungen, Pastelle, Lithographien aus der Sammlung Walther Groz*. Otto Conzelmann
1977 Albstadt, Städtische Galerie. *Otto Dix, der Krieg: Radierungen, Zeichnungen*. Alfred Hagenlocher
1977 Hamburg, Kunstverein. *Otto Dix: Zeichnungen, Aquarelle, Grafiken, Kartons*. Uwe M. Schneede
1979 Chambéry, Musées d'art et d'histoire de Chambéry. *Otto Dix: dessins, pastels, aquarelles, gravures, lithographies de la collection des arts graphiques de la Städtische Galerie Alstadt*
1981–1982 Stuttgart, Galerie der Stadt. *Dix: Otto Dix, Menschenbilder, Gemälde, Aquarelle, Gouachen und Zeichnungen*. Eugen Keuerleber
1983 Düsseldorf, Galerie Remmert und Barth. *Otto Dix und die Düsseldorfer Künstlerszene 1920–1925*. Peter Barth
1985 Brussel, Palais des beaux-arts. *Otto Dix*
1985 München, Museum Villa Stuck. *Otto Dix 1891–1969*. Rainer Beck
1986 Düsseldorf, Galerie Michael Neumann. *Otto Dix: Werke der zwanziger Jahre: Aquarelle, Zeichnungen, Graphik*
1986 Genova, Centro per le arti visive e Museo d'arte contemporanea di Villa Croce. *Otto Dix*
1986 Karlsruhe, Staatliche Kunsthalle. *Werke von Otto Dix*. (Bilderhefte der Staatlichen Kunsthalle Karlsruhe, Nr. 11)
1987 Berlin, Staatliche Kunsthalle; Hannover, Kestner-Gesellschaft; Wien, Museum des 20. Jahrhunderts. *Otto Dix*. Serge Sabarsky, and Ralph Jentsch
1987 New York, Lafayette Parke Gallery. *Otto Dix, Eros and Death: Watercolors, Drawings and Prints*
1989 Stuttgart, Galerie der Stadt. *Otto Dix: Bestandskatalog*
1990 Villingen-Schwenningen, Städtische Galerie. *Otto Dix zum 99. Geburtstag: "Kinderwelt und Kinderbildnis"*. Wendelin Renn

1991 Albstadt, Städtische Galerie. *Otto Dix zum 100. Geburtstag: Zeichnungen, Pastelle, Aquarelle, Kartons, Druckgraphik, Glasfenster aus eigenen Beständen*. Alfred Hagenlocher, and Adolf Smitmans
1991 Düsseldorf, Galerie Remmert und Barth. *Otto Dix zum 100. Geburtstag: Graphiken der 20er Jahre*
1991 Gera, Kunstgalerie. *Grüsse aus dem Krieg: Die Feldpostkarten der Otto-Dix-Sammlung in der Kunstgalerie Gera*. [Herausgegeben anlässlich des 100. Geburtstages von Otto Dix]. Ulrike Rüdiger
1991 London, Tate Gallery. *Otto Dix 1891–1969*. Keith Hartley, ed
1991 Stuttgart, Galerie der Stadt; Berlin, Staatliche Museen Preussischer Kulturbesitz, Nationalgalerie. *Dix: Otto Dix zum 100. Geburtstag 1891–1991*. Wulf Herzogenrath, and Johann-Karl Schmidt
1991–1992 Berlin, Galerie Nierendorf. *Otto Dix zum hundertsten Geburtstag: Gemälde, Aquarelle, Zeichnungen, Druckgraphiken*. (Kunstblätter der Galerie Nierendorf, Bd. 53/54)
1991–1992 Gera, Kunstgalerie, Orangerie und Dix-Haus. *Otto Dix 1891–1991: Arbeiten auf Papier: Ausstellung zum 100. Geburtstag*. Ulrike Rüdiger
1991–1992 Wein, Graphische Sammlung Albertina. *Otto Dix zum 100. Geburtstag: Die Dresdner Sammlung, Graphik und Zeichnungen; abridged English ed. Edinburgh, Scottish National Gallery of Modern Art. Otto Dix: The Dresden Collection of Works on Paper* Hans-Ulrich Lehmann
1993 Bietigheim-Bissingen, Galerie Bayer. *Otto Dix: Gemälde, Aquarelle, Zeichnungen, Graphik*. Rudolf Bayer
1995 Passau, Museum Moderner Kunst, Stiftung Wörlen. *Otto Dix: Die frühen Jahre*. Serge Sabarsky
1995–1996 Albstadt, Städtische Galerie. *Otto Dix: Bilder der Bibel und andere christliche Themen*
1995–1996 Berlin, Kunsthandel Wolfgang Werner. *Otto Dix: Dame mit Nerz und Schleier: Aquarelle, Zeichnungen und Graphik um ein neu entdecktes Bild von 1920*. Maria Wegener, and Wolfgang Werner
1996 Chemnitz, Städtische Kunstsammlungen. *Otto Dix*
1996 Colmar, Musée d'Unterlinden. *Otto Dix et les maîtres anciens*. Rainer Beck, ed.
1996 Gera, Kunstsammlung. *Otto Dix: Zeichnungen, Druckgrafik*. Ulrike Rüdiger, ed.

Lyonel Feininger
Reference Bibliography
HESS, HANS. *Lyonel Feininger*. New York: H. Abrams, 1961, p. 319-344

Oeuvre Catalogues
PRASSE, LEONA E. *Lyonel Feininger: A Definitive Catalogue of his Graphic Work: Etchings, Lithographs, Woodcuts = Das graphische Werk: Radierungen, Lithographien, Holzschnitte*. Cleveland: Cleveland Museum of Art, Distributed by Case Reserve University Press, 1972

Books
CINTI, ITALO. *Lyonel Feininger*. Bologna: Tamari, 1962
DEUCHLER, FLORENS. *Lyonel Feininger: Sein Weg zum Bauhaus-Meister*. Leipzig: E.A. Seemann, 1996
FEININGER, LORE, ed. *Aus der Werkstatt Lyonels: Fünfundzwanzig Zeichnungen und Holzschnitte*. (Archivarion-Kunst-Bibliothek. Sonderdruck, Nr. 307). Berlin: Archivarion, Deutsche Archiv-Verlag, 1958
FEININGER, T. LUX. *Die Stadt am Ende der Welt*. München: Rütten und Loening, 1965; *The City at the Edge of the World*. New York/London: Praeger, 1965
HENTZEN, ALFRED, ed. *Lyonel Feininger: Aquarelle*. (Piper-Bücherei, Nr. 124). München: R. Piper, 1958
HESS, HANS. *Lyonel Feininger*. [Mit einem Oeuvre Katalog der Gemälde von Julia Feininger]. Stuttgart: W. Kohlhammer, 1959; London: Thames & Hudson, 1961; reprint, Stuttgart/Berlin, 1991
HÜNEKE, ANDREAS. *Lyonel Feininger*. (Maler und Werk). Dresden: VEB Verlag der Kunst, 1989
LANGNER, JOHANNES. *Lyonel Feininger: Segelschiffe*. (Werkmonographien zur bildenden Kunst, Nr. 76). Stuttgart: P. Reclam, 1962
LUCKHARDT, ULRICH. *Lyonel Feininger*. München/New York: Prestel, 1989
LUCKHARDT, ULRICH. *Lyonel Feininger, die Karikaturen und das zeichnerische Frühwerk: Der Weg der Selbstfindung zum unabhängigen Künstler: Mit einem Exkurs zu den Karikaturen von Emil Nolde und George Grosz*. (Beiträge zur Kunstwissenschaft, Bd. 10). München: Scaneg, 1987
MÄRZ, ROLAND. *Lyonel Feininger*. (Welt der Kunst). Berlin: Henschelverlag, 1981

NESS, JUNE L., ed. *Lyonel Feininger*. (Documentary Monographs in Modern Art). New York: Praeger, 1974
RUHMER, EBERHARD. *Lyonel Feininger: Zeichnungen, Aquarelle, Graphik*. München: Bruckmann, 1961
SCHEYER, ERNST. *Lyonel Feininger: Caricature and Fantasy*. Detroit: Wayne State University Press, 1964
SCHREYER, LOTHAR. *Lyonel Feininger: Dokumente und Visionen*. (Langen-Müllers kleine Geschenkbücher, 62). München: Langen- Müller, 1957
TOBIEN, FELICITAS. *Lyonel Feininger*. Kirchdorf/Inn: Berghaus, 1988; English ed. Avon, England: Artline Editions, 1989
WOLFRADT, WILLI. *Lyonel Feininger*. (Junge Kunst, Bd. 47). Leipzig: Klinkhardt & Biermann, 1924

Exhibition Catalogues
1959–1960 San Francisco Museum of Art; Minneapolis, Institute of Arts; Cleveland Museum of Art; Buffalo, Albright Art Gallery; Boston, Museum of Fine Arts; York; London. *Lyonel Feininger: Memorial Exhibition*. Hans Hess
1961 Hamburg, Kunstverein; Essen, Museum Folkwang; Baden-Baden, Staatliche Kunsthalle. *Lyonel Feininger 1871–1956: Gedächtnis-Ausstellung*. Hans Hess
1962 Dortmund, Museum am Ostwall. *Lyonel Feininger: Kleine Blätter*
1963 Berlin, Amerikahaus. *Lyonel Feininger: Karikaturen 1898–1910*
1964 Detroit Institute of Arts. *Lyonel Feininger: The Formative Years*
1964 Milano, Galleria del Levante. *Lyonel Feininger: acquarelli e disegni*
1965 Campione d'Italia, Galerie Roman Norbert Ketterer L. *Feininger: Gemälde, Aquarelle, Zeichnungen, Graphik*. Wenzel Nachbaur
1966 Pasadena Art Museum; Milwaukee Art Center; Baltimore, Museum of Art. *Lyonel Feininger 1871–1956: A Memorial Exhibition*
1968 London, Marlborough Fine Art. *Lyonel Feininger 1871–1956: Drawings and Watercolours*
1969 New York, Marlborough-Gerson Gallery. *Lyonel Feininger*
1971 Hamburg, Altonaer Museum. *Lyonel Feininger: Zeichnungen von Schiff und See*
1972 München, Karl und Faber. *Ausgewählte Graphik von Lyonel Feininger*
1972 New York, Associated Ame-

rican Artists. *Lyonel Feininger: Etchings, Lithographs and Woodcuts from the Estate of the Artist*
1973 München, Haus der Kunst; Zürich, Kunsthaus. *Lyonel Feininger 1871–1956*
1974 Chicago, Allan Frumkin Gallery. *Lyonel Feininger: Etchings, Drypoints, Lithographs, Drawings 1902–1924*
1974 New York, American Associated Artists. *Lyonel Feininger: A Collection of Rare Proofs of Woodcuts used as Letterheads from the Estate of the Artist*. Leona Prasse
1974 Paris: Berggruen. *Feininger: huiles, aquarelles et dessins*. (Collection Berggruen, 56). William S. Lieberman
1975 London, Achim Moeller. *Lyonel Feininger: Visions of City and Sea: Watercolours, Drawings, Paintings: A Tribute to the Late Hans Hess*. Irene Leake, ed.
1981 Hamburg, Museum für Kunst und Gerwerbe; Hannover, Wilhelm-Busch-Museum. *Lyonel Feininger: Karikaturen, Comic Strips, Illustrationen 1888–1915*
1982 Kiel, Kunsthalle und Schleswig-Holsteinischer Kunstverein. *Lyonel Feininger: Gemälde, Aquarelle und Zeichnungen, Druckgraphik*
1985 New York, Achim Moeller Fine Art. *Lyonel Feininger: Visions of City and Sea II*
1985 Quedlinburg, Lyonel-Feininger-Galerie. *Lyonel Feininger: Druckgraphik-Aquarelle*. Ingrid Wernecke, ed.
1985–1986 New York, Acquavella Galleries; Washington, D.C., The Phillips Collection. *Exhibition Lyonel Feininger*
1987 London, Marlborough Fine Art. *Lyonel Feininger: The Early Years 1889–1919: Watercolours and Drawings = Lyonel Feininger: Die Frühzeit 1889–1919*
1988 Dortmund, Galerie Utermann. *Lyonel Feininger*
1989 Köln: Galerie Gmurzynska. *Lyonel Feininger 1871–1956*
1990 München, Staatliche Graphische Sammlung München. *Lyonel Feininger: Aquarelle, Zeichnungen, Druckgraphik: Eigener Bestand und Schenkung Michal*. Cathrin Klingsöhr-Leroy
1990 New York, Achim Moeller Fine Art. *Lyonel Feininger: Figurative Drawings 1908–1912*. Simon Taylor
1991 Baden, Stiftung "Langmatt" Sidney und Jenny Brown. *Lyonel Feininger 1871–1956: Lokomotiven und Eisenbahnlandschaften: 40*

Zeichnungen und Skizzen 1901–1913. Florens Deuchler in Zusammenarbeit mit Achim Moeller Fine Art, New York
1991 Lugano, Museo cantonale d'arte. *Lyonel Feininger: la variante tematica e tecnica nello sviluppo del processo creativo*. Manuela Kahn-Rossi, and Marco Franciolli
1991 Milano, Ruggerini e Zonca. *Lyonel Feininger: acquarelli e disegni dal 1908 al 1955*. (Arte moderna e contemporanea, 3)
1991 Quedlinburg, Lyonel-Feininger-Galerie. *Lyonel Feininger und die Romantik*. Ingrid Wernecke, ed
1992 Chicago, Davis and Alfred Smart Museum of Art, University of Chicago. *Lyonel Feininger: Awarenenss, Recollection, and Nostalgia*. Reinhold Heller
1992 München, Galerie Thomas. *Lyonel Feininger: Gemälde, Aquarelle, Graphiken*. Gabriele Karpf, and Giannina Spargnapani
1992 Nürnberg, Germanisches Nationalmuseum; New York, Achim Moeller Fine Art; Paris, Grand Palais. *Feininger in Paris: Lyonel Feininger: Die Pariser Zeichnungen von 1892 bis 1911*. Florens Deuchler
1992 Nürnberg, Kunsthalle. *Lyonel Feininger: Städte und Küsten: Aquarelle, Zeichnungen, Druckgrafik*
1992 Regensburg, Museum Ostdeutsche Galerie; Bremen, Kunsthalle. *Lyonel Feininger, Erlebnis und Vision: Die Reisen an die Ostsee 1892–1935*. Werner Timm
1993–1994 Emden, Kunsthalle; Köln, Museum Ludwig; Weimar, Kunstsammlungen. *Lyonel Feininger, Natur-Notizen: Skizzen und Zeichnungen aus dem Busch-Reisinger Museum, Harvard University*. Andrea Firmenich, and Ulrich Luckhardt, eds
1994 Leipzig, Galerie Michael Beck. *Feininger: Arbeiten aus seiner Zeit in Weimar und Dessau*. Ute Eggeling
1995 Halle, Staatliche Galerie Moritzburg; Wuppertal, Von der Heydt-Museum. *Lyonel Feininger, Gelmeroda: Ein Maler und sein Motiv*. Wolfgang Büche
1995–1996 Ludwigsburg, Kunstverein. *Lyonel Feininger*
1995–1996 Ludwigsburg, Kunstverein; Chemnitz, Städtische Kunstsammlungen. *Lyonel Feininger: 200 Holzschnitte aus Privatbesitz*
1996 Hannover, Sprengel Museum. *Lyonel Feininger: Originale auf Papier und Druckgraphik aus*

dem Besitz des Sprengel Museum Hannover. Norbert Nobis

Conrad Felixmüller
Reference Bibliography
GLEISBERG, DIETER. *Conrad Felixmüller: Leben und Werk*. Dresden: VEB Verlag der Kunst, 1982, p. 288-296

Written Works
HERZOG, G.H., ed. *Conrad Felixmüller: Legenden 1912–1976*. Tübingen: Wasmuth, 1977
SÖHN, GERHART, ed. *Conrad Felixmüller, von ihm, über ihn: Texte von und über Conrad Felixmüller*. Düsseldorf: Edition GS, 1977

Oeuvre Catalogues
SÖHN, GERHART, ed. *Conrad Felixmüller: Das graphische Werk 1912–1974*. Düsseldorf: Graphik Salon Gerhart Söhn, 1975; supplement, *Conrad Felixmüller: Das graphische Werk 1975–1997: Und Ergänzungen zum Hauptkatlog 1912–1974*. Düsseldorf, 1980; 2nd rev. ed. *Conrad Felixmüller: Das graphische Werk 1912–1977*. Düsseldorf, 1987
SPIELMANN, HEINZ, ed. *Conrad Felixmüller: Monographie und Werkverzeichnis der Gemälde*. Köln: Wienand, 1996

Books
GABELENTZ, HANNS-CONON VON DER. *Conrad Felixmüller: Ein Beitrag zur Frage der Tafelmalerei*. 2nd ed. (Veröffentlichungen aus den Sammlungen der Stadt Altenburg/Thür, 1). Altenburg: Kulturamt der Stadt Altenburg, 1946
GLEISBERG, DIETER. *Conrad Felixmüller: Leben und Werk*. Dresden: VEB Verlag der Kunst, 1982
HECKMANNS, FRIEDRICH W. *Felixmüller: Buch der Holzschnitte*. Düsseldorf: Dehnen, 1985
HEINZ, HELLMUTH. *Conrad Felixmüller: Maler und Werk*. Dresden: VEB Verlag der Kunst, 1978
RAABE, PAUL. *Felixmüller: Grösse und Wandlungen des späten Expressionismus*. (Wege und Gestalten). Biberach an der Riss: K. Thomas, 1968
SCHERF, HELMUT. *Conrad Felixmüller*. (Farbige Gemäldewiedergaben). Leipzig: E.A. Seemann, 1959
VORBRODT, GÜNTER W. *Fünf Regensburg-Zeichnungen von Conrad Felixmüller aus dem Jahre 1916*. Regensburg: Fremdenverkehrsverein, 1971
WÄCHTER, BERNHARD. *Das kleine*

Holzschnitthuch von Conrad Felixmüller. Rudolstadt: Greifenverlag, 1958

Exhibition Catalogues
1962 Eisenach, Thüringer Museum. *Conrad Felixmüller, Berlin: Druckgrahik und Zeichnungen*. Helmut Scherf
1965 Berlin, Galerie Nierendorf. *Conrad Felixmüller*. (Kunstblätter der Galerie Nierendorf, Nr. 8)
1967 Eisenach, Thüringer Museum. *Conrad Felixmüller: Malerei*. Helmut Scherf, and Hanns-Conon von der Gabelentz
1970 Roma, Hermes-Studio d'arte. *Conrad Felixmüller: acquarelli, incisioni, xilografie, litografie dal 1918 al 1970*. Wolfgang Kobbe
1972 Altenburg, Staatliches Lindenau-Museum; Leipzig, Museum der bildenden Künste. *Conrad Felixmüller: Grafik aus sechs Jahrzehnten*. Dieter Gleisberg
1972 Kaiserslautern, Pfälzische Landesgewerbeanstalt. *Conrad Felixmüller zum 75. Geburtstag des Malers*
1973 Berlin, Nationalgalerie; Galerie Verein Berliner Künstler. *Conrad Felixmüller: Malerei und Aquarelle*
1975–1976 Dresden, Staatliche Kunstsammlungen Dresden, Gemäldegalerie Neue Meister; Berlin, Staatliche Museen zu Berlin, Kupferstichkabinett und Sammlung der Zeichnungen. *Conrad Felixmüller: Gemälde, Aquarelle, Zeichnungen, Druckgrafik*
1977 Düsseldorf, Graphik Salon Gerhart Söhn. *Conrad Felixmüller: Aquarelle, Zeichnungen, Graphik*
1978 Dortmund, Museum am Ostwall. *Conrad Felixmüller: Retrospektive*
1978 Wolfenbüttel, Stadt- und Kreisheimatmuseum. *Conrad Felixmüller 1897–1977*. R. Busch, and B. Schnabel
1978–1979 Dortmund, Museum am Ostwall; Wiesbaden, Nassauischer Kunstverein; Saarbrücken, Saarland-Museum, Moderne Galerie. *Conrad Felixmüller 1897–1977*
1979 Charlottesville, VA, University of Virginia Art Museum. *Conrad Felixmüller 1897–1977: Prints and Drawings from the Collection of Dr. Ernst and Anne Fischer*. Titus Felixmüller, and Steven Schuyler
1980–1981 Nürnberg, Archiv für Bildende Kunst am Germanischen Nationalmuseum. *Conrad Felixmüller: Werke und Dokumente*. (Werke und Dokumente, n.F., Bd.

4). [Mit zahlreichen Selbstzeugnissen, Erinnerungen und Briefen Felixmüllers]
1981 Hamburg, Interversa Gesellschaft für Beteiligungen. *Conrad Felixmüller 1897–1977: Gemälde, Aquarelle, Zeichnungen.* (88. Ausstellung). Leonore Stege
1982 Düsseldorf, Graphik Salon Gerhart Söhn. *Conrad Felixmüller 1897–1977: Aquarelle, Zeichnungen, Skulpturen, Graphik: Ausstellung zum 85. Geburtstag*
1982 Münster, Westfälisches Museumsamt. *Conrad Felixmüller: Gemälde, Aquarelle, Zeichnungen, Druckgrafik.* Hartmut John, ed.
1985 Berlin, Galerie Nierendorf. *Conrad Felixmüller.* (Kunstblätter der Galerie Nierendorf, Nr. 47)
1986 Düsseldorf, Kunstmuseum. *Conrad Felixmüller: Das druckgraphische Werk 1912 bis 1976 im Kunstmuseum Düsseldorf, Schenkung Titus and Luca Felixmüller.* Friedrich W. Heckmanns
1987 Düsseldorf, Galerie Remmert und Barth. *Conrad Felixmüller: Die Dresdner Jahre 1913–1933.* Peter Barth
1990 Schleswig-Holsteinisches Landesmuseum, Schloss Gottorf; Düsseldorf, Kunstmuseum; Braunschweig, Kunstverein; Halle, Staatliche Galerie Moritzburg. *Conrad Felixmüller: Gemälde, Aquarelle, Zeichnungen, Druckgraphik, Skulpturen.* Christian Rathke
1993 Hemmenhofen, Otto-Dix-Haus. Conrad Felixmüller: Zeichnungen, Aquarelle und Druckgraphik. (Marginalien, Heft 3). Friedrich W. Heckmanns
1994 Leicester, Leicestershire Museum and Art Gallery. *Conrad Felixmüller 1897–1977: Between Politics and the Studio.* Shulamith Behr, and Amanda Wadsley
1994 London, Courtauld Institute Galleries. *Conrad Felixmüller 1897–1977: Works on Paper.* Shulamith Behr
1997 Dresden, Staatliche Kunstsammlungen Dresden, Gemäldegalerie Neue Meister; Hannover, Sprengel Museum. *Conrad Felixmüller zum 100. Geburtstag*

George Grosz
Reference Bibliographies
FLAVELL, M. KAY. *George Grosz: A Biography.* New Haven, CT/London: Yale University Press, 1988, p. 341-346
LEWIS, BETH. *George Grosz: Art and Politics in the Weimar Republic.* Rev. ed. Princeton, NJ: Prince-

ton University Press, 1991, p. 271-325. [Selected publications through 1990 that reflect his reputation and work in Germany before 1933]

Written Works and Books of Drawings
Abrechnung folgt! 57 politische Zeichnungen. (Kleine revolutionäre Bibliothek, Bd. 10). Berlin: Malik, 1923; reprint, Frankfurt am Main: makol verlag, 1972; Bari: Dedalo libri, 1973; Barcelona: Editoral Gustavo Gili, 1977; London/New York: Allison and Busby, 1984
The Autobiography of George Grosz: A Small Yes and a Big No. Arnold J. Pomerans, trans. London/New York: Allison and Busby, 1982; *George Grosz: an Autobiography.* Nora Hodges, trans. New York: Macmillan, 1983
DENKER, KLAUS PETER, ed. George Grosz: Ach knallige Welt, du Lunapark: Gesammelte Gedichte. München/Wien: C. Hanser, 1986
Ecce homo. Berlin: Malik, 1923; reprint, New York: Brusell and Brusell, 1965
Das Gesicht der herrschenden Klasse: 55 politische Zeichnungen. (Kleine revolutionäre Bibliothek, Bd. 4). Berlin: Malik, 1921; 3d rev. ed., Nov. 1921; reprint, [S.l.]: De Vrije, 1970; Frankfurt am Main: makol verlag, 1972; Milano: Biblioteca Universale Rizzoli, 1974; Barcelona: Editorial Gustavo Gili, 1977; London/New York: Allison and Busby, 1984
Die Gezeichneten: 60 Blätter aus 15 Jahren. Berlin: Malik, 1930; reprint, New York: Dover, 1971
GROSZ, GEORGE, and WIELAND HERZFELDE. *Die Kunst ist in Gefahr.* (Malik-Bücherei, Bd. 3). Berlin: Malik, 1925; Schneede, Uwe M., ed. *Die zwanziger Jahre: Manifeste und Dokumente deutscher Künstler.* Köln: Dumont, 1979, p. 61-64, 126-37. *Art is in Danger!* Paul Gorrell, trans. (Art on the Line, no. 5). Willimantic, CT/New York: Curbstone Press, 1987
HARTLEB, RENATE, ed. *George Grosz: Eintrittsbillett zu meinem Gehirnzirkus: Erinnerungen, Schriften, Briefe.* Herbert Knust, and Renate di Pol, trans. Leipzig: G. Kiepenheuer, 1989
HERZFELDE, WIELAND, and HANS MARQUARDT, eds, *Pass auf! Hier kommt Grosz: Bilder, Rhythmen und Gesänge 1915–1918.* Leipzig: P. Reclam, 1981
A Little Yes and a Big No: The Autobiography of George Grosz. Lola

Sachs Dorin, trans. New York: The Dial Press, 1946
Ein kleines Ja und ein grosses Nein: Sein Leben von ihm selbst erzählt. Hamburg: Rowohlt, 1955; unabridged ed. Hamburg, 1974; *Een klein Ja, Een Gjroot Nee.* Amsterdam: Uitgeverij de Arbeiderspers, 1978; *Un Petit Oui et un grand Non.* Nîmes: Éditions J. Chambon, 1990; *Un piccolo Si un grande No.* Milano: Longanesi, 1948; 2nd ed., 1975
Knust, Herbert, ed. *George Grosz: Briefe 1913–1959.* Reinbek bei Hamburg: Rowohlt, 1979
Mit Pinsel und Schere: 7 Materialisationen. Berlin: Malik, 1922

Oeuvre Catalogues
DÜCKERS, ALEXANDER. *George Grosz: Das druckgraphische Werk.* Frankfurt am Main/Berlin: Propyläen, 1979; 1st ed. in English, rev. and with a reprint of the original German text. San Francisco: A. Wofsy Fine Arts, 1996

Books
ANDERS, GÜNTHER. *George Grosz.* (Die kleinen Bücher der Arche). Zürich: Die Arche, 1961
BALLO, FERDINANDO, ed. *Grosz.* (Documenti d'Arte contemporanea, n. 3). Milano: Rosa e Ballo, 1946
BAUER, JOHN I.H. *George Grosz.* New York: Macmillan, and London: Thames and Hudson, 1954
BAZALGETTE, LÉON. *George Grosz: l'homme et l'oeuvre.* Paris: Les Ecrivains Réunis, 1926
BITTNER, HERBERT, ed. *George Grosz.* New York: Arts, 1960; Köln: DuMont Schauberg, 1961; London: P. Owen, 1962
BÜLOW, KJELD. *George Grosz: A Bibliography and other Check Lists.* Kopenhagen: The Booktrader, 1993
DESHONG, ANDREW. *The Theatrical Designs of George Grosz.* Ann Arbor, MI: UMI Research Press, 1982
FISCHER, LOTHAR. *George Grosz in Selbstzeugnissen und Bilddokumenten.* (Rowohlts Monographien, 241). Reinbek bei Hamburg: Rowohlt, 1976
FLAVELL, M. KAY. *George Grosz: A Biography.* New Haven, CT/London: Yale University Press, 1988
HESS, HANS. *George Grosz.* London: Studio Vista, 1974
HOFBAUER, IMRE. *George Grosz.* London: Nicholson and Watson, 1948

HOFFMANN-CURTIUS, KATHRIN. *George Grosz: John der Frauenmörder.* Stuttgart: G. Hatje, 1993
KANE, MARTIN. *Weimar Germany and the Limits of Political Art: A Study of the Work of George Grosz and Ernst Toller.* Tayport, Scotland: Hutton Press, 1987
KRANZFELDER, IVO. *George Grosz 1893–1959.* Köln: B. Taschen, 1994
LANG, LOTHAR, *George Grosz.* Berlin: Henschelverlag, 1966
LANG, LOTHAR. "*George-Grosz-Bibliographie*". In: *Marginalien, Zeitschrift für Buchkunst und Bibliophilie,* Heft 30 (Juli 1968)
LEWIS, BETH. *George Grosz: Art and Politics in the Weimar Republic.* Madison: University of Wisconsin Press, 1971; rev. ed. Princeton, NJ: Princeton University Press, 1991
McCLOSKEY, BARBARA. *George Grosz and the Communist Party: Art and Radicalism in Crisis 1918–1936.* Princeton, NJ: Princeton University Press, 1997
MYONOA (SALOMO FRIEDLAENDER). *George Grosz.* (Künstler der Gegenwart, Bd. 3). Dresden: R. Kaemmerer, 1922; reprint, Frankfurt am Main: makol verlag, 1975
NEUGEBAUER, ROSAMUNDE. *George Grosz: Macht und Ohnmacht satirischer Kunst: Die Graphikfolgen "Gott mit uns", Ecce homo und Hintergrund.* Berlin: Gebr. Mann, 1993
RAY, MARCEL. *George Grosz.* (Peintres et sculpteurs). Paris: G. Crès, 1927; first German ed. Dirk Heisserer, ed. and trans. Berlin: Das Arsenal, 1991
SABARSKY, SERGE. *George Grosz: The Berlin Years.* New York: Rizzoli, 1985
SAHL, HANS, ed. *George Grosz: Heimatliche Gestalten.* Frankfurt am Main: Fischer, 1966
SCHNEEDE, UWE M. *George Grosz: Der Künstler in seiner Gesellschaft.* (DuMont Kunst-Taschenbücher, 32). Köln: M. DuMont Schauberg, 1975; 2nd ed. Köln: DuMont, 1977; *George Grosz: The Artist in His Society.* Robert and Rita Kimber, trans. Woodbury, NY/London: Barron's, 1985
SCHNEEDE, UWE M., ed. *George Grosz: Leben und Werk.* Stuttgart: G. Hatje, 1975; *George Grosz: His Life and Work.* New York: Universe Books, and London: G. Fraser, 1979
TAVOLATO, ITALO. *George Grosz.* (Collection "Les artistes nouveaux"). Roma: Valori Plastici, 1924

WOLFRADT, WILLI. *George Grosz.* (Junge Kunst, Bd. 21). Leipzig: Klinkhardt und Biermann, 1921

Exhibition Catalogues
1962 Berlin, Akademie der Künste. *George Grosz.* Erwin Piscator, Walter Mehring, and Friedrich Ahlers-Hestermann
1962–1963 Berlin, Galerie Meta Nierendorf. *Ohne Hemmung: Gesicht und Kehrseite der Jahre 1914–1924.* Willi Wolfradt
1963 New York, Forum Gallery. *George Grosz 1893–1959: Berlin Period 1912–1932.* Hans Hess
1963 York, City Art Gallery; London, Arts Council Gallery; Bristol, City Art Gallery. *George Grosz 1893–1959.* Hans Hess
1964 Beverly Hills, Paul Kantor Gallery. *George Grosz: Drawings and Watercolors*
1965 Wien, Graphische Sammlung Albertina; Linz, Neue Galerie der Stadt, Wolfgang Gurlitt Museum; Graz, Neue Galerie am Landesmuseum Joanneum. *George Grosz 1893–1959.* Walter Koschatzky, Walter Kasten, and Erwin Piscator
1966 Paris, Galerie Claude Bernard. *George Grosz: dessins et aquarelles*
1968 New York, Peter Deitsch Fine Arts. *George Grosz 1893–1959: A Selection of Fifty Early Drawings from 1910–1920.* Catalogue no. 11
1969 Stuttgart, Württembergischer Kunstverein. *George Grosz.* Uwe M. Schneede
1970 Eindhoven, Van Abbemuseum. *Tekeningen van George Grosz.* Jaap Bremer, and Hein Reedijk
1970 Milano, Galleria del Levante. *George Grosz.* Catalogue no. 4. Emilio Bertonati
1971 Berlin-Dahlem, Staatliche Museen Preussischer Kulturbesitz, Kupferstichkabinett. *George Grosz: Frühe Druckgraphik: Sammelwerke, illustrierte Bücher 1914–1923.* Alexander Dückers
1971 Parma, Istituto di Storia dell'Arte, Università di Parma. *George Grosz.* [An exhibition circulated by the Museum of Modern Art, New York]
1975–1977 Hamburg, Kunstverein; Frankfurt am Main, Kunstverein; Braunschweig, Kunstverein; Münster, Landesmuseum; Wien, Museum des 20. Jahrhunderts; Karlsruhe, Badischer Kunstverein; Wuppertal, Von der Heydt-Museum; Berlin, Haus am Waldsee. *George Grosz: Leben und Werk.* Uwe M. Schneede, ed.

1977 Berlin, Staatliche Museen zu Berlin, Kupferstichkabinett und Sammlung der Zeichnungen, Grosz-Kabinett in der Nationalgalerie. *George Grosz.* Hans Ebert
1978 Los Angeles County Museum of Art; [Also shown at the Goethe Institutes in the USA and Canada]. *George Grosz 1893–1959: Drawings, Water-Colors, Photos, Books.* Walter Huder
1978–1979 Washington, D.C., Hirschhorn Museum and Sculpture Garden. *George Grosz.* Frank Gettings
1986–1987 Hamburg, Kunsthalle; München, Museum Villa Stuck; Hannover, Kestner-Gesellschaft; Tel Aviv Museum. *George Grosz: Die Berliner Jahre.* Serge Sabarsky
1990 Cambridge, MA, Busch-Reisinger Museum; Los Angeles County Museum of Art. *Envisioning America: Prints, Drawings, and Photographs by George Grosz and His Contemporaries 1915–1933.* Beeke Sell Tower
1990 New York, Soufer Gallery. *George Grosz*
1992 Valencia, IVAM Centre Julio González. *George Grosz: obra gráfica: los años de Berlin*
1993 Cambridge, MA, Busch-Reisinger Museum. *The Sketchbooks of George Grosz.* Peter Nisbet, ed.
1993 Hamburg, Kunsthalle. *"Im Blickfeld": George Grosz, John der Frauenmörder.* Uwe Schneede, ed.
1993 Passau, Museum Moderner Kunst, Stiftung Wörlen. *George Grosz: Die Berliner Jahre: Zeichnungen und Aquarelle.* Serge Sabarsky
1994–1995 Berlin, Neue Nationalgalerie; Düsseldorf, Kunstsammlung Nordrhein-Westfalen. *George Grosz: Berlin, New York.* Peter-Klaus Schuster, ed.
1997 London, Royal Academy of Arts.
1997 Venezia, Peggy Guggenheim Collection; Madrid, Museo Thyssen-Bornemisza. *George Grosz: Die Berliner Jahre 1893–1933.* Ralph Jentsch, ed.

Erich Heckel
Reference Bibliographies
VOGT, PAUL. *Erich Heckel.* Recklinghausen: A. Bongers, 1965, p. 329-333
ZDENEK, FELIX, ed. *Erich Heckel 1883–1970: Gemälde, Aquarelle, Zeichnungen und Graphik.* Exhibition catalogue. München: Prestel, 1983, p. 233-235

Oeuvre Catalogues
DUBE, ANNEMARIE, and WOLF-DIETER DUBE. *Das graphische Werk.* 2 vols. New York: E. Rathenau, 1964-65; 2nd ed., 3 vols. New York, 1974
RATHENAU, ERNEST. *Erich Heckel: Handzeichnungen.* New York: E. Rathenau, 1973
VOGT, PAUL. *Erich Heckel.* Recklinghausen: A. Bongers, 1965. [Monographie mit dem "Oeuvre-Katalog der Gemälde, Wandmalerei und Plastik"]

Books
BUCHHEIM, LOTHAR-GÜNTHER, ed. *Erich Heckel: Holzschnitte aus den Jahren 1905–1956.* Feldafing: Buchheim, 1957
Erich Heckel. (Graphik der Gegenwart, Bd. 1). Berlin: Euphorion, 1931
GEISSLER, HANS. *Erich Heckel zum Gedenken.* Hemmenhofen: Geissler, 1980
HENZE, ANTON. *Erich Heckel: Leben und Werk.* Stuttgart: Belser, 1983
JÄHNER, HORST. *Erich Heckel.* (Maler und Werk). Dresden: VEB Verlag der Kunst, 1975
LUCKE, MECHTHILD, and ANDREAS HÜNEKE. *Erich Heckel: Lebensstufen: Die Wandbilder im Angermuseum zu Erfurt.* Dresden: VEB Verlag der Kunst, 1992
KÖHN, HEINZ. *Erich Heckel: Aquarelle und Zeichnungen.* München: Bruckmann, 1959
MOELLER, MAGDALENA M. *Erich Heckel: Aquarelle, Zeichnungen, Druckgraphik aus dem Brücke-Museum Berlin.* München: Hirmer, 1991
RAVE, PAUL ORTWIN. *Erich Heckel.* (Kunst unserer Zeit, Heft 1). Berlin: K. Lemmer, 1949
THORMAEHLEN, LUDWIG. *Erich Heckel.* (Junge Kunst, Bd. 58). Berlin: Klinkhardt und Biermann, 1931

Exhibition Catalogues
1963 Essen, Museum Folkwang. *Erich Heckel zur Vollendung des achten Lebensjahrzehntes.* Paul Vogt
1963 München, Staatliche Graphische Sammlung. *Erich Heckel: Holzschnitte, Lithographien, Radierungen aus den Jahren 1903–1963*
1966 Campione d'Italia, Galerie Roman Norbert Ketterer; München, Galerie Wolfgang Ketterer; Hannover, Kunstverein. *Ausstel-*

lung Erich Heckel: Gemälde, Aquarelle, Zeichnungen. Wenzel Nachbaur
1968 Chicago, Allan Frumkin Gallery. *Erich Heckel: Woodcuts, Etchings, Lithographs*
1968 Karlsruhe, Staatliche Kunsthalle. *Erich Heckel: Gemälde, Aquarelle und Zeichnungen im Besitz der Staatlichen Kunsthalle.* (Bilderhefte der Staatlichen Kunsthalle Karlsruhe, Nr. 5). Johann Eckart von Borries
1969 Cambridge, MA, Gropper Art Gallery. *The Graphic Work of Erich Heckel: Woodcuts, Lithographs, Etchings from 1907–1968*
1970–1971 Hamburg, Altonaer Museum. *Erich Heckel 1883–1970: Aquarelle und Zeichnungen aus Norddeutschland.* Dorothy V. Hülsen
1973 Campione d'Italia, Galerie Roman Norbert Ketterer. *Erich Heckel zum 90. Geburtstag: Gemälde, Aquarelle, Zeichnungen, Graphik*
1973 Hamburg, Altonaer Museum. *Erich Heckel 1883–1970: Gemälde, Aquarelle, Graphik, Jahresblätter, gemalte Postkarten und Briefe aus dem Besitz des Museums.* Christine Knupp
1974 London, Achim Moeller. *Ernst Ludwig Kirchner, Erich Heckel: Selected Watercolours, Drawings and Graphics*
1974 Stuttgart, Staatsgalerie. *Erich Heckel: Farbholzschnitte, Zeichnungen, Aquarelle: Ausstellung zum 90. Geburtstag.* Gunter Thiem
1976 Berlin, Brücke-Museum. *Erich Heckel: Gemälde, Aquarelle und Zeichnungen aus dem Nachlass des Künstlers*
1976 Tübingen, Kunsthalle; Bielefeld, Kulturhistorisches Museum. *Erich Heckel: Zeichnungen*
1979 Hamburg, BAT Haus. *Erich Heckel 1883–1970: Das Menschenbild in der Grafik.* Gerhard Wietek
1980 Schleswig-Holsteinisches Landesmuseum, Schloss Gottorf. *Erich Heckel im Schleswig-Holsteinisches Landesmuseum.* Christian Rathke
1983 Berlin, Brücke-Museum. *Erich Heckel 1883–1970: Der frühe Holzschnitt: Zum Gedenken an den 100. Geburtstag des Künstlers.* Leopold Reidemeister
1983 Berlin, Galerie Pels-Leusden. *Erich Heckel zum 100. Geburtstag: Gemälde, Aquarelle, Handzeichnungen und Graphik*
1983 Essen, Museum Folkwang; München, Haus der Kunst. *Erich Heckel 1883–1970: Gemälde, Aqua-*

relle, Zeichnungen und Graphik. Felix Zdenek
1983 Würzburg, Städtische Galerie. *Erich Heckel 1883–1970: Aquarelle, Zeichnungen: Ausstellung zum 100. Geburtstag des Malers*
1983–1984 Karlsruhe, Städtische Galerie im Prinz-Max-Palais; Aschaffenburg, Schlossmuseum; Regensburg, Städtische Galerie; Frankfurt am Main, Jahrhunderthalle Hoechst. *Zeichnungen, Aquarelle*. Vol. 1; *Erich Heckel und sein Kreis: Dokumente, Fotos, Briefe, Schriften*. Vol. 2. Karlheinz Gabler
1985 Braunschweig, Kunstverein. *Erich Heckel*. Wilhelm Bojescul
1985 Los Angeles County Museum of Art. *Prints by Erich Heckel and Karl Schmidt-Rottluff: A Centenary Celebration*
1987 Campione d'Italia, Galleria Henze. *Das Thema Landschaft im Werk von Erich Heckel und Ernst Ludwig Kirchner*. Wolfgang Henze
1988 Köln: Galerie Glöckner. *Erich Heckel: Aquarelle, Graphik*
1988–1989 Reutlingen, Hans Thoma-Gesellschaft; Wiesbaden, Kunstverein Wiesbaden. *Erich Heckel 1883–1970: Aquarelle*
1995 Bietigheim-Bissingen, Städtische Galerie. *Erich Heckel: Die frühen Jahre*. Serge Sabarsky
1996 Saarbrücken, Saarland-Museum. *Erich Heckel*

Alexei Jawlensky
Reference Bibliographies
CHIAPPINI, RUDY, ANGELICA JAWLENSKY BIANCONI, and LUCIA PIERONI-JAWLENSKY, eds. *Alexej von Jawlensky*. Exhibition catalogue. Milano: Charta, 1995, p. 231-251
JAWLENSKY, MARIA, LUCIA PIERONI-JAWLENSKY, and ANGELICA JAWLENSKY, eds. *Alexej von Jawlensky: Catalogue Raisonné of the Oil Paintings*. London: Sotheby's, 1991–1992. Vol. 1, p. 517-519; vol. 2, p. 554-556

Oeuvre Catalogues
Alexej von Jawlensky: Catalogue Raisonné of the Oil Paintings. Vol. 1, 1890–1914; vol. 2, 1914–1933. Maria Jawlensky, Lucia Pieroni-Jawlensky, and Angelica Jawlensky. München: C. H. Beck, 1991–1992; English ed. London: Sotheby's, 1991–1992

Books
RATHKE, EWALD. *Alexej Jawlensky*. Hanau: Peters, 1968
ROSENBACH, DETLEV. *Alexej von*

Jawlensky: Leben und druckgraphisches Werk. Hannover: Edition Rosenbach, 1985
SCHULTZE, JÜRGEN. *Alexej Jawlensky*. (DuMont's neue Kunst Reihe). Köln: DuMont Schauberg, 1970
WEILER, CLEMENS. *A. Jawlensky: Köpfe, Gesichte, Meditationen*. Hanau: H. Peters, 1970; *A. Jawlensky: Heads, Faces, Meditations*. Edith Küstner, and J.A. Underwood, trans. New York: Praeger, 1970; London: Pall Mall Press, 1971
WEILER, CLEMENS. *Alexej Jawlensky*. Köln: M. DuMont Schauberg, 1959. [Mit "Katalog der Gemälde", p. 225-283]
WEILER, CLEMENS. *Alexej von Jawlensky: Der Maler und Mensch*. Wiesbaden: Limes, 1955
WEILER, CLEMENS. *Alexej von Jawlensky: Gemälde*. Feldafing: Buchheim, 1958

Exhibition Catalogues
1960 London, Redfern Gallery. *Jawlensky 1864–1941*
1960 Los Angeles, Dalzell Hatfield Galleries. *Alexei von Jawlensky 1864–1941: Oil Paintings 1906–1937*
1963 Genève, Galerie Krugier. *A. Jawlensky*
1964 Pasadena Art Museum. *Alexei Jawlensky: A Centennial Exhibition*. James T. Demetrion
1965 New York, Leonard Hutton Galleries. *A Centennial Exhibition of Paintings by Alexei Jawlensky 1864–1941*
1966 Irvine, Art Gallery, University of California; Riverside, Art Gallery, University of California. *Jawlensky and the Serial Image*. Shirley Hopps, and John Coplans
1967 Hamburg, Kunstverein. *Jawlensky*. Ewald Rathke
1978 München, Galerie Thomas. *Alexei Jawlensky, unbekannte Arbeiten: Zeichnungen, Aquarelle, Miniaturen, Bilder*
1983 München, Städtische Galerie im Lenbachhaus; Baden-Baden, Staatliche Kunsthalle. *Alexei Jawlensky 1864–1941*. Armin Zweite
1983–1984 Wiesbaden, Museum Wiesbaden. *Alexei Jawlensky: Zeichnung, Graphik, Dokumente*. Bernd Fäthke
1989–1990 Locarno, Pinacoteca Comunale Casa Rusca; Emden, Kunsthalle in Emden, Stiftung Henri Nannen. *Alexei Jawlensky*. Rudy Chiappini
1990 München, Galerie Thomas. *Alexei von Jawlensky: Eine Ausstellung zum 50. Todesjahr*. Gabriele

Karpf, and Christiane Schulze
1990 Pasadena, Norton Simon Museum. *Jawlensky*
1991 Milano, Galleria del Naviglio. *Alexei Jawlensky: disegni e pitture 1900–1936*
1991 Wiesbaden, Museum Wiesbaden. *Alexei von Jawlensky zum 50. Todesjahr: Gemälde und graphische Arbeiten*. Volker Rattemeyer, ed.
1992 Madrid, Fundacíon Juan March. *Alexej von Jawlensky*. Angelica Jawlensky
1993 Arles, Espace Van Gogh. *Alexei von Jawlensky*. Michèle Moutashar, and Alain Charron
1994 Bietigheim-Bissingen, Städtische Galerie. *Alexei von Jawlensky: Gemälde, Aquarelle, Zeichnugen*. Herbert Eichhorn
1994 Rotterdam, Museum Boymans-van-Beuningen. *Alexei von Jawlensky*. Volker Rattemeyer, and Talitha Schoon
1995 Genève, Musée Rath. *Alexei von Jawlensky*
1995 Milano, Palazzo Reale. *Alexei von Jawlensky*. Rudy Chiappini, Angelica Jawlensky Bianconi, and Lucia Pieroni-Jawlensky
1995 Murnau, Schlossmuseum. *Alexei von Jawlensky: Frühe Porträts 1908–1913*. Brigitte Salmen, ed.

Wassily Kandinsky
Reference Bibliographies
HAHL-KOCH, JELENA. *Kandinsky*. New York: Rizzoli, 1993: p. 413-425
ROETHEL, HANS K. *Kandinsky: Catalogue Raisonné of the Oil Paintings*. London: Sotheby's, 1984, vol. 2, p. 1071-1082

Written Works and Correspondence
Über das Geistige in der Kunst. München: R. Piper, 1912; 2nd ed. München, April 1912; 3rd ed. München, Herbst 1912; 4th-6th ed. Bern: Benteli, 1952–1959; *The Art of Spiritual Harmony*. Michael T.H. Sadler, trans. London: Constable, 1914; reprint, *On the Spiritual in Art*. Hilla Rebay, ed. and trans. New York: Solomon R. Guggenheim Foundation for the Museum of Non-Objective Painting, 1946; *Concerning the Spiritual in Art*. New York: Dover, 1977
Der Blaue Reiter. Wassily Kandinsky, and Franz Marc, eds. München: R. Piper, 1912; 2nd ed. München, 1914; New documentary ed. Klaus Lankheit, ed. München: R. Piper, 1965; *The Blaue Reiter Al-*

manac. New documentary ed. New York: Viking Press, 1974
Klänge. München: R. Piper, 1913; *Sounds*. Elizabeth R. Napier, trans. New Haven, CT: Yale University Press, 1981
Kandinsky 1901–1913. Berlin: Der Sturm, 1913. [Includes four essays by Kandinsky: "Rückblicke," "Komposition 4," "Komposition 6," and "Das Bild mit Weissem Rand"]; reprint of *Rückblicke*, *Rückblick*. Ludwig Grote, ed. Baden-Baden: W. Klein, 1955; Bern: Benteli, 1977.
Punkt und Linie zu Fläche: Beitrag zur Analyse der malerischen Elemente. Walter Gropius, and László Moholy-Nagy, eds. (Bauhausbücher, 9). München: A. Langen, 1926; 2nd ed. 1928; 3rd-4th ed. Bern: Benteli, 1955–1959; *Point and Line to Plane: Contribution to the Analysis of the Pictorial Elements*. Howard Dearstyne, and Hilla Rebay, trans. New York: Museum of Non-Objective Painting, 1947; reprint, New York: Dover, 1979
BILL, MAX, ed. *Kandinsky: Essays über Kunst und Künstler*. Stuttgart: G. Hatje, 1955; 2nd ed. Bern: Benteli, 1963
BOUILLON, JEAN PAUL, ed. *Regards sur le passé et autres textes 1912–1922*. Paris: Hermann, 1974
HAHL-KOCH, JELENA, ed. *Arnold Schönberg, Wassily Kandinsky: Briefe, Bilder und Dokumente einer aussergewöhnlichen Begegnung*. Salzburg/Wien: Residenz, 1980; *Arnold Schoenberg, Wassily Kandinsky: Letters, Pictures, and Documents*. John C. Crawford, trans. London/Boston: Faber and Faber, 1984
HOBERG, ANNEGRET, ed. *Wassily Kandinsky and Gabriele Münter: Letters and Reminiscences 1902–1914*. Ian Robson, trans. München/New York: Prestel, 1994
LANKHEIT, KLAUS, ed. *Wassily Kandinsky, Franz Marc, Briefwechsel*. München: R. Piper, 1983
LINDSAY, KENNETH C., and PETER VERGO, ed. *Kandinsky: Complete Writings on Art*. 2 vols. (Documents of Twentieth Century Art). Boston, MA: G.K. Hall, 1982
ROETHEL, HANS K., und JELENA HAHL-KOCH, ed. *Kandinsky: Die gesammelten Schriften*. Bd. 1, Autobiographische, ethnographische und juristische Schriften. Bern: Benteli, 1980
SERS, PHILIPPE, ed. *Wassily Kandinsky: Ecrits complets*. Paris: Denoël-

Gonthier, vol. 2, 1970; vol. 3, 1975 (vol. 1 forthcoming in 1994)

SERS, PHILIPPE, ed. *Wassily Kandinsky: Tutti gli scritti*. 2 vols. Libero Sosio, trans. Milano: Feltrinelli, 1973–1974

SONG, HAI-YOUNG. *Wassily Kandinsky: Von den frühen Landschaften zur Komposition 1901–1911*. (Theorie und Forschung, Bd. 370). Regensburg: S. Roderer, 1995

Oeuvre Catalogues

BARNETT, VIVIAN ENDICOTT. *Kandinsky: Werkverzeichnis der Aquarelle*. Vol. 1, 1900–1921; vol. 2, 1922–1944. München: C.H. Beck, 1992–1994; *Kandinsky Watercolors: Catalogue Raisonné*. Ithaca, NY: Cornell University Press, 1992–1994

ROETHEL, HANS K. *Das Graphische Werk*. Köln: DuMont Schauberg, 1970

ROETHEL, HANS K., and JEAN K. BENJAMIN. *Kandinsky: Catalogue Raisonné of the Oil Paintings*. Vol. 1, 1900–1915; vol. 2, 1916–1944. London: Sotheby's, 1982–1984

Books

BARNETT, VIVIAN ENDICOTT. *Das bunte Leben: Wassily Kandinsky im Lenbachhaus*. Köln: DuMont, 1996; *Vasily Kandinsky: A Colorful Life: The Collection of the Lenbachhaus*. Hugh Beyer, John Bjrogden, and Claudia Spinner, trans. New York: Distributed by H. Abrams, 1996

BARNETT, VIVIAN ENDICOTT, and ARMIN ZWEITE, ed. *Kandinsky: Watercolors and Drawings*. München/New York: Prestel, 1992

BARNETT, VIVIAN ENDICOTT. *Kandinsky at the Guggenheim*. New York: Solomon R. Guggenheim Museum, 1983

BECKS-MALORNY, ULRIKE. *Wassily Kandinsky 1966–1944: Aufbruch zur Abstraktion*. Köln: B. Taschen, 1994

BILL, MAX, *et al*. *Wassily Kandinsky*. Paris: Maeght Éditeur, 1951

BOWLT, JOHN E., and ROSE-CAROL WASHTON LONG, eds. *The Life of Vasilii Kandinsky in Russian Art: A Study of "On the Spiritual in Art"*. Newtonville, MA: Oriental Research Partners, 1980

CASSOU, JEAN. *Gegenklänge: Aquarelle und Zeichnungnen*. Köln: DuMont Schauberg, 1960

DEBRUNNER, HUGO. *Wir entdecken Kandinsky*. (Schriftenreihe "In medias res"). Zürich: Origo, 1947

DI SAN LAZZARO, G., ed. *Hommage à Wassily Kandinsky*. Paris: XXᵉ Siècle, 1975; *Homage to Wassily Kandinsky*. [Special issue of the XXe siècle review]. Wade Stevenson, trans. New York: L. Amiel, 1975

DZIERSK, HANS-MARTIN. *Abstraktion und Zeitlosigkeit: Wassily Kandinsky und die Tradition der Malerei*. Ostfildern: Edition Tertium, 1995

EICHNER, JOHANNES. *Kandinsky und Gabriele Münter*. München: Bruckmann, 1957

ELLER-RÜTER, and ULRIKE-MARIA. *Kandinsky: Bühnenkomposition und Dichtung als Realisation seines Synthese-Konzepts*. (Studien zur Kunstgeschichte, Bd. 57). Hildesheim/New York: G. Olms, 1990

GOLLEK, ROSEL. *Wassily Kandinsky: Frühe Landschaften*. München: R. Piper, 1978

GROHMANN, WILL. *Farben und Klänge: Erste Folge (Aquarelle)*. (Der Silberne Quell, 19). Baden-Baden: W. Klein, 1955

GROHMANN, WILL. *Farben und Klänge: Zweite Folge (Ölbilder)*. (Der Silberne Quell, 25). Baden-Baden: W. Klein, 1956

GROHMANN, WILL. *Wassily Kandinsky: Leben und Werk*. Köln: M. DuMont Schauberg, 1958; *Wassily Kandinsky: Life and Work*. New York: H. Abrams, 1958

HAHL-KOCH, JELENA. *Wassily Kandinsky*. Stuttgart: G. Hatje, 1992; *Kandinsky*. Karin Brown, Ralph Harratz, and Katharine Harrison, trans. New York: Rizzoli, and London: Thames and Hudson, 1993

HANFSTAENGL, ERIKA. *Wassily Kandinsky: Zeichnungen und Aquarelle: Katalog in der Sammlung der Städtischen Galerie im Lenbachhaus München*. (Materialien zur Kunst des 19. Jahrhunderts, Bd. 13). München: Prestel, 1974

HIRSCHFELD, SUSAN B. *Watercolors by Kandinsky at the Guggenheim Museum: A Selection from the Solomon R. Guggenheim Museum and the Hilla von Rebay Foundation*. New York: Guggenheim Museum, 1991; 2nd ed. with minor rev. New York, 1993

ILLETSCHKO, GEORGIA. *Kandinsky und Paris: Die Geschichte einer Beziehung*. München: Prestel, 1996

KANDINSKY, NINA. *Kandinsky und ich*. München: Kindler, 1976

KLEINE, GISELA. *Gabriele Münter und Wassily Kandinsky: Biographie eines Paares*. Frankfurt am Main: Insel, 1990

LASSAIGNE, JACQUES. *Kandinsky: étude biographique et critique*. (Le goût de notre temps, 41). Genève: Skira, 1964; *Kandinsky: Biographical and Critical Study*. (The Taste of our Time, 41). H.S.B. Harrison, trans. Cleveland: Distributed by World Pub. Co., 1964

LONG, ROSE-CAROL WASHTON. *Kandinsky: The Development of an Abstract Style*. (Oxford Studies in the History of Art and Architecture). Oxford: Clarendon, and New York: Oxford University Press, 1980

LONG, ROSE-CAROL WASHTON. *Vasily Kandinsky 1909–1913: Painting and Theory*. Ann-Arbor, MI: University Microfilms International, 1978

OVERY, PAUL. *Kandinsky*. New York: Praeger, 1969

RIEDL, PETER ANSELM, ed. *Wassily Kandinsky: Mit Selbstzeugnissen und Bilddokumenten*. (Rowohlts Monographien). Reinbek bei Hamburg: Rowohlt, 1983

ROSDAHL, ANDERS. *Nya perspektiv på Kandinsky = New Perspectives on Kandinsky*. Malmö: Malmö Konsthall, 1990

ROETHEL, HANS K., and JEAN K. BENJAMIN. *Kandinsky*. New York: Hudson Hills Press, 1979

SERS, PHILIPPE. *Kandinsky: Philosophe de l'abstraction: l'image métaphysique*. Genf: Skira, 1995

THÜRLEMANN, FELIX. *Kandinsky über Kandinsky: Der Künstler als Interpret eigener Werke*. (Schriftenreihe der Stiftung von Schnyder von Wartensee, Bd. 54). Bern: Benteli, 1986

TÍO BELLÍDO, RAMÓN. *Kandinsky*. Paris: Hazen, 1987; London: Bracken, 1988; rev. ed. London: Studio, 1993

VERGO, PETER. *Kandinsky Cossacks*. (Tate Modern Masterpieces). London: Tate Gallery, 1986

VOLBOUDT, PIERRE. *Die Zeichnungen Wassily Kandinskys*. Dagmar Daillant, and Karin Hafner, trans. (DuMont Dokumente. Graphik Serie, 4). Köln: M. DuMont Schauberg, 1974

VOLPI ORLANDINI, MARISA. *Kandinsky: dall'art nouveau alla psicologia della forma*. (Arte contemporanea, 2). Roma: Lerici, 1968

VOLPI ORLANDINI, MARISA. *Kandinsky e il Blaue Reiter*. Milano: F. Fabbri, 1970; *Kandinsky und der Blaue Reiter*. Herrsching: M. Pawlak, 1988

WEISS, PEG. *Kandinsky and Old Russia: The Artist as Ethnographer and Shaman*. New Haven, CT: Yale University Press, 1995

WEISS, PEG. *Kandinsky in Munich: The Formative Jugendstil Years*. Princeton, NJ: Princeton University Press, 1979

Exhibition Catalogues

1961 London, Marlborough Fine Art. *Kandinsky: The Road to Abstraction*. Hans K. Roethel

1963–1964 New York, Solomon R. Guggenheim Museum; Paris, Musée national d'art moderne; Den Haag, Gemeente Museum; Basel, Kunsthalle. *Vasily Kandinsky 1866–1944: A Retrospective Exhibition*. Thomas M. Messer

1965 Stockholm, Moderna Museet. *Kandinsky*. Pontus Hultén

1966 München, Städtische Galerie im Lenbachhaus. *Kandinsky: Das druckgraphische Werk zum 100. Geburtstag*. Hans K. Roethel

1970 New York, Museum of Modern Art; Fort Worth, TX, Art Center; Toronto, Art Gallery of Ontario. *Kandinsky Watercolors*

1971 Bern, Kunstmuseum. *Kandinsky: Aquarelle und Gouachen*. Sandor Kuthy, Text

1972 Basel, Galerie Beyeler. *Kandinsky: Aquarelle und Zeichnungen*. Nina Kandinsky

1972 New York, Solomon R. Guggenheim Museum. *Vasily Kandinsky 1866–1944 in the Collection of the Solomon R. Guggenheim Museum*

1972 Paris, Galerie Berggruen. *Kandinsky: aquarelles et dessins*

1973 Köln, Galerie Bargera. *Kandinsky 1866–1944: Gouachen, Aquarelle, Ölbilder und Zeichnungen*

1974–1975 New York, Solomon R. Guggenheim Museum; Cincinnati, OH; Little Rock, AR; San Antonio, TX; Houston, TX; Fort Worth, TX; Kansas City, MO; Davenport, IA; Detroit, MI; Worcester, MA; Washington, D.C., The Phillips Collection. *The Graphic Work of Kandinsky: a Loan Exhibition*. Hans K. Roethel. Circulated by The International Exhibitions Foundation

1976 München, Haus der Kunst; Städtische Galerie im Lenbachhaus. *Wassily Kandinsky 1866–1944*. 2nd rev. ed. Thomas M. Messer, Rosel Gollek, and Ingrid Krause

1976 Tokyo, Seibu Museum of Art. *Kandinsky*

1977 Paris, Galerie Karl Flinker. *Kandinsky: 82 œuvres sur papier de 1902 à 1944*

1979 Edinburg, Scottish Arts Council Gallery. *Kandinsky: The Munich Years 1900–1914*

1979 Paris, Musée national d'art moderne. *Kandinsky: Trente peintures des musées soviétiques.* Christian Derouet, text

1982 München, Städtische Galerie im Lenbachhaus. *Kandinsky und München: Begegnungen und Wandlungen 1896–1914.* Armin Zweite. ["Eine veränderte und erweiterte Fassung des vom Solomon R. Guggenheim Museum ... organisierten Projektes."]

1982 New York, Solomon R. Guggenheim Museum; San Francisco Museum of Modern Art. *Kandinsky in Munich 1896–1914.* Peg Weiss

1983–1984 New York, Solomon R. Guggenheim Museum. *Kandinsky: Russian and Bauhaus Years 1915–1933*; rev. and enl. ed. Berlin, Bauhaus-Archiv, Museum für Gestaltung; Zürich, Kunsthaus. *Kandinsky: Russische Zeit und Bauhausjahre 1915–1933.* Christian Wolsdorff

1984 Paris, Centre Georges Pompidou. *Kandinsky: œuvres de Vassily Kandinsky 1866–1944.* Christian Derouet, and Jessica Boissel

1984 Zürich, Kunsthaus. *Kandinsky in Russland und am Bauhaus 1915–1933.* Guido Magnaguagno

1989 Frankfurt am Main, Schirn Kunsthalle. *Wassily Kandinsky: Die erste sowjetische Retrospektive: Gemälde, Zeichnungen und Graphik aus sowjetischen und westlichen Museen.* S. Ebert-Schifferer

1989–1990 Malmö, Konsthall; Stockholm, Moderna Museet. *Kandinsky and Sweden: Malmö 1914–Stockholm 1916.* Vivian Endicott Barnett

1992 Düsseldorf, Kunstsammlung Nordrhein-Westfalen; Stuttgart, Staatsgalerie. *Kandinsky, kleine Freuden: Aquarelle und Zeichnungen.* Vivian Endicott Barnett, and Armin Zweite

1994–1995 Berlin, Brücke-Museum; Tübingen, Kunsthalle. *Der frühe Kandinsky 1900–1910.* Magdalena M. Moeller.

1995 Lugano, Museo cantonale d'arte. *Kandinsky: nelle collezioni svizzere.* Manuela Kahn-Rossi

1995 New York, Museum of Modern Art; Los Angeles County Museum of Art. *Kandinsky Compositions.* Magdalena Dabrowski

1996 München, Städtische Galerie im Lenbachhaus. *Das bunte Leben: Wassily Kandinsky im Lenbachhaus.* Vivian Endicott Barnett

Ernst Ludwig Kirchner

Reference Bibliography

KETTERER, ROMAN NORBERT, and WOLFGANG HENZE. *Ernst Ludwig Kirchner: Drawings and Pastels.* New York: Alpine Fine Arts, 1982, p. 249-309

Written Works and Correspondence

DÜMMLER, ELFRIEDE, and HANSGEORG KNOBLAUCH, eds. *Ernst Ludwig Kirchner: Briefwechsel mit einem jungen Ehepaar 1927–1937.* Bern: Kornfeld, 1989

GRISEBACH, LOTHAR, ed. *E.L. Kirchners Davoser Tagebuch: Eine Darstellung des Malers und eine Sammlung seiner Schriften.* Köln: DuMont Schauberg, 1968; new ed. *Ernst Ludwig Kirchners Davoser Tagebuch.* Ostfildern bei Ruit: G. Hatje, 1997

KIRCHNER, ERNST LUDWIG. *Briefe an Nele und Henry van de Velde.* München: R. Piper, 1961

KIRCHNER, ERNST LUDWIG. *Chronik KG Brücke.* Berlin: [S.n.], 1913

HENZE, WOLFGANG, ANNEMARIE DUBE-HEYNIG, and MAGDALENA KRAEMER-NOBLE, eds. *Ernst Ludwig Kirchner–Gustav Schiefler: Briewechsel 1910–1935/1938: Mit Briefen von und an Luise Schiefler und Erna Kirchner sowie weiteren Dokumenten aus Schieflers Korrespondenz-Ablage.* Stuttgart/Zürich: Belser, 1990

Œuvre Catalogues

DUBE, ANNEMARIE, and WOLF-DIETER DUBE. *Das graphische Werk.* 2 vols. München: Prestel, 1967; 2nd ed. München, 1980

GORDON, DONALD E. *Ernst Ludwig Kirchner: Mit einem kritischen Katalog sämtlicher Gemälde.* München: Prestel, 1968

DÜRST, FRITZ, and EBERHARD W. KORNFELD. *Lisa Gujer: Wirkereien nach Entwürfen von E.L. Kirchner.* Bern: Kornfeld, 1974

PRESLER, GERD, *Ernst Ludwig Kirchner, Die Skizzenbücher: 'Ekstase des ersten Sehens'.* Davos: Kirchner Verein, 1996

SCHIEFLER, GUSTAV. *Die Graphik Ernst Ludwig Kirchners bis 1924.* Berlin: Euphorion, 1926

SCHIEFLER, GUSTAV. *Die Graphik Ernst Ludwig Kirchners 1917–1927.* Berlin: Euphorion, 1931

Books

DUBE-HEYNIG, ANNEMARIE. *Ernst Ludwig Kirchner, Postkarten und Briefe an Erich Heckel im Altonaer Museum in Hamburg.* Köln: DuMont, 1984

FRONING, HUBERTUS. *E.L. Kirchner und die Wandmalerei im Museum Folkwang.* Recklinghausen: A. Bongers, 1991

GERCKEN, GÜNTHER. *Ernst Ludwig Kirchner Holzschnittzyklen: Peter Schlemihl, Triumph der Liebe, Absalom.* Stuttgart/Zürich: Belser, 1980

GRISEBACH, LUCIUS. *Ernst Ludwig Kirchner 1880–1938.* Köln/New York: B. Taschen, 1996

GROHMANN, WILL. *E.L. Kirchner.* Stuttgart: W. Kohlhammer, 1958; English ed. New York: Arts, 1961

GROHMANN, WILL. *Kirchner-Zeichnungen.* (Arnolds graphische Bücher, 2. Folge, Bd. 6). Dresden: E. Arnold, 1925

GROHMANN, WILL. *Das Werk Ernst Ludwig Kirchners.* München: K. Wolff, 1926

HENZE, ANTON. *Ernst Ludwig Kirchner: Leben und Werk.* Stuttgart: Belser, 1980

HENZE, WOLFGANG. *Gemälde, Aquarelle, Pastelle, Zeichnungen, Holzschnitte, Radierungen, Lithographien, Plastiken.* (Kirchner Museum Davos. Katalog der Sammlung, Bd. 1). Davos: Kirchner Verein, 1992

KETTERER, ROMAN NORBERT, ed. *Ernst Ludwig Kirchner: Zeichnungen und Pastelle.* Stuttgart/Zürich: Belser, 1979; *Ernst Ludwig Kirchner: Drawings and Pastels.* New York: Alpine Fine Arts, 1982

KORNFELD, EBERHARD W. *Ernst Ludwig Kirchner: Nachzeichnungen seines Lebens: Katalog der Sammlung von Werken ... im Kirchner-Haus Davos.* Bern: Kornfeld, 1979

KORNFELD, EBERHARD W. *Gut in den Lärchen: Die Geschichte eines Hauses in Frauenkirch.* Bern/Davos: Kornfeld, 1996

MOELLER, MAGDALENA, M. *Ernst Ludwig Kirchner: Die Strassenszenen 1913–1915.* München: Hirmer, 1993

MOELLER, MAGDALENA, M. *Ernst Ludwig Kirchner: Zeichnungen und Aquarelle.* München: Hirmer, 1993

SCHOOP, ALBERT. *Ernst Ludwig Kirchner im Thurgau: Die 10 Monate in Kreuzlingen 1917–1918.* Bern: Kornfeld, 1992

SYKORA, KATHARINA. *Weiblichkeit, Grossstadt, Moderne: Ernst Ludwig Kirchners Berliner Strassenzenen 1913–1915.* (Gegenwart Museum). Berlin: Museumspädagogischer Dienst, 1996

VOGT, PAUL. *Ernst Ludwig Kirchner: Skizzenbuch aus der Graphischen Sammlung des Museum Folkwang.* Freren: Luca, 1983

Exhibition Catalogues

1960 Düsseldorf, Kunsthalle. *E.L.Kirchner zum Gedächtnis an die 80. Wiederkehr des Geburtstages ....* Karlheinz Gabler, and Annemarie Dube-Heynig

1963 Campione d'Italia, Galerie Roman Norbert Ketterer. *E.L. Kirchner.* Wenzel Nachbaur

1963 Berlin, Galerie Nierendorf. *E.L. Kirchner zum fünfundzwanzigsten Todestag: Aquarelle, Bilder, Zeichnungen*

1967 Kassel, Staatliche Kunstsammlungen. *Ernst Ludwig Kirchner: Zeichnungen I, 1906–1925.* Karlheinz Gabler

1968 Berlin, Deutsche Akademie der Künste. *Ernst Ludwig Kirchner: Aquarelle, Zeichnungen, Druckgraphik.* Helga Weissgärber

1968 Seattle, Art Museum; Pasadena Art Museum; Boston, Museum of Fine Arts. *Ernst Ludwig Kirchner: A Retrospective Exhibition.* Donald E. Gordon

1969 London, Marlborough Fine Art. *Kirchner 1880–1938: Oils, Watercolours, Drawings and Graphics: First London Exhibition*

1971 Campione d'Italia, Galerie Roman Norbert Ketterer. *Ernst Ludwig Kirchner.* Wenzel Nachbaur

1974 Frankfurt am Main, Städtische Galerie im Städelschen Kunstinstitut. *Ernst Ludwig Kirchner: ... aus eigenem Besitz.* Christian Lenz

1978 Berlin, Brücke-Museum. *Ernst Ludwig Kirchner: Die Handzeichnungen, Aquarelle und Pastelle in eigenem Besitz.* Leopold Reidemeister

1978 Hamburg, Kunstverein; Frankfurt am Main, Kunstverein. *E.L. Kirchner: Zeichnungen und Druckgraphik 1905–1936.* Günther Gercken, and Uwe M. Schneede

1979 Basel, Kunstmuseum. *E.L. Kirchner.* Christian Geelhaar

1979–1980 Berlin, Nationalgalerie; München, Haus der Kunst; Köln, Museum Ludwig; Zürich, Kunsthaus. *Ernst Ludwig Kirchner 1880–1938.* Lucius Grisebach, and Annette Meyer zu Eissen

1980 Aschaffenburg, Museum der Stadt Aschaffenburg; Karlsruhe, Staatliche Kunsthalle; Essen, Mu-

seum Folkwang; Kassel, Staatliche Kunstsammlungen. 2 vols. *E.L. Kirchner: Dokumente: Fotos, Schriften, Briefe*; and *Ernst Ludwig Kirchner: Zeichnungen, Pastelle, Aquarelle*. Karl Heinz Gabler
1980 Campione d'Italia, Galerie Roman Norbert Ketterer. *Ausstellung Ernst Ludwig Kirchner*
1980 Chicago, Worthington Gallery. *Ernst Ludwig Kirchner 1880–1938: A Tribute Celebration of the Artist's Centennial Year*
1980 Chur, Bündner Kunstmuseum. *E.L. Kirchner und seine Schüler im Bündner Kunstmuseum Chur*. Hans Hartmann
1980 Frankfurt am Main, Städtische Galerie im Städelschen Kunstinstitut. *Ernst Ludwig Kirchner: ... aus dem Besitz des Städel*. Christian Lenz
1980 Stuttgart, Staatsgalerie. *Ernst Ludwig Kirchner in der Graphischen Sammlung ... Bestandskatalog*
1983 New York, Grace Borgenicht Gallery. *E.L. Kirchner: Paintings and Works on Paper*
1986 Duisburg, Wilhelm-Lehmbruck-Museum. *Ernst Ludwig Kirchner: Zeichnungen, Druckgraphik, Photographien, Dokumente*. Renate Heidt, and Winfried Wilhelmy
1988 Davos, Galerie Iris Wazzau. *E.L. Kirchner 1880–1938: Ausstellung zum 50. Todestag.*
1989 Davos, Kirchner Museum. *Ernst Ludwig Kirchner: Werke 1917–1923*. Eberhard W. Kornfeld
1990 Berlin, Brücke-Museum; Essen, Museum Folkwang; Bremen, Kunsthalle. *Ernst Ludwig Kirchner: Meisterwerke der Druckgraphik*. Magdalena M. Moeller, ed.
1991 Nürnberg, Kunsthalle. *Ernst Ludwig Kirchner: Zeichnungen, Aquarelle, Pastelle*. Lucius Grisebach, and Wolfgang Henze
1993 Davos, Kirchner Museum. *Ernst Ludwig Kirchner: Der Tanz, Gret Palucca zum Gedenken*. Gabriele Lohberg
1993–1994 Jena, Stadtmuseum Göhre. *Ernst Ludwig Kirchner: Von Jena nach Davos*. Anna-Maria Ehrmann, and Volker Wahl
1994 Davos, Kirchner Museum. *Ernst Ludwig Kirchner: Kunst und Technik der Radierung*. Gabriele Lohberg
1995 Davos, Kirchner Museum. *Ernst Ludwig Kirchner: Die Werke in Schweizer Museen*. Beat Stutzer
1995–1996 Chur, Bündner Kunstmuseum; Emden, Kunsthalle in Emden, Stiftung Henri Nannen; Schleswig-Holsteinisches Landesmuseum, Schloss Gottorf. *Ernst Ludwig Kirchner: Unbekannte Zeichnungen aus dem Kirchner Museum Davos: Ausgewählte Werke aus der Schenkung der Familienstiftung Benvenuta, Vaduz, 1994*. Gabriele Lohberg
1996 Davos, Kirchner Museum. *Ernst Ludwig Kirchner: Die Skizzenbücher: 'Ekstase des ersten Sehens'*. Gabriele Lohberg
1996 Davos, Kirchner Museum. *E.L. Kirchner: Gemälde und Zeichnungen*
1996 Salzburg, Galerie Welz. *Ernst Ludwig Kirchner 1880–1938: Holzschnitte, Radierungen, Lithographien*

Oskar Kokoschka
Reference Bibliography
WINGLER, HANS M. *Oskar Kokoschka: Das Werk des Malers*. Salzburg: Galerie Welz, 1956, p. 345-379

Written Works and Correspondence
Berichte aus einer eingebildeten Welt: Erinnerungen und erzählungen. Alfred Marnau, ed. Graz: Styria Graz, 1996
Briefe, Vol. 1, 1905–1919; Vol. 2, 1919–1934. Olda Kokoschka, and Heinz Spielmann, eds. Düsseldorf: Claassen 1984–1985
Der brennende Dornbusch; Mörder, Hoffnung der Frauen. (Der Jüngste Tag, 41). Leipzig: K. Wolff, 1917
Dramen und Bilder. Paul Stefan, introduction. Leipzig: K. Wolff, 1913
Mein Leben. Remigius Netzer, ed. München: Bruckmann, 1971; *My Life*. David Britt, trans. New York: Macmillan, 1974
Oskar Kokoschka: Letters 1905–1976. Olda Kokoschka, and Alfred Marnau, eds. New York: Thames and Hudson, 1992
Schriften 1907–1955. Hans M. Wingler, ed. München: Langen-Müller, 1956. [Verzeichnis der Schriften von Oskar Kokoschka, p. 480-484]
Das schriftliche Werk. Vols. I-IV. Heinz Spielmann, ed. Hamburg: H. Christians, 1973–1976
Spur im Treibsand: Geschichten. Zürich: Atlantis, 1956; *A Sea Ringed with Visions*. Eithne Wilkins, and Ernst Kaiser, trans. New York: Horizon Press, 1962; *Mirages du passé*. Louise Servicen, trans. (Collection l'imaginaire). [S.l.]: Gallimard, 1966
Vier Dramen. Berlin: P. Cassirer, 1919. ["Orpheus und Eurydike"; "Der brennende Dornbusch"; "Mörder, Hoffnung der Frauen"; and "Hiob"]
"Vom Erlebnis im Leben". In: *Schriften und Bilder*. Otto Breicha, ed. Salzburg: Galerie Welz, 1976

Books Illustrated and Written by Kokoschka
Der gefesselte Columbus. (Die neuen Bilderbücher, 3. Reihe). Berlin: F. Gurlitt, 1921
Hiob. Berlin: P. Cassirer, 1917
Menschenköpfe. Berlin: Der Sturm, 1916
Mörder, Hoffnung der Frauen. Berlin: Der Sturm, 1916
Die träumenden Knaben. Wien: Wiener Werkstätte, 1908; reprint, Wien: Jugend und Volk, 1968; *Die traeumenden Knaben = Les garçons qui rêvent = I Ragazzi sognanti*. Paris: Editions Chatelain-Julien; Lugano: Edizioni Pagine d'arte, 1995

Œuvre Catalogues
WINGLER, HANS M. *Oskar Kokoschka: Das Werk des Malers*. Salzburg: Galerie Welz, 1956; *Oskar Kokoschka: The Work of the Painter*. Frank S.C. Budgen, et al., trans. Salzburg, 1958
WINGLER, HANS M., and FRIEDRICH WELZ, eds. *O. Kokoschka: Das druckgraphische Werk*. Salzburg: Galerie Welz, 1975
WINGLER, HANS M., and FRIEDRICH WELZ, eds. *O. Kokoschka: Das druckgraphische Werk II*. Salzburg: Galerie Welz, 1981
WINKLER, JOHANN, and KATHARINA ERLING. *Oskar Kokoschka: Die Gemälde*. Vol. 1, 1906–1929. Salzburg: Galerie Welz, 1995

Books
BIERMANN, GEORG. *Oskar Kokoschka*. (Junge Kunst, Bd. 52). Berlin: Klinkhardt und Biermann, 1929
BORCHERT, BERNHARD. *Kokoschka*. Berlin: Safari, 1959; London: Faber and Faber, 1960
BULTMANN, GERHARD. *Oskar Kokoschka*. Salzburg: Galerie Welz, 1959
CALVOCORESSI, RICHARD. *Kokoschka*. (Meister der Moderne). Georg Hepermann, trans. Recklinghausen: A. Bongers, 1992
FAERNA, JOSÉ MARÍA, ed. *Kokoschka*. Diana Cobos, trans. (Great Modern Masters). New York: Abrams/Cameo, 1995
FENJÖ, IVAN. *OK: Die frühe Graphik*. Wien: Euro-Art Bücherkreis, 1976
GATT, GIUSEPPE. *Kokoschka*. Firenze: Sansoni, 1970; English ed. (Twentieth Century Masters). London/New York: Hamlyn, 1971
GOLDSCHEIDER, LUDWIG. *Kokoschka*. London: Phaidon, 1963
HEILMAIER, HANS. *Kokoschka*. (Les artistes nouveaux). Paris: G. Crès, 1929
HODIN, JOSEPH P. *Bekenntnis zu Kokoschka: Erinnerungen und Deutungen*. Berlin: F. Kupferberg, 1963
HODIN, JOSEPH P. *Oskar Kokoschka: The Artist and his Time: A Biographical Study*. Greenwich, CT: New York Graphic Society, 1966
HODIN, JOSEPH P. *Oskar Kokoschka: Eine Psychographie*. Wien: Europa, 1971
HOFFMANN, EDITH. *Kokoschka: Life and Work*. London: Faber and Faber, 1947
LESHKO, JAROSLAW. *Oskar Kokoschka: Paintings 1907–1915*. Ann Arbor, MI: University Microfilms International, 1977
LISCHKA, GERHARD JOHANN. *Oskar Kokoschka: Maler und Dichter: Eine literar-ästhetische Untersuchung zu seiner Doppelbegabung*. (Europäische Hochschulschriften. Reihe XVIII, Vergleichende Literaturwissenschaften, Bd. 4). Bern/Frankfurt am Main: H. Lang, P. Lang, 1972
MASCIOTTA, MICHELANGELO. *Kokoschka*. (Maestri moderni). Firenze: Del Turco Editore, 1949
MAURON, VÉRONIQUE. *Werke der Oskar Kokoschka-Stiftung*. Kathrin Braunschweig-Geller, trans. Mainz: P. von Zabern, 1994
PATKA, ERIKA. *Oskar Kokoschka: Symposium abgehalten von der Hochschule für Angewandte Kunst in Wien ... anlässlich des 100. Geburtstages des Künstlers*. Salzburg: Residenz Verlag, 1986
PLATSCHEK, HANS. *Oskar Kokoschka*. (Biblioteca Argentina de Arte). Buenos Aires: Poseidon, 1946
RATHENAU, ERNEST, ed. *Kokoschka: Drawings*. London: Thames and Hudson, 1962
RATHENAU, ERNEST, ed. *Handzeichnungen 1906–1965*. New York: E. Rathenau, 1966; *Drawings 1906–1965*. Heinz Norden, trans. Coral Gables, FL: University of Miami Press, 1970
RATHENAU, ERNEST, ed. *Handzeichnungen 1906–1969*. New York: E. Rathenau, 1971
RATHENAU, ERNEST, ed. *Handzeichnungen: Fünfter Band [1906–1976]*. New York: E. Rathenau, 1977
RECUPERO, JACOPO. *Oskar Kokoschka: scritti di Kokoschka*. (Edizioni dell'Ente premi Roma. Pittura,

artisti, stranieri, 3). Roma: De Luca Editore, 1959

SCHVEY, HENRY I. *Oskar Kokoschka: The Painter as Playwright.* Detroit: Wayne State University Press, 1982

SCHMALENBACH, FRITZ. *Oskar Kokoschka.* (Die blauen Bücher). Königstein im Taunus: K.R. Langewiesche, 1967; English ed. Violet M. Macdonald, trans. Greenwich, CT: New York Graphic Society, 1967

SCHRÖDER, KLAUS ALBRECHT, and JOHANN WINKLER, eds. *Oskar Kokoschka.* München: Prestel, 1991

SCHWEIGER, WERNER J. *Der junge Kokoschka: Leben und Werk 1904–1914.* (Schriftenreihe der Oskar Kokoschka-Dokumentation Pöchlarn, Bd. 1). Wien: C. Brandstätter, 1983

SPIELMANN, HEINZ. *Oskar Kokoschka: Die Fächer für Alma Mahler.* Hamburg: H. Christians, 1969; new ed. (Die Bibliophilen Taschenbücher, Nr. 462). Dortmund: Harenberg, 1985

WEIDINGER, ALFRED. *Kokoschka und Alma Mahler.* (Pegasus Library). München/New York: Prestel, 1996; English ed. Fiona Elliott, trans. München/New York, 1996

WELZ, FRIEDRICH, ed. *Oskar Kokoschka: Frühe Druckgraphik 1906–1912.* Salzburg: Galerie Welz, 1977

WESTHEIM, PAUL, ed. *Oskar Kokoschka: Das Werk Kokoschkas.* Potsdam-Berlin: G. Kiepenheuer, 1918

WESTHEIM, PAUL. *Oskar Kokoschka.* Berlin: P. Cassirer, 1925

WHITFORD, FRANK. *Oskar Kokoschka: A Life.* New York: Atheneum, 1986

WINKLER, JOHANN. *Begegnung mit Kokoschka: Eine Festschrift zur Eröffnung der Oskar Kokoschka-Dokumentation Pöchlarn.* Pöchlarn: Oskar Kokoschka-Dokumentation Pöchlarn, 1973

WINGLER, HANS M. *Kokoschka-Fibel.* Salzburg: Galerie Welz, 1957; *Introduction to Kokoschka.* Peter George, trans. London: Thames and Hudson, 1958; 2nd ed. London, 1963

WINGLER, HANS M. *Oskar Kokoschka: Ein Lebensbild in zeitgenössischen Dokumenten.* München: Langen-Müller, 1956

Exhibition Catalogues

1962 London, Tate Gallery. *Kokoschka: A Retrospective Exhibition of Paintings, Drawings, Lithographs, Stage Designs, and Books.* Organized by the Arts Council of Great Britain

1965 Hamburg, Museum für Kunst und Gewerbe. *Oskar Kokoschka: Illustrationen, Mappenwerke, Plakate, graphische Beiträge zu Zeitschriften und Büchern; Dichtungen; Schauspieler-Portraits und Bühnen-Entwürfe*

1966 London, Chelsea School of Art Gallery; Harrogate, Corporation Art Gallery; Derby, Museum and Art Gallery; Southampton Art Gallery. *Kokoschka Lithographs: An Exhibition Organized by the Arts Council of Great Britain to Mark the Occasion of the Artist's Eightieth Birthday*

1966 New York, Marlborough-Gerson Gallery. *Oskar Kokoschka: An Eightieth Birthday Tribute*

1966 Stuttgart, Staatsgalerie. *Oskar Kokoschka: Aquarelle und Zeichnungen: Ausstellung zum 80. Geburtstag*

1966 Zürich, Kunsthaus. *Oskar Kokoschka*

1971 Wien, Österreichische Galerie im Oberen Belvedere. *Oskar Kokoschka zum 85. Geburtstag.* Friedrich Welz

1975–1977 Middletown, CT: Wesleyan University Center for the Arts Gallery; Storrs, CT, William Benton Museum of Art. *Oskar Kokoschka: Literary and Graphic Works 1906–1923.* Richard S. Field

1976 London, Victoria and Albert Museum. *Homage to Kokoschka: Prints and Drawings Lent by Reinhold, Count Bethusy-Huc*

1976 Villingen-Schwenningen, Beethovenhaus. *Oskar Kokoschka zum 90. Geburtstag: Gemälde, Aquarelle, Zeichnungen, Graphik.* Margarete Willmann

1979 Albstadt, Städtische Galerie. *Oskar Kokoschka, Themen 1906–1976: Handzeichnungen, Druckgraphik, Buchkunst, Bildwerke, Leihgaben aus Privatbesitz.* Alfred Hagenlocher. [Includes continuation of Wingler and Welz oeuvre catalogue, p. 101-121, by Heinz Spielmann]

1980 Pöchlarn, Oskar Kokoschka-Dokumentation Pöchlarn im Geburtshaus des Künstlers. *Oskar Kokoschka: Gemälde und Graphik 1908–1976.* Johann Winkler

1980–1981 Salzburg, Residenzgalerie. *Oskar Kokoschka: Bilder zum Leben*

1981–1982 Roma, Palazzo Venezia. *Oskar Kokoschka 1886–1980.* Carmine Benincasa

1983 Bordeaux, Galerie des beaux-arts. *Oskar Kokoschka 1886–1980*

1983 Hannover, Kestner-Gesellschaft. *Oskar Kokoschka, die frühen Jahre: Aquarelle und Zeichnungen (1906–1924).* Carl Haenlein, ed.

1983 Pöchlarn, Oskar Kokoschka-Dokumentation Pöchlarn; Wien, Hochschule für Angewandte Kunst. *Der junge Kokoschka: Kunstgewerbeschule, Wiener Werkstätte, Carabet Fledermaus, Kunstschau 1908.* Werner J. Schweiger

1984 Vevey, Musée Jenisch. *Hommage à Oksar Kokoschka 1886–1980*

1985 New York, Serge Sabarsky. *Oskar Kokoschka, the Early Years: An exhibition of Paintings, Watercolors and Drawings Honoring the Forthcoming Centennial of the Artist*

1986 Hamburg, Kunsthalle. *Oskar Kokoschka: Die frühen Jahre 1906–1926: Aquarelle und Zeichnungen.* Serge Sabarsky

1986 New York, Solomon R. Guggenheim Museum. *Oskar Kokoschka 1886–1980.* Thomas Messer, Richard Calvocoressi, and Katharina Schulz

1986 Pöchlarn, Oskar Kokoschka-Dokumentation Pöchlarn. *Oskar Kokoschka: Der Sturm, die Berliner Jahre 1910–1916.* Werner J. Schweiger

1986–1987 London, Tate Gallery; Zürich, Kunsthaus; New York, Solomon R. Guggenheim Museum. *Oskar Kokoschka*

1987 Gent, Museum voor Schone Kunsten; Liège, Salle Saint-Georges. *Oskar Kokoschka.* Serge Sabarsky

1987 Santa Barbara Museum of Art; Kansas City, MO, Nelson-Atkins Museum of Art; Northampton, MA, Smith College Museum of Art. *Orbis Pictus: The Prints of Oskar Kokoschka 1906–1976: Selected from the Collection of Reinhold, Count Bethusy-Huc*

1989 Berlin, Obere Galerie, Haus am Lützowplatz. *Kokoschka in Berlin.* Paul Corazolla

1991 Wien, Kunstforum Wien. *Oskar Kokoschka.* Klaus A. Schröder, and Johann Winkler

1992 Cismar, Schleswig-Holsteinisches Landesmuseum, Kloster Cismar. *Oskar Kokoschka, Lebensspuren: Ausgewählte Gemälde, Aquarelle, Zeichnungen der Kokoschka-Stiftung Vevey aus den Jahren 1906–1976.* Heinz Spielmann

1992 Frankfurt am Main, Städtische Galerie im Städelschen Kunstinstitut. *Oskar Kokoschka und Alma Mahler, die Puppe: Epilog einer Passion.* Klaus Gallwitz, and Stephan Mann

1992 London, Courtauld Institute Galleries. *Kokoschka: Prints, Illustrated Books, Drawings in the Princes Gate Collection*

1994 Wien, Graphische Sammlung Albertina; New York, Solomon R. Guggenheim Museum. *Oskar Kokoschka, das Frühwerk (1897/98–1917): Zeichnungen und Aquarelle.* (Ausstellung der Graphischen Sammlung Albertina, 374); *Oskar Kokoschka, Works on Paper: The Early Years 1897–1917.* Alice Strobl, and Alfred Weidinger

1995 Bellinzona, Civica Galleria d'arte, Villa dei Cedri. *Oskar Kokoschka: Viaggi e figure = Voyages et figures = Reisen und Figuren: Scelta di opere dalla Fondazione Oskar Kokoschka, Museo Jenisch Vevey.* Véronique Mauron

1995 Jena, Städtische Museen. *Oskar Kokoschka: Zeichnungen, Bücher*

1995 Wien, Galerie Richard Ruberl. *Oskar Kokoschka 1886–1980: Aquarelle, Zeichnungen, Druckgraphiken.* Alice Strobl, and Alfred Weidinger

1995–1996 Salzburg, Rupertinum. *Oskar Kokoschka: Lithographien zu King Lear.* Alfred Weidinger

1995–1996 Würzburg, Städtische Galerie. *Oskar Kokoschka: Zeichnung und Druckgraphik*

1996 Schleswig, Schleswig-Holsteinisches Landesmuseum. *Oskar Kokoschka und die Musik.* Heinz Spielmann

1996–1997 Dresden, Staatliche Kunstsammlungen, Gemäldegalerie Neue Meister; Wien, Österreichische Galerie im Oberen Belvedere. *Kokoschka und Dresden.* Werner Schmidt, and Birgit Dalbajewa

1997 Helsinki, Amos Anderson Art Museum. *Oskar Kokoschka: Dreaming Boy and Enfant Terrible: Early Graphic Works 1902–1909*

Käthe Kollwitz

Reference Bibliography

FISCHER, HANNELORE, ed. *Käthe Kollwitz: Meisterwerke der Zeichnung.* Köln: Käthe Kollwitz Museum und DuMont, 1995, p. 246-252

Written Works and Correspondence

BOHNKE-KOLLWITZ, JUTTA, ed. *Briefe an den Sohn 1904–1945.* Berlin: Siedler, 1992

BOHNKE-KOLLWITZ, JUTTA, ed. *Die Tagebücher*. Berlin: Siedler, 1989

KOLLWITZ, HANS, ed. *Tagebuch Blätter und Briefe*. Berlin: Gebr. Mann, 1948; *Diary and Letters*. Richard and Clara Winston, trans. Chicago: H. Regnery, 1955; reprint, Evanston, IL: Northwestern University Press, 1988

KOLLWITZ, HANS, ed. *"Ich will wirken in dieser Zeit": Auswahl aus den Tagebüchern und Briefen, aus Graphik, Zeichnungen und Plastik*. Berlin: Gebr. Mann, 1952; unabridged ed. Frankfurt am Main: Ullstein, 1993

KOLLWITZ, HANS, ed. *Käthe Kollwitz: Aus meinem Leben: Ein Testament des Herzens*. (List Bücher, 92). München: P. List, 1958; new ed. Freiburg im Br.: Herder, 1992

WANDRY, HORST, ed. *Käthe Kollwitz: Aus Tagebüchern und Briefen*. (Künstlerschriften). Berlin: Henschelverlag, 1964

Oeuvre Catalogues

KLIPSTEIN, AUGUST. *Käthe Kollwitz: Verzeichnis des graphischen Werkes: Für die Jahre 1890–1912 unter Verwendung des 1913 erschienenen Oeuvrekataloges von Prof. Dr. Johannes Sievers*. Bern: Klipstein, 1955

KOLLWITZ, HANS, ed. *Käthe Kollwitz: Das plastische Werk*. Hamburg: C. Wagner, 1967. Leopold Reidemeister, introduction

NAGEL, OTTO. *Käthe Kollwitz: Die Handzeichnungen*. Berlin: Henschelverlag, 1972; 2nd ed. Berlin, 1980

SIEVERS, JOHANNES. *Die Radierungen und Steindrucke von Käthe Kollwitz innerhalb der Jahre 1890 bis 1912: Ein beschreibendes Verzeichnis*. Dresden: H. Holst, 1913

WAGNER, A. *Die Radierungen, Holzschnitte und Lithographien von Käthe Kollwitz: Eine Zusammenstellung der seit 1912 entstandenen graphischen Arbeiten in chronologischer Folge*. Dresden: E. Richter, 1927

Books

ACHENBACH, SIGRID. *Käthe Kollwitz 1867–1945: Zeichnungen und seltene Graphik im Berliner Kupferstichkabinett*. (Bilderheft der Staatlichen Museen zu Berlin, Preussischer Kulturbesitz, Heft, 79/81.) Berlin: Gebr. Mann, 1995

BACKHAUS, ANNIE, ed. *Käthe-Kollwitz-Museum Köln: Katalog der Handzeichnungen*. 2nd enlarged ed. Köln: Käthe-Kollwitz-Museum, 1989

BACKHAUS, ANNIE, ed. *Käthe Kollwitz Museum Köln: Handzeichnungen-Druckgraphik-Skulpturen*. (Kölner Museums-Bulletin. Sonderheft, 1-2/1991.) Köln: Museen der Stadt Köln, 1991

BITTNER, HERBERT. *Kaethe Kollwitz Drawings*. New York: T. Yoseloff, 1964

BONUS, ARTHUR. *Das Käthe Kollwitz-Werk*. New rev. and enlarged ed. Dresden: C. Reissner, 1930

BONUS-JEEP, BEATE. *Sechzig Jahre Freundschaft mit Käthe Kollwitz*. Boppard: K. Rauch, 1948; new ed. Berlin: Henschelverlag, 1963

DIEL, LOUISE. *Käthe Kollwitz, Mutter und Kind: Gestalten und Gesichte der Künstlerin*. Berlin: Furche-Kunstverlag, 1928

DIEL, LOUISE. *Käthe Kollwitz: Ein Weberaufstand, Bauernkrieg, Krieg: Die drei Folgen der Künstlerin*. Berlin: Furche-Kunstverlag, 1930

GURATZSCH, HERWIG. *Käthe Kollwitz: Druckgraphik, Handzeichnungen, Plastik*. Stuttgart: G. Hatje, 1990

HEILBORN, ADOLF. *Käthe Kollwitz*. (Die Zeichner des Volks, 1.) Berlin-Zehlendorf: Rembrandt, 1929; 4th ed. Berlin: K. Lemmer, 1949

HINZ, RENATE, ed. *Käthe Kollwitz: Druckgraphik, Plakate, Zeichnungen*. Berlin: Elefanten Press, 1980

JANSEN, ELMAR. *Ernst Barlach, Käthe Kollwitz: Berührungen, Grenzen, Gegenbilder*. Berlin: Gebr. Mann, 1989

KAEMMERER, LUDWIG. *Kaethe Kollwitz: Griffelkunst und Weltanschauung: Ein kunstgeschichtlicher Beitrag zur Seelen- und Gesellschaftskunde*. Dresden: E. Richter, 1923

KEARNS, MARTHA. *Käthe Kollwitz: Woman and Artist*. Old Westbury, NY: Feminist Press, 1976

KOERBER, LENKA VON. *Erlebtes mit Käthe Kollwitz*. Berlin: Rütten & Loening, 1957

KRAHMER, CATHERINE. *Käthe Kollwitz in Selbstzeugnissen und Bilddokumenten*. (Rowohlts Monographien, 294). Reinbek bei Hamburg: Rowohlt, 1981

KUHN, ALFRED. *Käthe Kollwitz*. (Graphiker der Gegenwart, Bd. 6). Berlin: Verlag Neue Kunsthandlung, 1921

MECKEL, CHRISTOPH, ULRICH WEISNER, and HANS KOLLWITZ. *Käthe Kollwitz 1867–1945*. Bad Godesberg: Inter Nationes, 1967

NAGEL, OTTO. *Käthe Kollwitz*. Dresden: VEB Verlag der Kunst, 1963

SCHMALENBACH, FRITZ. *Käthe Kollwitz*. (Die blauen Bücher). Königstein im Taunus: K.R. Langewiesche, 1965; English ed. Stella Humphries, trans. Greenwich, CT: New York Graphic Society, 1971

SCHNEEDE, UWE M. *Käthe Kollwitz: Das zeichnerische Werk*. München: Schirmer-Mosel, 1981

SCHUMANN, WERNER. *Ein Herz schlägt für die Mütter: 100 Handzeichnungen von Käthe Kollwitz*. Hannover: Fackelträger-Verlag, 1953

SCHUMANN, WERNER. *Käthe Kollwitz*. (Das kleine Buch, 86). Gütersloh: C. Bertelsmann, 1956

SINGER, HANS W. *Käthe Kollwitz*. (Führer zur Kunst, Bd. 15). Esslingen: P. Neff, 1908

STRAUSS, GERHARD. *Käthe Kollwitz*. (Künstlermonographien). Dresden: Sachsenverlag, 1950

TIMM, WERNER. *Käthe Kollwitz*. (Welt der Kunst). Berlin: Henschelverlag, 1974; 2nd ed. Berlin, 1980; 1st English ed. Lisabeth Gombrich, trans. Berlin: Henschelverlag, 1980

TIMM, WERNER. *Käthe Kollwitz: Meisterwerke*. München: Schirmer-Mosel, 1993

ZIGROSSER, CARL. *Kaethe Kollwitz*. New York: G. Braziller, 1951; rev. and enlarged ed. *Prints and Drawings of Käthe Kollwitz*. New York: Dover, 1969

Exhibition Catalogues

1962 Ottawa, National Gallery of Canada. *Kathe Kollwitz: An Exhibition*

1967 München, A. von der Becke. *Käthe Kollwitz: Handzeichnungen und graphische Seltenheiten: Eine Ausstellung zum 100. Geburtstag*

1967 New York, Galerie St. Etienne. *Kaethe Kollwitz: In the Cause of Humanity: Exhibition Arranged to Commemorate the Hundredth Birthday*

1967–1968 Berlin, Akademie der Künste in Verbindung mit den Staatlichen Museen Preussischer Kulturbesitz, Kupferstichkabinett und Nationalgalerie. *Käthe Kollwitz 1867–1945*

1971–1972 Tel Aviv Museum; Jerusalem, Israel Museum. *Kaethe Kollwitz: Zeichnungen, Radierungen, Lithographien, Holzschnitte, Skulpturen*. (Katalog/Israel Museum, Nr. 88)

1973 Düsseldorf, Galerie Vömel. *Die Bronze-Skulpturen von Käthe Kollwitz*

1973 Frankfurt am Main, Kunst-verein, Steinernes Haus am Römerberg; Stuttgart, Württembergischer Kunstverein; Berlin, Neue Gesellschaft für Bildende Kunst. *Käthe Kollwitz*. Georg Bussmann, ed.

1976 New York, Galerie St. Etienne. *Käthe Kollwitz*

1977 München, Museum Villa Stuck. *Käthe Kollwitz: Zeichnung, Graphik, Plastik*. Amélie Ziersch

1978 Riverside, CA, Art Gallery, University of California. *Käthe Kollwitz 1867–1945: Prints, Drawings, Sculpture*

1979 Esslingen, Kunstgalerie. *Käthe Kollwitz: Radierungen, Lithographien, Holzschnitte*. Ralph Jentsch

1980–1981 Hamburg, Kunstverein; Zürich, Kunsthaus. *Käthe Kollwitz: Die Zeichnerin*. Uwe M. Schneede

1981–1982 Cambridge, Kettle's Yard; Edinburgh, Scottish National Gallery of Modern Art; London, Institute of Contemporary Arts. *Käthe Kollwitz 1867–1945: The Graphic Works*

1985 Frankfurt am Main, Jahrhunderthalle Hoechst. *Käthe Kollwitz 1867–1945: Zeichnungen, Druckgraphik, Skulpturen aus dem Bestand der Galerie Pels-Leusden, Berlin und anderer Sammlungen*. Meyer-Herbert Ellinger

1987–1988 New York, Galerie St. Etienne. *Käthe Kollwitz: The Power of the Print*. Jane Kallir

1989 Köln, Käthe Kollwitz Museum. *Die Kollwitz-Sammlung des Dresdner Kupferstich-Kabinettes: Graphik und Zeichnungen 1890–1912*. Werner Schmidt, ed

1989 Hannover, Wilhelm-Busch-Museum; Regensburg, Ostdeutsche Galerie. *Käthe Kollwitz: Druckgraphik, Handzeichnungen, Plastik*. Herwig Guratzsch. [Continues the listing of the graphic works of Käthe Kollwitz subsequent to the Kollwitz oeuvre catalogue of August Klipstein, Bern 1955]

1990 Berlin, Galerie Pels-Leusden. *Käthe Kollwitz: Zeichnungen, Graphiken, Skulpturen*

1992 Feuchtwangen, In der Schranne; Wolfsburg, Schloss. *Käthe Kollwitz: Zeichnungen, Druckgraphik, Bronzen*. Jürgen Schilling, and Jana Marko, eds

1992 Washington, D.C., National Gallery of Art. *Käthe Kollwitz*. Elizabeth Prelinger

1994 Český Krumlov, Egon Schiele Centrum. *Käthe Kollwitz; Kresby a grafika = Zeichnungen und*

Graphik = Drawings and Graphic. 1995 Berlin, Käthe Kollwitz Museum. *Käthe Kollwitz: Schmerz und Schuld: Eine motivgeschichtliche Betrachtung: Ausstellung aus Anlass des 50. Todestages von Käthe Kollwitz und zum Gedenken der 50. Wiederkehr des Endes des Zweiten Weltkriegs.* Gudrun Fritsch, Martin Fritsch, and Annette Seeler, eds
1995 Köln, Käthe Kollwitz Museum. *Käthe Kollwitz: Meisterwerke der Zeichnung.* Hannelore Fischer
1995 London, South Bank Centre. *Käthe Kollwitz: Artist of the People.* Fiona Griffith
1995 Rotterdam, Chabot Museum. *Käthe Kollwitz: Tekeningen-grafiek-sculpturen = Zeichnungen-Grafik-Sculpturen.* Jisca Bijlsma, ed
1995 Schwerin, Staatliches Museum. *Käthe Kollwitz: "Ich will wirken in dieser Zeit": Radierungen, Lithographien, Holzschnitte 1892–1925*
1996 Galway, College Art Gallery, University College. *The Prints of Käthe Kollwitz.* Jack Rutberg
1996 Hannover, Sprengel Museum. *Ernst Barlach und Käthe Kollwitz: Verzeichnis der Bestände: Originale auf Papier und Druckgraphik*

Wilhelm Lehmbruck
Reference bibliographies
HÄNDLER, GERHARD. *Wilhelm-Lehmbruck-Sammlung: Plastik, Malerei, Bd. 1.* Recklinghausen: A. Bongers, 1964, p. 10-22. [Includes a list of Lehmbruck exhibitions from 1906–1964]
HOFF, AUGUST. *Wilhelm Lehmbruck: Leben und Werk.* Completely rev. and enlarged ed. (Die Kunst aller Zeiten, Bd. 13). Berlin: Rembrandt, 1961, p. 165-167
HELLER, REINHOLD. *The Art of Wilhelm Lehmbruck.* Exhibition catalogue. Washington, D.C.: National Gallery of Art, 1972, p. 186-197
SCHUBERT, DIETRICH. *Die Kunst Lehmbrucks.* 2nd ed. Worms: Werner'sche Verlagsgesellschaft, 1990, p. 325-336

Oeuvre Catalogues
PETERMANN, ERWIN. *Die Druckgraphik von Wilhelm Lehmbruck: Verzeichnis.* Stuttgart: G. Hatje, 1964

Books
BETHGE, HANS. *Wilhelm Lehmbruck zum Gedächtnis.* Berlin-Wilmersdorf: A.R. Meyer, 1920

EINSTEIN, CARL. *Wilhelm Lehmbrucks graphisches Werk.* Berlin: P. Cassirer, 1913
HÄNDLER, GERHARD. *Wilhelm-Lehmbruck-Sammlung: Plastik, Malerei, Bd. 1.* Recklinghausen: A. Bongers, 1964
HÄNDLER, GERHARD. *Wilhelm Lehmbruck: Die Zeichnungen der Reifezeit.* [With a catalogue of drawings]. Stuttgart: G. Hatje, 1985
HOFF, AUGUST. *Wilhelm Lehmbruck.* (Junge Kunst, Bd. 61/62). Berlin: Klinkhardt and Biermann, 1933
HOFF, AUGUST. *Wilhelm Lehmbruck: Seine Sendung und sein Werk.* Berlin: Rembrandt, 1936
HOFF, AUGUST. *Wilhelm Lehmbruck: Leben und Werk.* (Die Kunst aller Zeiten, Bd. 13). Berlin: Rembrandt, 1961. [With oeuvre catalogue and comprehensive bibliography]; *Wilhelm Lehmbruck: Life and Work.* New York: Praeger, 1969. [English translation lacks bibliography and oeuvre catalogue]
HOFMANN, WERNER. *Wilhelm Lehmbruck.* (Europäische Bildhauer). Köln: Kiepenheuer und Witsch, 1957; 2nd. ed. München/Ahrbeck: Knorr und Hirth, 1964; English ed. (Universe Sculpture Series). New York: Universe Books, 1959
LAHUSEN, MARGARITA C. *Wilhelm Lehmbruck: Gemälde und grossformatige Zeichnungen.* München: Hirmer, 1997
RODEN, GÜNTER VON, and SIEGFRIED SALZMANN, eds. *Wilhelm Lehmbruck, sieben Beiträge zum Gedenken seines 50. Todestages.* (Duisburger Forschnugen, Bd. 13). Duisburg: W. Braun, 1969
SALZMANN, SIEGFRIED, ed. *Wilhelm Lehmbruck: Katalog der Sammlung des Wilhelm-Lehmburg-Museums der Stadt Duisburg.* Recklinghausen: A. Bongers, 1981
SCHUBERT, DIETRICH. *Die Kunst Lehmbrucks.* Worms: Werner'sche Verlagsgesellschaft, 1981; 2nd rev. and enlarged ed. Worms, 1990.
TRIER, EDUARD. *Wilhelm Lehmbruck: Zeichnungen und Radierungen.* (Piper-Bücherei, Bd. 84). München: R. Piper, 1955
TRIER, EDUARD. *Wilhelm Lehmbruck: Die Kniende.* (Werkmonographien zur bildenden Kunst in Reclams Universal Bibliothek, Nr. 32). Stuttgart: P. Reclam, 1958
WESTHEIM, PAUL. *Wilhelm Lehmbruck: Das Werk Lehmbrucks.* Potsdam: G. Kiepenheuer, 1919; 2nd ed. Potsdam, 1922

Wilhelm-Lehmbruck-Museum, Duisburg. Duisburg: C. Lange, 1964

Exhibitions
1963 New York, Otto Gerson Gallery. *Wilhelm Lehmbruck and other German Sculptors of His Time*
1964 Duisburg, Wilhelm-Lehmbruck-Museum. *Das graphische Gesamtwerk Wilhelm Lehmbrucks*
1969 Duisburg, Wilhelm-Lehmbruck-Museum. *Wilhelm Lehmbruck: Frühwerk, Plastik, Zeichnungen, Bd. III.* Gerhard Händler, ed
1972–1973 Washington, D.C., National Gallery of Art; Los Angeles, University of California; San Francisco Museum of Art; Boston, Museum of Fine Arts. *The Art of Wilhelm Lehmbruck.* Reinhold Heller
1973 Berlin, Staatliche Museen Preussischer Kulturbesitz, Nationalgalerie. *Wilhelm Lehmbruck.* Henning Bock, Ursula Prinz, and Angela Schneider
1977 Duisburg, Wilhelm-Lehmbruck-Museum. *Duisburger Akzente, Shakespeare 1977: Wilhelm Lehmbruck Zeichnungen und Radierungen zu Shakespeare.* Ernst-Gerhard Güse
1978 Duisburg, Wilhelm-Lehmbruck-Museum. *Lehmbruck + Italien: Zeichnungen, Graphik, Plastik.* Ernst-Gerhard Güse
1981 Heilbronn, Städtische Museen, Deutschhof; Mainz, Mittelrheinisches Landesmuseum. *Wilhelm Lehmbruck.* Andreas Pfeiffer, ed
1981–1982 Duisburg, Wilhelm-Lehmbruck-Museum. *Hommage à Lehmbruck: Lehmbruck in seiner Zeit.* Siegfried Salzmann, and Karl-Egon-Vester
1987–1988 Gotha, Museum der Natur; Berlin, Nationalgalerie der Staatlichen Museen zu Berlin im Alten Museum; Leipzig, Museum der Bildenden Künste. *Wilhelm Lehmbruck 1881–1919: Plastik, Malerei, Graphik aus den Sammlungen des Wilhelm-Lehmbruck-Museums der Stadt Duisburg.* Peter Betthausen, and Christoph Brockhaus
1990–1991 Zürich, Kunsthaus; Münster, Westfälisches Landesmuseum für Kunst und Kulturgeschichte. *Wilhelm Lehmbruck: Zeichnungen aus dem Wilhelm-Lehmbruck-Museum Duisburg.* Erich Franz
1991 Hamburg, Kunsthalle. *Wilhelm Lehmbruck.* Uwe M. Schneede, ed

1992–1993 New York, Michael Werner. *Wilhelm Lehmbruck*

August Macke
Reference Bibliographies
FIRMENICH, ANDREA, ed. *August Macke: Gesang von der Schönheit der Dinge.* Köln: Wienand, 1992: p. 295
GÜSE, ERNST-GERHARD. *August Macke: Gemälde, Aquarelle, Zeichnungen.* München: Bruckmann, 1986, p. 515-525

Written Works and Correspondence
FRESE, WERNER, and ERNST-GERHARD GÜSE, eds. *Briefe an Elisabeth und die Freunde.* München: Bruckmann, 1987
MACKE, WOLFGANG, ed. *August Macke-Franz Marc, Briefwechsel.* Köln: M. DuMont Schauberg, 1964

Œuvre Catalogues
HEIDERICH, URSULA. *August Macke: Die Skizzenbücher.* 2 vols. Stuttgart: G. Hatje, 1987
HEIDERICH, URSULA. *August Macke, Zeichnungen: Werkverzeichnis.* Stuttgart, G. Hatje, 1993
VRIESEN, GUSTAV. *August Macke.* Stuttgart: W. Kohlhammer, 1953; 2nd substantially enlarged ed. Stuttgart, 1957

Books
BARTMANN, DOMINIK. *August Macke, Kunsthandwerk: Glasbilder, Stickereien, Keramiken, Holzarbeiten und Entwürfe.* (Gebr. Mann Studio-Reihe). Berlin: Gebr. Mann, 1979
BITTER, RUDOLF VON. *August Macke.* München: Bruckmann, 1993
BRÜCHER, ERNST, und MAJELLA BRÜCHER. *Die Tunisreise: Aquarelle und Zeichnungen.* Köln: M. DuMont Schauberg, 1958; 3rd ed. Köln: DuMont, 1982; *Tunisian Watercolors and Drawings.* Milton S. Fox, ed. New York: H. Abrams, 1959
BUSCH, GÜNTER. *August Macke: Das russische Ballett.* Stuttgart: P. Reclam, 1966
BUSCH, GÜNTER. *August Macke: Handzeichnungen.* Mainz/Berlin: Kupferberg, 1966
COHEN, WALTER. *August Macke.* (Junge Kunst, Bd. 32). Leipzig: Klinkhardt and Biermann, 1922
ENGELS, MATHIAS T. *August Macke.* 2nd ed. Recklinghausen: A. Bongers, 1958
ERDMANN-MACKE, ELISABETH. *Erin-*

nerung an August Macke. Stuttgart: W. Kohlhammer, 1962; unabridged ed. Frankfurt am Main: Fischer Taschenbuch Verlag, 1987

FRIESEN, ASTRID VON. *August Macke: Ein Maler-Leben*. Hamburg: Ellert & Richter, 1989

GUSTAV, JÜRGEN. *August Macke*. Velbert: Edition Cicero, 1990; English ed. Thornbury, England: Artline Editions, 1990

HEIDERICH, URSULA. *August Macke: Zeichnungen aus den Skizzenbüchern*. Stuttgart: G. Hatje, 1986

HOLZHAUSEN, WALTER. *August Macke*. München: Bruckmann, 1956

Macke und die Tradition: Zeichnungen aus den Skizzenbüchern von 1904 bis 1914. Münster: Westfälisches Landesmuseum für Kunst- und Kulturgeschichte, 1979

MACKE, WOLFGANG. *August Macke: Aquarelle*. München: R. Piper, 1958

MACKE, WOLFGANG. *August Macke*. (Bastei Galerie der grossen Maler, Nr. 44). Bergisch Gladbach: Bastei-Verlag, 1968

MARTIN, KURT. *Reise nach Kairouan: Zwölf farbige Aquarelle*. Baden-Baden: W. Klein, 1954

MESEURE, ANNA. *August Macke 1887–1914*. Köln: B. Taschen, 1990; English ed. Köln, 1991

MOELLER, MAGDALENA M. *August Macke*. (DuMonts Bibliothek grosser Maler). Köln: DuMont, 1988

MOELLER, MAGDALENA M. *August Macke: Die Tunisreise*. München: Prestel, 1989

STADLER, WOLF. *August Macke: Er gab der Farbe den hellsten Klang: 24 Gemälde*. Freiburg im Br.: Herder, 1987

WEYANDT, BARBARA. *Farbe und Naturauffassung im Werk von August Macke*. (Studien zur Kunstgeschichte, Bd. 86). Hildesheim/New York: G. Olms, 1994

Exhibitions

1962 München, Städtische Galerie im Lenbachhaus. *August Macke*. Hans K. Roethel, introduction

1964 Bonn, Städtische Kunstsammlungen. *August Macke 1887–1914: Zeichnungen, Aquarelle, Graphik*

1964–1965 Bremen, Kunsthalle. *August Macke: Handzeichnungen und Aquarelle*

1968–1969 Hamburg, Kunstverein. *August Macke: Gemälde, Aquarelle, Zeichnungen*

1973 Berlin, Haus am Waldsee; Bonn, Städtisches Kunstmuseum. *August Macke und die rheinischen Expressionisten: Gemälde, Zeichnungen, Graphik 1906–1930 aus dem Städtischen Kunstmuseum Bonn*

1976–1977 Münster, Westfälisches Landesmuseum für Kunst und Kulturgeschichte; Bonn, Städtisches Kunstmuseum; Krefeld, Kaiser Wilhelm Museum. *August Macke 1887–1914: Aquarelle und Zeichnungen* Klaus, and Brigitte Kühn, eds.

1977–1978 Berlin, Galerie Pels-Leusden. *Franz Marc: Gouachen, Aquarelle und Zeichnungen: August Macke: Gemälde, Pastelle, Aquarelle, Zeichnungen und Plastik*. Paul Vogt

1978–1979 Hannover, Kestner-Gesellschaft. *August Macke und die rheinischen Expressionisten aus dem Städtischen Kunstmuseum Bonn* C.-A. Haenlein, and Dierk Stemmler, eds.

1979 Bonn, Städtisches Kunstmuseum; Krefeld, Kaiser Wilhelm Museum; Wuppertal, Von der Heydt-Museum. *Die rheinischen Expressionisten: August Macke und seine Malerfreunde*. Aurel Bongers, Joachim Heusinger von Waldegg, and Dierk Stemmler, eds.

1982–1983 Münster, Westfälisches Landesmuseum für Kunst und Kulturgeschichte; Bonn, Städtisches Kunstmuseum. *Die Tunisreise: Klee, Macke, Moilliet*. Ernst-Gerhard Güse, ed.

1986–1987 Münster, Westfälisches Landesmuseum für Kunst und Kulturgeschichte; Bonn, Städtisches Kunstmuseum; München, Städtische Galerie im Lenbachhaus. *August Macke: Aquarelle, Zeichnungen*. Ernst-Gerhard Güse

1991 Bonn, Kunstmuseum. *August Macke und die rheinischen Expressionisten im Kunstmuseum Bonn: Die Sammlung*. Katharina Schmidt, and Mario-Andreas von Lüttichau

1992–1993 Emden, Kunsthalle in Emden, Stiftung Henri Nannen; Ulmer Museum; Bonn, Kunstmuseum. *August Macke: "Gesang von der Schönheit der Dinge": Aquarelle und Zeichnungen*. Andrea Firmenich, ed.

1994 Paderborn, Städtische Galerie in der Reithalle, Schloss Neuhaus. *Durchfreuen der Natur: Blumen, Gärten, Landschaften; August Macke und die Expressionisten in Westfalen … .* Klaus Bussmann, and Ursula Heiderich

Franz Marc

Reference Bibliography

LANKHEIT, KLAUS. *Franz Marc: Sein Leben und seine Kunst*. Köln: DuMont, 1976, p. 212-221

Written Works Aufzeichnungen und Aphorismen. München: Galerie Günther Franke, 1946

Briefe, Aufzeichnungen und Aphorismen. 2 vols. Berlin: P. Cassirer, 1920

Briefe aus dem Feld. Berlin: Rembrandt Verlag, 1940; new ed. Klaus Lankheit, and Uwe Steffen, eds. (Serie Piper, Nr. 233). München: R. Piper, 1982

LANKHEIT, KLAUS, ed. *Schriften*. Köln: DuMont, 1978

LANKHEIT, KLAUS, ed. *Skizzenbuch aus dem Feld*. Berlin: Gebr. Mann, 1956

LANKHEIT, KLAUS, ed. *Wassily Kandinsky, Franz Marc: Briefwechsel: Mit Briefen von und an Gabriele Münter und Maria Marc*. München: R. Piper, 1983

MACKE, WOLFGANG, ed. *August Macke-Franz Marc: Briefwechsel*. Köln: M. DuMont Schauberg, 1964

MEISSNER, GÜNTER, ed. *Briefe, Schriften und Aufzeichnungen*. Weimar: G. Kiepenheuer, 1980; 2nd enlarged and rev. ed. Weimar, 1989

Oeuvre Catalogues

LANKHEIT, KLAUS. *Franz Marc: Katalog der Werke*. Köln: DuMont Schauberg, 1970

Books

BÜNEMANN, HERMANN. *Franz Marc: Zeichnungen und Aquarelle*. New 3rd rev. ed. München: Bruckmann, 1960

DÜCHTING, HAJO. *Franz Marc*. Köln: DuMont, 1991

ECKARDT, ANNETTE SIMON VON. *Web-Muster entworfen von Franz Marc*. München: W. Plessmann, 1908

HÜNEKE, ANDREAS. *Franz Marc, Tierschicksale: Kunst als Heilgeschichte*. Original ed. Frankfurt am Main: Fischer Taschenbuch Verlag, 1994

HÜNEKE, ANDREAS. *Zitronenpferd und Feuerochse: 100 Grafiken*. (Reclam-Bibliothek, Bd. 1370). Leipzig: P. Reclam, 1990

LANKHEIT, KLAUS. *Franz Marc*. (Kunst unserer Zeit, Bd. 3). Berlin: K. Lemmer, 1950

LANKHEIT, KLAUS. *Franz Marc im Urteil seiner Zeit*. Köln: M. DuMont Schauberg, 1970

LANKHEIT, KLAUS. *Franz Marc: Sein Leben und seine Kunst*. Köln: DuMont, 1976

LANKHEIT, KLAUS, ed. *Franz Marc, Tierstudien: 36 Handzeichnungen*. (Insel-Bücherei, Nr. 567). Wiesbaden: Insel-Verlag, 1953

LANKHEIT, KLAUS. *Führer durch das Franz Marc Museum, Kochel am See*. 3rd rev. ed. München: Deutscher Kunstverlag, 1989

LANKHEIT, KLAUS, ed. *Unteilbares Sein: Aquarelle und Zeichnungen*. Köln: M. DuMont Schauberg, 1959; *Franz Marc: Watercolors, Drawings, Writings*. New York: H. Abrams, 1960

LEVINE, FREDERICK S. *The Apocalyptic Vision: The Art of Franz Marc as German Expressionism*. New York: Haper and Row, 1979

MÄRZ, ROLAND. *Franz Marc*. Berlin: Henschelverlag, 1984

NIGRO COVRE, JOLANDA. *Franz Marc: dal pensiero alla forma*. Torino: Martano, 1971

PARTSCH, SUSANNA. *Franz Marc 1880–1916*. Köln: B. Taschen, 1991

PAULI, GUSTAV. *Franz Marc: Der Mandrill*. Hamburg: Hamburger Kunsthalle, 1922

PESE, CLAUS. *Franz Marc: Leben und Werk*. Stuttgart/Zürich: Belser, 1989

PESE, CLAUS. *Franz Marc: Aquarelle*. München: Schirmer/Mosel, 1990

ROSENTHAL, MARC. *Franz Marc*. München/New York: Prestel, 1989

SCHARDT, ALOIS J. *Franz Marc*. (Die Zeichner des Volkes). Berlin: Rembrandt, 1936

SCHUSTER, PETER-KLAUS. *Franz Marc: Postcards to Prince Jussuf*. Abridged ed. München/New York: Prestel, 1988

SEILER, HARALD. *Franz Marc*. München: Bruckmann, 1956

TOBIEN, FELICITAS. *Franz Marc*. Ramerding: Berghaus, 1982

Exhibitions

1963 München, Städtische Galerie im Lenbachhaus. *Franz Marc*. 2nd rev. ed

1963–1964 Hamburg, Kunstverein. *Franz Marc: Gemälde, Gouachen, Zeichnungen, Skulpturen*

1967 Bern, Kunstmuseum. *Franz Marc: Das graphische Werk*. Hans Christoph von Tavel

1977–1978 Berlin, Galerie Pels-Leusden. *Franz Marc: Gouachen, Aquarelle und Zeichnungen: August Macke: Gemälde, Pastelle, Aquarelle, Zeichnungen und Plastik*. Paul Vogt

1979–1980 Berkeley, University of California, Art Museum; Fort Worth Art Museum; Minneapolis, Walker Art Center. *Franz Marc 1880–1916*. Mark Rosenthal
1980 München, Städtische Galerie im Lenbachhaus. *Franz Marc 1880–1916*. Rosel Gollek; 3rd enlarged ed. München, 1985
1984 Düsseldorf, Wolfgang Wittrock Kunsthandel. *Franz Marc 1880–1916: Gemälde, Aquarelle, Zeichnungen, Graphik*. Werner Haftmann, introduction
1987–1988 München, Staatsgalerie Moderner Kunst. *Franz Marc, Else Lasker-Schüler, "Der Blaue Reiter präsentiert eurer Hoheit sein blaues Pferd": Karton und Briefe*. Peter-Klaus Schuster, ed.
1989–1990 Berlin, Brücke-Museum; Essen, Museum Folkwang; Tübingen, Kunsthalle. *Franz Marc: Zeichnungen und Aquarelle*. Magdalena M. Moeller
1993 Münster, Westfälisches Landesmuseum für Kunst und Kultur; München, Staatsgalerie Moderner Kunst; Emden, Kunsthalle in Emden, Stiftung Henri Nannen. *Franz Marc: Kräfte der Natur: Werke 1912–1915*. Erich Franz, and Andrea Witte
1995–1996 München, Städtische Galerie im Lenbachhaus. *Franz Marc: Skulpturen*

Ludwig Meidner

Reference Bibliography
BREUER, GERDA, and INES WAGEMANN, eds. *Ludwig Meidner: Zeichner, Maler, Literat 1884–1966*. Darmstadt: Mathildenhöhe, 1991, vol. 2, p. 489-502

Written Works
Dichter, Maler und Cafés. Ludwig Kunz, ed. Zürich: Die Arche, 1973
Im Nacken das Sternemeer. Leipzig: K. Wolff, 1916
Septemberschrei: Hymen, Gebete, Lästerungen. Berlin: P. Cassirer, 1920

Books
BERANKOVA, LJUBA, and ERIK RIEDEL. *Apokalypse und Offenbarung: Religiöse Themen im Leben von Ludwig Meidner*. Sigmaringen, J. Thorbecke, 1996
BRIEGER, LOTHAR. *Ludwig Meidner*. (Junge Kunst, Bd. 4). Leipzig: Klinkhardt und Biermann, 1919
GROCHOWIAK, THOMAS, ed. *Ludwig Meidner*. Recklinghausen: A. Bongers, 1966
HODIN, JOSEPH PAUL. *Ludwig Meidner: Seine Kunst, seine Persönlichkeit, seine Zeit*. Darmstadt: Justus-von-Liebig-Verlag, 1973
LEISTNER, GERHARD. *Idee und Wirklichkeit: Gehalt und Bedeutung des urbanen Expressionismus in Deutschland, dargestellt am Werk Ludwig Meidners*. (Europäische Hochschulschriften. Reihe 28, Kunstgeschichte, Bd. 66). Frankfurt am Main/New York: P. Lang, 1986

Exhibitions
1963 Recklinghausen, Kunsthalle; Berlin, Haus am Waldsee; Darmstadt, Kunsthalle. *Ludwig Meidner*. Thomas Grochowiak
1965 Milano, Galleria del Levante. *Disegni di Ludwig Meidner*. Edouard Roditi
1968 Heidelberg, Kunstkabinett Dr. Helmut Tenner. *Ludwig Meidner: Gemälde, Zeichnungen, Graphik, Bücher*. Petra Tenner
1970 Frankfurt am Main, Kunstkabinett Hanna Bekker vom Rath. *Ludwig Meidner: Zeichnungen von 1902–1927*
1971 Regensburg, Ostdeutsche Galerie. *Ludwig Meidner 1884–1966: Aquarelle, Zeichnungen, Druckgraphik*
1972 Notre Dame, IN, University of Notre Dame Art Gallery. *The Graphic Work of Ludwig Meidner: Drawings and Prints from the D. Thomas Bergen Collection*. Frank Whitford
1973 Los Angeles, University of Southern California, Art Galleries. *Prints and Drawings of Ludwig Meidner: The Ernest and Lilly Jacobson Collection*. Donald J. Brewer
1975–1976 Frankfurt am Main, Galerie Meyer-Ellinger. *Ludwig Meidner: Zeichnungen 1912–1915*
1976 Milwaukee, Art Center. *Ludwig Meidner: Apocalyptic German Expressionist: From the Collection of Marvin and Janet Fishman*
1977 München, Galleria del Levante. *Ludwig Meidner*. Franco Fortini
1978 Ann Arbor, University of Michigan, Museum of Art. *Ludwig Meidner: An Expressionist Master: Drawings and Prints from the D. Thomas Bergen Collection: Paintings from the Marvin and Janet Fishman Collection*
1979 Köln, Galerie Ruchti. *Ludwig Meidner: Zeichnungen aus dem Nachlass*
1984 Berlin, Akademie der Künste. *Meisterzeichnungen von Ludwig Meidner zum 100. Geburtstag*
1984 Darmstadt, Saalbau-Galerie. *Ludwig Meidner zum Hundertsten: Ölbilder, Zeichnungen, Druckgraphik*
1985 Wolfsburg, Kunstverein. *Ludwig Meidner 1884–1966*. Klaus Hoffmann
1989–1990 Los Angeles County Museum of Art. *The Apocalyptic Landscapes of Ludwig Meidner*; Berlin, Berlinische Galerie, Martin-Gropius-Bau. *Apokalyptische Landschaften*. Carol S. Eliel
1991 Darmstadt, Mathildenhöhe. *Ludwig Meidner: Zeichner, Maler, Literat 1884–1966*. 2 vols. Gerda Breuer, and Ines Wagemann
1991 Hofheim am Taunus, Stadthalle. *Ludwig Meidner 1884–1966: Das druckgraphische Werk: Ein Überblick*. Winfried Flammann
1994 Grafenau, Galerie Schlichtenmaier, Schloss Dätzingen. *Ludwig Meidner 1884 Bernstadt – 1966 Darmstadt: Zeichnungen, Radierungen*
1994 Leverkusen, Museum Morsbroich, Studiogalerie. *Ludwig Meidner: Expressionistische Graphik*. Uta Kiksche
1994–1995 Hofheim am Taunus, Stadtmuseum. *Ludwig Meidner 1884–1966: Kneipe und Café: Aquarelle, Zeichnungen, Druckgraphik*. Winfried Flammann
1996–1997 Frankfurt am Main, Jüdisches Museum. *Ludwig Meidner*

Otto Müller

Reference Bibliographies
BUCHHEIM, LOTHAR-GÜNTHER. *Otto Müller: Leben und Werk*. Feldafing: Buchheim, 1963, p. 283-286
MOELLER, MAGDALENA M., ed. *Otto Müller: Gemälde, Aquarelle, Pastelle, und Druckgraphik aus dem Brücke-Museum Berlin*. München: Hirmer, 1996, p. 110-111

Oeuvre Catalogues
KARSCH, FLORIAN. *Otto Müller zum hundertsten Geburtstag: Das graphische Gesamtwerk: Holzschnitte, Radierungen, Lithographien, Farblithographien*. Berlin: Galerie Nierendorf, 1974

Books
BUCHHEIM, LOTHAR-GÜNTHER. *Otto Müller: Leben und Werk*. [Mit einem Werkverzeichnis der Graphik von Florian Karsch]. Feldafing: Buchheim, 1963
BUCHHEIM, LOTHAR-GÜNTHER. *Otto Müller*. Feldafing: Buchheim, 1968
DECKER-JANSSEN, MARLENE. *Gestaltungselemente im Bildwerk von Otto Müller*. Dortmund: Projekt Verlag, 1993
FLEMMING, HANNS THEODOR. *Otto Müller: Farbige Zeichnungen und Lithographien*. Feldafing: Buchheim, 1957
JÄHNER, HORST. *Otto Müller*. Dresden: VEB Verlag der Kunst, 1974
LÜTTICHAU, MARIO-ANDREAS VON. *Otto Müller: Ein Romantiker unter den Expressionisten*. (DuMont-Taschenbücher, Nr. 292). Köln: DuMont, 1993
SCHEIDIG, WALTHER, ed. *Otto Müller: Zigeuner Mappe*. München: Berghaus, 1958
SCHMELLER, ALFRED, ed. *Otto Müller: Mädchenbilder und Zigeunerleben*. München: R. Piper, 1959
TROEGER, EBERHARD. *Otto Müller*. Freiburg im Br.: Crone, 1949

Exhibitions
1963 Köln: Dom Galerie. *Otto Müller*
1964 Berlin, Galerie Nierendorf. *Otto Müller*. (Kunstblätter der Galerie Nierendorf, Nr. 4/5)
1968 Berlin, Galerie Nierendorf. *Otto Müller*. (Kunstblätter der Galerie Nierendorf, Nr. 15)
1969 München, Galerie Günther Franke. *Otto Müller: Bilder, Aquarelle, Zeichnungen und Druckgraphik*
1974 Mulheim an der Ruhr, Städtisches Museum. *Otto Müller: Eine Ausstellung von Gemälden, Zeichnungen und Druckgraphik aus Privatbesitz und öffentlichen Sammlungen*
1978 München, Galerie Thomas. *Otto Müller: Bilder, Aquarelle, Kreiden, Lithographien*
1987–1988 Regensburg, Museum Ostdeutsche Galerie; Moers, Städtische Galerie Peschkenhaus. *Otto Müller und Zeitgenossen: Expressionistische Kunst in Privatbesitz*. (Veröffentlichung / Ostdeutsche Galerie Regensburg, Nr. 3/1987). Anne-Dore Ketelsen-Volkhardt
1988 München, Art Forum Thomas. *Otto Müller: Gemälde, Aquarelle, Graphik*. Janina Briggs-Forell, and Gabriele Karpf
1990 Berlin, Galerie Nierendorf. *Otto Müller zum sechzigsten Todestag: Gemälde, Aquarelle, Zeichnungen, Graphiken*. (Sonderkatalog der Galerie Nierendorf, Nr. 22). Florian Karsch
1996–1997 Berlin, Brücke-Museum; Frankfurt am Main, Jahrhunderthalle Hoechst; Leip-

zig, Museum der Bildenden Künste; Freiburg im Br., Städtische Museen, Museum für Neue Kunst. *Otto Müller: Gemälde, Aquarelle, Pastelle und Druckgraphik aus dem Brücke-Museum.* Magdalena M. Moeller

Max Pechstein
Reference Bibliography
MOELLER, MAGDALENA M. *Max Pechstein: Sein malerisches Werk.* Exhibition catalogue. München: Hirmer, 1996, p. 327-330

Written Works
Erinnerungen. Wiesbaden: Limes Verlag, 1960; 2nd ed., Stuttgart: Deutscher Verlags-Anstalt, 1993
"Gedichte und Aufzeichnungen aus Palau", in: *Künstlerbekenntnisse: Briefe, Tagebuchblätter, Betrachtungen heutiger Künstler.* Paul Westheim, ed. Berlin: Propyläen Verlag, 1921
Palau: Zeichnungen und Notizen aus der Südsee. Hans Gerd Sellenthin, ed. Feldafing: Buchheim, 1956
Reisebilder: Italien, Südsee: 50 Federzeichnungen auf Stein. Berlin: P. Cassirer, 1919
"Tagebuch", in: *Almanach auf das Jahr 1919.* Berlin: F. Gurlitt, 1919

Œuvre Catalogues
FECHTER, PAUL. *Das graphische Werk Max Pechsteins.* Berlin: F. Gurlitt, 1921
GURLITT, FRITZ. "Max Pechstein", in: *Das graphische Jahr.* Berlin: F. Gurlitt, 1921, p. 29-34
KRÜGER, GÜNTER. *Das druckgraphische Werk Max Pechsteins.* Tökendorf, R.C. Pechstein Verlag, 1988

Books
BIERMANN, GEORG. *Max Pechstein.* (Junge Kunst, Bd. 1). Leipzig: Klinkhardt und Biermann, 1919
HEYMANN, WALTHER. *Max Pechstein.* München: R. Piper, 1916
LEMMER, KONRAD, ed. *Max Pechstein und der Beginn des Expressionismus.* (Kunst unserer Zeit, Heft 2). Leipzig: Volk und Buch Verlag, 1949
OSBORN, MAX. *Max Pechstein.* Berlin: Propyläen, 1922
SCHILLING, JÜRGEN, and JANA MARKO, eds. *Max Pechstein: Zeichnungen und Aquarelle.* Hamburg: [S.n.], 1987

Exhibitions
1960 Wolfsburg, Kunstverein. *Max Pechstein: Der Maler und Graphiker*

1965 Baden-Baden, Galerie Elfriede Wirnitzer. *Max Pechstein: Ernte eines Sommers*
1969 Bremen, Graphisches Kabinett Ursula Voigt. *Max Pechstein: Gemälde, Aquarelle, Graphik aus den Jahren 1909–1924*
1972 Hamburg, Altonaer Museum; Frankfurt am Main, Jahrhunderthalle Hoechst. *Max Pechstein 1881–1955: Graphik.* Gerhard Wietek, and Günter Krüger
1981 Berlin, Brücke-Museum. *Max Pechstein 1881–1955: Zeichnungen und Aquarelle, Stationen seines Lebens.* Leopold Reidemeister
1981 Bremen, Graphisches Kabinett Kunsthandel Wolfgang Werner. *Max Pechstein 1881–1955: Zeichnungen, Druckgraphik zum 100. Geburtstag*
1982 Braunschweig, Kunstverein; Kaiserslautern, Pfalzgalerie. *Max Pechstein.* Giesela Fiedler-Bender
1982 Karl-Marx-Stadt, Städtische Kunstsammlungen. *Hermann Max Pechstein 1881–1955*
1984 New York, Helen Serger/La Boetie; Bremen, Graphisches Kabinett Wolfgang Werner. *Max Pechstein: Brücke Period and Works by Heckel, Nolde, Kirchner, Schmidt-Rottluff in Collaboration with Kunsthandel Wolfgang Werner*
1986–1987 Köln: Galerie Glöckner. *H.M. Pechstein: Graphik*
1987–1988 Wolfsburg, Kunstverein; Bremen, Gerhard-Marcks-Haus; Salzburg, Rupertinum; Wien, Hochschule für angewandte Kunst; Stade, Schwedenspeicher-Museum. *Max Pechstein: Zeichnungen und Aquarelle.* Jürgen Schilling, and Jana Marko
1988 Wedel, Ernst-Barlach-Museum. *Max Pechstein: Graphische Werke*
1989 Regensburg, Museum Ostdeutsche Galerie. *Max Pechstein 1881–1955: Druckgraphik.* Ingrid Stilijanov-Nedo
1989 Unna, Schloss Cappenberg. *Max Pechstein: Eine Ausstellung des Kreises Unna.* Jürgen Schilling, and Jana Marko
1995–1996 Reutlingen, Städtisches Kunstmuseum Spendhaus; Zwickau, Städtisches Museum. *Max Pechstein, Das ferne Paradies: Gemälde, Zeichnungen, Druckgraphik*
1996 Hamburg, Altonaer Museum. *Künstlerpost von Max Pechstein an Eduard Plietzsch*
1996–1997 Berlin, Brücke-Museum; Tübingen, Kunsthalle; Kiel, Kunsthalle. *Max Pechstein: Sein*

malerisches Werk. Magdalena M. Moeller

Karl Schmidt-Rottluff
Reference Bibliography
WIETEK, GERHARD. *Schmidt-Rottluff: Oldenburger Jahre 1907–1912.* Mainz: P. von Zabern, 1995, p. 609-616

Œuvre Catalogues
GROHMANN, WILL. *Karl Schmidt-Rottluff.* Stuttgart: W. Kohlhammer, 1956. [Monographie mit "Chronologischer Oeuvrekatalog der Gemälde", p. 281-308]
RATHENAU, ERNEST, ed. *Karl Schmidt-Rottluff: Das graphische Werk seit 1923.* New York: E. Rathenau, 1964
SCHAPIRE, ROSA. *Karl Schmidt-Rottluffs graphisches Werk bis 1923.* Berlin: Euphorion, 1924

Books
BRIX, KARL. *Karl Schmidt-Rottluff.* Wien: A. Schroll, 1972
DIRKSEN, VIKTOR. *Karl Schmidt-Rottluff.* (Kleine Führer der Kunsthalle Hamburg). Hamburg: Kunsthalle Hamburg, 1921
REIDEMEISTER, LEOPOLD. "Der Holzstock als Kunstwerk: Karl Schmidt-Rottluff: Holzstöcke von 1905 bis 1930". In: *Brücke-Archiv,* Heft 13/14. Berlin: Brücke-Museum, 1983
VALENTINER, WILHELM R. *Schmidt-Rottluff.* (Junge Kunst, Bd. 16). Leipzig: Klinkhardt und Biermann, 1920
WIETEK, GERHARD. *Karl Schmidt-Rottluff: Bilder aus Nidden 1913.* (Werkmonographien zur bildenden Kunst, Nr. 91). Stuttgart: P. Reclam, 1963
WIETEK, GERHARD. *Schmidt-Rottluff: Graphik.* München: K. Thiemig, 1971
WIETEK, GERHARD. *Karl Schmidt-Rottluff in Hamburg und Schleswig-Holstein.* (Kunst in Schleswig-Holstein aus dem Schleswig-Holsteinisches Landesmuseums, Bd. 25). Neumünster: K. Wachholtz, 1984
WIETEK, GERHARD. *Schmidt-Rottluff: Oldenburger Jahre 1907–1912.* Mainz: P. von Zabern, 1995

Exhibitions
1963 Hannover, Kunstverein. *Karl Schmidt-Rottluff: Aquarelle und Zeichnungen.* Gunther Thiem
1964 Berlin, Staatliche Museen Preussischer Kulturbesitz, Kupferstichkabinett. *Karl Schmidt-Rot-*

luff: Druckgraphik ... zum 80. Geburtstag. Dierk Stemmler
1964 Hannover, Kunstverein; Essen, Museum Folkwang; Frankfurt am Main, Kunstverein; Berlin, Akademie der Künste. *Karl Schmidt-Rottluff: Gemälde, Aquarelle, Graphik.* Gunther Thiem
1969 Stuttgart, Staatsgalerie. *Karl Schmidt-Rottluff: Aquarelle, Farbstift- und Tuschpinselblätter: Ausstellung zum 85. Geburtstag*
1969–1970 Hamburg, Altonaer Museum; Bielefeld, Städtische Kunsthalle. *Karl Schmidt-Rottluff: Graphik aus Norddeutschland zum 85. Geburtstag des Künstlers*
1972 New York, Helen Serger/La Boetie. *A Selection of Works by Karl Schmidt-Rottluff*
1973 Baden-Baden, Galerie Elfriede Wirnitzler. *Karl Schmidt-Rottluff: Holzschnitte 1909–1919*
1973 München, Günther Franke. *Karl Schmidt-Rottluff: Bilder und Aquarelle*
1974 Berlin, Brücke-Museum. *Karl Schmidt-Rottluff: Das graphische Werk zum 90. Geburtstag des Künstlers.* Leopold Reidemeister
1974 Hamburg, Altonaer Museum. *Schmidt-Rottluff: Gemälde, Landschaften;* B.A.T. Haus. *Aquarelle aus den Jahren 1909 bis 1969.* Gerhard Wietek, and Christine Knupp
1974 Karl-Marx-Stadt, Städtische Kunstsammlung; Dresden, Staatliche Kunstsammlungen Dresden, Gemäldegalerie Neue Meister; Berlin, Nationalgalerie der Staatlichen Museen. *Karl Schmidt-Rottluff: Malerei und Grafik aus sieben Jahrzehnten ... zum 90. Geburtstag.* Karl Brix
1974 Reutlingen, Spendhaus. *Karl Schmidt-Rottluff: Graphik der Jahre 1906–1921: Ausstellung zum 90. Geburtstag.* Alfred Hagenlocher
1974 Stuttgart, Staatsgalerie. *Karl Schmidt-Rottluff: Die Schwarzblätter ... zum 90. Geburtstag.* Gunther Thiem
1979–1980 Braunschweig, Kunstverein. *Karl Schmidt-Rottluff: Werke 1905 bis 1961.* Jürgen Schilling, and Dieter Blume
1983–1984 Berlin, Brücke-Museum. *Der Holzstock als Kunstwerk: Karl Schmidt-Rottluff Holzstöcke von 1905 bis 1930: Eine Schenkung des Künstlers von 1975 an das Brücke-Museum*
1984 Berlin, Brücke-Museum. *Karl Schmidt-Rottluff: Ausstellungen zum 100. Geburtstag des Künstlers.* Leopold Reidemeister

1984 Berlin, Galerie Nierendorf. *Karl Schmidt-Rottluff zum 100. Geburtstag: Holzschnitte, Lithographien, Radierungen: Gedächtnisausstellung*
1984 Bremen, Graphisches Kabinett Kunsthandel Wolfgang Werner. *Karl Schmidt-Rottluff 1884–1976: Aquarelle, Druckgraphik: Ausstellung zum 100. Geburtstag*
1984 Würzburg, Städtische Galerie. *Karl Schmidt-Rottluff 1884–1976: Aquarelle und Zeichnungen: Ausstellung zum 100. Geburtstag des Malers*
1985 Los Angeles County Museum of Art. *Prints by Erich Heckel and Karl Schmidt-Rottluff: A Centenary Celebration.* Gunther Thiem
1987 Frankfurt am Main, Kunstkabinett Hanna Bekker vom Rath. *Vierzig Jahre Frankfurter Kunstkabinett ... Jubiläumsausstellung Karl Schmidt-Rottluff*
1989 Bremen, Kunsthalle; München, Städtische Galerie im Lenbachhaus. *Karl Schmidt-Rottluff Retrospektive.* Gunther Thiem, and Armin Zweite
1991 Berlin, Brücke-Museum. *Karl Schmidt-Rottluff: Aquarelle.* Magdalena M. Moeller
1992 Düsseldorf, Städtische Kunsthalle. *Karl Schmidt-Rottluff der Maler.* Magdalena M. Moeller, and Hans-Werner Schmidt
1993 Chemnitz, Städtische Kunstsammlungen. *Karl Schmidt-Rottluff: Malerei und Grafik.* (Bestandskatalog der Sammlung Malerei und Plastik und des Graphik-Kabinettes der Städtischen Kunstsammlungen Chemnitz, Bd. 1). Susanne Anna
1995 Nice, Musée Matisse. *Karl Schmidt-Rottluff.* Xavier Girard
1995–1996 Frankfurt am Main, Jahrhunderthalle Hoechst; Salzburg, Rupertinum, Graphische Sammlung. *Karl Schmidt-Rottluff: Tuschpinselzeichnungen.* Magdalena M. Moeller
1997 Kassel, Neue Galerie. *Kraft der Linie: Karl Schmidt-Rottluff, Graphik und Plastik*
1997 München, Kunsthalle der Hypo-Kulturstiftung; Wien, Kunstforum. *Karl Schmidt-Rottluff: Werke aus der Sammlung des Brücke-Museums Berlin.* Magdalena M. Moeller

Georg Scholz
Reference Bibliography
HOLSTEN, SIEGMAR. *Georg Scholz: Gemälde, Zeichnungen, Druckgraphik.* Exhibition catalogue. Karls-ruhe: Staatliche Kunsthalle Karlsruhe, 1990, p. 74-75

Books
MÜCK, HANS-DIETER. *Den Zeitgeist im Visier: Kritischer Realismus in Baden 1914–1933: Georg Scholz, Karl Hubbuch, Wilhelm Schnarrenberger, Hanna Nagel.* Stuttgart: H. Matthaes, 1991

Exhibitions
1961 Berlin, Haus am Waldsee. *Neue Sachlichkeit.* Eberhard Marx
1968 München and Roma, Galleria del Levante, *Aspetti della "Nuova Oggettività" = Aspekte der "Neuen Sachlichkeit".* Emilio Bentornati
1971 Milano, Rotonda di via Besana, Comune di Milano. *Il Realismo in Germania*
1971 Stuttgart, Württembergischer Kunstverein. *Realismus zwischen Revolution und Machtergreifung 1919–1933*
1975 Karlsruhe, Badischer Kunstverein. *Georg Scholz: Ein Beitrag zur Diskussion realistischer Kunst*
1976 Bonn, Rheinisches Landesmuseum. *Die zwanziger Jahre im Porträt: Porträts in Deutschland 1918–1933*
1978 London, Hayward Gallery. *Neue Sachlichkeit and German Realism of the Twenties*
1978–1979 Berlin, Nationalgalerie, Kupferstichkabinett und Sammlung der Zeichnungen. *Revolution und Realismus in Deutschland 1917–1933*
1980 Karlsruhe, Künstlerhaus-Galerie. *Realistische Kunst der 20er Jahre in Karlsruhe*
1982 Karlsruhe, Künstlerhaus-Galerie. *Georg Scholz: Das druckgrafische Werk.* Barbara Bessel, et al
1990 Karlsruhe, Staatliche Kunsthalle. *Georg Scholz: Gemälde, Zeichnungen, Druckgraphik.* (Bildhefte der Staatlichen Kunsthalle Karlsruhe, Nr. 13). Siegmar Holsten
1990 Waldkirch, Georg Scholz-Haus. *Georg Scholz 1890–1945: Malerei, Zeichnung, Druckgraphik.* Hans-Dieter Mück, ed.

Jakob Steinhardt
Œuvre Catalogues
KOLB, LEON. *The Woodcuts of Jakob Steinhardt: Chronologically Arranged and Fully Reproduced.* San Francisco: Genuart, 1959

Books
AMISHAI-MAISELS, ZIVA. *Jacob Steinhardt: Etchings and Litho-graphs.* Jerusalem/Tel Aviv: Dvir, 1981
GAMZU, HAIM. *The Graphic Art of Jakob Steinhardt.* New York/London: T. Yoseloff, 1963
MERTENS, HEINRICH A. *Jakob Steinhardt: Propheten.* Essen: Fredebeul & Koenen, 1963
NADEL, ARNO. *Jacob Steinhardt.* (Graphiker der Gegenwart, Bd. 4). Berlin: Verlag Neue Kunsthandlung, 1920
SCHIFF, FRITZ. *Die Holzschnitte von Jakob Steinhardt.* Jerusalem: Jerusalem Art Society, 1950
PFEFFERKORN, RUDOLF. *Jakob Steinhardt.* Berlin: Stapp, 1967
TIETZE, HANS. *Jakob Steinhardt.* Berlin-Frohnau: J.J. Ottens, 1928

Exhibitions
1962 Jerusalem, Bezalel Museum. *Steinhardt*
1963 Berlin. *Jakob Steinhardt, Jerusalem: Holzschnitte, Farbholzschnitte aus den Jahren 1913–1962.* Rudolf Pfefferkorn
1964 Tel Aviv, Beth Dizengoff. *Steinhardt*
1966 Berlin, Haus am Lützowplatz. *Jakob Steinhardt*
1967 Jerusalem, Israel Museum. *Jakob Steinhardt: His Graphic Work.* (Catalogue no. 86)
1968 Berlin, Kunstamt Wedding. *Jakob Steinhardt*
1968 Haifa, Museum of Modern Art. *Jakob Steinhardt: Graphic Work*
1987 Berlin, Kunstamt Wedding. *Jakob Steinhardt: Das graphische Werk.* Stefan Behrens
1987 New York, Jewish Museum. *The Unknown Steinhardt: Prints by Jakob Steinhardt Produced between 1907 and 1934.* Arthur A. Coen
1995 Berlin, Martin-Gropius-Bau. *Jakob Steinhardt, Der Prophet: Ausstellungs- und Bestandskatalog, Jüdisches Museum im Berlin Museum* Dominik Bartmann, ed.

Gert Wollheim
Reference Bibliography
WIESE, STEPHAN VON. *Gert H. Wollheim 1894–1974: Monographie und Werkverzeichnis.* Köln: Wienand, 1993, p. 358-362

Books
EULER-SCHMIDT, MICHAEL. *Gert Heinrich Wollheim 1894–1974: Leben und Werk bis 1947: Werkverzeichnis des Gesamtwerkes bis 1947.* 4 vols. Ph.D. diss. Bremen, Universität, 1986
WIESE, STEPHAN VON. *Gert H. Wollheim 1894–1974: Monographie und Werkverzeichnis.* Köln: Wienand, 1993
WOLLHEIM, MONA, ed. *Gert H. Wollheim: Gedanke und Werk.* München: Thiemig, 1977

Exhibitions
1961 Düsseldorf, Kunstmuseum. *Gert H. Wollheim.* Irene Markowitz
1971 Berlin, Staatliche Museen Preussischer Kulturbesitz. *Gert H. Wollheim: Malerie, Graphik, Plastik.* Alheidis von Rohr
1984 Düsseldorf, Galerie Remmert und Barth. *Gert H. Wollheim: Die wilden Jahre 1919–1925.* [Mit dem Werkverzeichnis der Druckgraphik 1912–1922]. Eberhard Roters, and Michael Euler-Schmidt, essays; Michael Euler-Schmidt, and Herbert Remmert, œuvre catalogue
1984 Düsseldorf, Stadtmuseum. *Gert H. Wollheim 1894–1974, im Schützengraben: Gemälde, Zeichnungen, Dokumente zum 90. Geburtstag des Künstlers.* Michael Euler-Schmidt, text
1989 Düsseldorf, Galerie Remmert und Barth. *Dix-Pankok-Wollheim: Freunde in Düsseldorf 1920–1925*
1993 Düsseldorf, Kunstmuseum im Ehrenhof; Berlin, Grundkredit-Bank. *Gert H. Wollheim 1894–1974: Eine Retrospektive.* Stephan von Wiese

Index of Names

Index of Authors and Works

Photos Credits

Jorg P. Anders, Berlin - 96, 176-178, 192-194, 207, 209, 216-221, 236-245, 258-267, 276, 278-281, 285, 286-288, 314-315

Archiv der Schött's Söhne, Mainz - 83

Archiv der Universal Edition A.G., Vienna - 81 bottom, 82 top, 82 center, 84

Archivio RCS Libri, Milan - 30, 32 top, 33 top, 34 center, 43 bottom, 59, 60, 62 center, 74, 79, 80, 81, 95 2nd and 4th, 345-352

Graziano Arici, Venice - 62

Artothek, Peissenberg - 211, 300

© Bildarchiv Preussischer Kulturbesitz, Berlin - 63-68, 353-360

Foto Jorg P. Anders, Berlin - 155, 158, 166, 167, 174, 188, 189, 204, 214, 269, 282, 283, 287, 304, 309, 310, 312

Foto Karin März, Berlin - 173

Foto Nationalgalerie, Berlin - 153, 206, 270, 293

Foto Reinhard Saczewski, Berlin - 268

Foto Sachsse, Bonn - 164

Foto Jens Ziehe, Berlin - 198

© Ernst und Hans Barlach GBR Lizenzverwaltung, Ratzeburg - 34 top, 36

Blauel/Gnam - Artothek, Peissenberg - 182, 307

Joachim Blauel - Artothek, Peissenberg - 159, 186, 313

Brunzel Foto, Kassel - 228, 229, 230, 231

Camera Foto, Venice - 61 top

Cineteca Comunale di Bologna - 90-98 All the images (taken straight from frames) are from restored copies of the films cited, in which the original color has also been restored. Worth noting is *Von morgens bis mitternachts* originally released in black and white for expressive reasons. *Faust* also seems to have been released exclusively in black and white. The restored copies are archived at the Cineteca Comunale, Bologna, for whom my deepest thanks.

County Museum of Art, Los Angeles - 24 2nd, 25 bottom, 26 bottom, 27 2nd and 3rd, 31 top, 37

County Museum of Art, Los Angeles, The Robert Gore Rifkind Center for German Expressionist Studies, purchased with funds provided by Anna Bing Arnold, Museum Associates Fund and deaccession funds - 36, 38, 39, 40 bottom, 41 bottom, 42 top, 43 top, 44 top

Courtauld Institute of Art, London - 45 bottom, 46 bottom, 47 bottom, 51 top

Deutsches Historisches Museum, Berlin - 316-325

© Ursula Edelmann, Frankfurt - 190

M.L. Fishman Realty Co., Milwaukee - 157, 224, 226, 274

© 1993 Klaus E. Gotz, Halle - 201

Sophie-R. Gnamm - Artothek, Peissenberg - 172

David Heald - 33 center

David Heald © Solomon R. Guggenheim Foundation, New York - 223

Michael Harling, Hannover - 305

Imaging Service © 1997 The Art Institute of Chicago, All Rights Reserved - 222

Dietmar Katz - Kunstbibliothek, Berlin - 45 top, 47, 53, 54 bottom, 69, 74, 85-88

Bernd Kirtz Fotograf BFF, Duisburg - 196

Walter Klein Fotomeister, Dusseldorf - 185, 273

Niedersächsisches Landesmuseum, Landesgalerie, Hannover - 32 center

Roberto Leydi, Milano - 80 center

Roman März Werkfoto, Berlin - 179, 183, 208, 328-344

Collezione André Meyer, Parigi - 80 bottom, 82 bottom

Parisini Imaging, Vienna - 154

Rheinisches Bildarchiv, Koln - 180, 253, 292

Giuseppe Schiavinotto, Rome - 61 bottom

Ullstein Bilderdienst, Berlin - 75-78

Giorgio Vasari, Rome - 99-149

Rudolf Wakonigg, Münster - 250

© Elke Walford - Fotowerkstatt Hamburger Kunsthalle - 31 bottom

This catalogue has been published with the support of Cartiere Burgo
and it is printed on R4 New Matt Satin 150 g/m² paper manifactured by Cartiere Burgo

Fotocomposizione Grande - Monza (Milan)

Printed in August 1997
by New Interlitho-Italia - Caleppio di Settala (Milan)